D0285974

Lawyers in Practice

THE CHICAGO SERIES IN LAW AND SOCIETY

Edited by John M. Conley and Lynn Mather

ALSO IN THE SERIES:

Additional series titles follow index

Lawyers in Practice

Ethical Decision Making in Context

Edited by
LESLIE C. LEVIN AND LYNN MATHER

THE UNIVERSITY OF CHICAGO PRESS • *Chicago and London*

Leslie C. Levin is professor of law at the University of Connecticut School of Law.

Lynn Mather is professor of law and political science at the University at Buffalo Law School, State University of New York. She is coeditor of the Chicago Series in Law and Society and coauthor of several books, including *Private Lawyers and the Public Interest*.

The University of Chicago Press, Chicago 60637
The University of Chicago Press, Ltd., London
© 2012 by The University of Chicago
All rights reserved. Published 2012.
Printed in the United States of America
21 20 19 18 17 16 15 14 13 12   1 2 3 4 5

ISBN-13: 978-0-226-47515-8   (cloth)
ISBN-13: 978-0-226-47516-5   (paper)
ISBN-10: 0-226-47515-8   (cloth)
ISBN-10: 0-226-47516-6   (paper)

Library of Congress Cataloging-in-Publication Data

Lawyers in practice : ethical decision making in context / edited by Leslie C. Levin and Lynn Mather.
     p. cm.
   Includes bibliographical references and index.
   ISBN-13: 978-0-226-47515-8 (hardcover: alkaline paper)
   ISBN-13: 978-0-226-47516-5 (paperback: alkaline paper)
   ISBN-10: 0-226-47515-8 (hardcover: alkaline paper)
   ISBN-10: 0-226-47516-6 (paperback: alkaline paper)   1. Legal ethics. 2. Prosecution—Decision making—Moral and ethical aspects. 3. Decision making—Moral and ethical aspects.   I. Levin, Leslie C. II. Mather, Lynn M.
   K123.L395 2012
   174'.3—dc23

                                                              2011038791

♾ This paper meets the requirements of ANSI/NISO Z39.48-1992 (Permanence of Paper).

Contents

Preface

There is a tendency in law schools and the legal profession to look at lawyers' conduct from a narrow legalistic perspective—that is, do lawyers follow the rules and laws that govern them, and if not, how can we get them to do so? This focus on the law of lawyering ignores the reality that lawyers are people, too (notwithstanding lawyer jokes to the contrary), and their conduct is inevitably affected by a host of factors that have little to do with the substantive law. This book investigates these factors along with the governing law to understand what influences lawyers' conduct.

By examining lawyers' decision making in the context of their day-to-day practices, the book also fills a gap in sociolegal research by fleshing out many specialty areas of lawyers' work that have not been systematically explored. The book brings together leading and emerging legal scholars and social scientists (including an anthropologist, sociologists, and political scientists) to describe and explain lawyers' conduct in different areas of legal practice with a particular focus on ethical dilemmas. Because this research field is still growing, we are not able to cover in this first volume all the practice areas we would like to address. Nevertheless, our contributors describe lawyers who work in a wide range of settings, including private practice, government service, legal services, and in-house counsel, and who represent individuals, organizations, and the public interest.

The book should appeal to anyone interested in the everyday work of lawyers. Most obviously, it will interest law students, lawyers, judges, and legal regulators. It is also designed for undergraduate and graduate students in courses in sociology of law, law and society, and legal studies, and for anyone considering a career in law.

In order to generate conversation about lawyers' decision making and to provide feedback on the authors' research, we held a conference at the University at Buffalo Law School in April 2010. We would like to thank the Baldy Center for Law and Social Policy at the University at Buffalo and the University of Connecticut for funding this conference. We are grateful to the Baldy Center for logistical support and, in particular, to Laura Wirth, assistant director of the Center. The book benefited from the comments of conference speakers whose views are not represented here: Milton Regan, Tanina Rostain, and Eli Wald. We also thank Buffalo faculty, students, and other attendees who participated in the discussion.

Most important, we want to thank all of our authors. Each of their chapters constitutes an important contribution to the literature on the legal profession. They uncomplainingly responded to numerous requests for revision, often under very tight deadlines. We also thank the many lawyers—well over 1,000 overall—who cooperated with our contributors by answering their survey questions, sitting for lengthy interviews, or allowing themselves to be observed.

The book is much improved as a result of careful reading and suggestions from Richard Abel and two anonymous outside reviewers for the University of Chicago Press. We especially thank John Tryneski for his encouragement and wise counsel, and Rodney Powell for his fine attention to detail.

Finally, Lynn Mather would like to thank Sue Martin for her excellent administrative support and the Baldy Center for Law and Social Policy for financial assistance. She also thanks Mike for his love and understanding for the many occasions on which this project took over our lives. Leslie Levin is grateful to the University of Connecticut School of Law for financial assistance and to Claudia Norsworthy for administrative support. She also thanks Steve, David, Rachel, and Adam Kaplan for knowing when to act as cheerleaders and when to suffer in silence.

Contributors

Elizabeth Chambliss is Professor of Law and Co-Director of the Center for Professional Values and Practice at New York Law School. Chambliss received her JD and PhD in sociology from the University of Wisconsin–Madison.

John M. Conley is the William Rand Kenan Jr. Professor of Law at the University of North Carolina at Chapel Hill. He received his JD and PhD in anthropology from Duke University.

Scott L. Cummings is Professor of Law at the UCLA School of Law, where he is faculty director of the Epstein Program in Public Interest Law and Policy.

Stephen Daniels is Visiting Lecturer at the Sturm College of Law, University of Denver, and Research Professor at the American Bar Foundation.

John Flood is Professor of Law and Sociology at the University of Westminster, London. He is also Visiting Professor of Law at the University of Miami and Bremen University. He received his PhD in sociology from Northwestern University, his LLB from the London School of Economics, and LLMs from Warwick University and Yale Law School.

Bruce A. Green is the Louis Stein Professor at Fordham Law School, where he directs the Louis Stein Center for Law and Ethics. He is a member of the Multistate Professional Responsibility Examination drafting committee and served on the ABA Standing Committee on Ethics and Professional Responsibility.

Sung Hui Kim is Acting Professor of Law at UCLA School of Law. Prior to law teaching, she spent six years as a corporate lawyer in large law firms and four years as general counsel to Red Bull North America, Inc., a leading beverage company.

Kimberly Kirkland is Professor of Law at the University of New Hampshire School of Law. Before she began teaching, Kirkland spent four years as a litigator in a large corporate law firm and six years as a litigator at a small firm in New Hampshire.

Herbert M. Kritzer is the Marvin J. Sonosky Chair of Law and Public Policy and Adjunct Professor of Political Science, University of Minnesota. For many years he was Professor of Political Science and Law at the University of Wisconsin–Madison.

Leslie C. Levin is Professor of Law at the University of Connecticut School of Law. She served as Secretary to the Committee on Professional and Judicial Ethics of the New York City Bar Association.

Joanne Martin is a Research Professor Emerita at the American Bar Foundation in Chicago. She holds a JD from Loyola University of Chicago and an MM from Northwestern University's Kellogg School of Management.

Lynn Mather is Professor of Law and Political Science at the University at Buffalo Law School, State University of New York. She was previously Director of the Baldy Center for Law and Social Policy at the University at Buffalo and President of the Law and Society Association.

Craig A. McEwen is the Daniel B. Fayerweather Professor of Political Economy and Sociology at Bowdoin College. He previously served as chair of the Grievance Commission of the Maine Board of Overseers of the Bar and as a member of Maine's Board of Overseers of the Bar.

Patrick Schmidt is Associate Professor of Political Science and Co-Director of Legal Studies at Macalester College.

Corey S. Shdaimah is Assistant Professor at the University of Maryland, School of Social Work. She holds law degrees from Tel Aviv University and the University of Pennsylvania and a PhD in social work from Bryn Mawr College.

Nicole Martorano Van Cleve is Assistant Professor of Criminal Justice at Temple University with courtesy appointments in the Department of Sociology and the Beasley School of Law. She received her PhD in sociology from Northwestern University and served as Research Director for Chicago Appleseed Fund for Justice.

David B. Wilkins is the Lester Kissel Professor of Law, Vice Dean for Global Initiatives on the Legal Profession, and Faculty Director of the Program on the Legal Profession and the Center for Lawyers and the Professional Services Industry at Harvard Law School. He is also Senior Research Fellow at the American Bar Foundation.

Ellen Yaroshefsky is Clinical Professor of Law and the Director of the Jacob Burns Ethics Center at the Benjamin N. Cardozo School of Law. She is co-chair of the Ethics, Gideon and Professionalism Committee of the American Bar Association's Criminal Justice Section.

Part I

Introductory Perspectives on Ethics in Context

CHAPTER ONE

Why Context Matters

Lynn Mather and Leslie C. Levin

How do lawyers resolve ethical problems in the everyday context of law practice? Does zealous advocacy mean the same thing for corporate litigators, criminal defense attorneys, and divorce lawyers? How are lawyers' decisions influenced by their roles within an organization, such as in-house counsel or law firm associate? What do disclosure requirements mean in practice for prosecutors—or for securities lawyers? This book examines lawyers' ethical decision making in context, that is, through close attention to different office settings and practice areas. Lawyers now specialize in specific legal fields more than ever before. Hence, the research reported here deconstructs the general obligations of professional responsibility to show how lawyers specializing in different areas of law understand them. While there are continuities across fields, we also find that each practice area has its own particular norms and challenges, shaped not only by substantive, procedural, and ethical legal rules, but also by clients, practice organizations, economics, and culture.

Rather than address the professional responsibility of lawyers primarily through professional rules and the substantive "law of lawyering," or through individual case studies, this book combines empirical research on lawyers with analysis of ethical issues that arise in particular areas of legal practice. A central feature of the volume is its interdisciplinary nature, in which lawyers' decision making is firmly embedded both in the professional world of regulation and the sociological and economic setting of the workplace. By situating lawyers in their everyday practices, this book also builds on existing research to explore how organizational, economic, and client differences across the legal profession actually matter for the work that lawyers do and the decisions that they make.

A generation of sociolegal scholarship has pointed out the implications of legal stratification for the construction of bar rules, differences in the meaning and enforcement of ethical codes for different segments of the bar, the ways in which personal identity intersects with professionalism, and the limited ability of a single set of professional rules to promote appropriate conduct in work settings as diverse as those that exist within the legal profession (Wilkins 1990; Nelson and Trubek 1992). Yet the organized bar and many law schools continue to focus their discussion of legal ethics primarily on bar rules of professional conduct. That approach, this book suggests, is a serious mistake. Those rules are extremely general, unevenly understood and enforced, and sometimes at odds with the realities of legal practice. But that does not mean that lawyers lack normative ideals and constraints. We agree with Robert Nelson and David Trubek that legal professionalism exists "not [as] a fixed unitary set of values, but instead . . . [as] multiple visions of what constitutes proper behavior by lawyers" (1992, 179). Through empirical studies of ethical decision making by lawyers in different practice areas, this book provides a partial answer to the challenge Nelson and Trubek posed: "to explain how different professional ideologies emerge in various contexts and with what effects" (179).

To identify and understand lawyers' professional ideologies and the informal norms that shape their conduct requires engagement with particular "communities" of legal practice—"groups of lawyers with whom practitioners interact and to whom they compare themselves and look for common expectations and standards" (Mather, McEwen, and Maiman 2001, 6). The ideals and norms of professionalism vary across networks or groups of lawyers practicing in different areas of law, among lawyers in the same practice area but with different clienteles, between large law firms and small firms, and across firms with different law firm cultures (Mather, McEwen, and Maiman 2001; Carlin 1966; Kelly 1994). Definitions of acceptable lawyering conduct are constructed by lawyers within their offices; in interactions with one another in negotiations and litigation; in contacts with agencies; through appearances before judges; as well as through professional rules, disciplinary boards, and other third parties that regulate lawyer conduct. Legal professionalism, in other words, emerges from the bottom up as well as the top down, and indeed, the most powerful normative constraints on lawyers likely stem from their clients, colleagues, and practice organizations and not from edicts of the organized bar.

In order to examine the ethical decision making of lawyers, it is necessary to fully understand—in a fundamental sense—the context in which they work.

Jerome Carlin (1966) was one of the first to do so when he studied the social setting of lawyers' work and its impact on lawyers' ethics. He described significant differences in the work lives and ethical responses of New York City lawyers in large firms and those in solo and small firm practice. Carlin documented the stratification of the New York City bar and found that the type of clients a lawyer serves affected the lawyer's ability to conform to ethical standards, as did the lawyer's work setting (166–167). In a similar vein, but with a focus on geographic community rather than firm size, Joel Handler (1967) studied the bar in a middle-sized midwestern city. He showed how the continuing relationships and homogeneity of the local community powerfully affected lawyers' conduct and their understanding of their professional responsibilities. Donald Landon's (1990) account of rural lawyers added further to our knowledge of how geographic context can shape lawyers' norms and behavior.

John Heinz and Edward Laumann's (1982) study of the Chicago bar provided even more information about the differences in the backgrounds, work, incomes, and status of urban lawyers. In particular, they emphasized the importance of clients—organizational or individual—to distinguish the "two hemispheres" of the legal profession according to the type of client a lawyer represents. In a follow-up survey conducted in 1995, Heinz et al. (2005) found that almost two-thirds of Chicago lawyers' time was devoted to working for large organizations (including work for nonbusiness entities such as labor unions and the government), while only 29% was devoted to individuals and small business clients. David Wilkins revisits the two hemispheres thesis in chapter 2. He explains how this evidence on contextual differences among lawyers led to his 1990 proposal for context-specific rules for lawyer regulation. Wilkins also identifies six major trends in the profession that have emerged in recent years. These trends—lawyer mobility, technology, unbundling and outsourcing of legal tasks, new organizational forms for providing legal services, institutionalization of pro bono, and globalization—break down and complicate some of the contextual distinctions among groups of lawyers. Wilkins also cites more recent Chicago data showing that substantive or skill-type specialization now plays a greater role than it did 20 years earlier in explaining differences in the bar. His conclusions point to the vital importance of understanding context when thinking about the ethical decisions lawyers make in their everyday work.

Substantive legal specialization provides the organizational framework for this book in order to highlight the contextual differences and informal norms that influence lawyers' decision making in different communities of practice. The idea that attorneys in different fields of law might have different ethical standards and display different ethical conduct is something of a truism, but it receives some support in reputational rankings of Chicago lawyers by practice area (Heinz and Laumann 1982; Heinz et al. 2005). Evidence of ethical differences also comes from observations of lawyers about practitioners in their own areas of practice. Data from 5,892 Michigan alumni surveyed from 1997–2006 (including graduates 5, 15, 25, 35, and 45 years out of law school) found considerable variation in lawyers' responses to the following: "The lawyers with whom I deal (other than those in my own office) are highly ethical in their conduct."[1] Although only 57.1% of lawyers overall agreed (mildly to strongly) that their peers were highly ethical, more than 65% of attorneys in the areas of energy, securities, real property, and estates viewed lawyers in their fields as highly ethical. By contrast, less than 50% of lawyers in the areas of criminal (prosecution and defense), labor, antitrust, communications, and civil rights/discrimination law agreed that lawyers with whom they deal outside their offices were highly ethical.

While the Michigan survey data reveal differences by field of practice in lawyers' perceptions of their peers, no definition of "ethical conduct" was provided to respondents. Thus, they relied on their own definitions, so it is possible that lawyers who choose to work in different fields of law bring different ethical standards with them. Alternatively, it could be that lawyers were all using the same bar definition of ethical conduct (or perhaps their own moral sensibility) so that the resulting variation reflects real differences across areas of practice. Such speculation raises the crucial question Elizabeth Chambliss explores in chapter 3, "Whose Ethics? The Benchmark Problem in Legal Ethics Research." Chambliss identifies the difficulties in empirically assessing lawyers' ethics: "Should lawyers' ethical standards and conduct be compared to ordinary (lay) morality? To the formal rules of legal ethics? Or to the prevailing professional norms within a specialized area of practice (which may or may not be consistent with the formal rules)?" (chapter 3, 48). These questions, as she explains, have profound theoretical and practical implications for research on lawyers' professional conduct.

1. The survey was sent annually to Michigan law graduates over 40 years, with an average response rate of 67%. Respondents used a 7-point scale to indicate the strength of their agreement with the statement. For further details and analysis of responses to this question, see Mather (forthcoming). We thank David Chambers, co-director of the Michigan alumni survey, for making the data available for use in this chapter.

Before proceeding, it is important to define what *we* mean by "ethical" decision making. David Luban identifies four strands of legal ethics: the hard law of ethics, ethics of role, ethics of professionalism, and ethics of honesty (Luban 2005). When lawyers talk about "ethical" conduct, they often mean the first strand—conduct that is permitted or prohibited by the formal rules of professional responsibility (Suchman 1998; Levin 2004). Somewhat related to this conception is the second, the role morality lawyers assume when they act as one-sided partisans for clients, zealously advocating for them within the adversary system (Wasserstrom 1975). The third strand considers what values and conduct are expected of lawyers (and lawyers expect of themselves) as professionals, balancing obligations to the public and their clients with the need to make a living. Finally, legal ethics consists of basic honesty and truthfulness, what Chambliss refers to in chapter 3 as "ordinary (lay) morality" (48). We include in our definition of ethical decision making all four of these strands. The formal rules of professional conduct and the law of lawyering provide a useful starting point for analysis, along with the concept of role morality. But both "the rules" and lawyers' conceptions of professional role leave considerable room for individual discretion. Consequently, we define ethical decision making much more broadly to include the ways in which the rules and norms of lawyering, individual values, and considerations of justice, clients, and practice organizations, shape individual conduct.

With this broad definition in mind, we deferred to our contributors to select which ethical issues to address. Our only other criterion was that the ethical dilemmas be common or particularly troubling in the area of practice about which they were writing. As a result, the dilemmas discussed in part 2 of this book range from narrower ones involving possible violations of law or formal rules (e.g., responding to a lying client, how to advertise professionally, how much disclosure to provide an adversary) to broader ones of professional role and identity (e.g., the corporate litigator's obligation to the truth, the role of in-house counsel, the accountability of public interest lawyers). Each chapter describes the resolution of the ethical dilemma *from the practitioners' point of view in that particular area of practice.* Our goal in this book is to help students and scholars understand *how and why* lawyers make the decisions they do, invoking or ignoring formal rules, succumbing to self-interest or furthering the public good, acting in ways they consider moral or not. Such knowledge, we believe, could increase ethical self-awareness in lawyers as well as provide information to help construct more effective systems of professional regulation.

The Legal Profession and the Rise in Specialization

In order to understand the importance of context, it is first necessary to understand the composition of the US legal profession. There are almost 1.2 million US lawyers who work in a wide range of office settings, both in the United States and abroad. More than 75% work in private practice, approximately 10% work for the government, 8% work for private organizations as in-house counsel, and less than 1% work for legal services organizations or as public defenders (Nelson 2008). Despite the emphasis in the popular and scholarly press on the growth of large law firms, more than 60% of all lawyers in private practice still work in offices of 1 to 5 lawyers (Nelson 2008). These sole and small firm practitioners often represent individual clients in personal plight matters such as divorce, criminal law, and consumer bankruptcy, and small businesses, although some represent large corporate clients (Seron 1996; Levin 2004). Almost 22% of all private practitioners work in firms of 6 to 100 lawyers, while about 16% of all private practitioners work in large firms of more than 100 lawyers, with some firms having more than 1,000 lawyers (Nelson 2008). In-house attorneys work for organizations that employ from 1 to over 1,000 lawyers. Government lawyers and legal services lawyers also work in offices ranging in size from a few to several hundred lawyers.

Differences such as these in practice sites and firm size have substantial implications for how attorneys think about and do their work. Office size can affect the ways in which lawyers are socialized to the norms of the profession and influence the availability of internal monitoring and ethical support. It is also associated with major differences in the economics of law practice, which in turn affects incentives and constraints on attorneys. For example, lawyers' 2009 starting salaries in private practice varied by firm size with new lawyers in small firms (2–10 lawyers) earning a median salary of $50,000, compared to large firm lawyers (over 250 lawyers) earning a median salary of $160,000 (NALP 2010a). In contrast, new law school graduates in legal service jobs earned a median income of $42,000 annually, while the median income for new prosecutors in local government jobs was $50,000 (NALP 2010b).

Other economic incentives for lawyers may come from the ways in which they are compensated for their work. In theory, compensation is unrelated to professional conduct, but common sense and research suggest otherwise. While in-house lawyers work for fixed salaries, their bonuses—often a large component of their income—are not fixed, creating potential ethical conflicts since their sole client is also their employer. Lawyers in private practice charge clients directly for their services, and they depend on those fees to pay for the overhead associated with running a firm. Their fee arrangements include a flat fee (often charged by lawyers when working for individuals), a contingent fee (meaning that their ability to collect a fee depends on the case outcome), or an hourly fee. Each of these fee arrangements raises potential ethical issues for lawyers because of the conflicts of interest inherent in them (Fortney 2000; Kritzer 2004). For instance, the flat fee incentivizes lawyers to limit the time spent on a case, whereas the hourly fee might encourage inflated hours.

Changes in the economy and the economics of law practice over the last 20 years have brought many challenges for lawyers. Recent evidence suggests that the large firm business model built on high associate salaries and an intense tournament for partnership cannot be sustained (Galanter and Henderson 2008). Large firm clients more closely watch and contain law firm costs and are much more price sensitive when making decisions about legal representation. Large firm lawyers report less client loyalty, which puts increased pressure on them to satisfy their clients' demands and to constantly seek new clients (Suchman 1998; Kirkland, chapter 8). These lawyers increasingly confront competition for business from foreign law firms and from nonlawyers, including accounting firms. Law firm mergers and individual lawyer mobility present challenges for law firm management and for maintaining the ethical culture of law firms (Suchman 1998; Kelly 2007).

Economic challenges also affect lawyers working in smaller firms. Private practitioners who represent individual clients often struggle with cash flow and with finding new clients (Seron 1996). Many individuals, unable to afford lawyers' fees, are turning to self-help through books, computer programs, and the Internet to address their legal needs. They are also, in some cases, turning to nonlawyer providers, who may be engaged in the unauthorized practice of law. Competition for clients and concerns about cash flow may tempt lawyers to interpret professional rules in self-serving ways that allow them to address these pressures (Mather and McEwen, chapter 4; Levin, chapter 5; Daniels and Martin, chapter 6).

Lawyers in different office settings and practice specialties do not always share the same incentives and concerns. Law firm associates seek to satisfy partners, on whom they rely for promotion (Kirkland, chapter 8). Midsize to large firm partners seek to satisfy clients in order to maintain their income and positions within their firms. Solo and smaller firm lawyers face constant pressure to bring in new clients so that they can pay the rent. In-house lawyers do not need to bring in business, but still seek to facilitate their client's goals for personal advancement and other reasons (Kim, chapter 10). Prosecutors have no traditional clients or direct economic incentives, but are concerned with conviction rates, which provide a measure of status and aid in promotion (Yaroshefsky and Green, chapter 13).

The concerns of these lawyers suggest some of the pressures that encourage particular visions of professionalism and might also give rise to deviant conduct in different practice settings. Eagerness to make partner may cause young associates to engage in questionable behavior to please a powerful partner. A small firm lawyer who is facing a financial crunch might be tempted to "borrow" money from a client trust account or to take on more cases than she can reasonably handle, resulting in client neglect. In-house counsel may feel pressure to accommodate his client-employer because of concerns about receiving a bonus or retaining his job. A prosecutor focused on conviction rates may be tempted to bend the rules to achieve that goal. In short, the economic and political incentives and constraints of practice organizations motivate lawyers to think in particular ways about their professional responsibilities.

We must also consider the variation in lawyers' work contexts due to the substantive area of law in which they practice. As the law becomes increasingly complex and the legal market for clients becomes more competitive, many lawyers now specialize in particular fields. In their 1995 survey of the Chicago bar, Heinz et al. (2005) found that 33% of all lawyers they interviewed worked in only one field, a much higher percentage than they found 20 years earlier. And a more recent study of law school graduates reveals that 54% of lawyers describe themselves as specialists just seven years after graduation (Dinovitzer et al. 2010). Large law firms often hire for specific departments or areas of practice within the firm. While solo and small firm lawyers used to practice in several personal plight areas (Carlin 1962), more recently, even solo and small firm lawyers often limit their practices primarily to one or two practice areas (Levin 2004).

Even specialists are becoming more specialized. The Chicago lawyer study identified 42 different legal specialties, but it also noted many subspecialties within these areas (Heinz et al. 2005). For example, within the "securities" specialty, large firm lawyers further specialize in practice areas such as "asset management," "capital markets," "commodities futures and derivatives," "finance," "financial institutions advisory and financial regulatory," and "structured finance" (Shearman & Sterling 2011). In immigration, some lawyers perform business immigration work exclusively, representing large organizations that seek to hire foreign nationals, but "they wouldn't touch an asylum case; they wouldn't touch a removal case. They wouldn't touch an incarcerated alien" (Levin 2009, 414). Criminal defense lawyers who engage in white-collar defense work in federal court do not typically represent defendants in state court who are charged with ordinary street crimes.

Finally, individual differences among lawyers also affect their construction of their professional identities in ways we do not yet fully understand. Although the traditional ideology of the bar presumes that any personal values lawyers have stemming from their gender, race, or religion are put aside—or "bleached out"—of their professional identities, the reality is far more complex (Levinson 1993, 1578). The bar continues to be dominated by white males, but it is becoming increasingly feminized, with women making up almost 29% of all lawyers and close to half of all law students (ABA 2009). Although women now enter private practice at about the same rate as men, they continue to be underrepresented in the partnership ranks (NALP 2010c). Instead, women work disproportionately in government, in legal services, and for corporations. Minority groups also continue to make inroads into the legal profession, but the number of black, Hispanic, and Asian lawyers lags well behind what would be predicted based on the percentage of these groups in the US population. Approximately 3.9% of all lawyers are black, 3.3% are Hispanic, and 2.3% are Asian (Chambliss 2004). Minority lawyers also continue to be underrepresented in large law firms—at least among the partner ranks (NALP 2010c)—and overrepresented among lawyers who work for the government (Chambliss 2004).

The Regulation of Lawyers

Multiple normative frameworks exist for guiding lawyers' decisions. Ethical rules take precedence in the rhetoric of the bar, but they often do not provide clear answers to real-world dilemmas. Some of these rules reflect the views of the elite bar, and not the norms or values of many lawyers (Carlin 1966; Auerbach 1976). A considerable body of substantive law also guides lawyers' conduct and shapes their views through administrative or court sanctions or through malpractice liability. Finally, informal norms and shared values influence lawyers through collegial control in specific communities of practice. These shared ways of defining and answering ethical problems develop in conjunction with bar rules and substantive law to influence ethical decision making in practice. The chapters in this book look at lawyers' decisions from the bottom up—that is, from the perspective of lawyers in practice—and not from top-down rules that often reveal more about the aspirations of the profession than the reality.

For more than 100 years, the organized bar has devoted considerable effort to defining and refining its statement of the professional rules and values that govern lawyers. Those professional rules, embodied in state-adopted variations on the American Bar Association's (ABA) Model Rules of Professional Conduct, are a one-size-fits-all effort to define the responsibilities of lawyers and guide them in resolving ethical dilemmas.[2] But, as Richard Abel notes, "the Rules do not resolve those dilemmas; they merely restate them in mystifying language that obscures the issues through ambiguity, vagueness, qualification and hypocrisy" (1981, 685). In substance, these rules are often vague, and in many cases, they leave considerable discretion to lawyers' judgments. In practice, lawyers do not often consult the rules when addressing ethical issues. Not surprisingly, a few specialty bars, such as divorce, have drafted their own professional standards to guide the conduct of lawyers who practice in those areas, but they lack enforcement mechanisms.

Unquestionably, many of the ABA's rules do align with or inform some practice norms (most notably, in the area of confidentiality), but the rules' power to directly shape conduct is undercut in a variety of ways. Some of the rules—like those governing advertising and the duty to report lawyer misconduct—are notoriously under- or unenforced by disciplinary authorities (Zacharias 2002; Greenbaum 2003; Daniels and Martin, chapter 6). Courts sometimes disregard the rules, for example, in conflicts of interest and malpractice cases. The ABA's rules occasionally diverge from substantive law, and that law almost invariably trumps the bar rules.

In fact, efforts to influence lawyer conduct through substantive law have increased steadily in recent years. Most notably, Congress responded to corporate scandals in the early 2000s by directly imposing gatekeeping functions on lawyers who practice before the Securities and Exchange Commission (SEC) (Sarbanes-Oxley 2002). This occurred notwithstanding vigorous opposition from the ABA, which publicly charged that the new law conflicted with the lawyer's duties of confidentiality and privately feared that the law undermined the bar's claim to be a self-regulating profession. But efforts outside the bar to regulate lawyer conduct pre-date that legislation. Since the 1960s,

---

2. The ABA Model Rules of Professional Conduct set forth lawyers' duties to clients, the courts, third parties, and the public. The Model Rules can be found at http://www.americanbar .org/groups/professional_responsibility/publications/model_rules_of_professional_conduct .html. Virtually every state has adopted some version of the ABA Model Rules to govern the conduct of lawyers, and violations of a state's rules can result in the imposition of lawyer discipline

prosecutors have shown an increased willingness to indict lawyers who aid their clients in illegal conduct (*United States v. Benjamin*, 1964). The SEC began to pursue enforcement actions against lawyers in the 1970s (*SEC v. National Student Marketing*, 1978). The Office of Thrift Supervision sent shock waves through the elite bar when it sought to freeze the assets of the Kaye Scholer law firm in connection with its representation of the failed Lincoln Savings and Loan (Simon 1998). Less famously, other federal agencies, such as the Internal Revenue Service, the US Patent and Trademark Office (PTO), and the Executive Office for Immigration Review (EOIR) have sanctioned lawyers who violate their rules and standards of conduct.

The ethical rules of the legal profession are enforced through state disciplinary systems that are underfunded and largely reactive (Levin 2007). Disciplinary agencies are reasonably effective at monitoring lawyer behavior with respect to the money maintained in client trust accounts due to arrangements with banks that notify the agencies when there are overdrafts in these accounts. For other misconduct, discipline agencies lack sufficient investigative resources and primarily rely on reporting by clients, who may not know that they have been victimized by their lawyers or may have reasons not to report the misconduct (Wilkins 1992). Discipline complaints are most often filed for neglect of client matters and failure to communicate with clients (Abel 2008; Daniels and Martin, chapter 6). Initial complaints come most frequently against lawyers practicing in certain areas of law such as divorce, criminal, tort, and real estate (Mather and McEwen, chapter 4). Solo and small firm practitioners who practice in these areas receive a disproportionate number of discipline sanctions, as they often lack the resources of larger firms to manage their practices or the financial means to hire lawyers to represent them in discipline proceedings (Levin 2007). Moreover, larger firm clients often do not file complaints as they have more resources and options for seeking redress from their lawyers (Wilkins 1992).

The threat of malpractice liability also shapes the conduct of lawyers—or at least those in private practice. For example, fear of malpractice actions arising out of missed deadlines leads many firms to use sophisticated calendaring software and to implement backup systems to avoid such problems. Certain areas of law consistently rank high on the list of malpractice claims filed, including plaintiffs' personal injury and real estate (with family law often third) (ABA Standing Committee 2008). Most legal malpractice claims are brought against solo and small firm lawyers. However, midsize and large law firm lawyers are also sued frequently for malpractice. Settlements can range in the millions of dollars, and even large law firms have closed their doors in the face of significant malpractice claims (Fairbank and Maxon 2007).

Malpractice insurance also plays an important role in regulating some lawyer behavior (Ramos 1994; Cohen 1997). For instance, malpractice suits based on conflicts of interest have prompted carriers to require their insureds to use conflicts checking software (Fortney and Hanna 2002). Malpractice carriers promote competent conduct by requiring lawyers to identify the areas in which they practice and then limiting coverage to those areas. They also set premiums according to what they view as riskiest areas of law practice and place caps on coverage, require high deductibles, and impose exclusions from coverage for certain activities. In exchange for lower premiums, many insurers require in-house ethics committees and other internal mechanisms that will help avoid lawsuits. They often offer seminars, firm audits, and hotlines (Cohen 1997). But a substantial minority of private lawyers do not carry malpractice insurance (Qualters 2006; Illinois ARDC 2009); thus, insurers' efforts to reduce risky practices have no impact on this group.

As this discussion suggests, legal and regulatory efforts affect lawyers in different practice contexts unevenly. Enforcement efforts by various agencies matter only for the lawyers who practice before them. And enforcement varies tremendously from agency to agency: PTO and SEC enforcement efforts have ramped up in recent years while the EOIR lacks the resources to mount significant enforcement efforts (Conley and Mather, chapter 12; Schmidt, chapter 11; Levin, chapter 5). Discipline is a concern for solo and small firm lawyers, but is imposed on large firm lawyers infrequently, and on prosecutors almost never (Yaroshefsky and Green, chapter 13). Malpractice liability matters especially to private practitioners, but malpractice claims against legal services lawyers, government lawyers, or in-house counsel are rare.

Informal collegial control operates alongside the formal mechanisms of regulation to influence lawyers' conduct. In large law firms, such control might be seen in the organizational logic of the firm, the incentive structure, or even cultural ties. Emmanuel Lazega (2001), for example, analyzes the ways in which overlapping networks, competition for status, and social niches within a large firm create powerful collegial controls over lawyers. For lawyers working in solo or in small firms, informal norms and practices often develop that teach newcomers how to behave and also sanction those who deviate. The importance of an attorney's reputation has been noted in numerous studies (Landon 1990; Mather, McEwen, and Maiman 2001; Kritzer 2004), in particular the way in which peer pressure induces conformity to local practice norms or to the norms of specialized communities of practice. Shared identities and values, such as those that characterize attorneys working in legal services or public interest law firms, may also act as informal mechanisms of control. Some law firms or specialized communities of practice seem to be quite cohesive and have widely shared norms, whereas others—for whatever reason—have weaker collegial control (Kelly 1994; Mather 2010).

The Legal Profession's Sites of Socialization

How do lawyers come to learn the rules and norms of practice? They learn through direct instruction, through conversations they overhear, and from observation of the lawyers around them (Zemans and Rosenbaum 1981; Garth and Martin 1993; Seron 1996). Robert Nelson and David Trubek (1992, 179) use the term "arenas of professionalism" to describe the four institutional settings in which lawyers construct their understanding of professional norms and values. One of these arenas, disciplinary enforcement, has already been discussed. The other arenas are legal education, bar associations, and the workplace.

The first arena, legal education, plays an important role in socializing lawyers into the norms and values of the profession (Granfield 1992; Mertz 2007). Law schools teach the formal professional rules, respect for the law, certain habits of mind, and the hierarchy of the profession, which places large firm corporate practice at the top. But the impact of law school on the ethical decisions that lawyers make in practice may be limited (Pipkin 1979). Granfield and Koenig reported in their follow-up study of Harvard law school graduates that respondents "almost uniformly felt that their ethics training in law school had done little to prepare them for the issues they now confront as practicing attorneys" (2003, 508). They observed that the focus on formal rules was insufficient because it severed the cases from the social and other contexts in which they were embedded.

Bar associations also play an important role in the construction of lawyers' understanding of professionalism. As previously noted, the ABA drafts the model professional rules that govern lawyers, and a few other specialty bars construct guidelines that have persuasive effect. Even a quick glance at their mission statements reveals that bar associations consciously promote their visions of professionalism, which include high-quality lawyer performance and strong advocacy for clients. At the same time, those statements reflect their members' unique interests and values, which they disseminate through educational materials and programming efforts. More important, bar associations introduce lawyers with similar interests to one another, both in person and via the Internet. They help lawyers identify effective office management practices, which reduce the likelihood of discipline complaints. They also facilitate informal information exchange among lawyers, both with respect to the law and professional norms (Kilpatrick 1997–1998). They do this through substantive meetings and social gatherings, through mentoring programs and listservs, and through lobbying and other advocacy efforts (Levin 2011).

The most powerful arena of professionalism, however, is probably the workplace. It is here that professional values are most powerfully communicated and inculcated. Attorneys working in large law firms or other large organizations learn values and guides for decision making within the organization. In the solo and small firm context, however, the workplace may be a looser association of lawyers who share office space or provide advice, even if they are not formally associated or even physically proximate (Carlin 1966; Levin 2004). For these lawyers, Mather, McEwen, and Maiman's (2001, 6) concept of "communities of practice" may be more useful. For example, divorce lawyers, who practice mostly in solo and small firms, work within overlapping communities that include the bar as a whole, lawyers in particular locales, specialists and nonspecialists in family law, and individual law firms. Communities of practice not only communicate norms through example, but they can also exert limited control over lawyers.

The impact of these communities on lawyers' decisions has been found in a variety of practice contexts. The communities of practice within which divorce lawyers work encourage the norm of the reasonable lawyer (Mather, McEwen, and Maiman 2001; Sarat and Felstiner 1995). The norm of reasonableness also permeates the local professional community of legal aid lawyers when dealing with judges, opposing counsel, and clients (Katz 1982). Cooperativeness, courtesy, and trust were hallmarks of the country lawyers that Donald Landon studied (1990), and that community of lawyers imposed informal sanctions against those who did not comply with those norms. In the large law firm setting, one of the communities may be a single practice group or work group, from which younger lawyers learn the norms of aggressive discovery practice (Suchman 1998).

Social psychology, in addition to the economic, organizational, and cultural incentives discussed above, helps to explain why lawyers learn informal norms in these communities. Ralph Hertwig (2006) notes that "social learning—of which imitation is an example—allows individuals to learn about their environment without engaging in potentially hazardous learning trials or wasting large amounts of time" (398). But imitation is not the only social process at work. The psychological pressure on individuals to conform to the behavior of a group can be powerful. A group is more effective at inducing conformity if (1) it consists of experts, (2) the members are important to the individual, or (3) the members are comparable to the actor in some way (Aronson 1999). In this way, experienced lawyers transmit their norms and induce compliance with them, especially in organizations or in communities with repeated social interactions.

Interestingly, some evidence suggests that the longer lawyers work at their jobs, the more they come to see other attorneys' behavior as ethical. According to the Michigan law alumni survey data discussed above, there is a correlation between years in practice and perceptions of behavior as "highly ethical." Although only 51% of lawyers 5 years from graduation viewed the conduct of attorneys they worked with (other than in their own firm) as highly ethical, that percentage increased with each group: 55% of 15-year graduates, 59% of 25-year graduates, and 63% of 35- and 45-year graduates agreed that their peers' conduct was highly ethical. As Chambliss (chapter 3) explains these data, they could support a narrative of "ethical fading" in which younger attorneys come to accept as ethical lawyer behavior that they once decried. Alternatively, however, they could support a more positive narrative of professional specialization, socialization, and ethical learning. That is, as lawyers become more experienced in certain areas of law, they learn the nuances of their specific field of practice, including what constitutes ethical conduct in that field. Increased specialization in particular areas of legal practice thus may have significant implications for legal ethics, affecting the very definition of what constitutes ethical behavior for lawyers.

Organization of the Book

The chapters in this book examine ethical decision making in different areas of practice and the role that ethical rules—*and other factors*—play in everyday legal work. While the bar's rules may be interpreted and experienced differently by individuals due to their personal characteristics (e.g., gender, race, religion, personality) and by type of office setting (e.g., solo, firm, other organization), we chose to organize the book according to areas of practice instead. A primary focus on personal characteristics or office setting runs the risk of missing other important commonalities and differences in decision making. This book therefore is organized around what we believe is one of the most significant influences on ethical decision making: the practice area in which lawyers work.

Following the introductory chapters in part 1, the 13 chapters in part 2 examine different communities of legal practice, including legal specialty areas such as divorce, personal injury, criminal, securities, patents, and public interest law. In some of these practice areas, client characteristics are highly salient and thus require separate chapters for personal injury plaintiffs' lawyers and insurance defense lawyers, and for prosecutors and criminal defense attorneys. Corporate legal work encompasses so much variation that it is more appropriate to think of decision making in certain corporate settings—such as the chapters here on litigation, in-house counsel, or transnational practice. Obviously, many additional chapters could be included—ranging from other legal specialties such as environmental, tax, labor, or bankruptcy law to chapters on government lawyers at the local, state, and federal levels. We hope that future editions of this book will expand on the fields presented here.

Readers can easily start with any of the chapters depending on their primary interest in different sectors of the legal profession. Since each chapter addresses lawyers' decision making about one or more ethical issues, an alternative approach for readers might be to read the book according to the ethical issues presented, thus facilitating comparisons across legal fields in how lawyers think about and resolve such dilemmas. Decisions about disclosure are discussed in chapters on securities (chapter 11), patents (chapter 12), and prosecutors (chapter 13). Conflicts of interest are discussed in chapters on insurance defense (chapter 7), transnational lawyering (chapter 9), and patents (chapter 12). Issues of the lawyer/client relationship are explored in chapters on divorce (chapter 4), insurance defense (chapter 7), in-house counsel (chapter 10), criminal defense (14), and legal services (chapter 15). The meaning of advocacy in practice is examined in chapters on divorce (chapter 4), corporate litigators (chapter 8), criminal defense (chapter 14), legal services (chapter 15), and public interest lawyers (chapter 16). Other ethical decisions include how to handle the lying client (chapter 5) and lawyer advertising (chapter 6).

Another way to approach the chapters is in the order in which they appear. The first two chapters in part 2 look at lawyers who practice in personal plight areas and often deal with emotional and vulnerable clients. In chapter 4 on divorce lawyers, Lynn Mather and Craig McEwen report that the grievance complaints against these lawyers often arise out of the difficulties of communicating and working with emotional clients and their spouses on problems that include many nonlegal issues as well as legal ones. Divorce lawyers learn about what constitutes appropriate conduct from their communities of practice, but the ways in which they resolve issues of professional responsibility depend heavily on client resources and attorney caseloads, the structure of law firms, and the degree of specialization. Those with less affluent clients and fewer firm resources are more likely to face grievances. In chapter 5, Leslie Levin explores how immigration lawyers deal with the client who lies or wishes to lie in order to obtain the right to live and work in the United States. Lawyers' responses to the lying client are informed by the professional rules, but are also influenced by what they learn from their communities of practice—often early in their careers. The fear of discipline or criminal prosecution constrains some of these lawyers; but the need for clients and the perceived unfairness of the immigration system affects the willingness of others to close their eyes or even knowingly assist a lying client.

The next two chapters concern lawyers who work on opposite sides in tort cases and who also struggle to reconcile their vision of themselves as professionals with their need to earn a living. Stephen Daniels and Joanne Martin in their study of plaintiffs' personal injury lawyers (chapter 6) explore how the need for clients in a contingent fee practice shapes personal injury lawyers' views. They report that although violations of the formal rules concerning advertising and solicitation rarely result in discipline, personal injury lawyers construct their own understanding of what type of advertising a lawyer may engage in—if any—while still maintaining their self-respect as professionals. The community's approach to these norms is pragmatic, recognizing that some lawyers must advertise simply to stay in business. Similarly, in chapter 7, Herbert Kritzer also addresses a problem that arises out of lawyers' need to earn a living: How do insurance defense lawyers maintain good relations with the insurance companies that pay them while at the same time provide professional representation to the insured client? As a practical matter, most insurance defense lawyers work closely with the insurance company—which has the contractual right to direct the defense—to resolve the lawsuit. But insurance defense lawyers do draw some lines to preserve the traditional attorney-client relationship, so that they can also protect the interests of the insured client.

Shifting gears, the next three chapters investigate lawyers who work in large corporate settings. In chapter 8, Kimberly Kirkland examines how the norms of the adversary system affect how the lawyers come to view their obligations to the truth, and how this affects their approach to the discovery process. She shows how the corporate law firm's organizational structure, institutional demands, and changing norms also shape the ways in which corporate litigators understand their roles and responsibilities as lawyers. John Flood, in chapter 9, examines how lawyers in large transnational law firms that handle complex international transactions—in which clients may change shape and sides—address conflicts of interest. Like Kirkland, he explores how corporate lawyers view their obligations to the truth—in this case, when corporate clients seek to create a transaction on paper that is at odds with reality in order to conform with regulatory requirements. In chapter 10, Sung Hui Kim looks at lawyers working in a different corporate context when she considers "The Ethics of In-House Practice." She explores the ways in which in-house counsel balance their roles as facilitators of their client's business objectives with their professional gatekeeping function, especially when the corporation is considering conduct that could be both unlawful and substantially harmful to the organization.

The next section considers lawyers who work in specific corporate specialties that routinely require clients to make affirmative public disclosure, that is, who work in a very different regulatory environment than the lawyers described above. Patrick Schmidt's "The Ethical Lives of Securities Lawyers" (chapter 11) describes securities lawyers who share a culture favoring disclosure and transparency, not only because of the legal requirements of Sarbanes-Oxley, but also because of fear of shareholders' suits against their clients and malpractice actions against their firms. These lawyers have a legal duty to serve as gatekeepers, which they continually balance against their visions of themselves as creative professionals seeking to advance their clients' interests. In some cases, the actual disclosure is more a matter of form than substance, but it protects the client (and the lawyer) from risk of criminal penalties and financial harm. In contrast, in chapter 12, John Conley and Lynn Mather discuss the community of patent lawyers, who share a culture of disclosure that seems even more robust. The culture is encouraged by the law and consequences of nondisclosure (which can result in the invalidation of valuable patent rights), but also by the fact that patent lawyers come from a science background and seemingly share a stronger allegiance to the "truth" as a result of their training as scientists.

The final two sections of the book focus on lawyers working in various capacities on public law problems. First are attorneys who work on opposite sides of criminal cases—prosecutors and defense attorneys. In chapter 13, Ellen Yaroshefsky and Bruce Green systematically consider the many factors that influence how prosecutors interpret and execute their disclosure obligations to defense counsel. Since discipline against prosecutors is rare and malpractice is not a meaningful constraint on these lawyers, prosecutors are much more affected by the norms and values they learn in court and from their office colleagues in interpreting their obligation to disclose. Nicole Martorano Van Cleve, in chapter 14, shows how urban criminal defense lawyers interpret their obligations as advocates—generally seeking outcomes other than acquittal and exploring mental health or drug treatment alternatives for clients. Defense lawyers reinterpret the meaning of advocacy in part because they repeatedly face the same prosecutor and judge, both of whom may be hostile and unsympathetic to their clients.

The final two chapters look at lawyers who work to further the public interest through legal services or public interest advocacy. Corey Shdaimah (chapter 15) describes the ways in which legal services lawyers struggle with their desire to encourage client autonomy—even when their low-income clients may not seek it. These lawyers also wonder how they can ever effect real social change when their day-to-day work involves small victories that have little structural impact on a legal system that facilitates the disempowerment of their clients. Explicitly addressing the issue of how lawyers can effectively advocate for structural change, Scott Cummings (chapter 16) discusses how public interest lawyers from multiple practice settings (government, public interest, private practice) come together on behalf of a variety of clients (public interest organizations, government, unions, etc.) to promote law reform efforts. He explores how these lawyers devise strategies and negotiate conflict while still remaining accountable to their clients.

We hope this book will help narrow the gap between what sociolegal scholars are learning about lawyers' ethical decision making in context and the legal profession's approach to the teaching and regulation of lawyers. The book deliberately focuses on empirical research rather than on normative perspectives. Normative perspectives are well represented in the literature, but to be useful, they must be grounded in the realities of lawyers' professional lives. Knowing what "is" can help the bar, lawmakers, and other regulators construct and enforce what lawyers "ought" to do.

References

Abel, Richard L. 1981. "Why Does the ABA Promulgate Ethical Rules?" *Texas Law Review* 59:639–688.

———. 2008. *Lawyers in the Dock: Learning from Attorney Disciplinary Proceedings.* New York: Oxford University Press.

American Bar Association (ABA). 2009. "Lawyer Demographics." http://new.abanet.org/marketresearch/PublicDocuments/Lawyer_Demographics.pdf.

ABA Standing Committee on Lawyers' Professional Liability. 2008. *Profile of Legal Malpractice Claims: 2004–2007.* Chicago: ABA.

Aronson, Elliot. 1999. *The Social Animal.* 8th ed. New York: W. H. Freeman.

Auerbach, Jerold S. 1976. *Unequal Justice: Lawyers and Social Change in Modern America.* New York: Oxford University Press.

Carlin, Jerome E. 1962. *Lawyers on Their Own: A Study of Individual Practitioners in Chicago.* New Brunswick, NJ: Rutgers University Press.

———. 1966. *Lawyers' Ethics: A Survey of the New York City Bar.* New York: Russell Sage Foundation.

Chambliss, Elizabeth. 2004. *Miles to Go: Progress of Minorities in the Legal Profession.* Chicago: ABA Commission on Racial and Ethnic Diversity in the Profession.

Cohen, George M. 1997. "Legal Malpractice Insurance and Loss Prevention: A Comparative Analysis of Economic Institutions." *Connecticut Insurance Law Journal* 4:305–350.

Dinovitzer, Ronit, Robert L. Nelson, Gabriele Plickert, Rebecca Sandefur, and Joyce S. Sterling. 2010. *After the JD II: Second Results from a National Study of Legal Careers.* Chicago: American Bar Foundation and NALP Foundation for Law Career Research and Education.

Fairbank, Katie, and Terry Maxon. 2007. "How Jenkens & Gilchrist Lost Its Way: As Law Firm Dissolves, Leaders Have No Doubt Tax Scheme to Blame." *Dallas Morning News,* April 1.

Fortney, Susan Saab. 2000. "Soul for Sale: An Empirical Study of Association Satisfaction, Law Firm Culture, and the Effects of Billable Hour Requirements." *UMKC Law Review* 69:239–309.

Fortney, Susan Saab, and Jett Hanna. 2002. "Legal Malpractice and Professional Responsibility: Fortifying a Law Firm's Ethical Infrastructure: Avoiding Legal Malpractice Claims Based on Conflicts of Interest." *St. Mary's Law Journal* 33:669–720.

Galanter, Marc, and William Henderson. 2008. "The Elastic Tournament: A Second Transformation of the Big Law Firm." *Stanford Law Review* 60:1867–1929.

Garth, Bryant G., and Joanne Martin. 1993. "Law Schools and the Construction of Competence." *Journal of Legal Education* 43:469–509.

Granfield, Robert. 1992. *Making Elite Lawyers: Visions of Law and Harvard and Beyond.* New York: Routledge.

Granfield, Robert, and Thomas Koenig. 2003. "'It's Hard to be a Human Being and a Lawyer': Young Attorneys and the Confrontation with Ethical Ambiguity in Legal Practice." *West Virginia Law Review* 105:495–524.

Greenbaum, Arthur F. 2003. "The Attorney's Duty to Report Professional Misconduct: A Roadmap for Reform." *Georgetown Journal of Legal Ethics* 16:259–332.

Handler, Joel. 1967. *The Lawyer and His Community: The Practicing Bar in a Middle-Sized City.* Madison: University of Wisconsin Press.

Heinz, John P., and Edward O. Laumann. 1982. *Chicago Lawyers: The Social Structure of the Bar.* New York: Russell Sage Foundation.

Heinz, John P., Robert L. Nelson, Rebecca Sandefur, and Edward O. Laumann. 2005. *Urban Lawyers: The New Social Structure of the Bar.* Chicago: University of Chicago Press.

Hertwig, Ralph. 2006. "Do Legal Rules Rule Behavior?" In *Heuristics and the Law,* edited by Gerd Gigerenzer and Christoph Engel, 391–410. Cambridge, MA: MIT Press.

Illinois Attorney Registration and Disciplinary Commission (ARDC). 2009. *2008 Annual Report.* Chicago: Illinois ARDC.

Katz, Jack. 1982. *Poor People's Lawyers in Transition*. New Brunswick, NJ: Rutgers University Press.

Kelly, Michael J. 1994. *Lives of Lawyers: Journeys in the Organizations of Practice*. Ann Arbor: University of Michigan Press.

———. 2007. *Lives of Lawyers Revisited: Transformation and Resilience in the Organization of Practice*. Ann Arbor: University of Michigan Press.

Kilpatrick, Judith. 1997–1998. "Specialty Lawyer Associations: Their Role in the Socialization Process." *Gonzaga Law Review* 33:501–569.

Kritzer, Herbert M. 2004. *Risks, Reputations, and Rewards: Contingency Fee Legal Practice in the United States*. Palo Alto, CA: Stanford University Press.

Landon, Donald. 1990. *Country Lawyers: The Impact of Context on Professional Practice*. New York: Praeger.

Lazega, Emmanuel. 2001. *The Collegial Phenomenon: The Social Mechanisms of Cooperation among Peers in a Corporate Law Partnership*. Oxford: Oxford University Press.

Levin, Leslie C. 2004. "The Ethical World of Solo and Small Law Firm Practitioners." *Houston Law Review* 41:309–392.

———. 2007. "The Case for Less Secrecy in Lawyer Discipline." *Georgetown Journal of Legal Ethics* 20:1–50.

———. 2009. "Guardians at the Gate: The Backgrounds, Career Paths, and Professional Development of Private US Immigration Lawyers." *Law & Social Inquiry* 34:399–436.

———. 2011. "Specialty Bars as a Site of Professionalism: The Immigration Bar Example." *St. Thomas Law Journal* 8:194–225.

Levinson, Sanford. 1993. "Identifying the Jewish Lawyer: Reflections on the Construction of Professional Identity." *Cardozo Law Review* 14:1577–1612.

Luban, David J. 2005. "Introduction." In *Legal Ethics: Law Stories*, edited by Deborah L. Rhode and David J. Luban, 1–15. New York: Foundation Press.

Mather, Lynn. 2010. "How and Why Do Lawyers Misbehave? Lawyers, Discipline, and Collegial Control." In *An Unfinished Project: Legal Professionalism in Crisis*, edited by Scott L. Cummings, 109–131. New York: Cambridge University Press.

———. forthcoming. "Lawyers' Ethical Conduct Across Different Areas of Practice." *St. Thomas Law Journal*.

Mather, Lynn, Craig A. McEwen, and Richard J. Maiman. 2001. *Divorce Lawyers at Work: Varieties of Professionalism in Practice*. New York: Oxford University Press.

Mertz, Elizabeth. 2007. *The Language of Law School: Learning to "Think Like a Lawyer."* New York: Oxford University Press.

NALP. 2010a. "Class of 2009 National Summary Report." http://www.nalp.org/uploads/NatlSummaryChartClassof09.pdf.

———. 2010b. "Some Associate Salaries Retreat from Their High But Remain Far Ahead of Salaries for Public Service Attorneys." Press release, September 9. http://www.nalp.org/uploads/PressReleases/2010NALPSalPressRelease.pdf.

———. 2010c. "Women and Minorities in Law Firms by Race and Ethnicity." *NALP Bulletin*, January. http://www.nalp.org/race_ethn_jan2010.

Nelson, Robert L. 2008. "Trends in the Legal Profession: Demographic, Economic, and Early Careers." PowerPoint presentation at American Bar Foundation, Chicago, IL, September.

Nelson, Robert L., and David M. Trubek. 1992. "Arenas of Professionalism: The Professional Ideologies of Lawyers in Context." In *Lawyers Ideals/Lawyers Practices: Transformations in the American Legal Profession,* edited by Robert L. Nelson, David M. Trubek, and Rayman L. Solomon, 177–214. Ithaca, NY: Cornell University Press.

Pipkin, Ronald M. 1979. "Law School Instruction in Professional Responsibility: A Curricular Paradox." *American Bar Foundation Research Journal* 1979:247–275.

Qualters, Sheri. 2006. "No Malpractice Insurance? You Must Tell." *National Law Journal,* August 3.

Ramos, Manuel R. 1994. "Legal Malpractice: No Lawyer or Client is Safe." *Florida Law Review* 47:1–62.

Sarat, Austin, and William L. F. Felstiner. 1995. *Divorce Lawyers and Their Clients: Power and Meaning in the Legal Process.* New York: Oxford University Press.

Seron, Carroll. 1996. *The Business of Practicing Law: The Work Lives of Solo and Small-Firm Attorneys.* Philadelphia: Temple University Press.

Shearman & Sterling LLP. 2011. "Practices." http://www.shearman.com/practices/.

Simon, William H. 1998. "The Kaye Scholer Affair : The Lawyer's Duty of Candor and the Bar's Temptations of Evasion and Apology." *Law & Social Inquiry* 23:243–295.

Suchman, Mark. 1998. "Working Without a Net: The Sociology of Legal Ethics in Corporate Litigation." *Fordham Law Review* 67:837–874.

Wasserstrom, Richard. 1975. "Lawyers as Professionals: Some Moral Issues." *Human Rights* 5:1–24.

Wilkins, David B. 1990. "Legal Realism for Lawyers." *Harvard Law Review* 104:468–524.

———. 1992. "Who Should Regulate Lawyers?" *Harvard Law Review* 105:801–887.

Zacharias, Fred. 2002. "What Lawyers Do When Nobody's Watching: Legal Advertising as a Case Study of the Impact of Underenforced Professional Rules." *Iowa Law Review* 87:971–1022.

Zemans, Frances Kahn, and Victor G. Rosenbaum. 1981. *The Making of a Public Profession.* Chicago: American Bar Foundation.

Cases and Statutes

SEC v. National Student Marketing, 457 F. Supp. 682 (D.D.C. 1978).

United States v. Benjamin, 328 F.2d 854 (2d Cir. 1964).

Sarbanes-Oxley Act of 2002, Pub. L. No. 107-204, 116 Stat. 745.

CHAPTER TWO

Some Realism about Legal Realism for Lawyers

Assessing the Role of Context in Legal Ethics

David B. Wilkins

Twenty years ago, I wrote an article in the Harvard Law Review entitled *Legal Realism for Lawyers* (Wilkins 1990). It was the first substantial piece I ever published, and in many ways it has defined my research agenda ever since.

The article addressed a curious gap in the scholarship about the legal profession. Although a furious debate was then raging about the application of legal realism to legal theory and to the practice of judges, relatively little attention had been paid to how these same insights might affect legal ethics or, more generally, the traditional understanding of the lawyer's role. This omission was especially surprising since even a cursory examination of how the legal system functions makes plain that if there is a large amount of indeterminacy in the law, it is lawyers who are largely responsible for creating and exploiting it. Given their central role, as Karl Llewellyn famously observed more than six decades before when discussing legal ethics, "Why should you expect the ethics of the game to be different from the game itself?" (1930, 180).

The article's main contribution, however, was less to underscore that the rules of legal ethics are indeterminate—although, as I argued, not as radically indeterminate as some others had suggested. Instead, my goal was to emphasize *why* this was so, and what might be done to narrow the discretionary space that any plausible ethical regime would leave practitioners. The main culprit, I argued, was not so much the rules themselves (many of which are undoubtedly indeterminate on their face) but rather the underlying ethos that whatever

Thanks to the participants at the conference that gave rise to this volume and the editors for helpful comments on prior drafts. Cory Way provided invaluable editorial and research assistance.

rules are developed should apply equally, as stated in the preamble to the original American Bar Association (ABA) Model Code of Professional Responsibility (1969): "to all lawyers, regardless of the nature of their professional activity." This universalist assumption, I argued, obscures important distinctions in the roles lawyers are expected to play (e.g., litigation versus counseling), the clients that they represent (e.g., individuals versus corporations), and the potentially conflicting normative obligations (e.g., duties to clients versus duties to the legal system) that the ethical rules assume should guide their actions. Failing to pay attention to these contextual distinctions, I asserted, undermines the determinacy of the profession's meta-ethical norm that practitioners should represent their clients zealously but only "within the bounds of the law." As a result, even seemingly determinant ethical constraints on lawyer conduct can be, and as a practical matter often are, rendered indeterminate by clients and lawyers who have the resources and incentives to seek out (or help to create) gaps, conflicts, and ambiguities in the governing rule structure. If legal ethics is to escape this trap, I concluded, the profession should abandon its commitment to universalism and instead move to put in place a system of "middle-level" rules tailored to specific lawyering contexts.

In critiquing the universalist assumptions of the traditional model of legal ethics, *Legal Realism for Lawyers* was taking on one of the legal profession's most sacred cows. Far more than simply the basis for the formal rule structure, as I argued in a subsequent article, the image of *the* legal profession is deeply rooted in the stories, habits, and practices that lawyers have used for more than a century to understand themselves and their work (Wilkins 1992). The organized bar has long conceived of the practice of law as fundamentally a "generalist" profession in which differences among lawyering roles are largely unimportant with respect to the task of defining professional norms, or even assessing professional competence. All that matters is that the person *is* a lawyer and therefore has adopted a professional identity that subsumes all other personal characteristics (Nelson and Trubek 1992). For many US lawyers, this universalist assumption applies not only to all of the lawyers in all of the different lawyering roles in this country, but is the lens through which they understand and evaluate legal professionals around the world as well.

As Charles Wolfram (1986) has noted, even when the ABA enacted its first code of ethics in 1908, the assumption that all US lawyers shared enough in common to create a uniform set of professional expectations and rules was very likely false. By the time I wrote *Legal Realism for Lawyers* in 1990, it was demonstrably so. Virtually every significant study of the profession had documented wide disparities in the working conditions, experiences, professional status, and economic rewards enjoyed by lawyers in different parts of the profession (Auerbach 1976; Carlin 1966). According to this research, lawyers who represent large corporations were different from practitioners who primarily represent individuals (Heinz and Laumann 1982). Plaintiffs' lawyers were different from defendants' lawyers (Rosenthal 1974). Lawyers in large cities were different from lawyers in small towns (Handler 1967; Landon 1990). Lawyers who litigate were different from lawyers who primarily negotiate or offer office counseling (Macaulay 1979). Given this empirical evidence, I argued, any sensible regime of legal regulation would have to be sensitive to how contextual differences among lawyers in different parts of the bar would affect the way that these practitioners understood and interpreted ethical rules.

Acknowledging that context matters, however, is not the same thing as explaining *how* it should matter and for what purposes. In *Legal Realism for Lawyers* I acknowledged that this was no easy task given the large number of contextual factors that arguably might influence how lawyers understand and interpret ethical rules. In many respects, the sociolegal scholars on whose work I based my argument for a contextual approach to professional ethics did not have to face this challenge. For the most part, these researchers viewed their task as primarily descriptive. As indicated above, this research suggests a number of important differences among lawyers working in different parts of the profession. Any proposal that purported to direct regulatory officials to develop "middle-level" context-specific norms of professional practice would have to develop workable and effective principles for deciding which of these various contextual factors should be considered most important in particular circumstances.

The Two Hemispheres of the Legal Profession

This daunting task was made much easier by John Heinz and Edward Laumann in their path-breaking book *Chicago Lawyers* (1982). Using data from a random sample of over 800 lawyers throughout the Chicago bar, Heinz and Laumann argued that many of the contextual differences we observe among lawyers cluster around one central distinction—the "client" level difference between lawyers who represent individuals and those who represent corporations and other large organizations. As their data persuasively demonstrate, corporate lawyers in Chicago tended to work in larger firms, make more money, and have greater professional status and occupational mobility than lawyers who primarily represented individuals. Similarly, corporate and individual lawyers concentrated in different fields of law and interacted with different state and regulatory officials. The result was that the Chicago legal profession was divided into two hemispheres—a "personal plight" hemisphere comprised of immigrant, Catholic, and Jewish lawyers working in small firms for relatively little money and prestige, and a "corporate" hemisphere comprised of high-status WASP lawyers working in prestigious and highly paid positions in larger law firms handling corporate and securities matters for their equally high-status organizational clients.

Over the years, scholars like me built on the "hemispheres" framework to move from the descriptive to the prescriptive or regulatory level of analysis. Thus, in *Legal Realism for Lawyers*, I argued that the clustering effect around certain areas of practice—for example, tax law or securities—meant that it was possible to develop effective middle-level rules for practitioners in these areas without worrying about the complexities that might be caused by differences among the arguably relevant contextual factors (Wilkins 1990). Similarly, two years later in *Who Should Regulate Lawyers?* I argued that understanding the differences between the two hemispheres was central to constructing a plausible enforcement system that would encourage lawyers to fulfill both their duties to clients and to the public regulatory framework (Wilkins 1992). The next year, I combined these perspectives to argue in favor of context-specific rules and enforcement practices for law firms like Kaye Scholer that represent federally insured depository institutions such as Lincoln Savings and Loan (Wilkins 1993). Other scholars followed a similar path (Rapoport 1998; Sporkin 1993).

Indeed, some scholars have employed the hemispheres thesis to support a third level of analysis beyond the descriptive level for which it was originally intended and the prescriptive level of rulemaking and enforcement represented by *Legal Realism for Lawyers* and other similar work. For these scholars, the descriptive differences produced by the profession's division between lawyers for corporate and individual clients justify redefining the profession's entire identity and structure to reflect this central contextual reality. Thus, Professor Gillian Hadfield (2000) uses the hemispheres thesis to argue in favor of a fundamental restructuring of legal education and professional regulation designed to divide lawyers into two largely separate professions: The first would concentrate on corporate clients and managing the economy, while the second would serve individuals and the broader public purposes supporting the rule of law.

The fact that scholars could rely on the hemispheres thesis as a factual predicate for our normative analysis has been crucial in eliding certain tricky problems associated with calling for a contextual approach to regulation, or more broadly, to resolving questions of professional identity and structure. While contextual rules are, on the one hand, more likely to reflect the actual ethical tensions that arise in particular areas of law practice, they also inevitably risk creating—as Duncan Kennedy (1976) argued—"jurisdictional" conflicts as regulators attempt to identify which contextual rule to apply to which aspect of a particular problem. Is a lawyer who advises her client about how to present testimony at a public hearing before a government regulatory commission engaged in "litigation" or "counseling"? Is a lawyer whose client is being sued by a group of private plaintiffs for securities fraud governed by the "civil" or the "criminal" paradigm if the plaintiffs are cooperating with the government and the statute of limitations for criminal charges has yet to run? Is a lawyer temporarily working in the neighborhood legal services clinic of a large multicity law firm governed by the rules applicable to "corporate" or "individual" lawyers? A system of middle-level contextual rules must develop mechanisms for efficiently resolving these kinds of jurisdictional disputes— without becoming so complex that lawyers who simultaneously occupy more than one relevant context cannot understand or follow the rules. By focusing on the fact that these inevitable tensions were likely to be rare given that most relevant differences among lawyers could be subsumed within the overarching hemispheres framework, it was easier for scholars like me to set these complexities to one side.

Trends in the legal profession in the years since Heinz and Laumann first wrote in 1982 appeared to confirm the soundness of this approach. Thus, specialization, already an important fact of legal life in the 1970s, became pervasive in the last decades of the twentieth century (Heinz et al. 2005). Gone are the days when even in large law firms, a lawyer might dabble in a range of litigation and corporate matters before picking an area of practice in which to specialize. Instead, young lawyers today are increasingly required to join a particular department of a law firm or other legal organization—a department that is itself likely to be far more specialized than the old generic distinctions between "litigation" and "corporate"—and immediately begin steeping themselves in the minutiae of a particular area of practice. Moreover, as the largest law firms grew ever larger during this period, most shed the smaller clients and "full-service" practices that previously allowed them to dabble in work that more closely resembled the work done by their brethren in the personal plight hemisphere of the bar (Galanter and Henderson 2008). As more and more law firms strive to do only "premium work for premium clients," the distance between lawyers in the largest law firms and those in other parts of the bar has grown increasingly large.

This increasing distance has been dramatically reflected in the starting salaries of lawyers in the two hemispheres. By 2000, the "going rate" for first-year associates had climbed to $125,000, often accompanied by bonuses and other perks (Leonhardt 2000). Median salaries for public sector lawyers, on the other hand, were less than half of that amount, averaging between $45,000 and $63,000 per year (Dinovitzer et al. 2004). Indeed, as William Henderson (2009) has documented, by 2000 there was a clear bimodal distribution of starting salaries, with the overwhelming majority of new lawyers clustered around two poles: the first around $90,000 representing the amount made by entering associates in law firms, and the second around $40,000 representing virtually everyone else. As he notes, this distribution contrasts sharply with the picture for the class of 1991, where the overwhelming majority of graduates were clustered around a median salary of $40,000. And in every year between 2000 and 2008, the two parts of the distribution moved further away from each other so that by the last year the difference between the "corporate" peak of $160,000 and the "individual and public" peak of $50,000 amounted to $110,000, roughly double their separation in 2000.

Picking up on these disparities, a growing number of sociolegal scholars began to document the unique and often divergent culture and practices of lawyers in different parts of the bar. The rapidly growing number of corporate lawyers with their outsized incomes and expanding exposure in the professional and popular press received the lion's share of the attention (e.g., Regan 2004; Kronman 1993; Galanter and Palay 1991). But there were also excellent studies demonstrating the unique norms and practices of lawyers in the personal plight hemisphere, including divorce lawyers (Mather, McEwen, and Maiman 2001), plaintiffs' tort lawyers (Daniels and Martin 2000; Kritzer 2001), and solo and small firm practitioners (Seron 1996).

Given this research, those of us who study the legal profession were not surprised when Heinz, Laumann, and their new collaborators, Robert Nelson and Rebecca Sandefur, concluded in in 2005 (based on a new exhaustive study of Chicago lawyers conducted in 1995) that, notwithstanding all of the changes over the last 20 years, "the division between the two classes of clients . . .

endures" (Heinz et al. 2005, 7). Indeed, the most surprising thing about this second study was the degree to which the two hemispheres had pulled away from each other over the intervening two decades, both at the level of individual careers and in the aggregate amount of services rendered to entities and individuals. Although acknowledging that "lawyers employed by large law firms do, of course, handle legal work for individuals as well as for corporations," the research done by Heinz and his collaborators confirmed that as lawyers within these organizations have become increasingly specialized—"as lawyers who do securities work are now less likely to do probate or commercial law as well"— that "fewer lawyers will cross the boundaries" between the two hemispheres, leading to an increase in separation between the two domains (8).

At the same time, the corporate sector had grown so rapidly over the previous 20 years that the relative amount of legal work devoted to these two increasingly distinct and distant parts of the bar had shifted dramatically. In 1975, 53% of the work of Chicago lawyers was devoted to representing corporations and other organizational clients, while 40% was devoted to individuals (with another 7% not clearly assignable). By 1995, 64% of legal effort was devoted to serving the needs of organizational clients and only 29% was directed at providing services to individuals. As the researchers observed in a 1998 article announcing this finding, because "'hemi' means 'half,'" it may no longer be appropriate to use this metaphor to describe the state of the Chicago bar since "it is now hard to argue that the two parts are of approximately equal size" (Heinz et al. 1998, 773). Notwithstanding this terminological quibble, both of these findings further solidified the feeling among most sociolegal scholars that the hemispheres thesis represented a powerful descriptive tool for understanding the current state of the American legal profession, and a firm foundation for developing normative ideas about professional regulation and ideology.

Indeed, the idea that the bar is increasingly fragmented along client lines has become so pervasive that it is now an unquestioned part of the self-image of many practicing lawyers. The following two anecdotes are typical of the kind of comments that I have heard from lawyers with increasing frequency over the last several years. The first occurred in the late 1990s as I was moderating a discussion at Harvard Law School on the public responsibilities of lawyers. Toward the end of the discussion, a partner from one of the large New York law firms stood up to say that he recognized the long tradition of lawyers being "officers of the court," but in his world this tradition now applied only to litigators. "I'm a corporate lawyer," he declared, "and we don't have these kinds of public responsibilities." The second occurred in 2010 at a meeting organized by the ABA where I was speaking to a group of managing partners on the impact of globalization on the market for legal services. At the conclusion of my presentation, the president of the ABA explained that the association wanted to work with large firms to address some of the issues I raised. But when she asked for comments, the head of a major international law firm said that he was surprised to hear of her interest since in his view the ABA had been completely captured by solo and small firm practitioners who had no understanding of the issues facing large law firms and who insisted on maintaining a set of antiquated rules and practices that were destroying the profession. Virtually all of the other managing partners in attendance nodded their heads in agreement.

Not surprisingly, others have a different view about which segments of the profession are destroying professionalism. Thus, in the wake of the charges brought by the Office of Thrift Supervision against the New York law firm of Kaye, Scholer, Fierman, Handler & Hayes, many commentators pointed to the law firm's decision to place a litigator in charge of the thrift's response to the government's regulatory audit as being responsible for the overly aggressive manner in which the law firm counseled the client to respond to the regulator's requests for information (Wilkins 1993). Similarly, the New York State Bar Association (2000) issued a report criticizing the excessive commercialism of many large law firms and instead arguing that "medium sized law firms (11–50 lawyers) . . . have frequently been the backbone of activities within the organized bar, stressing 'professionalism' and providing leadership for professional organizations." The fact that the number of "specialty" bar associations representing the interests of lawyers in different sectors of the profession has increased dramatically in recent years underscores just how fragmented the profession has become (Kilpatrick 1997–1998).

In the wake of corporate scandals from Enron, to Options-gate, to the 2008 financial meltdown, it is easy (albeit painful) to dismiss this kind of squabbling over whose culture is more destructive of professionalism as just another manifestation of the entire legal profession's failure to take responsibility for the role lawyers have played in corporate misconduct. But the fact that this kind of disassociation and finger pointing has become increasingly common among lawyers from different parts of the profession should also be a tip that there may be troubling consequences to pushing an approach to professional identity that encourages lawyers to define their most basic professional responsibilities solely in relation to what have become the ever narrower boundaries of their own practices.

Context 2.0: The Shifting Boundaries of Legal Practice

Not surprisingly, sociolegal researchers are in the forefront of helping us to identify these dangers and, more generally, to understand the complexity of generating a descriptively accurate and normatively attractive contextual account of legal practice and legal ethics in the increasingly volatile global market for legal services. Although this scholarship continues to document such trends as specialization and the accelerated growth of large law firms that reinforce the hemispheres thesis, recent studies also document six trends that complicate the goal of creating a rich context-specific descriptive or normative account of the contemporary legal profession.

The first complication is mobility. While Heinz and his fellow researchers acknowledge that lawyers had become increasingly mobile by the end of the twentieth century, this trend has escalated rapidly in the first decade of the twenty-first. The *After the JD* study (AJD), of which I am one of a number of principal researchers, makes this point plain. In AJD, we are following 4,000 lawyers who entered the bar in the year 2000 during the first 10 years of their practice (Dinovitzer et al. 2004). We have now surveyed these lawyers in 2003 and in 2007. In the four years between these two snapshots, an astounding 50% of the sample had changed jobs more than once (Dinovitzer et al. 2010). Nor were all of these job changes simply lawyers moving from one large or small firm to another. Although many respondents have remained in similar kinds of jobs even as they change employers, almost 50% of the lawyers who moved had not just changed jobs but job sectors as well (Dinovitzer et al. 2010). Thus, of all of the lawyers who began their careers in law firms of over 250 lawyers, only 43% were still working in similar institutions seven years after graduation. Of the remaining 57%, 17% had moved in-house, in all likelihood remaining firmly within the corporate hemisphere. Another 5% had abandoned law practice altogether for business jobs, often within companies for which they previously did legal work. But 10% had moved to significantly smaller firms (21–100 lawyers), with 6% working in organizations with fewer than 20 attorneys. Another 16% were working in government, public service, or education. Although some of these lawyers are undoubtedly continuing to represent corporate clients or work in traditionally corporate fields of law (e.g., doing securities work for a federal or state agency), the fact that they are now doing so in a context where they are also likely to either represent individual clients—or, in the case of government lawyers, have responsibility for their interests—changes the straightforward picture portrayed by the hemispheres thesis. Significantly, women were less likely to still be working in large law firms (only 40.9% as compared to 44.3% of men), and more likely to have moved down in firm size (16% as compared to 12.8% of men), than their male counterparts. Given that women now constitute approximately 50% of all law school graduates, this disparity suggests that as the percentage of women in the profession increases, there is likely to be more, not less, movement across the hemispheres.

The fact that lawyers are increasingly mobile complicates the task of creating middle-level rules governing particular areas of legal practice. To the extent that professional socialization is one of the forces that helps lawyers to internalize distinctive norms and practices, that process is potentially disrupted by lawyers moving across traditional boundaries. Philosophers have long worried, for example, that lawyers who move from private practice into government bring an overly adversarial and client-centered approach to legal practice that is often inconsistent with their new role as protectors of the public interest (Wasserstrom 1975). As lawyers move with greater frequency across sectors and specialties, creating stable, practice-specific norms will arguably become increasingly difficult.

Second, both mobility and the weakening of the correlation that Heinz and his fellow researchers observed between firm size and client type are likely to be accelerated by the increasing importance of information technology in the legal market. To be sure, large law firms have continued to shed the smaller clients and matters that used to constitute a sizeable part of their practices at the time of the first *Chicago Lawyers* study. At the same time, however, smaller firms are increasingly using technology to leverage their ability to provide the kinds of services that we have come to think of as being the exclusive province of larger firms. There are now a number of "boutique" litigation firms that compete directly with global megafirms for the most sophisticated legal work (Bario 2009). Advances in information technology are likely to make it possible for even smaller and more geographically dispersed groups of lawyers to collaborate on important matters for global clients (Glater 2001). These smaller and more loosely organized networks are likely to pull recruits from the growing number of lawyers who are dissatisfied with the working conditions typically found in large law firms and in-house legal departments (Zimmett 2007). The rapid growth of Axiom Legal, a loosely affiliated network of refugees from the country's most prestigious law firms and companies who work on a project-by-project basis for top corporate clients while reserving the right to temporarily "go on the beach" to pursue their other professional and personal interests (some of which have to do with working on causes in the personal plight hemisphere), underscores how these new organizational forms are likely to further destabilize existing career patterns and relationships (Jones 2008). As Richard Suskind (2008) suggests in his provocatively titled book *The End of Lawyers?*, we are only at the forefront of seeing the kind of changes that technology is likely to bring to legal practice.

Needless to say, these changes will also have a profound effect on how we think about regulating lawyers. The ability to deliver legal services over the Internet is already challenging standard assumptions about who can practice law, how it should be practiced, and which jurisdictions should be entitled to regulate this conduct (Blades and Vermylen 2004). The even more radical changes contemplated by Suskind and others will undoubtedly destabilize existing regulatory patterns even further.

These changes in turn will reinforce a third trend toward the unbundling—and, equally important, repackaging—of legal tasks. Sophisticated general counsel are increasingly breaking down legal work into its component parts and then shipping these parts to service providers around the globe whom they believe can accomplish these tasks in the most efficient and effective ways possible (Regan 2010). As a result, Indian lawyers are now finding themselves working for legal process outsourcing companies (LPOs) doing discovery work for Fortune 500 companies—often cheek by jowl with relocated American ex pats who are leaving US and UK law firms and companies to train these new soldiers in the legal global value chain (Krishnan 2007). As law firms and companies embrace "nearsourcing" work to lower-cost cities in this country as a way to drive efficiency while avoiding some of the complexities currently associated with offshoring legal work to places like India, a growing number of US lawyers who previously would have worked in small law firms in the personal plight hemisphere may find themselves (at least temporarily) doing back-office work for large companies (Schmitt 2008).

Although outsourcing and offshoring by global companies have received most of the attention in this area, the ability to use technology and global supply chains to disaggregate and repackage legal work need not be confined solely to the corporate hemisphere. Theoretically, there is no reason why enterprising lawyers cannot develop ways to leverage these resources to package and process transactions for individuals that can be handled more efficiently at the aggregate level. There are already indications that some Indian LPOs are beginning to do just that by offering solo and small firm practitioners the ability to send legal work overseas as a means of expanding their resources as needed without the cost and risk of hiring new lawyers (Sherman 2005). The fact that some of these LPOs are also marketing themselves to global companies to provide similar services is yet another example of how the two hemispheres are likely to interact in unexpected ways in the years ahead.

Once again, these changes are already straining existing regulatory patterns and practices. The ABA has recently issued an advisory opinion concerning the use of LPOs (ABA Standing Committee 2008). This is likely only the opening salvo in what is becoming an increasingly bitter battle both in the United States and around the world about how this practice is going to be regulated. More fundamentally, the growing use of offshoring, nearshoring, and other similar methods for disaggregating legal work raise long-term issues about the training of junior lawyers and the structure of law firms (Owen 2008). As these trends become more pervasive, they are likely to further destabilize our existing understandings of what constitutes "legal services" and the ways these services are delivered—and therefore should be understood and potentially regulated—across a broad range of lawyering contexts (Terry 2008).

The fourth trend toward eliminating regulatory restrictions on the organizational forms through which law can be practiced is likely to facilitate these new ventures. The UK has already enacted reforms that effectively eliminate virtually all of the traditional restrictions on the kinds of institutions that can "practice law," including expressly authorizing nonlawyer ownership of law firms and multidisciplinary partnerships (Clementi 2005). Although once again most of the attention has been focused on how this will affect the corporate hemisphere, an express goal of these reforms was to make it easier for supermarkets and other consumer-oriented companies to go into the business of efficiently providing legal services to individuals (Flood 2008). As Flood argues, if the United Kingdom authorizes "Tesco Law" (named after a large UK supermarket chain that under the new law will be able to set up legal clinics next to the produce aisle), there will be increasing pressure, both through the normal processes of the marketplace and through the operation of international agreements such as the General Agreement on Trade in Services, for the United States to follow suit by allowing Tesco to operate similar clinics in its stores in this country.

Indeed, in Australia where publicly traded law firms are already legal, the first firm to take advantage of this option was not a large firm serving corporate clients. Instead, it was Slater & Gordon, a classic personal plight plaintiffs' law firm serving accident victims and other individuals (Regan 2008). Since the initial public offering, Slater & Gordon has used its new capital to acquire six smaller plaintiffs' law firms, thereby allowing it to achieve the kinds of economies of scale and scope previously reserved for law firms catering to the corporate hemisphere (Parker 2008). Plaintiffs' firms—and those who would like to invest in them—in the United States and around the world are taking notice.

Moreover, the bigger and more successful plaintiffs' firms become, the more overlap there is likely to be between plaintiff and defense lawyers—and not just across the "v" as opposing parties in litigation. There are already a number of firms that defy the traditional separation between the plaintiff and defense bar. Some, like Boies, Schiller & Flexner LLP, do most of their work for companies suing other companies in the rapidly expanding market for business-to-business litigation (Goldhaber 2001). But some, like Susman Godfrey LLP, started out life as plaintiffs' firms representing individuals and class actions and gradually morphed into also doing defense work for major corporations (Frankel 2005). Indeed, the recession has led some traditional defendants'-side firms to take on plaintiffs'-side cases as a means of boosting their sagging profits (Kamping-Carder 2010). At the same time, the status and incomes of the traditional insurance defense bar have declined to such an extent that their profiles have begun to look increasingly similar to the "bread and butter" tort lawyers whom they traditionally have opposed (Kritzer 2006).

The fifth trend blurring the boundary between the two hemispheres is what Scott Cummings (2004) aptly describes as the "institutionalization of pro bono." As Cummings documents, law firms and other corporate legal employers now provide more services to individuals than government-sponsored legal aid does. Not surprisingly, legal services and public interest organizations are reorienting their missions and practices to take account of this changing reality.

The growing interdependence between large firms and public interest organizations became blindingly obvious when the market cratered in the fall of 2008, taking the corporate legal market down with it. Suddenly, law firms had many more lawyers than they needed, with more on the way. Many simply laid off these newly unnecessary assets the way General Motors lays off autoworkers. But many firms decided to soften the blow (or the negative publicity) by "furloughing" their unwanted or deferred associates to legal services and public interest organizations, often paying salaries that far exceeded what the lawyers already working in these organizations could make after many years of experience (Breitman 2009). Although it appears that this particular gambit is unlikely to be repeated, the fact that firms continue to look to pro bono and public service to provide everything from training for their associates to legitimacy in the eyes of clients and regulators underscores that at least in this area, the "corporate" and the "personal plight" hemispheres are closer than they might appear.

Nor is pro bono work the only place where lawyers are finding themselves straddling divisions that sociolegal scholars have traditionally thought of as defining separate sectors of the bar. Beginning with the tobacco litigation in the 1990s, a growing number of state attorneys general have begun to sue private companies for damages that these entities have allegedly caused to state citizens (Erichson 2000). In a significant number of these cases, state officials have brought in private lawyers to litigate alongside government lawyers. Although the courts that have blessed these arrangements insist that these private lawyers should act indistinguishably from the public lawyers who are ultimately responsible for the conduct of the litigation, these arrangements in fact require lawyers serving in this capacity to balance a complex mix of public and private duties and incentives (Wilkins 2010).

Globalization, the last and arguably the most important of the six trends, seems likely both to encourage this complex and symbiotic relationship between the public and the private sectors as it also problematizes the content of the "public interest" norms on which pro bono, public service, and indeed the very idea of law as a "public" profession are based. As anyone who follows the legal profession is well aware, American lawyers are going global (Flood, chapter 9). Nor is this phenomenon confined to the corporate hemisphere. In fields as diverse as immigration, family law, personal injury, and human rights, lawyers who represent individuals are increasingly finding themselves in situations in which clients, opposing parties, or relevant third parties or legal issues reach beyond the US border (Velaigam 2007).

Indeed, it is not just US lawyers who are being reshaped by globalization. China, India, Brazil, and a host of other emerging nations are joining the United States and Europe in developing sophisticated commercial law firms and new "American-style" law schools to train lawyers to staff them (Krishnan 2010; Liu 2008). As these firms attempt to capture their share of the expanding market for corporate legal services both in their own countries and elsewhere, they are also increasingly being asked to demonstrate that they have all of the attributes of a "modern" legal profession, including a commitment to pro bono and public service. The fact that corporate lawyers and their counterparts in nongovernmental and human rights organizations both find themselves with a shared interest in expanding at least the trappings of the rule of law will only accentuate this trend (Dezalay and Garth 2010).

As lawyers seek to understand and adapt to the ways that globalization is blurring and reshaping contextual boundaries, they increasingly face expanding regulation by various public and private actors—regulation that is itself being reshaped by globalization. Since there is no international government that can regulate transnational legal practice, new legal forms are emerging through dispersed rule setting (Quack 2007). Some of this regulation attempts to target specific issues or areas of practice, such as money laundering or international arbitration (Rogers 2010). The task of creating even this kind of context-specific regulation, however, is becoming increasingly difficult as globalization throws new kinds of parties, lawyers, and issues into institutions that were set up to deal with a more homogeneous environment (Rogers 2007). The task of organizations like the International Bar Association that seek to create a new code of conduct that would regulate lawyers across the full range of international and transnational practice settings is even more daunting (Boon and Flood 1999).

Conclusion: Context as Process and Paradox

Collectively these six trends—mobility, technology, unbundling and repackaging, new organizational forms for delivering legal services, the institutionalization of pro bono, and the connected set of changes falling under the general heading of globalization—complicate both the descriptive and the normative task faced by those of us who seek to analyze the legal profession "in context." Descriptively, each of these developments makes it more difficult to identify which contextual factors are relevant and for which purposes. Are large publicly traded plaintiffs' firms more like large defense firms or like traditional plaintiffs' firms? Are organizations that use technology and global supply chains to aggregate and process individual claims part of the corporate or individual hemisphere? Will deferred associates who spend time in a legal services or public interest organization think or practice differently when they return to their corporate law firms? These and the many other complexities introduced by the large-scale trends discussed above are likely to destabilize many of our traditional ways of thinking about context.

The regulatory and normative implications of these new contextual realities are even more perplexing. In *Legal Realism for Lawyers*, I argued that the traditional model's preference for general, universally applicable rules addressed to all lawyers in all contexts created a significant risk that these commands would acquire unintended, perhaps even perverse, meanings once they were interpreted by real lawyers operating in the real and distinct contexts in which they worked. While I believe that this remains true, the growing complexity and fluidity resulting from the six trends discussed above creates a parallel risk that regulation that is too narrowly tailored to fit a single context will produce similarly unforeseen consequences as lawyers, clients, and legal norms increasingly cross established contextual boundaries. My point, therefore, is not that we should abandon our attempt to craft context-specific rules. Instead, we need to temper our efforts to create appropriate middle-level rules with an equally vigilant search for the ways in which the increasingly blurred and porous boundaries that now characterize a significant amount of legal practice should also be incorporated into the regulatory process.

Consider, for example, the hotly debated question of the scope and content of the regulation that should be applied to private lawyers who are deputized as "substitute" attorneys general in damage actions against private parties (Rubenstein 2004, 2143). Several prominent commentators argue that just as regulations and precedents have long prohibited a prosecutor from being paid a salary that is in any way contingent on the outcome of the case, private lawyers hired to assist public lawyers in prosecuting public cases should also be banned from being compensated on the basis of contingent fees (Redish 2008; Erichson 2000). This contention, however, overlooks the benefits to the state of being able to engage private lawyers on different terms than it could pay its own employees. More fundamentally, the argument that substitute attorneys general should be treated in exactly the same way as lawyers who are actually full-time government employees ignores the crucial fact that those who serve in the former capacity remain private lawyers subject to the demands of the private marketplace, even as they serve public ends. Given this important distinction, as I argue elsewhere, there are good reasons to believe that these private-public lawyers should be regulated differently than public lawyers who are not subject to these private market demands (Wilkins 2010). Those designing middle-level rules to govern this new form of public-private practice must be attuned to these differences.

Indeed, an appropriate regulatory regime should take advantage of the fact that many (although by no means all) of the lawyers who are currently engaged in this new form of public-private practice were themselves full-time government lawyers before entering private practice. The existence of this revolving door clearly creates the risk, as the Model Rules warn, that lawyers who move between public service and private practice will "exploit" the benefits of their public roles for the benefit of their private clients (Model Rule 1.11 cmt. 3). But it also creates a cadre of private lawyers who at least potentially understand the benefits of public service and are committed to the public norms that are supposed to guide public lawyering, even when it is conducted by private lawyers who have been deputized to do so. At the same time, the private lawyers who assume these public positions can help the government lawyers who employ them to understand what it is like to be on the receiving end of government power in a manner that could improve the overall efficiency and fairness of these kinds of public actions. To be sure, there is no guarantee that this kind of cross-pollination will produce lawyers who will effectively discharge their complex public and private responsibilities in this new setting. My point simply is that an effective regulatory regime for this area of practice should take account of how mobility and professional socialization are likely—for better or for worse—to affect the ways that both government and private lawyers operate in this context.

In the last analysis, however, it is the task of creating a credible and normatively attractive understanding of professional identity that is most challenged by the developments I have chronicled in this chapter. In the past, lawyers had a fairly simple and straightforward way of thinking about their identity. Lawyers, according to this traditional view, are simultaneously and indivisibly both zealous advocates for the interests of their private clients and officers of the legal system with a special obligation to protect democratic values and the rule of law. Today, such confident pronouncements about the seamless and mutually reinforcing connection between private practice and public service ring hollow against the backdrop of the increasingly competitive and cutthroat global market for legal services. There is a widespread feeling among younger and older lawyers alike that the once interconnected worlds of private practice and public service have grown increasingly distant from each other, with lawyers and even law students forced to stake their claim to one or the other realm at an ever earlier time (Rhode 1998).

The series of connected trends discussed in this chapter, however, point to a more complex reality. Even as lawyers continue to become more and more specialized, their public and private roles are arguably more inextricably intertwined than they have been at any other time in the profession's history. As the remark from the New York corporate partner cited above underscores, lawyers both in the United States and around the world have always tried to separate these competing obligations, either by prioritizing client interest in a way that effectively eviscerates public duties or by outsourcing these latter norms to some other part of the bar (Gordon 1988). But as I have argued elsewhere, these attempts are ultimately self-destructive since the only thing that gives lawyers both legitimacy and access to top talent is the claim that law is, notwithstanding all of the market trappings to the contrary, ultimately a public profession. This "paradox of professional distinctiveness" (Wilkins 2007, 1273–1277), I believe, is now being replicated around the world as lawyers attempt to both conform their institutions and practices to the demands of the global economy while at the same time hold on to the norms, myths, and habits that ultimately make them distinct. For all of its power, the hemispheres thesis does not tell us how to help lawyers achieve this fundamental unification.

As they have in so many other areas, Jack Heinz and his fellow researchers at the American Bar Foundation anticipated this problem. While indicating that the hemispheres thesis still applied notwithstanding all of the changes that had occurred since their study in 1975, the researchers noted that "in 1995 . . . it appears that . . . specialization by client type played a lesser role and substantive or skill-type specialization played a greater role than in the 1975 analysis." Moreover, as the researchers went on to note, these changes should make one cautious about whether the patterns they discerned in 1995 would persist. In the typically understated tone that pervades all of their work, Heinz and his co-authors warned, "It may be a mistake to assume that the structure of the bar will eventually settle into stability once again" (Heinz et al. 2005, 9). As sociolegal scholars, it is our obligation to heed this warning and to look for the new structures that are reshaping lawyers both in the United States and around the world. In so doing, we should continue to pay careful attention to context— including how the six factors discussed in this chapter are reshaping how we understand what context means in the twenty-first century. This is exactly why I am so delighted to be a part of this important volume—and proud to have played some small role in beginning the inquiry that got it started.

References

American Bar Association (ABA) Standing Committee on Ethics and Professional Responsibility. 2008. "Lawyer's Obligations When Outsourcing Legal and Nonlegal Support Services." Formal Opinion 08-451, August 5. http://www.aapipara.org/File/Main%20Page/ABA%20Outsourcing%20Opinion.pdf.

Auerbach, Jerold S. 1976. *Unequal Justice: Lawyers and Social Change in Modern America.* New York: Oxford University Press.

Bario, David. 2009. "Litigation Boutique of the Year Winner Bartlit Beck: Unique Model, Unmatched Results." *American Lawyer,* January 1. http://www.law.com/jsp/tal/Pub ArticleTAL.jsp?id=1202426960171&slreturn=1&hbxlogin=1.

Blades, Melissa, and Sarah Vermylen. 2004. "Virtual Ethics for a New Age: The Internet and the Ethical Lawyer." *Georgetown Journal of Legal Ethics* 17:637–658.

Boon, Andrew, and John Flood. 1999. "The Globalization of Professional Ethics? The Significance of Lawyers' International Codes of Conduct." *Legal Ethics* 2:29–58.

Breitman, Rachel. 2009. "Law Firms Scramble to Place Deferred Associates in Volunteer Posts." *American Lawyer Daily,* March 19. http://www.law.com/jsp/article.jsp?id= 1202429198615 .

Carlin, Jerome E. 1966. *Lawyers' Ethics: A Survey of the New York City Bar.* New York: Russell Sage Foundation.

Clementi, David. 2005. *The Future of Legal Services: Putting Consumers First.* Norwich: Her Majesty's Stationery Office.

Cummings, Scott L. 2004. "The Politics of Pro Bono." *UCLA Law Review* 52:1–150.

Daniels, Stephen, and Joanne Martin. 2000. "'The Impact That It Has Had Is between People's Ears': Tort Reform, Mass Culture, and Plaintiffs' Lawyers." *DePaul Law Review* 50:453–496.

Dezalay, Yves, and Bryant G. Garth. 2010. *Asian Legal Revivals: Lawyers in the Shadow of Empire.* Chicago: University of Chicago Press.

Dinovitzer, Ronit, Bryant G. Garth, Richard Sander, Joyce Sterling, and Gita Z. Wilder. 2004. *After the JD: First Results of a National Study of Legal Careers.* Chicago: American Bar Foundation and NALP Foundation for Law Career Research and Education.

Dinovitzer, Ronit, Robert L. Nelson, Gabriele Plickert, Rebecca Sandefur, and Joyce S. Sterling. 2010. *After the JD II: Second Results from a National Study of Legal Careers.* Chicago: American Bar Foundation and NALP Foundation for Law Career Research and Education.

Erichson, Howard M. 2000. "Coattail Class Actions: Reflections on Microsoft, Tobacco, and the Mixing of Public and Private Lawyering in Mass Litigation." *University of California Davis Law Review* 34:1–48.

Flood, John. 2008. "Will There be Fallout from Clementi? The Global Repercussions for the Legal Profession after the UK Legal Services Act 2007." Jean Monnet/Robert Schuman Paper Series, Volume 8, Number 6, Coral Gables, Florida, April. Available on SSRN: http://papers.ssrn.com/so13/papers.cfm?abstract_id=1128398.

Frankel, Alison. 2005. "Risky Business: Susman Godfrey Likes Placing the Big Bets Almost as Much as it Likes Taking in the Big Fees." *American Lawyer,* January. http://www .susmangodfrey.com/default/Attorney%20Articles/AmericanLawyerTopLitigation Boutiqueso1_2005.pdf.

Galanter, Marc, and William Henderson. 2008. "The Elastic Tournament: A Second Transformation of the Big Law Firm." *Stanford Law Review* 60:1867–1930.

Galanter, Marc, and Thomas Palay. 1991. *Tournament of Lawyers: The Transformation of the Big Law Firm.* Chicago: University of Chicago Press.

Glater, Jonathan D. 2001. "Making a Network of Lawyers: Small Firms Find Way to Compete with Giants." *New York Times,* June 8.

Goldhaber, Michael D. 2001. "Boies Schiller's Big Year." *National Law Journal,* February 12.

Gordon, Robert W. 1988. "The Independence of Lawyers." *Boston University Law Review* 68:1–84.

Hadfield, Gillian. 2000. "The Price of Law: How the Market for Lawyers Distorts the Justice System." *Michigan Law Review* 98:953–1006.

Handler, Joel F. 1967. *The Lawyer and His Community: The Practicing Bar in a Middle-Sized City.* Madison: University of Wisconsin Press.

Heinz, John P., Robert L. Nelson, and Edward O. Laumann. 2001. "The Scale of Justice: Observations on the Transformation of Urban Law Practice." *Annual Review of Sociology* 27:337–362.

Heinz, John P., and Edward O. Laumann. 1982. *Chicago Lawyers: The Social Structure of the Bar.* New York: Russell Sage Foundation.

Heinz, John P., Edward O. Laumann, Robert L. Nelson, and Ethan Michelson. 1998. "The Changing Character of Lawyers' Work: Chicago in 1975 and 1995." *Law & Society Review* 32:751–775.

Heinz, John P., Robert L. Nelson, Rebecca L. Sandefur, and Edward O. Laumann. 2005. *Urban Lawyers: The New Social Structure of the Bar.* Chicago: University of Chicago Press.

Henderson, William. 2009. "The End of an Era: The Bi-Modal Distribution for the Class of 2008." *Legal Profession Blog,* June 29. http://lawprofessors.typepad.com/legal_profession/2009/06/the-end-of-an-era-the-bi-modal-distribution-for-the-class-of-2008.html.

Jones, Ashby. 2008. "Newcomer Law Firms Are Creating Niches with Blue-Chip Clients." *Wall Street Journal,* July 2.

Kamping-Carder, Leigh. 2010. "Plaintiff-Side Work for BigLaw Can Bring Profit, Pain." *Law360,* March 30. http://www.law360.com/articles/158727.

Kennedy, Duncan. 1976. "Form and Substance in Private Law Adjudication." *Harvard Law Review* 89:1685–1778.

Kilpatrick, Judith. 1997–1998. "Specialty Lawyer Associations: Their Role in the Socialization Process." *Gonzaga Law Review* 33:501–70.

Krishnan, Jayanth K. 2007. "Outsourcing and the Globalizing Legal Profession." *William & Mary Law Review* 48:2189–2246.

———. "Globetrotting Law Firms." 2010. *Georgetown Journal of Legal Ethics* 23:57–99.

Kritzer, Herbert M. 2001. "The Fracturing Legal Profession: The Case of Plaintiffs' Personal Injury Lawyers." *International Journal of the Legal Profession* 8:225–250.

———. 2006. "The Commodification of Insurance Defense Practice." *Vanderbilt Law Review* 59:2053–2094.

Kronman, Anthony T. 1993. *The Lost Lawyer: Failing Ideals of the Legal Profession.* Cambridge, MA: Harvard University Press.

Landon, Douglas D. 1990. *Country Lawyers: The Impact of Context on Professional Practice.* New York: Praeger.

Leonhardt, David. 2000. "Law Firm Pay Soars to Stem Dot-Com Defections." *New York Times,* February 2. http://query.nytimes.com/gst/fullpage.html?res=9901EEDD153FF931A35751C0A9669C8B63.

Liu, Sida. 2008. "Globalization as Boundary-Blurring: International and Local Law Firms in China's Corporate Law Market." *Law & Society Review* 42:771–804.

Llewellyn, Karl N. 1930. *The Bramble Bush: Some Lectures on Law and Its Study.* New York: Columbia University Press.

Macaulay, Stewart. 1979. "Lawyers and Consumer Protection Laws." *Law & Society Review* 14:115–171.

Mather, Lynn, Craig A. McEwen, and Richard J. Maiman. 2001. *Divorce Lawyers at Work: Varieties of Professionalism in Practice.* New York: Oxford University Press.

Nelson, Robert L., and David M. Trubek. 1992. "Arenas of Professionalism: The Professional Ideologies of Lawyers in Context." In *Lawyers' Ideals/Lawyers' Practices: Transformations in the American Legal Profession,* edited by Robert L. Nelson, David M. Trubek, and Rayman L. Solomon, 177–214. Ithaca, NY: Cornell University Press.

New York State Bar Association Special Committee on the Law Governing Firm Structure and Organization. 2000. *Preserving the Core Values of the American Legal Profession: The Place of Multidisciplinary Practice in the Law Governing Lawyers.* Albany: New York State Bar Association. http://www.law.cornell.edu/ethics/mdp1.htm.

Owen, Michael G. 2008. "Legal Outsourcing to India: The Demise of New Lawyers and Junior Associates." *Pacific McGeorge Global Business & Development Law Journal* 21: 175–190.

Parker, Jon. 2008. "Is Slater's IPO a Model that UK Firms Could Follow?" *Lawyer,* March 3. http://www.thelawyer.com/is-slaters-ipo-a-model-that-uk-firms-could-follow?/131546 .article.

Quack, Sigrid. 2007. "Legal Professionals and Transnational Law-Making: A Case of Distributed Agency." *Organization* 14:643–666.

Rapoport, Nancy B. 1998. "Our House, Our Rules: The Need for a Uniform Code of Bankruptcy Ethics." *American Bankruptcy Institute Law Review* 6:45–102.

Redish, Martin H. 2008. "Private Contingent Fee Lawyers and Public Power: Constitutional and Political Implications." Paper presented at the Research Roundtable on Expansion of Liability under Public Nuisance, Chicago, IL, April 7–8. http://www.law.northwestern .edu/searlecenter/papers/Redish_revised.pdf.

Regan, Milton C., Jr. 2004. *Eat What You Kill: The Fall of a Wall Street Lawyer.* Ann Arbor: University of Michigan Press.

———. 2008. "Lawyers, Symbols, and Money: Outside Investment in Law Firms." *Pennsylvania State International Law Review* 27:407–439.

———. 2010. "Supply Chains and Porous Boundaries: The Disaggregation of Legal Services." *Fordham Law Review* 78:2137–2191.

Rhode, Deborah L. 1998. "The Professionalism Problem." *William & Mary Law Review* 39:283–326.

Rogers, Catherine A. 2007. "The Arrival of the Have-Nots in International Commercial Arbitration." *Nevada Law Journal* 8:341–384.

———. 2010. "The Ethics of Advocacy." In *The Art of Advocacy in International Arbitration,* 2nd ed., edited by Doak Bishop and Edward Kehoe, 49–66. Huntington, NY: Juris.

Rosenthal, Douglas E. 1974. *Lawyer and Client: Who's in Charge?* New York: Russell Sage Foundation.

Rubenstein, William B. 2004. "On What a 'Private Attorney General' Is—and Why it Matters." *Vanderbilt Law Review* 57:2129–2173.

Schmitt, Kellie. 2008. "Orrick's Ops Center: One Small Town's Salvation." *Recorder,* May 9. http://www.law.com/jsp/article.jsp?id=1202421246077.

Seron, Carroll. 1996. *The Business of Practicing Law: The Work of Solo and Small-Firm Attorneys.* Philadelphia: Temple University Press.

Sherman, Ann. 2005. "Should Small Firms Get on Board with Outsourcing?" *Small Firm Business,* September 12. http://www.naukri.com/gpw/quislex/press.html.

Sporkin, Stanley. 1993. "The Need for Separate Codes of Professional Conduct for the Various Specialties." *Georgetown Journal of Legal Ethics* 7:149–152.

Suskind, Richard. 2008. *The End of Lawyers?* New York: Oxford University Press.

Terry, Laurel S. 2008. "The Future Regulation of the Legal Profession: The Impact of Treating the Legal Profession as 'Service Providers.'" *Journal of the Professional Lawyer* 2008:189–211.

Velaigam, Malar. 2007. "Mills & Reeve Goes All Out for Divorce Market." *Lawyer*, November 29. http://www.thelawyer.com/mills-and-reeve-goes-all-out-for-divorce-market/130165.article.

Wasserstrom, Richard. 1975. "Lawyers as Professionals: Some Moral Issues." *Human Rights* 5:1–24.

Wilkins, David B. 1990. "Legal Realism for Lawyers." *Harvard Law Review* 104:468–524.

———. 1992. "Who Should Regulate Lawyers?" *Harvard Law Review* 105:799–887.

———. 1993. "Making Context Count: Regulating Lawyers After *Kaye, Scholer.*" *Southern California Law Review* 66:1145–1220.

———. 1998. "Everyday Practice *Is* the Troubling Case: Confronting Context in Legal Ethics." In *Everyday Practices and Trouble Cases,* edited by Austin Sarat, Marianne Constable, David Engel, Valerie Hans, and Susan Lawrence, 68–108. Chicago: Northwestern University Press.

———. 2007. "Partner Shmartner! *EEOC v. Sidley Austin Brown & Wood.*" *Harvard Law Review* 120:1264–1277.

———. 2010. "Rethinking the Public-Private Distinction in Legal Ethics: The Case of 'Substitute' Attorneys General." *Michigan State Law Review* 2010:423–470.

Wolfram, Charles W. 1986. *Modern Legal Ethics.* St. Paul: West.

Zimmett, Mark P. 2007. "Lessons from a Large-Firm Partner Who Set Up His Own Shop." *American Lawyer,* April 9. http://www.law.com/jsp/law/sfb/lawArticleSFB.jsp?id=1175850240358.

Whose Ethics?

The Benchmark Problem in Legal Ethics Research

Elizabeth Chambliss

A recent survey of workplace culture in 15 Australian law firms found "strong differences" between junior and senior lawyers' perceptions of ethics support within their firms and perceptions of their own capacity to raise ethical issues (Parker and Aitken 2011, 402). Among junior lawyers, only 44% said that they are always "able to raise ethical issues in confidence," compared to 75% of senior lawyers (441). Junior lawyers were also less likely to know where to turn for ethical advice, and to report that their ethical concerns are given consideration in the firm. Among junior lawyers, less than 40% said that their ethical concerns are always given consideration, compared to nearly 80% of senior lawyers (441).

David Chambers also found significant differences between junior and senior lawyers in his analysis of data from the University of Michigan Law School alumni survey (Mather and Levin, chapter 1). Among law graduates surveyed five years after graduation, only 51% agreed that "the lawyers with whom I deal . . . are highly ethical," compared to 63% of those surveyed 35 or 45 years after graduation. This finding was generally consistent across practice specialties.

How should we interpret such differences between junior and senior lawyers? One theory holds that junior lawyers are more reliable informants—that their perceptions are not yet corrupted by self-interest and the demands of practice and therefore will tend to be closer to universal or ordinary morality. This is the predominant theory in the academic literature on large law

Thanks to Molly Land, Leslie Levin, Lynn Mather, and Christine Parker for their very helpful comments.

firms, which tends to portray large law firms as being in perpetual moral decline (Chambliss 2010) and to portray new associates as sheep to the slaughter. Patrick Schiltz (1999) has described professional socialization in large law firms as the process of "becoming unethical" (915). To some extent, this corruption narrative informs all critical legal ethics research.

An alternative theory holds that junior lawyers are inexperienced and/or naïve and therefore may be unreliable informants about professional matters. This theory views professional socialization as the process of acquiring knowledge and ethical judgment in complex situations. Junior lawyers, by definition, have not had time to acquire such knowledge and therefore are in no position to assess law firm management practices or senior lawyers' work. Perhaps not surprisingly, this is the dominant theory among large firm partners and managers (Chambliss 2006).

These two theories of lawyer socialization are not necessarily incompatible. Research on lawyers provides examples of both "ethical fading" (Tenbrunsel and Messick 2004), whereby lawyers gradually lose sight of ordinary morality (Regan 2004; Schiltz 1999), and "ethical learning," whereby lawyers gradually acquire specialized ethical expertise (Chambliss and Wilkins 2002a). Moreover, lawyers may experience both ethical fading and ethical learning at different stages of their careers, in different practice contexts, and with respect to different issues in their work.

The challenge, however, is defining the benchmark for theoretical analysis. Should lawyers' ethical standards and conduct be compared to ordinary (lay) morality? To the formal rules of legal ethics? Or to the prevailing professional norms within a specialized area of practice (which may or may not be consistent with the formal rules)? The definition of the normative benchmark itself has theoretical implications and is not always explicit in legal ethics research.

This chapter examines the use of benchmarks in legal ethics research and shows how different benchmarks may produce competing—but partial—theoretical claims. It argues, specifically, that the literature is biased toward critical accounts of "ethical fading" that are based on unspecified and/or internally inconsistent benchmarks. The goal of the chapter is to promote a more consistent specification of benchmarks in order to build a more holistic theory of lawyer socialization. A clearer definition of the normative baseline for analysis would allow more focused comparisons between junior and senior lawyers, as well as between different types of lawyers, and between lawyers and the members of other occupational groups.

The Corruption Narrative: Ethical Fading

Perhaps the most compelling corruption narrative in the legal ethics literature is Patrick Schiltz's (1999) provocative and widely read critique of large law firm practice. According to Schiltz, large law firms systematically socialize young lawyers to lie, cheat, and steal, while at the same time modeling a variety of strategies for rationalizing such conduct. His detailed phenomenology of corruption and rationalization is worth quoting at length:

> Unethical lawyers do not start out being unethical; they start out just like you—as perfectly decent young men or women who have every intention of practicing law ethically. They do not become unethical overnight; they become unethical just as you will (if you become unethical)—a little bit at a time. And they do not become unethical by shredding incriminating documents or bribing jurors; they become unethical just as you are likely to—by cutting a corner here, by stretching the truth a bit there.
>
> Let me tell you how you will start acting unethically: It will start with your time sheets. One day, not too long after you start practicing law, you will sit down at the end of a long, tiring day, and you just won't have much to show for your efforts in terms of billable hours. It will be near the end of the month. You will know that all of the partners will be looking at your monthly time report in a few days, so what you'll do is pad your time sheet just a bit. Maybe you will bill a client for ninety minutes for a task that really took you only sixty minutes to perform. However, you will promise yourself that you will repay the client at the first opportunity by doing thirty minutes of work for the client for "free." In this way, you will be "borrowing," not "stealing."
>
> And then what will happen is that it will become easier and easier to take these little loans against future work. And then, after a while, you will stop paying back these little loans. . . .
>
> And then you will pad more and more—every two minute telephone conversation will go down on the sheet as ten minutes, every three hour research project will go down with an extra quarter hour or so. You will continue to rationalize your dishonesty to yourself in various ways until one day you stop doing even that. And, before long—it won't take you much more than three or four years—you will be stealing from your clients almost every day, and you won't even notice it.
>
> You know what? You will also likely become a liar. A deadline will come up one day, and, for reasons that are entirely your fault, you will not be able

to meet it. So you will call your senior partner or your client and make up a white lie for why you missed the deadline. . . . And then you will be reading through a big box of your client's documents—a box that has not been opened in twenty years—and you will find a document that would hurt your client's case, but that no one except you knows exists, and you will simply "forget" to produce it in response to your opponent's discovery requests.

Do you see what will happen? After a couple years of this, you won't even notice that you are lying and cheating and stealing every day that you practice law. None of these things will seem like a big deal in itself—an extra fifteen minutes added to a time sheet here, a little white lie to cover a missed deadline there. But, after a while, your entire frame of reference will change. . . . (916–918)

Schiltz's portrayal vividly illustrates the process of ethical fading, whereby one learns to "behave self-interestedly while, at the same time, falsely believing that one's moral principles were upheld" (Tenbrunsel and Messick 2004, 223). One of the principal enablers of this type of self-deception is the "slippery slope of decision making," whereby repeated exposure to ethical dilemmas in a series of small decisions leads to progressively unethical conduct (228–229). As Schiltz (1999, 916) argues, young lawyers "do not become unethical overnight" but rather "a little bit at a time." Ethical fading also is facilitated by language euphemisms (Tenbrunsel and Messick 2004, 227), such as "borrowing" versus "stealing" and "forgetting" versus "withholding" documents (Schiltz 1999, 917–918). As Schiltz observes, "after a couple years" of relabeling such decisions, "you won't even notice that . . . your entire frame of reference" has changed (918).

Ethical fading is a powerful framework for thinking about lawyers' ethical socialization and for explaining the difference between junior and senior lawyers' perceptions. The empirical literature offers numerous examples of dubious practices that are taken for granted within specialized "communities of practice" (Mather, McEwen, and Maiman 2001) such as those explored in this volume: for instance, corporate litigators who learn to withhold potentially relevant documents in deposition defense (Kirkland, chapter 8; Suchman 1998, 867); prosecutors who learn to hold onto exculpatory material until right before trial (Yaroshefsky and Green, chapter 13); real estate lawyers who learn to "go get a cup of coffee" when cash passes under the table (Levin 2004, 364); and personal injury lawyers who "accept every case with significant damages, serve a complaint, and wait for the check" (Abel 2008, 96). This phenomenon is not limited to law. Ann Tenbrunsel and David Messick (2004) illustrate their theory of ethical fading with examples of corporate misconduct. They argue that the psychological tendencies that lead to ethical fading "are constant and pervasive in individuals' lives" (225).

As applied to *legal* ethics, however, ethical fading has a benchmark problem. Unlike some other specialized groups that succumb to ethical fading or "groupthink" (Janis 1972), lawyers are required to adhere to norms that depart from ordinary morality and therefore may justify (and/or rationalize) their conduct in terms of positive professional norms. For instance, lawyers are required to keep client confidences even when doing so imposes high costs on third parties and societal interests (Liptak 2008). Litigators are expected to be zealous advocates of the client's interests even when a neutral observer might view the client's cause as unjust (Freedman 1975). Lawyers are expected to counsel their clients to withhold apologies (Cohen 1999), serve up scapegoats (Duggin 2008), and protect the client's own private interests even when public and other private interests may suffer. These professional norms complicate the definition of "ethics" in legal ethics research. Who decides whether a practice is dubious or unethical? That is, who defines the normative benchmark from which ethical fading is measured?

In some contexts, it may seem obvious. For instance, Schiltz (1999, 917) focuses on fraudulent billing, missing deadlines "for reasons that are entirely your fault," and secretly withholding an obviously relevant document in discovery. Most lawyers and laypersons would agree that these are examples of dubious or unethical conduct. Indeed, the power of Schiltz's portrayal depends on this universal appeal.

But what about less obvious questions? The relevance of documents in discovery, for instance, is a notoriously complex question. Experienced litigators define the ethics of discovery practice primarily in terms of being civil to opponents and "sending honest signals" about gray areas and strategic decisions to withhold (Kirkland 2005, 722). Academics and other nonlitigators may find this troubling and interpret it as evidence of ethical fading or some other process of moral corruption (Kirkland 2005; Suchman 1998). But this interpretation devalues litigators' experience and specialized expertise. Litigators are taught to balance the requirements of an adversary system with the truth-seeking functions of the adversary process. Thus, litigators may use a different benchmark for normative assessment than nonlitigators. This difference complicates the theoretical analysis of ethical fading. Whose benchmark should be used to distinguish between (undesirable) ethical fading and (desirable) ethical learning?

Of course, all research on norms and culture confronts this problem to some extent. Anthropologists have long debated the relative merits of "etic" approaches, in which theoretical and normative benchmarks are defined by the researcher, and "emic" approaches designed to understand and describe the natives' point of view (Martin 2002, 36–37). But the problem is compounded when the group under study has a specialized normative code—especially insofar as the code is inaccessible to nonspecialists. Moreover, the code itself is not a solution to the problem of benchmarks because experienced lawyers may debate the merits and application of particular rules. Thus, the specialization of legal ethics—both as a body of positive law and as a subject of debate among lawyers—makes the choice of benchmarks especially thorny in legal ethics research.

The Specialization Narrative: Ethical Learning

Lawyers tend to view the process of ethical socialization as the process of acquiring specialized knowledge and judgment in complex situations. Legal ethical learning typically begins in law school with the formal study of the American Bar Association (ABA) Model Rules of Professional Conduct and preparation for the Multistate Professional Responsibility Exam, a national examination that is required for bar admission in every state (Levin 1997). Yet while the Model Rules tend to be the focus of students' initial exposure, the actual rules of professional conduct vary substantially from state to state and are increasingly enmeshed in a web of other state, federal, and international sources of professional regulation (Chambliss 2001). Moreover, even these increasingly complex rules provide inadequate guidance for the many legal risks and moral dilemmas that lawyers and law practice organizations confront (Bernstein 2009; Chambliss 2000; Levin 1997).

Legal ethical learning continues, therefore, within particular practice contexts, both formally, through continuing legal ethics education requirements and in-house training programs within practice organizations such as large law firms (Chambliss and Wilkins 2002a) and prosecutors' offices (Yaroshefsky 2010); and informally, though "advice networks" (Levin 2004) and specialized communities of practice (Mather, McEwen, and Maiman 2001). Thus, legal ethical learning has both doctrinal and experiential components.

Both of these components may be relatively inaccessible to laypeople and junior lawyers (Raymond 2005) and even to experienced lawyers who do not specialize in legal ethics as a substantive field (Chambliss 2006). Large law firms increasingly employ full-time general counsel and other ethics and risk management specialists to answer lawyers' day-to-day questions and keep abreast of changes in professional regulation (Chambliss and Wilkins 2002a; Chambliss 2006; Davis 2008). Midsized law firms, too, are increasingly investing in specialized ethics and risk management personnel (Chambliss 2009). Likewise, many public practice organizations, such as prosecutors' offices and legal services organizations, have created specialized ethics resources and compliance infrastructure to address the various complex and recurring issues that they confront.

Thus, within many practice contexts, nonspecialists—such as junior lawyers and even law-trained researchers—will have less doctrinal and/or experiential expertise than the lawyers they observe. Arguably, therefore, these nonspecialists are not fully equipped to judge the technical—or normative—quality of the work.

Large firm partners, for instance, tend to view new associates as unreliable informants about most professional matters (Chambliss 2006). According to partners, many so-called ethical issues raised by associates are actually the result of misunderstandings or lack of expertise. In the words of one law firm general counsel:

> Associates can be naïve. You get a breathless phone call, "The partner is asking me to back date documents!" And it turns out this is a closed corporation, five guys who have been working together for months, it's a start up, and now they need a current board ratification of prior decisions, perfectly legal. No one is defrauding anyone. (1546)

Large firm partners also tend to be skeptical of legal academics, whom they view as overly critical of the ethics of large firm practice. As one in-house ethics specialist remarked:

> People in firms are reluctant to talk to academics because they tend to view academics as ideological. There is this idea that lawyers are always trying to cut corners. But lawyers call me all the time with questions. Once the firm began providing this service, and lawyers knew there was someone there who had an answer—lawyers are big rules followers. (Chambliss 2006, 1565)

Such skepticism about the judgment of junior lawyers and other nonspecialists is not limited to large firm partners, but rather is characteristic of experienced lawyers in many practice specialties. Divorce lawyers, legal services lawyers, prosecutors, patent lawyers: As this volume illustrates, different types of lawyers face very different practice environments and tend to operate within distinct and sometimes insular communities of practice. Each of these groups has its own set of professional values and concerns, and develops specialized norms of practice that go beyond—and, in some cases, depart from—the formal rules. Thus, not only do lawyers, as a group, have a specialized ethical code, but experienced lawyers tend to have their own specialized views on the code, backed up by claims of even-more-specialized technical and normative expertise.

Nonspecialists, naturally, may be skeptical of specialists' normative claims. Indeed, the central theoretical debate within the sociology of professions is the extent to which professional claims to authority are justified by specialized expertise. Functional theory holds that professional authority—including ethical self-regulation—is justified by the asymmetry of expertise between professionals and nonprofessionals (Parsons 1994). "Professional" ethics, in other words, both presumes and requires specialized expertise. As Talcott Parsons (1994) has written:

> Among the . . . basic characteristics [of the professions] is a level of special technical competence that must be acquired through formal training and that necessitates special mechanisms of social control in relation to the recipients of services because of the "competence gap" which makes it unlikely that the "layman" can properly evaluate the quality of such services or the credentials of those who offer them. (679)

Critics of functionalism question the scope and validity of professional expertise (Collins 1979), including claims about the public purpose and effectiveness of professional ethics codes. Critics view professional ethics codes primarily as a means of legitimating professional monopoly and staving off external regulation (Abel 1989; Caplow 1954). According to Richard Abel (1989), for instance:

> The suspicion that professional associations promulgate ethical rules more to legitimate themselves in the eyes of the public than to engage in effective regulation is strengthened by the inadequacy of enforcement mechanisms. . . . Surveys repeatedly show that lawyers are ignorant of many rules and fail to internalize those that they do know. . . . More disturbing, most lawyers never even perceive moral dilemmas in their practice. (143)

These competing narratives provide a rich framework for empirical ethics research, including research about the sources and mechanisms of ethical fading and other undesirable outcomes of lawyer socialization. The increasing specialization of lawyers and legal ethics as a substantive field does not mean that "nonspecialists"—such as students, junior lawyers, and academic research-ers—must abandon critical analysis of legal ethics doctrine or lawyers' ethics in practice. Grounding such critiques, however, requires a rigorous separation between empirical and normative claims. This separation, in turn, requires the systematic specification of normative benchmarks in research.

Implications for Understanding Lawyers' Ethics in Practice

One implication of this analysis for students and legal ethics scholars is the need to pay close attention to the ways researchers define "ethics." Some re-search focuses on the development of ethics policies, committees, and other "ethical infrastructure" (Chambliss and Wilkins 2002b; Schneyer 1998) and lawyers' use of such infrastructure (Chambliss and Wilkins 2002a; Davis 2008), whereas other research focuses on lawyers' ethical values and consciousness (Alfieri 2006; Kirkland 2005; Suchman 1998). These two sets of variables, though related in potentially significant ways, nevertheless may operate ac-cording to very different dynamics and have different implications for theo-retical and normative analysis.

For instance, this chapter opened with two examples of differences between junior and senior lawyers' perceptions of "ethics," as if the two examples sug-gested a single, normative theme. Yet the first example focused primarily on junior lawyers' access to structural (ethical and supervisory) supports within firms, rather than their ethical values. As Christine Parker and Lyn Aitken (2011, 430) explain, such findings are open to competing interpretations and may primarily reflect junior lawyers' place within the organizational hierarchy. Research on business organizations has found that lower-level employees gen-erally have more negative perceptions of organizational ethical culture than senior employees and managers (Treviño 2005; Treviño, Weaver, and Brown 2008)—particularly lower-level employees who are dissatisfied with their jobs (Key 1999, 222). Junior lawyers also may be unaware of the existence or opera-tion of ethical infrastructure due to their short tenure in the firm (Parker and Aitken 2011, 426–427). Parker and Aitken defined junior lawyers as lawyers with one to three years of experience (417). Thus, differences between junior and senior lawyers' perceptions of and access to ethical supports within firms do not necessarily suggest differences in their underlying values or changes in lawyers' values over time. Instead, such differences may stem primarily from their structural positions in the firm.

The second example, likewise, did not focus directly on lawyers' values, but rather on lawyers' perceptions of other lawyers' ethicality. The Michigan data were drawn from a question about whether "the lawyers with whom I deal (other than those in my own office) are highly ethical in their conduct," in which the term "ethical" was left undefined. Here, too, the differences between junior and senior lawyers are open to competing interpretations. One interpretation, as implied by the initial pairing of the two examples, is that lawyer socialization involves a shift from one set of ethical values and commitments (for instance, those most consistent with universal or ordinary morality) to another set of (arguably narrower and distorted or corrupted) commitments. Another interpretation, however, consistent with the structural explanation offered above for the Australian results, is that junior lawyers are more likely to have negative perceptions of senior lawyers' ethics—or of senior lawyers, generally—than senior lawyers themselves. Such perceptions are typical not only of junior employees but of people in general. One of the most consistent findings in the business ethics literature is that most people view themselves as more ethical than other people (Ford and Richardson 1994, 219). This tendency may be most pronounced when evaluating people outside one's own group (such as people outside one's own office or hierarchical status) (Regan 2007).

Thus, while the two opening examples may be theoretically related, in suggesting an undesirable shift in lawyers' ethical values over time, neither is based on the direct measurement of lawyers' values (or changes over time). Moreover, both sets of findings may be explained by variables that are unrelated to lawyers' ethical values but rather stem from more general organizational or psychological factors, such as respondents' hierarchical positions or the dynamics of group identification. This is not to say that such findings are unimportant for lawyers and law practice organizations, but rather that closer analysis is required to ground theoretical and normative claims.

A second implication of the benchmark problem and foregoing analysis is that researchers must pay closer attention to what lawyers mean when *they* talk about "ethics." As a threshold matter, this means distinguishing between lawyers' references to legal ethics—in particular, the formal rules of legal ethics—and lawyers' references to broader, universal ethics and values.

Lawyers in practice tend to use the term "ethics" to refer to the formal rules of legal ethics (Chambliss 2010; Suchman 1998) or a specific regulated issue that is particularly salient in their practice. For instance, large firm partners tend to use the term "ethics" to refer to conflicts of interest, which in large firm practice is a central and highly technical issue (Chambliss and Wilkins 2002a,

567). Corporate litigators may use the term "ethics" to refer to the acceptable level of aggressiveness in discovery (Suchman 1998, 854). Divorce lawyers may use the term "ethics" to refer to their obligation to protect children's interests in accord with the guidelines for matrimonial lawyers (Mather and McEwen, chapter 4).

Moreover, lawyers themselves tend to distinguish between these regulated or doctrinal issues and broader, universal questions of ethics and values. For instance, Michael Kelly (1994, 2007) began his ethnographic research on lawyers by looking for ethical issues and problems that he could use to enrich classroom teaching in the required law school course on legal ethics. He found, however, that he quickly "had to abandon this approach" (1994, 229) because "the lawyers I interviewed were largely disinterested in the kinds of ethical issues I was addressing with my students" (2007, 9). Instead, the lawyers he interviewed were concerned with "their lives in practice" (9) or what Kelly called "meaning-of-life ethics" (13). He noted, "Lawyers worry about their group practice, its direction, its future, and its quality. . . . There is a lot of talk about friendship, about the value of a working life spent with (at least some) colleagues whom one admires, respects, and enjoys. . . . Talk about values is common" (9–10).

Likewise, Mark Suchman (1998, 843) found that the litigators he interviewed "repeatedly distinguished between ethics (meaning the letter and, to a limited extent, the spirit of the professional rules) and morals (meaning substantive issues of right and wrong)." He reported: "A large-firm associate captured this sense of the distance between 'ethics' and 'right and wrong' by noting that 'most of the issues that we're talking about here aren't issues of ultimate justice or even specific justice. They are questions of following the rules so that the cases will come out, and the right information will be presented, and ultimately, justice will be served.'"

Lawyers also may distinguish between regulated issues with broad normative implications, such as billing fraud, and those with primarily tactical and/ or risk management implications, such as the rules of discovery and large law firm conflicts of interest (Chambliss 2005, 2006). In the words of one law firm general counsel:

We take risks all the time and we know what they are. God knows the courts get them confused. Able lawyers come in and say, "There's a conflict of interest, what could be worse?" Thirty to forty percent of malpractice claims have in them a conflict of interest, although it is often hard to connect the conflict with any actual harm. But the jury goes to town. What you and I would consider a risk issue, not a moral issue, gets treated by the courts and juries as indistinct from the drug addict lawyer who stole money from his client trust accounts. It is something that really frosts me. . . . There are lots of foaming-at-the-mouth moralists in the field. (Chambliss 2006, 1566)

Of course, the way lawyers talk about ethics and the distinctions they draw between doctrinal, tactical, and normative issues may be highly theoretically significant. The theory of ethical fading is precisely about the ways in which ethical issues become drained of normative content over time, for instance, through cognitive narrowing, repetition, and self-deception (Tenbrunsel and Messick 2004). This theory suggests that the specialization of lawyers—and legal ethics as a substantive field—may tend to crowd out or inhibit more universal moral awareness and engagement among lawyers (Alfieri 2006; Raymond 2005).

For instance, Alfieri (2006) has argued that the increased focus on "risk management" in large law firms has diminished lawyers' appreciation of the moral choices they face and undermined "classical norms of . . . fraternity and community" (1926). Raymond (2005), too, has argued that the "professionalization of ethics" in large law firms has led lawyers to view ethics as "just another area of specialization" (159) and "runs the risk of . . . taking ethical issues out mainstream discourse" (160). Richard Moorhead (2010, 227) has referred to this as the "paradox of specialization." As he notes, "Specialization is capable of giving rise to benefits (in terms of improved quality) and detriments (reduced access, increased cost, and an inability to see problems beyond one's own specialty . . .)."

But while lawyer specialization may encourage ethical fading, not every example of specialized ethics necessarily represents ethical fading. Grounding the theory of ethical fading—and, by implication, ethical learning—requires attention to different sources of "ethics," as well as to lawyers in different settings and stages of their careers. Only through systematic descriptions of lawyers' ethics in practice can empirical ethics research provide the foundation for theoretical and normative critique.

References

Abel, Richard L. 1989. *American Lawyers*. New York: Oxford University Press.
———. 2008. *Lawyers in the Dock*. New York: Oxford University Press.
Alfieri, Anthony V. 2006. "The Fall of Legal Ethics and the Rise of Risk Management." *Georgetown Journal of Legal Ethics* 94:1909–1955.
Bernstein, Anita. 2009. "Pitfalls Ahead: A Manifesto for Training of Lawyers." *Cornell Law Review* 94:479–517.

Caplow, Theodore. 1954. *The Sociology of Work*. Minneapolis: University of Minnesota Press.

Chambliss, Elizabeth. 2000. "Professional Responsibility: Lawyers, A Case Study." *Fordham Law Review* 69:817–857.

———. 2001. "Regulation of Lawyers." In *International Encyclopedia of the Social and Behavioral Sciences*, edited by Neil J. Smelser and Paul B. Baltes, 8559–8564. Amsterdam: Elsevier.

———. 2005. "The Nirvana Fallacy in Law Firm Regulation Debates." *Fordham Urban Law Journal* 33:119–151.

———. 2006. "The Professionalization of Law Firm In-House Counsel." *North Carolina Law Review* 84:1515–1576.

———. 2009. "New Sources of Managerial Authority in Large Law Firms." *Georgetown Journal of Legal Ethics* 22:63–95.

———. 2010. "Measuring Law Firm Culture." In *Law, Politics and Society: Law Firms, Legal Culture and Legal Practice*, edited by Austin Sarat, 1–31. Bingley, UK: Emerald.

Chambliss, Elizabeth, and David B. Wilkins. 2002a. "The Emerging Role of Ethics Advisors, General Counsel, and Other Compliance Specialists in Large Law Firms." *Arizona Law Review* 44:559–592.

———. 2002b. "Promoting Ethical Infrastructure in Large Law Firms: A Call for Research and Reporting." *Hofstra Law Review* 20:691–716.

Cohen, Jonathan R. 1999. "Advising Clients to Apologize." *Southern California Law Review* 72:1009–1069.

Collins, Randall. 1979. *The Credential Society*. New York: Academic Press.

Davis, Anthony E. 2008. "Legal Ethics and Risk Management: Complementary Visions of Lawyer Regulation." *Georgetown Journal of Legal Ethics* 21:95–131.

Duggin, Sarah Helene. 2008. "The McNulty Memorandum, the KPMG Decision and Corporate Cooperation: Individual Rights and Legal Ethics." *Georgetown Journal of Legal Ethics* 21:341–409.

Ford, Robert C., and Woodrow D. Richardson. 1994. "Ethical Decision-Making: A Review of the Empirical Literature." *Journal of Business Ethics* 13:205–221.

Freedman, Monroe H. 1975. *Lawyers' Ethics in an Adversary System*. Indianapolis: Bobbs-Merrill.

Janis, Irving L. 1972. *Groupthink: Psychological Studies of Policy Decisions and Fiascoes*. 2nd rev. ed. Boston: Houghton Mifflin.

Kelly, Michael J. 1994. *Lives of Lawyers: Journeys in the Organizations of Practice*. Ann Arbor: University of Michigan Press.

———. 2007. *Lives of Lawyers Revisited: Transformation and Resilience in the Organizations of Practice*. Ann Arbor: University of Michigan Press.

Key, Susan. 1999. "Organizational Ethical Culture: Real or Imagined?" *Journal of Business Ethics* 20:217–225.

Kirkland, Kimberly. 2005. "Ethics in Large Law Firms: The Principle of Pragmatism." *University of Memphis Law Review* 35:631–730.

Levin, Leslie C. 1997. "The MPRE Reconsidered." *Kentucky Law Journal* 86:395–412.

———. 2004. "The Ethical World of Solo and Small Law Firm Practitioners." *Houston Law Review* 41:309–392.

Liptak, Adam. 2008. "When Law Prevents Righting a Wrong." *New York Times*, May 4.

Martin, Joanne. 2002. *Organizational Culture: Mapping the Terrain*. London: Sage.

Mather, Lynn, Craig A. McEwen, and Richard J. Maiman. 2001. *Divorce Lawyers at Work: Varieties of Professionalism in Practice.* New York: Oxford University Press.

Moorhead, Richard. 2010. "Lawyer Specialization—Managing the Professional Paradox." *Law & Policy* 32:226–259.

Parker, Christine, and Lyn Aitken. 2011. "The Queensland 'Workplace Culture Check': Learning from Reflection on Ethics Inside Law Firms." *Georgetown Journal of Legal Ethics* 24:399–441.

Parsons, Talcott. 1994. "Equality and Inequality in Modern Society, or Social Stratification Revisited." In *Social Stratification: Class, Race, & Gender in Sociological Perspective,* edited by David B. Grusky, 670–685. Boulder, CO: Westview Press.

Raymond, Margaret. 2005. "The Professionalization of Ethics." *Fordham Urban Law Journal* 33:153–170.

Regan, Milton C. 2004. *Eat What You Kill: The Fall of a Wall Street Lawyer.* Ann Arbor: University of Michigan Press.

———. 2007. "Moral Intuitions and Organizational Culture." *Saint Louis Law Journal* 51:941–987.

Schiltz, Patrick J. 1999. "On Being a Happy, Healthy, and Ethical Member of an Unhappy, Unhealthy, and Unethical Profession." *Vanderbilt Law Review* 52:871–951.

Schneyer, Ted. 1998. "A Tale of Four Systems: Reflections on How Law Influences the 'Ethical Infrastructure' of Law Firms." *South Texas Law Review* 39:245–277.

Suchman, Mark C. 1998. "Working Without a Net: The Sociology of Legal Ethics in Corporate Litigation." *Fordham Law Review* 67:837–874.

Tenbrunsel, Ann E., and David M. Messick. 2004. "Ethical Fading: The Role of Self-Deception in Unethical Behavior." *Social Justice Research* 17:223–236.

Treviño, Linda Klebe. 2005. "Out of Touch: The CEO's Role in Corporate Misbehavior." *Brooklyn Law Review* 70:1195–1211.

Treviño, Linda Klebe, Gary R. Weaver, and Michael E. Brown. 2008. "It's Lovely at the Top: Hierarchical Level, Identities, and Perceptions of Organizational Ethics." *Business Ethics Quarterly* 18:233–252.

Yaroshefsky, Ellen. 2010. "Foreword: New Perspectives on *Brady* and Other Disclosure Obligations: What Really Works?" *Cardozo Law Review* 31:1943–1959.

Part II

Decision Making in Communities of Legal Practice

Client Grievances and Lawyer Conduct

The Challenges of Divorce Practice

Lynn Mather and Craig A. McEwen

In their study of Chicago lawyers, Heinz et al. (2005, 87–88) report that the ethical conduct imputed to divorce attorneys was the lowest of 42 fields rated. What does this negative reputation of divorce lawyers for ethical conduct tell us about the challenges of working in this area of law? Part of the answer lies in the taint of dealing with messy human problems and the stigma of legally undoing marriages. The reputation also finds support in the disproportionately high percentage of grievances filed against divorce lawyers for professional misconduct. This evidence does not necessarily mean, however, that the lawyers who represent divorce clients are less ethical than their professional peers. Rather, it could indicate that they face particular problems of practice due to client expectations, the nature of divorce, and resource limits.

In this chapter we argue that the high rate of grievance complaints—and divorce lawyers' negative reputation—grow out of the difficult challenges of dealing with the social, economic, emotional, and legal conflicts of divorcing couples and with the problematic circumstances of divorce representation, especially when client—and lawyer—resources are limited. Divorce attorneys share common, day-to-day professional choices that can give rise to grievances: choices about how to deal with "nonlegal" issues, work and communicate with emotional clients, support client autonomy while asserting professional authority, and determine the extent of appropriate advocacy. The choices that lawyers make often reflect varying professional identities—for example, as

We thank Jackie Rogers of the Maine Board of Overseers of the Bar and Thomas Trevethick of the New Hampshire Attorney Discipline Office for providing us with the raw data for some of the calculations that appear in this chapter. We also thank the National Science Foundation for research support for our initial study.

specialists or generalists—and widely differing client capacities to pay for legal work and attorney resources to carry that work out.

We begin with a brief profile of the divorce bar based on research in Maine and New Hampshire and then use bar disciplinary data as a lens through which to examine decision making by divorce lawyers. Bar complaints lead us to focus on professional conduct in the area of the client-lawyer relationship, including competence, allocation of authority between client and lawyer, communication, and diligence. To put the particular client-lawyer issues into context, we describe the challenges to professionally responsible behavior that are embedded in divorce practice generally and in key practice variations—by degree of specialization in family law, by resources of clients and attorney caseload, and by law firm structures. We then link common grievances about divorce lawyers—and day-to-day practice issues—to these different kinds of practices.

Profile of the Divorce Bar and the Market for Clients

Domestic relations cases constitute a significant proportion of civil matters in state courts, with 5.7 million cases nationwide in 2007; most of those cases involved divorce or child support (NCSC 2009). While that number might suggest an enormous market for divorce attorneys, the economics of divorce point in a very different direction. Divorce cases generally have at most one lawyer involved, not two. An increasing number of divorcing parties have no legal counsel on either side because they cannot afford a lawyer or because they prefer to try and resolve their issues themselves. Rates of pro se (self-) representation in divorce in the late 1980s to 1990s ranged from 56% to 89% in different courts and states (Mather 2003), and since then, they have continued to increase (Herman 2006; Goldschmidt 2008). The legal market for divorce thus includes a wide range of clients with quite different needs and resources but overrepresents parties with deeper conflicts and more assets. At the low end, clients choose between self-representation and a lawyer they can afford, while high-end parties typically both hire attorneys.

In this chapter, we draw on interviews with a sample of 163 divorce lawyers in Maine and New Hampshire, analysis of divorce docket records, and data on lawyer discipline in these states and others.[1] We found that many of the lawyers

---

1. Lawyer interviews were conducted in 1990–1991 by the authors, along with Richard J. Maiman. The lawyers were identified in divorce dockets in three New Hampshire and four Maine counties. In addition, the research team coded docket records of 6,971 divorce cases (e.g., duration of case, number of motions filed) in those counties for several years. Details of this

who represent divorce clients are regulars—that is, they do not consider them-selves divorce specialists but they rely on a continuing stream of divorce clients to complement their other—and widely variant—areas of practice. Other law-yers with divorce clients could be considered "general practice" lawyers (or gen-eralists), representing clients in a wide array of subject areas—criminal defense, real estate, wills/trusts, incorporations, and divorce. We found a surprisingly high percentage of lawyer names listed in divorce dockets associated with only one or two divorce cases for the entire year, suggesting that many lawyers repre-sent only an occasional divorce client. At the other end of the spectrum are the "specialist" family lawyers who account for a significant portion of all divorce representations in court.

Twenty percent of our interviewees were specialists, reporting that divorces constituted 75% or more of their caseload. An additional 15% said that divorces comprised at least half of their cases. Specialists (over 75% divorce practice) were particularly likely to be women (67% compared to 24% of nonspecial-ists). The high proportion of women lawyers in divorce practice has been noted since the 1920s when matrimonial law was one of the few fields open to them (Epstein 1993). More recently, some women law graduates have purposely chosen family law to advocate on behalf of women and children.

Lawyers varied considerably with regard to the social class of their divorce clients; 20% of all the lawyers we interviewed described them as mostly "upper middle class," compared to 38% reporting a cross-section of clients or mostly "middle class," and 42% describing a largely working- and lower-middle-class clientele. Divorce specialists were especially likely to represent upper-middle-class clients (48% of clients compared to 13% for nonspecialists). Differences in the social class of their clienteles were reflected in lawyers' widely varying fees (ranging in 1990 dollars from $45 to over $200 per hour) and policies about re-tainers (from zero to $10,000). A New Hampshire divorce specialist interviewed in 2009 said that he only takes divorces involving "a million or more in assets." High-end attorneys—whether specialist or not—have relatively small caseloads. The more limited the resources of the clients represented, the larger the attor-neys' caseloads. Several lawyers who organized their practices to be accessible to low-income individuals, for example, reported 200 or more open cases. A few of these attorneys charged flat fees rather than the typical hourly fees of their peers. Lawyers with higher-income clients reported closer to 40 to 50 open cases.

---

research are reported more fully in Mather, McEwen, and Maiman (2001). The different types of data allow us to have greater confidence in conclusions drawn from the interviews.

Unlike some areas of law in which teams of lawyers pour through myriad documents and handle depositions, successful divorce practice requires attorneys to work closely with emotional clients. Such work cannot be delegated to a junior lawyer. Not surprisingly, then, most divorce lawyers—even high-end ones—work in solo practice or in small firms (although some large law firms have family law specialists to accommodate their business clients). Twenty-eight percent of the Maine and New Hampshire divorce lawyers whom we interviewed were sole practitioners, with another 45% in firms of two to four lawyers, and 25% in firms of five or more; this is consistent with Heinz et al.'s (2005) finding that lawyers who represent individual (rather than organizational) clients are much less likely to practice in large law firms.

These differences among divorce lawyers influenced how they viewed their professional responsibilities. Specialists and generalists each constituted distinct "communities of practice," that is, layered and overlapping sets of attorneys who interact regularly and provide reference points for one another about the nature of appropriate professional conduct. When specialists and generalists found themselves to be adversaries on the same case, their differing views sometimes clashed. Divorce specialists filed more formal motions, submitted interrogatories, and engaged in other litigation activities that the more informal general practice lawyers seldom employed. But when specialists or generalists faced a pro se party on the other side, they both struggled to find appropriate ways to behave in relation to someone so unfamiliar with the ordinary legal procedures that they took for granted. All of these lawyers faced the potential of client grievance complaints and experienced common challenges that arise from having divorce clients. But those attorneys with fewest resources were likely to struggle the most to meet the expectations of the bar and their clients.

Formal Grievances in Family Law

State discipline agencies report that family law attorneys rank among the legal specialties that receive the highest number of grievances filed against them. Family law ranked first in New Hampshire and Maine on the list of practice areas that generate complaints, and second in Arizona, Illinois, Indiana, and Michigan.[2] Thus, for example, in the years 2004–2007, 27% to 46% of all initial

---

2. Lawyer grievance systems publish surprisingly little data about the nature of complaints against lawyers. Searches of websites of disciplinary authorities in 20 states yielded few web-

complaints to the bar arose from divorce matters in New Hampshire and 19% to 24% arose from divorce matters in Maine.[3] Lawyer discipline processes in all states—as discussed by Stephen Daniels and Joanne Martin for Texas (chapter 6)—show a tremendous winnowing of initial complaints with dismissal of the vast majority (as unfounded or not involving issues of bar rules), investigation of those remaining, hearings on a still smaller number, and then sanctions imposed on only a tiny fraction of attorneys who faced those initial complaints. In Maine, for example, of all complaints against attorneys in family law cases from 2005–2009, 90% were ultimately dismissed, similar to the overall dismissal rate of 91%.

Although few states reveal much detail about the discipline process, we can begin to answer three questions about complaints filed against divorce lawyers: Who complains against them? What are the lawyers' practice settings? And what is the nature of the complaints? Drawing on data from several years, we found that out of the total complaints against family lawyers, 35% came from the opposing party in Maine (36% in New Hampshire) and 41% came from clients in Maine (51% in New Hampshire). Other complaints came from relatives of parties, judges, and opposing counsel. Thus, in both states, three out of every four complaints filed against domestic relations lawyers came from one of the divorcing parties. Clients are a frequent source of complaints against attorneys, but only in divorce do the opposing parties file nearly as many complaints against attorneys as do their clients. In Maine, for example, only 22% of the complainants in non-family cases were opposing parties compared to 35% in family cases, while clients constituted 44% of complainants in non-family and 41% in family cases.

Solo practitioners received 50% of all family law grievance complaints in Maine (55% in New Hampshire). Thirty-nine percent of the family law complaints in Maine were directed at attorneys in firms of two to five, while 34% in New Hampshire were against attorneys in two- to four-person firms. These findings are consistent with research that shows that lawyers in solo and small firm practice receive disproportionately more complaints against them than

published annual reports, and most of those provided numbers of complaints and sanctions but little else. For disciplinary data reported in this section for Maine, see Maine Board of Overseers of the Bar (2009); and for New Hampshire, see New Hampshire Supreme Court Attorney Discipline Office (2011). For other states, see State Bar of Arizona (2011), Illinois Attorney Registration and Disciplinary Commission (2009), Indiana Supreme Court Disciplinary Commission (2010), and Michigan Attorney Grievance Commission (2009).

3. That percentage was 25% in New Hampshire and 24% in Maine at the time of our research, according to Trevethick (1995) and Davis (1991).

do lawyers in other firms (Levin 2004; Abel 2008). Of all private practitioners in Maine, 67% worked in firms of one to five attorneys but lawyers in these firms received 89% of all family law complaints filed, and 65% of New Hampshire lawyers worked in firms of one to four attorneys but received 89% of all family law complaints.[4]

State disciplinary reports show the concerns giving rise to complaints. Neglect (lack of diligence) leads the list in all studies of the lawyer discipline process (Abel 2008, 57). Other common complaints include inadequate communication with clients, fees, and lack of candor (meaning honesty with clients and/or courts). For example, the Illinois Attorney Registration and Disciplinary Commission (2010) reports neglect (37%), failing to communicate with client (including failing to communicate the basis of the fee) (17%), and fraudulent or deceptive activity (15%) as the three most common types of misconduct alleged.

Excerpts from Connecticut Grievance Committee decisions in two different divorce cases illustrate the interwoven aspects of rule violations.[5]

> In one case, the client was unable to obtain information about her divorce. The lawyer did not return her numerous phone messages and at one point the lawyer's answering machine was full, preventing the client from leaving a message. This continued for six months at which point the client terminated the relationship.
>
> In the second case, the client retained a lawyer for two separate matters, a criminal proceeding and a marital dissolution, and paid an initial $2,000.00 retainer. After one month, the client asked for divorce papers to be filed. The lawyer failed to initiate the divorce, despite telling the judge in the criminal matter that the divorce was pending. The lawyer also did not keep appointments with the client or communicate court dates for the criminal matter. A year later, the client asked again for papers to be filed and paid an additional $970 to the lawyer. The lawyer still failed to do so despite telling the client that he had filed them.

---

4. Data on distribution of private lawyers in each state by firm size comes from Curran (2004) based on figures for 2000 (compared to the Maine data for 2005–2008 and New Hampshire data for 1991–1993).

5. J. Scott Davis, Maine's bar counsel for more than 20 years, observed that the Connecticut cases not only typify the divorce cases leading to sanctions that he sees, but also typify the kinds of issues raised from all areas of practice (interview, January 14, 2010). The case descriptions paraphrase the decisions in Grievance Complaint #97-0751 and Grievance Complaint #00-0601. See Connecticut Statewide Grievance Committee (2011).

Nonresponsiveness to client communications runs through both cases. Neglect in responding to telephone calls and letters can also reflect failures to take timely steps in the divorce or reluctance to talk with clients about fee disagreements. The second case also exemplifies "lack of candor," essentially lying to the client about what the attorney had done (or not done). Rules of professional responsibility, as vague as they may be on some issues, leave little doubt that the conduct described in these cases falls outside the norms of acceptable professional conduct.

Learning Professional Responsibility in Family Law Practice

Lawyers gain most of their lessons about what constitutes appropriate professional conduct from practice experience. Family law attorneys learn from their clients and their clients' spouses, from judges, and particularly from other attorneys doing divorce work. New lawyers pick up tips from court clerks on matters ranging from the appropriate forms to the personalities and reputations of different lawyers and judges. Lawyers also observe and talk with more experienced attorneys as they interact with them in divorce negotiations. Lawyers in a family law specialty firm receive training and advice from junior peers and senior partners. The interactions among lawyers help constitute communities of practice within law firms, in particular courts, and among lawyers who meet one another repeatedly.

As lawyers look for help in dealing with the difficult professional decisions of divorce practice, they find that bar rules provide limited guidance. The American Bar Association (ABA) Model Rules of Professional Conduct, as adapted by each state, ignore the highly variable circumstances of legal practice even within a particular specialty such as divorce because they must be framed at a level of generality that crosses practice areas. In addition, day-to-day professional choices sometimes implicate several rules at the same time, which may provide inconsistent guidance. Moreover, some rules suggest behavior (such as zealous advocacy) that experienced divorce lawyers believe often runs counter to what is in the best interest of divorcing couples and families.

As Robert Nelson and David Trubek observe, "It is in the legal workplace that we find real conflicts over how practice should be organized," that is, over "what constitutes proper behavior by lawyers" (1992, 179). Clients are a key part of that legal workplace. Communication with bewildered, distraught, and legally inexperienced clients must take different forms than communication with legally sophisticated clients with well-defined objectives. Moreover, the amount of time devoted to cases and the plausible courses of legal action depend directly on the capacity of clients to pay attorneys' hourly rates. The resources of attorneys themselves—shaped by the structure and nature of their law firms—also affect choices about how to communicate with clients, which clients to accept and drop, and how aggressively to engage in advocacy. Thus, no serious understanding of professionally responsible and irresponsible lawyering can ignore the particularized and highly variable contingencies of practice.

What reference points do lawyers in different practice settings use in making responsible and ethical decisions in their day-to-day practices? The Model Rules assert that the conscience of individual lawyers is a key touchstone for these decisions, but the preamble goes on to note the importance of the "approbation of peers" for lawyer's conduct. In recognizing the role that lawyers play for one another, the Rules thus anticipate the findings of empirical research on the informal normative frameworks provided by communities of practice. Among the attorneys we interviewed, we heard repeated reference to the judgment of peers as a major criterion for evaluating their own personal success. According to one, "The way to measure it [my success] largely is how I'm perceived by other attorneys and for that matter judges. It's a small bar, and I want to be respected for my forthrightness." Another described his community of practice and its shared normative standards: "The lawyers that I deal with on divorce work . . . we usually know one another. We've had cases together. We both tend to view the case similarly. We're going to be advocates for our clients, but we will obviously talk to one another and try to effectuate a satisfactory result without a lot of discord and difficulty." This quote articulates "the norm of the reasonable lawyer"—the widely shared view that divorce lawyers should anticipate likely case outcomes, argue only for "realistic" positions (not whatever the client wants), show respect for other lawyers, and avoid unnecessary conflict in settling cases (see also Katz 1982, 56–59). While this view characterizes the norms of the general community of divorce lawyers, smaller communities of practice also exist and overlap; they include, for example, law firm partners and associates, lawyers who regularly appear as adversaries in cases, and groups of lawyers who practice in the same courts and who may observe, and at times second-guess, at least some of their conduct as lawyers.

The informal norms emerging from these communities of practice provide divorce lawyers with cues and signals about appropriate behavior and thus constitute crucial reference points for decisions. Since most divorce cases settle after negotiations, lawyers have numerous opportunities to interact with their peers and observe other lawyering styles in handling divorce cases.

Many of the specific ideas and values embodied in informal norms for divorce practice are also found in the formal guidelines of the specialty family law bar, the American Academy of Matrimonial Lawyers (AAML). The AAML was founded in 1962 by leading divorce attorneys to elevate the professionalism of the matrimonial bar and address the unique problems of family law. Although membership is highly selective—only three New Hampshire attorneys and eight Maine attorneys are current members—the AAML guidelines, *Bounds of Advocacy: Goals for Family Lawyers* (AAML 2000), are posted online and are influential in "provid[ing] clear, specific guidelines in areas most important to matrimonial lawyers."[6] The AAML criticizes bar rules for not providing "adequate guidance to the matrimonial lawyer. The ABA's Model Rules . . . are addressed to all lawyers, regardless of the nature of their practices. . . . Many Fellows of the American Academy of Matrimonial Lawyers have encountered instances where the [Model Rules] provided insufficient, or even undesirable, guidance" (AAML, *Bounds* Preliminary Statement). Although *Bounds of Advocacy* sets higher and, on some issues, somewhat different standards for matrimonial lawyers than those found in the Model Rules, no attorney can be disciplined for violating the AAML guidelines. Nevertheless, *Bounds* remains an important guide, articulated and disseminated especially by specialists in the matrimonial area, to address some of the difficult challenges divorce lawyers face in practice.

The Common Challenges of Divorce Practice

All divorce lawyers face the problem of representing clients who, in addition to the legal hurdles of divorce, often face significant emotional turmoil as well as painful life choices about disposition of property and remaking living arrangements with reduced income. Many divorce clients have little or no prior experience with the legal system and bring with them a naiveté about what the law can and cannot do. In some divorces, the well-being of children looms over the legal process and concerns both attorneys and their clients. For many divorce lawyers, as one interviewee said, "The hardest part of divorce practice is . . . not

---

6. See the AAML website for membership by state and for *Bounds of Advocacy:* http://www .aaml.org/library/publications/19/bounds-advocacy.

the other side, not the courts. It's dealing with your own client." These qualities of divorce clients and cases present divorce lawyers with four particularly difficult professional issues: defining the scope of their responsibilities in representation; acting diligently with emotional, demanding clients; allocating decision-making responsibilities between attorney and client; and defining the meaning of advocacy.

Interviews with divorce lawyers underlined the emotional dimensions of many of these cases. "Divorce is *all* emotion," said one attorney. Another asserted, "You're seeing people at their absolute worst. I mean, I represent people who've killed other people . . . and they're emotionally much easier to deal with than . . . many divorcing people!" Perhaps more important, lawyers also recognized the lack of fit between clients' needs and what the law could deliver: "I am asked to legally solve an emotional problem." No-fault divorce heightens this challenge by generally making legally irrelevant the powerful feelings of anger and blame that parties may bring to a divorce. Part of the "emotional divorce" for clients may be to show that their spouse was wrong, deceitful, or irresponsible. The no-fault legal process gives little room to play out the emotional need to establish blame (Mather, McEwen, and Maiman 2001, 119–120; Sarat and Felstiner 1995).

The law also falls short in guiding people about how to remake their lives. As *legal* specialists, divorce attorneys often find themselves in the middle of a broad array of nonlegal issues that are generally beyond their competence to handle. One attorney summarized the expectations that clients may bring with them about how "their lawyer" can and should help them: "I see people who are dealing with so many issues that the actual legal issue many times is the easiest thing. . . . They have the feeling that if they are hiring an expert, that expert can give them advice in all areas—in their love life, in how to parent their children, should they sell their home for such and such a price?"

This common situation raises serious questions about boundaries and about responsibilities to clients with interlinked legal and nonlegal needs— what kinds of advice are lawyers competent and comfortable in providing? Although Model Rule 2.1 states that lawyers "may" consider "moral, economic, social and political" issues in giving advice to a client, Model Rule 1.1 defines competence with reference to *legal representation*, that is, "the legal knowledge, skill, thoroughness and preparation reasonably necessary for the representation." On the other hand, the AAML asserts that an attorney is responsible for *all* aspects of a representation, including legal and financial details—tax, pensions, trusts, and estates—but also "knowledge [that] is not limited to legal information. For example, custody and visitation cases require knowledge of child development and, at times, understanding of mental and emotional disorders" (*Bounds* 1.1 cmt.). It also provides that "an attorney should advise the client of the emotional and economic impact of divorce and explore the feasibility of reconciliation" (1.2).

Not surprisingly, we found substantial differences in the ways that divorce lawyers understood their professional obligations. As one said, "Divorce requires the attorney to be not only a legal technician [but] a general problem-solver, helping people cope, sort of handholding." In a similar vein, another observed that "sensitive" lawyers also should know what community resources—for example, counseling for children, financial advice—are available to assist clients, perhaps at low cost. Lawyering for the "whole person" in collaboration with professionals from other disciplines has been one innovative bar response to assisting clients in dealing with nonlegal issues. Indeed, the emergence of mediation, collaborative lawyering, and holistic lawyering can be understood as new structures for responding to the nonlegal needs of clients (Rubinson 2008). This perspective, as advocated by the AAML and building on Binder, Bergman, and Price's (1991) client-centered approach to lawyering, was much more common among divorce specialists, many of whom in Maine participated in Resources for Divorced Families, an organization of judges, divorce attorneys, and mediators focused on establishing collaboration across disciplines and providing support services for divorcing families. Specialists were especially likely to refer clients to other professionals or community agencies for assistance. Many other lawyers, however, resisted an overly broad advisory role and drew a line with their clients: "When conversations get to that point, where somebody is just constantly looking for that kind of [nurturing] support, I'll cut those conversations short." For these attorneys, especially common among generalists, professional conduct meant reorienting clients to the narrow legal role that these lawyers preferred to play.

A second challenge in divorce lies in the lawyer's duty to manage client communication and act with "reasonable diligence and promptness" (Rule 1.3). The emotional character of divorce, the general neediness of some divorce clients, and their inexperience with the legal system compound these responsibilities. The Model Rules on communication generally assume the client is a rational and knowledgeable actor, and allow exceptions only for clients with diminished capacity or when immediate communication would be harmful (Rule 1.4 cmt.). But the AAML's *Bounds of Advocacy* acknowledges practice realities with divorce clients whose emotions and stress may impede thoughtful deliberation. It underlines the importance of listening to and respecting clients but also urges lawyers to assess whether a "client's decision-making ability appears to be impaired," and if so, it urges the attorney "to protect the client from the harmful effects of the impairment" (*Bounds* 2.5). Moreover, although both sets of rules describe the lawyer's duty to communicate promptly with the client, the AAML also recognizes that lawyers should educate clients to temper their expectations—"the client should understand that a successful lawyer has many clients, all of whom believe their case to be the most important" (*Bounds* 2.3 cmt.).

Our interviews with attorneys highlighted both these communication challenges and the difficulty of deciding what "reasonable . . . promptness" means in divorces. Most divorce lawyers charged hourly fees, and they learned from bitter experience that clients often balked at bills that reflected the time spent on phone calls. Lawyers also worried about the "people . . . who . . . think that they are my only clients. . . . Someone who is going to want to be able to pick up the phone and call you four, five, six times a week and want you to be there to hold your hand and to talk with them about everything." Consequently, attorneys at times found themselves reluctant to return phone calls and would let the phone messages pile up from especially demanding clients. Many divorce attorneys practiced defensively and tried to screen out clients they thought would be unusually difficult and needy. But others, because of the economics of their practice—either as generalists or as divorce specialists for low-income clients—would take virtually all clients but then be unable to give the most demanding ones the time and emotional attention they expected.

Some divorce attorneys used delay strategically with clients who were bent on revenge and unable to be reasonable in their expectations. These lawyers were concerned about moving cases too quickly in light of the emotional state of clients who were focused on their anger and retribution. As one lawyer explained, "I have to say that court delays are a help. . . . Time heals. I hate temporary hearings held three weeks after the libel gets filed. These people are angry and hurt. They can't think straight." A second agreed, noting that "a lot of that [unreasonable demands] I find is easy to deal with by just delaying things, by letting things calm down. I'm a great believer in delay in the system in situations like that. It really works to defuse the divorce."

Attorneys also worried about clients who were so exhausted by conflict that they wanted to "throw in the towel."

> I try to make them [despondent clients who want to walk away] realize that
> they will go through a series of emotions as the case ages and that what

they're telling me at this moment is not what they'll be feeling two months down the road. And in those cases I'll stop an attempt to make a quick settlement if I feel that what they're settling for is insufficient.

I quite often intentionally delay a case until the party is ready to make a reasonable decision and until you know how the two parties are going to function in their separate lives.

Thus, faced with "unreasonable" clients, divorce attorneys not infrequently delayed moving cases forward, even in the face of pressures from their clients to take the next steps and the requirement of Model Rule 3.2 "to expedite litigation." Under these circumstances, especially, communications with clients were often intentionally limited. These responses could be construed by clients as lack of diligence and poor communication.

In the context of this pressure to strip away some or all of a client's unreasonable expectations, a third professional challenge emerges and has special salience in divorce: to define the meaning in practice of abiding "by a client's decisions concerning the objectives of representation" (Rule 1.2(a)). This challenge takes on additional importance in light of the legal naiveté of many clients and the "unreasonable expectations" that at least some have about how the case should be resolved. In our interviews, we commonly heard this issue defined as that of the "unreasonable client" who needed to be reeducated about attainable goals. Although the Model Rules depict a bright line between the objectives of representation (which the client controls) and the means (which the lawyer controls), that line is often hard to decipher in divorce—or in criminal defense (Van Cleve, chapter 14). The AAML, in contrast, calls for shared decision making between lawyer and client, adding that lawyers have "responsibility for the propriety of the objectives sought" (*Bounds* 2.4).

Divorce clients' emotions can create unrealistic goals. Noting this problem, attorneys describe their frequent attempts to overcome it: "I spend a lot of time trying to defuse what I call the nonsense or the bullshit, and I will be very firm with my client that this is not a matter of spite, and I have a whole pitch I give to them." Another said, "There are a lot of times when you have to say, 'It isn't going to happen. The judge is not going to do that,' when they start telling you, 'I want this and I want that.'" Two other interviewees describe similar challenges:

In some cases obviously it's just impossible to get what your client wants. They come in asking for custody and that just may not be realistic at all. They come in asking for some large amount of alimony that may not be realistic. I mean, people do have unrealistic expectations sometimes. I try and reduce their expectations right away if that's in fact what it looks like to me.

There's a great gradation between how much beating over the head you have to do as far as getting them to comprehend that what they want is unreasonable. It's not that you're telling them what to do but telling them that the positions that they are taking are unreasonable and unsupportable.

These strong interventions may dominate the early sessions with clients and challenge attorneys to think about the appropriate balance between lawyer and client control over decision making. They can also raise that question in the minds of clients. One interviewee observed, "I have had a number of people [clients] say, 'Wait a minute, who are you representing?' And usually I can straighten that out by explaining that part of what I perceive to be my role is to help a person come to the right expectations as far as what's going to happen." In other words, the informal norms of divorce lawyers reflect their knowledge of law and typical case outcomes, and also recognize their clients' emotional and personal plights.

A fourth issue of professional responsibility centers on the meaning of advocacy given the difficulty that divorce lawyers experience when "the best interests of children" are at stake. Although obligated to represent only the parent (their client), attorneys are influenced by both the law's general emphasis on the best interests of children and their own personal concerns for the well-being of children. What does and should this mean for the role that they take as strong advocates for their clients, in shaping or accepting client goals, and in pursuing them? Instead of advocating exclusively for the client's position, as the Model Rules suggest, many divorce lawyers believe that they have an "ethical obligation" to protect the interests of children and that they "should consider the welfare of, and seek to minimize the adverse impact of the divorce on, the minor children" (*Bounds* 6.1). The AAML also asserts that advocacy of client interests should not be done at the expense of the children, and that attorneys should not contest custody or visitation for reasons of "financial leverage or vindictiveness" (*Bounds* 6.2).

The attorneys we interviewed approached this issue in different ways. One noted how he tried to pressure "unreasonable" clients with children: "If children are involved, I'll use the metaphor of 'If you do not . . . soften, and we have a contested hearing, the approximate cost of the contested hearing—with your contribution and your husband's . . . will approximate eight years of child support. . . . If you soften, isn't it better to go to the kids?'" Another attorney, observing variable conduct among colleagues noted the special pressures of cases involving children: "Some attorneys are very resolution-minded . . . to try to keep the [divorcing spouses] friends if they can, particularly if there are children involved, to try to minimize the areas of dispute, to try to control their clients, to try to keep them from driving each other crazy during the process." Interviews with family law specialists (particularly as compared to generalists) typically reflected the perspective of the AAML. That is, family law specialists were more likely than the general practitioners to articulate a concern for the children and to explain how it shaped their advocacy for clients.

More generally, attorneys expressed quite different views about how they advocated for clients in divorce negotiations, varying in the degree to which they emphasized fairness for both parties or promoted the most advantageous position for their client. These varying views also reflect the divergent stances of the ABA and the AAML. Whereas the former describes the advocacy role in the preamble as "zealously assert[ing] the client's position under the rules of the adversary system" and the negotiator's task as "seek[ing] a result advantageous to the client but consistent with requirements of honest dealings with others," the AAML questions the role of zealous advocacy in the context of family law:

> The emphasis on zealous representation of individual clients in criminal and some civil cases is not always appropriate in family law matters. Public opinion . . . has increasingly supported other models of lawyering and goals of conflict resolution in appropriate cases. A counseling, problem-solving approach . . . in resolving difficult issues and conflicts within the family is one model. . . . Mediation and arbitration offer alternative models. (*Bounds* Preliminary Statement)

Our interviews indicated that divorce lawyers themselves were divided and uncertain about advocacy norms in divorce. One observed that "some attorneys are strictly advocates of their clients. They don't care if the case settles. Their client gave them a position and gave them their marching orders, and they're out there to try to achieve that." Another respondent noted the apparent tension between his reading of the bar rules and his own sense of what was best in divorce cases: "The right answer from the bar association stand is probably to get as much as I can for my client, *but it is the other one, that's what I do: a reasonable settlement, I guess, fair to both parties.*" In our research we also quantified responses to this issue. When asked whether their primary goal in divorce was best described as reaching a settlement fair to both parties or as getting as much as possible for their client, 35% of the lawyers selected "fair settlement"; 23% opted for getting the "most for client"; and 42% resisted the forced choice and instead combined the possibilities, as in, for example, "reaching a settlement fair to my client." The fact that less than one in four lawyers we interviewed embraced the traditional zealous advocacy role underscores the importance of context in understanding how divorce attorneys define advocacy.

Variations and Contingencies in Divorce Work

In discussing these common challenges and lawyers' general responses to them, we have suggested some possible explanations for the differences in those responses. Here we focus particularly on three contingencies in divorce work—specialization, client resources and caseload, and law firm structure—that influence divorce lawyers' interpretations of professional responsibilities. These three contingencies highlight the informal norms and values as well as the incentives and disincentives of lawyers working in different practice settings.

Specialization

Divorce specialists viewed their professional responsibility to advocate for clients differently than did general practice lawyers. Specialists more often acknowledged the broad needs of clients, including the nonlegal issues that they knew from experience could create havoc for clients and for case settlement if ignored. Competence for the specialists (whose clients also tended to be wealthier) involved knowledge of tax and pensions and of resources for counseling and emotional support. Generalists more frequently said, as one lawyer did, that expertise in divorce law is "not that important" since "it's not hard to be an expert at a level that is appropriate for the cases that I handle." Because clients of most specialists could pay their generally higher retainers and hourly rates and afford more billable hours in their cases, these clients were also more likely to receive regular communications from their lawyers (including, for example, copies of all correspondence in the case). Nonetheless, specialist divorce attorneys were some of the most forceful in describing their control over the timing of case progress, including the use of delay, to respond to vulnerable clients who were unable or not yet ready, in their lawyers' eyes, to have "realistic" objectives.

Many specialists embraced family law as an important and challenging area of practice that should use the tools of civil litigation to advance the interests of clients. Thus, they often saw interrogatories and other discovery techniques as necessary. General practice lawyers, on the other hand, worked more often with clients with more limited resources, saw divorce practice as important but best accomplished through informal exchanges of information with opposing lawyers, and limited their retainers, hourly rates, and use of formal discovery techniques. When specialists and general practitioners met in cases, their perspectives on appropriate professional conduct—and the nature of advocacy—clashed. For example, a specialist criticized general practice lawyers for "not work[ing] a file the way a divorce file should be worked" and for not responding to discovery requests. But from the viewpoint of general practice lawyers, the specialists were at fault since they "would make a federal case of every divorce."

Specialists varied, however, both when it came to advocacy in cases that involved children and in their criteria for success as attorneys. Many held strong views, consistent with the AAML, that the interests of children should temper zealous advocacy on behalf of a client. Some said they would withdraw from representation before they would engage in unwarranted legal combat over custody. One specialist said that child custody "is not a fight I'm going to fight. They're not going to use the kids that way." Another explained, "I might go along with it if they want to go around mudslinging. . . . But if there are children involved, I don't go through with it." Other specialists, however, did not let the presence of children moderate their advocacy role. Another variation among specialists was that women specialists were less likely than men to define their success as lawyers purely in terms of legal case outcomes and showed instead a greater concern for clients' emotional and personal adjustment.

These variations among specialists, and between general practice lawyers and specialists, thus reflect ideological differences situated in the contingencies of practice about the meaning of competent representation, diligence, client objectives, and zealous advocacy. These ideologies lie not only in the minds of the attorneys but also link closely to other aspects of their practices—variations in client resources and caseload, and law firm structure. Attorneys with similar practices draw on shared knowledge, incentives, and constraints as they decide how to respond to professional challenges.

Client Resources and Caseload

To pay the bills and themselves, attorneys need to keep busy, and to ensure that busyness, they must continue to bring in new clients. For lawyers representing one-shot individual clients, there is no certain stream of work, so there is constant pressure to take on whoever comes in the door—whether in divorce, immigration (Levin, chapter 5), or plaintiff personal injury (Daniels and Martin, chapter 6). As one matrimonial lawyer put it 50 years ago, "A lawyer to live must have volume. I have volume, but it is killing me" (O'Gorman 1963, 47). Many of the divorce lawyers whom we interviewed pushed the boundaries of manageable caseload levels for their practices. As one hard-pressed lawyer put it, "You've got to keep all balls in the air at one time without letting one fall." Another complained: "There is simply more than I can do. It is not even time management. It is just the fact that there are times when there are crises in cases, and things happen, and it all happens at once, and there is only so much of you." Most important, high caseloads expose attorneys to client concerns about communication and meeting deadlines, particularly if law office resources are limited. Client concerns may be exacerbated by the fact that such lawyers are unable to spend much time on any one case. This means often giving short shrift to a client's emotions and being too pressed for time to be able to educate the client about realistic objectives, all things that lawyers with fewer cases and better-paying clients can more easily do.

Client resources and attorney caseloads also carry important implications for lawyers' choices about how aggressively to approach representation. Competent representation involves the "thoroughness and preparation reasonably necessary for the representation" (Model Rule 1.1). But what is "reasonable," and how does or should that relate to resources? Many lawyers are emphatic about this point: "The amount of work that will be done on a case will be based on the client's ability to pay. . . . Clients who want a Cadillac of a divorce but only will be able to spend $1,000 to $1,500 aren't going to get it." And another lawyer observed wistfully: "I wish, you know, that everybody paid, and we could bill less, and money was never a problem. And we could concentrate solely on the legal issues and not the financial impact of following one course or another. That's a factor that you have to consider: How much justice can this client reasonably afford?" Advocacy is limited when clients cannot afford to pay for the hours required for motions or lengthy hearings. Some lawyers serving lower-income clients purposely set a flat fee to avoid the obvious injustice clients see when they cannot afford the attorney's hours for aggressive representation. But the flat fee (typically low) may simply hide the problem since lawyers will lose money if they engage in lengthy proceedings.

Further evidence that client resources affect the nature of lawyers' advocacy comes from statistical data we collected on case disposition processes and length. Lawyers with working-class or middle-class clienteles initiated far fewer "adversarial" motions per divorce case than did those with upper-middle-class clients. And the mean length of divorces handled by our interviewees varied from 251 days (working-class clients), to 264 days (middle-class clients), to 341 days (upper-middle-class clients). Obviously, wealthier clients presented more financial issues to investigate and contest than did clients of modest means, but the better-off couples also tended to have two lawyers involved, which further escalated the level of advocacy.

Facing a self-represented party on the other side, lawyers said they rarely filed motions, encouraged their client to negotiate directly with the other party, and took less time between filing and disposition than in cases with opposing counsel (Mather 2003). Both communication and advocacy can be ethical minefields for lawyers facing pro se litigants. Lawyers are allowed to provide legal information to the pro se party, but they may not give legal advice (Rule 4.3). They also must take care not to outmaneuver or aggravate the pro se spouse and "cause him or her to become more litigious in turn" (Goldschmidt 2008, 142). An aggravated pro se spouse who is unhappy with the case outcome could easily vent that unhappiness on the lawyer through a grievance complaint.

Because parties in divorce often struggle to find sufficient funds to pay them, lawyers also face difficult decisions about responsible conduct when their clients run out of money or delay paying bills. For example, delay can be a lever to extract payments from clients. Some attorneys (mostly those with working-class clients) admitted that on occasion they simply stopped work on a case or delayed a final hearing to pressure a client to pay. According to one, "If I have the plaintiff, then I will probably tell my client that I will schedule a final hearing when my fees are paid. I will hold the papers to the extent I can." Another admitted, "I am sitting on one where the father sent me $500 from Virginia, and now it is contested, and he is supposed to send me another $500, and it has been two or three months. So I am just not working the case." For these attorneys, what looks from the client's perspective to be lack of diligence is justified as a necessary step to stay in business. And state bar rules are often expansive enough to justify such action. Other attorneys (whose clients had more resources) avoided this problem by structuring their retainer and fee schedules according to the steps in the divorce case. Still others maintained that they did not let a client's nonpayment interrupt what they saw to be the appropriate professional course of legal action. Such decisions about what constitutes professionally responsible practice relate not only to client resources but also to the structures of law firms.

Law Firm Structure

The structure of legal practice provides crucial context for lawyer decision making, creating or mitigating pressures leading to misconduct. Firms with multiple lawyers provide collegial support systems (communities of practice) to give advice about difficult decisions and also help to establish infrastructures to manage cases, deadlines, documents, and communication. Both of these presumably help to diminish violations of rules of professional responsibility. At the same time, firms also reorient lawyer decision making to take account of firm interests, discouraging attorneys from taking on clients who might not be able to pay their bills fully.

Divorce lawyers who have one or more partners or associates have immediate access to colleagues with whom to confer about professional decisions and ways to handle difficult clients. By contrast, sole practitioners often lack support networks of colleagues, although some do have informal relationships with attorneys they have met as opposing counsel or at bar meetings. The relative isolation of sole practitioners helps to explain their overrepresentation among those accused of bar violations—but an even more likely explanation is their weaker office structures for managing caseloads and for responding to grievances once they are filed.

Logistical resources vary across firm types with solo practitioners facing greater economic difficulty in developing the basic infrastructure of support—clerical assistance, filing systems, adequate computer resources, and so on. Inadequate resources can directly lead to bar grievances, relating particularly to communication and diligence. These problems appear vividly in a Maine discipline case of a relatively new solo practitioner working on a family law case:

> Attorney B first neglected her client, Mr. W., by filing a motion for modification of child support but then never served the motion upon the opposing party. Then, when Mr. W. retained another lawyer and asked for his file, Attorney B discovered that she had misplaced the file and was unable to locate it. But she avoided telling this to Mr. W. and ignored follow up requests for the file from Mr. W. and his new counsel.[7]

In this case, the Grievance Commission Panel found Attorney B in violation of the Maine Rules of Professional Conduct concerning communication and

---

7. *Board of Overseers of the Bar v. Bartlett*, Report of Findings of Panel E of the Grievance Commission, December 10, 2004.

safekeeping property, and issued a reprimand. When the violation occurred, the attorney lacked support staff and was in the middle of an office move. Since then, she has improved her law office management in ways that would make a recurrence of the problems unlikely (e.g., hiring full-time clerical staff, maintaining files onsite, updating records by computer).

The strong office support more likely to be found in larger firms also helps attorneys charged with grievances to avoid findings of actual misconduct by aiding in the production of documents such as cancelled checks, telephone records, daily calendars, and office memos that can be powerful defenses against grievances. Bar counsel in both Maine and New Hampshire emphasized the importance of having effective office systems to help attorneys avoid findings of misconduct.

Not only can law firm structures provide office support to help lawyers communicate promptly with clients, keep track of their files, and defend against grievances, but firms also can create pressures, incentives, and procedures for screening out impecunious clients, for regular billing and account keeping, and for dropping clients who cannot pay their bills promptly. We found that sole and small firm practitioners were somewhat more likely to accept divorce clients out of altruism and to make downward adjustments to bills than were attorneys in larger firms. Solo practice attorneys, in particular, have only themselves to answer to and often lack office rules about retainers, payments, and billing—and the monitoring systems to enforce them. One sole practitioner explained how hard it was to ask for a new retainer when clients would complain and act insulted by the request: "You try to give them the usual stock line that, 'I'm sorry, it's office policy' . . . [but] it's tough to say when you're the only person that's saying it!" By contrast, law partners often look askance at firm members who take on clients who cannot pay, and firm structures help stiffen the spines of overly empathetic attorneys.

Law firm structure and size thus both provide lawyers resources to avoid violating rules of professional conduct and for operating in a more business-like manner. Sole and small firm practitioners are likely to work with fewer of these resources. Firm structures thus serve to advance the interests of clients in many instances. However, they also create pressures for sympathetic lawyers to resist accepting or continuing to represent clients with limited resources because doing so could diminish firm income. As a result, firms can also act as powerful counterweights to the attorneys' commitment to make legal services more widely accessible.

Conclusion

Attorneys in divorce cases face a higher likelihood of complaints from clients and opposing parties than do lawyers in most other areas of law. The volume of complaints grows out of the nature of divorce work and clients, but vulnerability to violations of codes of professional responsibility is unequally distributed across the varied settings of divorce practices. Clients with sufficient resources, law offices with well-developed business practices, and available professional colleagues to advise on problem cases all reduce significantly the conditions that can lead to complaints and rule violations. Overtaxed and underresourced sole and small firm practitioners appear to face a higher likelihood of sanctions, particularly for neglect and poor communication with clients. As Abel (2008) shows in his six case studies of lawyer misconduct, explanations for their irresponsible behavior often lie in the individual circumstances of attorneys (e.g., family or health stresses, financial pressures). However, as we have seen in our consideration of divorce lawyers and as Levin (2009) and Mather (2011) note as well, certain communities of practice and working conditions may facilitate attorney misconduct by reinforcing informal norms and understandings (in the case of generalist attorneys) or by not providing office support (in the case of sole or small firm practitioners).

Much more common than clear rule violations and sanctions—in fact inherent in the daily challenges of divorce practice—are unanswered questions about what professionally responsible divorce practice means, especially in light of the difficulties that divorce clients can pose and the variable contingencies of practice. The characteristics of many divorce clients (high emotion, legal naiveté, immediate practical concerns, frequently limited resources, and the needs of children) also often apply to clients of legal services (Shdaimah, chapter 15), immigration (Levin, chapter 5), and criminal defense lawyers (Van Cleve, chapter 14). Not surprisingly, lawyers representing such clients often respond in similar ways, such as teaching "realism" to clients and trying to be reasonable with peers to resolve issues as expeditiously as possible. This chapter has shown how lawyers' ways of addressing several issues of professional responsibility vary in relation to the degree of specialization, the resources of clients and attorney caseloads, and the structure of law firms in divorce. The Model Rules provide incomplete guidance in identifying and addressing these questions, and the practice-specific AAML guidelines offer somewhat greater help. Nonetheless, each attorney is left to define professionally responsible practice in her own terms, most often in relation to the expectations of colleagues in firms and other communities of practice.

References

Abel, Richard. 2008. *Lawyers in the Dock: Learning from Attorney Disciplinary Proceedings.* New York: Oxford University Press.

American Academy of Matrimonial Lawyers (AAML). 2000. *Bounds of Advocacy: Goals for Family Lawyers.* http://www.aaml.org/library/publications/19/bounds-advocacy.

Binder, David A., Paul B. Bergman, and Susan C. Price. 1991. *Lawyers as Counselors: A Client-Centered Approach.* St. Paul: West.

Connecticut Statewide Grievance Committee. 2011. "Grievance Decisions." http://www.jud.ct.gov/SGC/decisions.

Davis, J. Scott. 1991. *Maine Bar Counsel's 1991 Annual Report.* http://www.mebaroverseers.org/board/annual_reports/pdf/1991%20Annual%20Report.pdf.

Epstein, Cynthia Fuchs. 1993. *Women in Law.* 2nd ed. Urbana: University of Illinois Press.

Goldschmidt, Jona. 2008. "Strategies for Dealing with Self-Represented Litigants." *North Carolina Central Law Review* 30:130–150.

Heinz, John P., Robert L. Nelson, Rebecca L. Sandefur, and Edward O. Laumann. 2005. *Urban Lawyers: The New Social Structure of the Bar.* Chicago: University of Chicago Press.

Herman, Madelynn. 2006. "Self-Representation: Pro Se Statistics." National Center for State Courts. http://www.ncsconline.org/wc/publications/memos/prosestatsmemo.htm.

Illinois Attorney Registration and Disciplinary Commission. 2010. *2009 Annual Report.* https://www.iardc.org/AnnualReport2009.pdf.

Indiana Supreme Court Disciplinary Commission. 2010. "Disciplinary Commission Annual Reports." http://www.in.gov/judiciary/discipline/about.html.

Katz, Jack 1982. *Poor People's Lawyers in Transition.* New Brunswick, NJ: Rutgers University Press.

Levin, Leslie C. 2004. "The Ethical World of Solo and Small Law Firm Practitioners." *Houston Law Review* 41:309–392.

———. 2009. "Bad Apples, Bad Lawyers or Bad Decisionmaking: Lessons from Psychology and from *Lawyers in the Dock*." *Georgetown Journal of Legal Ethics* 22:1549–1594.

Maine Board of Overseers of the Bar. 2009. *2009 Annual Report.* http://www.mebaroverseers.org/board/annual_reports/pdf/2009%20Annual%20Report.pdf.

Mather, Lynn. 2003. "Changing Patterns of Legal Representation in Divorce: From Lawyers to Pro Se." *Journal of Law and Society* 30:137–155.

———. 2011. "How and Why Do Lawyers Misbehave? Lawyers, Discipline, and Collegial Control." In *The Paradox of Professionalism: Lawyers and the Possibility of Justice,* edited by Scott L. Cummings, 109–131. New York: Cambridge University Press.

Mather, Lynn, Craig A. McEwen, and Richard J. Maiman. 2001. *Divorce Lawyers at Work: Varieties of Professionalism in Practice.* New York: Oxford University Press.

Michigan Attorney Grievance Commission. 2009. *2009 Annual Report.* http://www.agcmi.com/pages/AGCStatistics.html.

National Center for State Courts (NCSC). 2009. "Trial Courts: Domestic Relations Caseloads." In *Examining the Work of State Courts: An Analysis of 2007 State Court Caseloads,* by Robert C. LaFountain, Richard Y. Schauffler, Shauna M. Strickland,

Chantal G. Bromage, Sarah A. Gibson, Ashley N. Mason, and William E. Raftery, 12–20. Williamsburg, VA: National Center for State Courts. http://www.ncsconline.org/d_research/csp/2007B_files/EWSC-2007-v21-online.pdf.

Nelson, Robert R., and David M. Trubek. 1992. "Arenas of Professionalism: The Professional Ideologies of Lawyers in Context." In *Lawyers' Ideals/Lawyers' Practices*, edited by Robert L. Nelson, David M. Trubek, and Rayman L. Solomon, 177–214. Ithaca, NY: Cornell University Press.

New Hampshire Supreme Court Attorney Discipline Office. 2011. "Annual Reports." http://nhattyreg.org/annual.php.

O'Gorman, Hubert J. 1963. *Lawyers and Matrimonial Cases: A Study of Informal Pressures in Private Professional Practice.* New York: Free Press.

Rubinson, Robert. 2008. "The Model Rules of Professional Conduct and Serving the Non-Legal Needs of Clients: Professional Regulation in a Time of Change" *Journal of the Professional Lawyer* 2008:119–135.

Sarat, Austin, and William L. F. Felstiner. 1995. *Divorce Lawyers and Their Clients: Power and Meaning in the Legal Process.* New York: Oxford University Press.

State Bar of Arizona. 2011. "Reports of Lawyer Discipline." http://www.azbar.org/lawyerconcerns/disciplineprocess/reportsoflawyerdiscipline.

Trevethick, Thomas V. 1995. "Is There a Pattern in the Madness? A Statistical Survey of Conduct Complaints." *New Hampshire Bar Journal* 36:13–22.

Immigration Lawyers and the Lying Client

Leslie C. Levin

[There are] always ethical issues in immigration practice. The question is: Does anyone want to recognize them? You know, the client will come into the office for a marriage case: Is it a bona fide marriage, or not? Are you going to take the case, or not? I think right away it's an ethical question (Attorney #23).[1]

The practice of immigration law is ethically challenging. Clients are often desperate, the law is harsh, and decision makers can be hostile. Competition for business is fierce, and fees are often low. Clients may lie—even to their lawyers—to escape persecution, remain with their families, or secure work in the United States. How do the law, the conditions under which these lawyers operate, their colleagues and clients, and the threat of sanctions affect lawyers' ethical decision making in practice?

The substantive law and the formal rules governing lawyers help shape lawyer conduct, but are not the only factors that affect their ethical decisions. Lawyers learn professional norms through their communities of practice—that is, the groups of lawyers with whom they interact and to whom they compare themselves (Mather, McEwen, and Maiman 2001). Their ethical commitments vary significantly based on the kinds of clients they represent, the office settings in which they work, and the legal authorities with whom they interact (Carlin 1966). Personal identity also affects how lawyers conceive and negotiate their role as professionals, as do complex psychological processes (Wilkins

---

1. Immigration attorneys were interviewed by the author and promised anonymity in a 2006 study described below. Throughout this chapter, the number following each quotation signifies the attorney quoted.

1998; Langevoort 2000). The perceived fairness of the legal system within which they operate may further influence their decisions.

In an effort to explore ethical decision making in the immigration law context, this chapter draws on interviews conducted in 2006 with a random sample of 71 lawyers in the New York City metropolitan area who were primarily engaged in the private practice of immigration law. These lawyers were asked to participate in a study of the work lives and professional development of immigration lawyers.[2] Toward the end of the interviews, they answered questions about the ethical issues they encountered in their practices. One issue that many confronted—at least occasionally—was the lying client.

The term "lying client" is used here to include the client who lies to the lawyer and wishes to lie to authorities; the client who reveals to the lawyer that he wishes to lie to authorities; and the client who realizes during the course of the representation that lying would help to attain a legal goal. Of course, lying clients are not unique to the immigration field. They are found in every practice specialty. Ordinarily, lying contravenes not only lawyers' professional codes, but also lay notions of morality. The lying immigration client presents a useful vehicle for exploring the factors that affect lawyers' responses to (what arguably should be) a simple ethical issue in an especially challenging practice context.

Overview of the Immigration Bar

While the immigration bar is small, the clients whom they represent and the types of work these lawyers do are varied. Clients range from Fortune 100 companies that are seeking to hire foreign-born employees, to foreign nationals who seek legal status based on their familial relationship to someone who is already legally residing in the United States, to individuals who are seeking asylum from persecution, to noncitizens facing removal proceedings based on criminal offenses or unlawful status. Business immigration lawyers—who perform the work that must be done for organizations to sponsor a foreign national to enter and work legally in the United States—are considered at the top of the immigration bar's status hierarchy (Levin 2009). Most immigration lawyers who do not focus primarily on business immigration do at least some family-based immigration. Some immigration lawyers also handle asylum

---

2. A detailed description of the lawyers in the study and the method of data collection appears in Levin (2009).

claims or deportation defense work. These differences affect the pressure that clients can bring to bear on their lawyers to achieve the clients' ends (e.g., repeat player business clients versus one-shot individuals and families) and the economic stability that lawyers have to resist such pressures.

Most immigration lawyers work in solo and small firms (2 to 5 lawyers). Even some business immigration lawyers with substantial corporate clients work in this setting. Immigration lawyers also work in larger boutique immigration firms—typically of less than 20 lawyers—although the world's largest immigration firm, Fragomen LLP, has over 60 lawyers in its New York office (Levin 2009). A small number of large corporate law firms (more than 100 lawyers) employ a few business immigration lawyers, primarily as a way to service their existing corporate clients (Levin 2009).[3]

At the same time, members of this bar share some significant commonalities. One-third of the lawyers in the study are immigrants,[4] and almost one-third of the US-born lawyers have at least one foreign-born parent (Levin 2009). Some are drawn to the work because it resonates with their own history or because of a desire to help others. These lawyers compete for clients but they are not adversaries in practice, as they do not negotiate or litigate against each other. Their adversary is the US government. Immigration lawyers often communicate with each other to keep abreast of frequent changes in the law. They view their colleagues within the bar as a closely knit community.

Coping with a Challenging Legal System

Immigration lawyers navigate and advocate within an extremely difficult legal system (Coutin 2000; Morando 2010). As one lawyer noted, it is a "really lousy" system with a "total lack of logic" (#19). It has an overlapping administrative structure, with problems in administration and rules that are in continual flux. Another lawyer explained, "If you read *Alice in Wonderland, Catch 22, Metamorphosis, The Trial* and Machiavelli, you will know more about

---

3. The lawyers in the study were disproportionately solo practitioners because only one lawyer from any given firm was interviewed. The breakdown was 54% solo practitioners, 24% in firms of 2–5 lawyers, 11% in firms of 6–20 lawyers, 6% in firms of 21–49 lawyers, and 4% in firms of more than 50 lawyers.

4. This group may not be representative of immigration lawyers elsewhere because New York is one of the few jurisdictions that permit foreign-born lawyers to take the bar examination without obtaining a JD or LLM from a US law school (NCBE and ABA 2011).

immigration law than most attorneys. You see so many things that don't make sense" (#24).

Immigration law became tougher after the passage of the Illegal Immigration Reform and Immigration Responsibility Act of 1996 and again after September 11, 2001. One lawyer noted, "September 11th put a whole other spin on immigration, and different laws and procedures. And the mentality about immigration that is very negative! That has permeated everything! . . . It really has. It is—the impact has been tremendous. Formally, in some ways, with actual changes in laws and rules and procedures, and informally in terms of the mentality. So that's also a very, very big challenge" (#31). Another lawyer voiced the frustration shared by many attorneys that "basically there are very few avenues for people to legalize. It's not that they don't want to be legalized; it's that there are so few avenues open right now" (#39). Lawyers increasingly found themselves telling potential clients that under the current law, there was nothing the lawyers could do for them.

An example of the problem is seen in the shrinking "cap" on H-1B visas, which are the temporary visas that enable US employers to employ foreign workers in jobs that require educational degrees in fields such as law, medicine, and engineering. There were 195,000 H-1B visas available annually during 2001–2003, but the current "cap" is 65,000 visas (Wasem 2006; US Citizenship and Immigration Services 2011). At the time of the study, the available visas were gone within a few months, and lawyers could do no more for clients than to suggest they reapply the following year. These lawyers were understandably frustrated. As one noted:

> They're making being an immigration lawyer very difficult. I can't work if I can't get someone what they want. H-1B's is the bread and butter of any immigration attorney who practices. In the old days, when they had 195,000 visas . . . H-1B's was a great source of income. But you know, it's gone! Everything is gone! H-1B's are completely tapped out! . . . So you're basically telling an employer, "I can't hire you until next October" [when visas are next available]. I mean, it makes no sense! (#12).

Several lawyers described other areas of immigration law in equally negative terms. Another lawyer echoed the views of several of others when she commented, "Our law doesn't make any sense and it hurts a lot." She later concluded that "in every way it stinks" (#60).

Immigration practice is also complicated by the fact that numerous administrative agencies are involved. As one lawyer explained, immigration law is very complex, but often not clear. And they pass new laws, and we could live for years, literally years, without implementing regulations. So we don't really know: What is the agency interpretation of this? So we get memos, [laughs] and you know, talk to each other. And people pontificate. But without clear guidance, [it] can be very, very difficult to practice. You know . . . there can be several bureaucracies, because you're dealing with DHS [Department of Homeland Security] and all its different parts, the Department of Labor, the Department of State. They can be really impenetrable bureaucracies, very difficult to deal with (#31).

The involvement of so many agencies contributes to a common perception that the law and procedures are constantly changing. Indeed, some lawyers claimed that "it changes every day" (#7). The changes may relate to filing fees or where to file a document, or they can be more substantive. These changes lead lawyers to feel that they are practicing law in an unpredictable and chaotic setting. One lawyer noted:

Out my window, I can see Federal Plaza, but you know, just there! It's fourteen floors of all sorts of chaos going on, and just getting something filed in the court can be, like, you know: elevator here, elevator there. Going here, talking to this person—I mean, it's a very inefficient system. . . . [I]t can be very frustrating and challenging to deal with the people that don't understand, really, what the law is. Or they think they know, because they heard it from somebody. Or, they're telling you "no" all the time, when you know the answer should be "yes" (#4).

Several lawyers described the large amounts of time they spent simply trying to stay up to date with the changes (Levin 2011).

These changes are not only stressful and costly, but they can cause delay and make it very difficult to predict outcomes for clients. On the most basic level, papers are filed in the wrong places or are rejected because a new form or filing fee is required. More significant, because of the changes in the law, "it's hard to . . . have a strategy in place—you can't really duplicate that strategy for a series of clients because things change from day to day and what was working yesterday is not going to work today and so you're constantly having to redevelop your strategy" (#59). As a result of frequent changes, mistakes by attorneys are difficult to avoid.

Some lawyers experience practice as more difficult because some immigration officials are "cold hearted" and "meaner" than they used to be. One lawyer observed that since September 11, 2001, "there's sort of a more negative feeling towards immigrants at DHS" (#16). Another lawyer, when asked whether his job had gotten harder since September 2001, stated:

> Well, Immigration's harder. They're more difficult about so many things! I've never seen them like this before! I mean, Immigration's always been a bad agency. They've always messed up in lots of cases. But I've never seen such a nasty attitude. So you deal with that, and that makes life a lot harder, because the cases that five years ago would have gone through without a problem, now you get some officer with a bad attitude, and they give you a problem (#15).

Even if decision makers are not nasty, they can be culturally insensitive. One lawyer recalled a judge who was "screaming at my clients that they need to apologize to him for saying—[for] lying to him and they did lie, but they're from China, and if you know anything about Chinese culture you don't say 'I'm sorry' in China" (#68). Another lawyer described the difficulty clients encounter when asked a question that "makes no sense in their own culture." He continued with an example:

> A witness said they were shooting Bob, okay. "They were shooting Bob. I saw them. They drove by. They were shooting Bob," and he was referring to a drive-by shooting of Bob's house in Albania. But they don't say they were shooting at the house. They were shooting at Bob, because that's Bob. Bob owns the land. Bob's associated with the land. Bob's family has been there for who knows how many decades or generations. That's Bob's place. If they're attacking the house or any part of the house or anybody at the house, inside the house, outside the house, in front of the house, on top of the house, it's all directed at Bob. It's an attack on Bob. So the judge would say, "Well, what do you mean? He didn't say that. He said that they were shooting Bob. You didn't say that they were shooting the house." And so it was used to infer negative credibility (#51).

Cultural differences when testifying, which may cause clients to avert their eyes, answer questions indirectly, or avoid certain sensitive topics, may also cause judges to discredit truthful testimony (Kalin 1986; Lustig et al. 2008). This is extremely frustrating for lawyers and can produce devastating consequences for clients.

Not surprisingly, many immigration lawyers experience the system as arbitrary and unfair (Coutin 2000). Echoing complaints by several lawyers, one noted, "There's a lot of discretion on the part of poorly-trained immigration officers that may or may not understand the law" (#4). As a result, the system is "unpredictable and it's full of weird things, and you are often at the mercy of people who are not very well-trained or sophisticated" (#16). In addition, decision makers may misapply the law. A lawyer explained, "The statute says one thing, but the government disobeys the law, will not apply the law, will apply the law in a draconian fashion. This is something they don't teach you in law school" (#40).

Some immigration judges also contribute to the perception of unfairness (Coutin 2000). An analysis of asylum case outcomes from 1999–2005 revealed substantial disparities in the decisions of New York City immigration judges: Two judges granted no more than 8% of asylum claims while three judges awarded asylum at rates of 80% or higher (Ramji-Nogales, Schoenholtz, and Schrag 2007). These findings are consistent with the observations of one lawyer in the study:

> Immigration, especially asylum, it's just the judging seems to be very subjective, okay? And I know that's a bad word to use, but there's no other way to put it, because everything falls under the catch-all of credibility. And anything can make your client seem not credible. And overcoming a credibility finding, if that's all it is, it's nearly impossible! It's one of these things where you can go before one judge, and you know you're going to lose. You go before another judge, you know you're going to win! . . .
>
> So that's—it's almost like going to Atlantic City and putting your coin in a machine. If I get the right judge, my client's going to be very happy! [Laughs] But [if] I get the wrong judge, it could be very bad (#29).

Another lawyer described the difficulty of walking "into a courtroom where there's a judge that you know is going to deny your case—you know those— any other judge in that courthouse would grant it." This lawyer recalled:

> I had a judge that was writing—I believe was writing the decision while my client was testifying after I'd asked him to recuse himself and I put that on the record that I thought he was doing that and I asked him to mark his notes into the—into the record because I saw him literally turning the pages that he'd been writing while my client was testifying—so you see some really horrible injustices (#70).

The reports of unfairness are echoed by outside observers. In a damning indictment, Judge Richard Posner of the Seventh Circuit Court of Appeals observed that some immigration judges are "hostile" and "abusive . . . [and that] the adjudication of these cases at the administrative level has fallen below the minimum standards of legal justice" (*Benslimane v. Gonzales* 2005, 829–830).

Earning a Living as an Immigration Lawyer

Immigration lawyers typically charge flat fees for their work because their clients expect it and their competitors do the same. The work that must be performed to provide competent immigration representation can be substantial, and the fee must be low enough so that the client can afford it. As one lawyer explained, the "number one absolutely biggest challenge in this practice is that you're helping people who almost always cannot afford your services—that's number one and it's amazing—it's a very complicated area of law and there's a government bureaucracy with tens of thousands of employees that don't understand it" (#58). Government employees are sometimes disorganized and "inept" (Morando 2010, 16; Coutin 2000); not surprisingly, they make mistakes. Those mistakes make legal representation of immigrants more time consuming and, consequently, more expensive. One lawyer described how a client was mistaken for another immigrant and it took an additional year of the lawyer's efforts, including numerous phone calls, letters, and an office visit to a supervisor, to straighten out the mistake. When lawyers charge on a flat-fee basis, it is difficult to obtain compensation for the time expended dealing with such mistakes.

Competition for business can also be intense. Immigration clients often decide which lawyer to hire based on price. Consequently, even business immigration lawyers in large law firms are cost conscious due to competition. One noted his firm charged mostly flat fees for immigration work, even though large firms typically charge on an hourly basis. "We regularly have meetings about that, to determine whether or not it's comparable to other law firms. Because in New York, I mean, you have people charging pennies to do things all over town, so there's a lot of competition here" (#4). A small firm lawyer explained:

> In general you can get a sense of how many hours it will take you, but you're dealing with the additional problem of market forces. And there are other people who are going to charge certain prices, and while I'm not going to lower my prices to somebody who's some hack out there, who is really not doing a good job, just to compete with that person. There are respectable practitioners, and if they're offering certain things at a certain fee level, and I don't do the same, I'm going to lose the business (#32).

A solo lawyer noted, "Clients are fussy and fickle in general. There's a lot of immigration lawyers they can go to . . . and if a situation comes up that you don't handle so well, whether it's your fault or not, they start to question whether they should be working with a bigger outfit" (#15).

A second source of competition—especially for lawyers who do family-based and asylum work—is from nonlawyers variously known as notarios, travel agents, or multiple service agencies, who engage in the unauthorized practice of law (a felony in New York). These nonlawyers often mislead immigrants about their likelihood of success in the immigration process and guarantee positive outcomes. They frequently submit fraudulent immigration applications for clients (Coutin 2000, 81) and then use a lawyer who works for them to appear in court. As one lawyer explained:

> There are those who are appearing on behalf of agencies who are seeing the clients at the interview or at the court, and going to court not having seen them, or even necessarily their file or anything else about them, until just as they're walking into the courtroom, or maybe minutes before, and probably not even speaking to the client before. And just going in and putting in their appearance, and doing the representation, and obviously getting paid, possibly in cash, a hundred or two hundred bucks or something like that, to show up, and doing ten of those a day, and making a reasonable living, and have no responsibility, really, for the case, for the file, which they don't even have in their possession if they give it right back to the person from the office (#23).

Immigrants often seek help from individuals in these agencies because their offices are in immigrant communities, they can speak the same language, and they offer their services for less money than lawyers. As one lawyer explained, "They look for the cheapest one, to pay the least amount of money. They often go to travel agencies and preparers. And often the preparers screw up their applications, because, oh, they think it's just a form! And then when they screw it up . . . they find themselves in deportation removal proceedings" (#14). Another lawyer, when asked whether the existence of nonlawyer providers affected his business, responded: "Absolutely! It affects the fees that I charge. People think it's just filling out pieces of paper, which it's not. It's far more sophisticated than that!" (#40).

Some lawyers were visibly frustrated by the government's failure to rein in the illegal activities of these nonlawyers. A few lawyers described efforts to file complaints against the agencies and the failure of New York authorities to take action. Immigrants are often scared to step forward, and law enforcement resources are limited (Rivlin 2006; Spragens 2005). One lawyer recounted his conversation with an immigration official who said, "'You have to understand,' he goes, 'the amount of people that are doing this, we would need a workforce ten times bigger than we are right now to handle this'" (#50).

Lying Clients and Lawyers' Responses

Immigration lawyers—like other lawyers—encounter clients who are lying, wish to lie, or are seeking help with constructing their lies. One lawyer described some of the scenarios as follows:

> Well, you know, "Find me a husband to marry." . . . "We're not living together; it's a business marriage. What kinds of documents do I need?" "I committed a crime overseas, but I don't want to tell Immigration about it, so don't divulge anything about it." I mean, you know, "My employer wants to sponsor me, but I'm not working for them; I'm working for somebody else" (#8).

Some clients want to make up stories—or enhance their stories—about persecution in their home countries to qualify for asylum. Others seek to lie about the ways in which they entered the country because the answer affects the likelihood they can legally remain in the United States. Clients also lie about their work experience or the terms of an employment relationship so that they can legally work in the United States.

Some clients lie because they come from corrupt legal systems and believe that lawyers in the United States are equally corrupt. One lawyer explained:

> They have a different concept of how the government works, and therefore they have a different concept of what your place in the process is. And that becomes an issue. You have to be able to convince them that the legal fee that they're paying you is not going to wind up in some envelope for a government official, because that is the way they operate! (#6).

As a result of coming from corrupt legal systems, some clients view lying as acceptable or even desirable. For example, one lawyer noted:

> With Russians, if you're honest, you're stupid! And it's playing the system, and you ask them a question, and they say, "Well, what answer do you want? Do you want me to have a degree? I'll come back with it tomorrow." And like, they're blowing the ink dry while they're handing it to you! (#9).

Some clients seek to lie because of their own experiences—or the experiences of others in their community—with nonlawyers who are willing to manufacture stories to help them attain their goals:

> Sometimes [the clients] have the idea, from their experience in this community of working with these non-attorney places, that they just can walk in, and I'm going to make up a story for them. Whereas, I have no intention of doing anything like that. I'll explore with them what happened in their lives, and try to find things that are useful, but I'm certainly not going to say, "No, you can't say that. You better say you did this, or you were that. Go home and make up a story, and come back tomorrow." . . . But sometimes they seem to expect that, because that's what they do in these non-attorney offices. They have like a whole set of stories, and they just pick one, you know, and try to fit it to the guy's age and background. . . . I mean sometimes they'll be, like, "You're the lawyer! Tell me what to say" (#16).

Clients also lie because of fear or desperation. One lawyer explained that some clients "have a real fear of the government. I mean, it's really palpable, and it's there. And, they're really scared of going back, so they will sometimes do whatever they have to, even if it involves dishonesty, to stay here" (#1). Clients may also feel desperate because adverse immigration decisions can physically separate spouses from one another and parents from their children. To put it in perspective, another lawyer said, "If you thought about it, what would you do to keep your American citizenship? Ninety-nine percent of Americans would probably lie" (#24).

How did lawyers respond to lying clients? The clearest evidence came from lawyers' descriptions of clients who lied or wished to lie about a marriage that was not "real"—that is, a marriage entered into solely to obtain legal immigration status. Lawyers who did family-based immigration reported that this problem arose at least occasionally, and for some lawyers, it arose frequently. Some lawyers attempted to avoid the problem by refusing to represent clients from certain countries because of the prevalence of fake marriages or fake documents in those communities. Virtually all of the lawyers who discussed their approach to the problem said that if a client told them directly that the marriage was not "real," they would not take the case.[5] One lawyer described

---

5. The limits of self-reported data are apparent here. I could rely only on demeanor evidence, follow-up questions, and the lawyers' later willingness to reveal how they handled clients whom they suspected—but did not know—were involved in fake marriages to assess the truthfulness of these answers.

the firm's "zero tolerance policy" if an individual even alluded to the marriage not being legitimate (#59).

When these lawyers merely suspected that a marriage was not real, they took a variety of approaches. Almost one-third of the lawyers said if they had suspicions, they would refuse to proceed with the representation. The remainder of the lawyers would represent the clients even if they suspected the marriage was not real, but many would try to dissuade their clients from going forward. For instance, a few gave warnings about the consequences of lying. One lawyer explained:

> I make it clear to them, "I don't deal with cases where, if you're not married, I don't want you here. You better be," and I try to read them the riot act, because they're going to find out by the interview, so, "This better be a completely legitimate situation here. Otherwise, not only are you, foreign national, but you, Mrs. American citizen, are going to end up fined, or possibly in jail." And if they, at the end of the day, say, "No, we understand that," but I still may think that they're—but if they say that, I mean, for me not to represent them, if they're asking for my help, is the same ethical quandary as to represent them. So, if they're telling me, and I've warned them, even if I feel it may not be an appropriate situation, I'd represent them to the best of my ability, and that's it (#32).

More often, rather than confront the clients directly, the lawyers explain what the couple would need to prove in order to prevail, including that they live together and have documentation to prove it. An experienced lawyer said:

> Well look, I'd never ask someone, you know. I've never doubted them. If they come to me saying that they're married, I've never said . . . "Well, can you document it?" I don't think it's my job. . . . Certain questions you just don't—you basically say, "Let's see how you can document it," and then, "We'll try it." I'm not going to—I don't know if it's my job to say that. I could be wrong, you know? Is it my job to say I don't believe? It's the same thing like a criminal lawyer. Am I supposed to say . . . "I think your marriage is fake?" They're swearing it's real; they're signing a paper that says under penalty of perjury, it's real, I'm going to still say, "Oh, no?" . . . I just don't ask that question. Even Immigration doesn't usually. They'll just deny a case (#16).

Several immigration lawyers—including some who attempted to discourage fraud—expressed the view that their clients were entitled to representation even if they personally did not believe their clients' stories, as long as they did not "know" they were false. A few lawyers adopted a "don't ask, don't tell" policy to avoid "knowing" a marriage was not real. Another explained, "The rule of thumb is, you know, what I tell my Eastern European clients, because it's knowingly providing false information: 'If you don't tell me, then I'm protected. So I know you look like a duck and quack like a duck, but if you don't tell me you're a duck, then I'm protected'" (#12). The lawyers who provide representation even when they suspect fraud rely on their role as advocates to justify their approach. As one lawyer noted, "It's the government's job to say, 'Your marriage is bullshit,' not mine" (#13). These immigration lawyers, much like criminal defense attorneys, defer judgments about their clients' truthfulness to third parties.

Business immigration lawyers also encounter lying clients. Sometimes it is the employer who seeks to lie. One lawyer explained, "Clients want to lie about things. They want to call somebody a manager who's not a manager. They want to say that somebody's a subordinate who's not a subordinate. They want to say a salary is a salary that's not a salary" (#41). In other cases, business immigration lawyers are retained and paid by the employee/beneficiary, and these clients may seek to lie about their education, their work history, or their job offers. The issues that business immigration lawyers encounter can also be more subtle:

> When you're dealing with these companies, a lot of the time they're saying, "Listen, we really need to bring this guy. Can he come first on a tourist visa, and then we'll change it?" And then just the mere asking of the question is the answering of the question, which means that it will involve telling an embassy and the State Department, "I don't intend to stay," when you do. This comes up a lot, and it's a very gray area, because obviously someone's intent can change (#2).

Some business immigration lawyers viewed their work as "cleaner" and less ethically problematic than other areas of immigration practice. As one explained:

> Most of my clients are pretty reputable. And [these are] corporate clients, you know, it's not like this is the only case they're ever going to have. They don't want to spoil things for the next case or the next case or the next case. And then some of them are public, so they have Sarbanes-Oxley concerns, and things like that! So they tend to be pretty cautious. But then there are a few who tend to be a little bit more, you know, push the envelope. They just consider expediency versus what's the right thing (#22).

One lawyer who had previously done family-based and asylum work said that he had seen more ethical issues in those areas than in business immigration (#4). It was not possible to determine from this study, however, whether business immigration lawyers actually encountered fewer lying clients than lawyers in other types of immigration practices.

In fact, it appears that some business immigration lawyers encounter lying clients with some frequency. Analysis by the US Citizenship and Immigration Services (2008) of a random sample of H-1B petitions filed in 2005–2006 revealed a fraud rate of 13.4%. Organizations with 25 or fewer employees and with annual gross incomes of less than $10 million had higher rates of fraud (e.g., fraudulent documents, shell businesses, no bona fide job offers) than larger organizations. It is possible that larger clients that are repeat players in seeking work visas have more at stake than businesses that only occasionally seek visas and thus are more careful. Or it may be that larger organizations have internal structures or procedures that make them less likely to engage in business immigration fraud. It is also conceivable that lawyers in larger firms—which tend to represent the largest business immigration clients—are less likely to accommodate lying clients. Whatever the reasons, this government study suggests that the size of the organizational client affects the likelihood that the business immigration lawyer will encounter or assist a lying client.

Virtually all of the business immigration lawyers in the study indicated that they would not knowingly represent clients engaged in obvious deception about the employee's past work history, education, or actual compensation, although some were willing to be very flexible if they did not "know." One lawyer explained:

> Well, you know, I have a young woman who has a degree as an economist, and so she got a job as a market research analyst. But in reality she's just a store clerk. She does some sort of marketing, but she's a store clerk.... If the Immigration Service were to walk in, she would lose her—but there's nothing wrong, because she had an actual degree, and if the company says she's a market research analyst, who I am to say no, unless it's clearly pointed out to me? So that's like, kind of pushing the envelope (#12).

Business immigration lawyers also routinely confront an ethical issue that implicates the honesty of both lawyers and clients. These lawyers help employers submit job descriptions or write ads for positions that will satisfy the requirements of the immigration regulations, while arguably not crossing the line into fraud. This scenario is so much a part of their everyday lives that they come to regard it as a "slight" ethics problem (#12), if they recognize it at all. Challenges arise, for example, when writing job descriptions for employees whose work does not neatly fit into the job descriptions that the US Citizenship and Immigration Services recognize. As one large firm lawyer noted:

> You just have to focus on making sure that you balance between what they really do, and what is expected of the position, and write the best support letter that you can, disclosing everything they do, but essentially: this is their job function, and hope it works out. And then you've got the employer, you know, talking in your ear about, "That's not really what they do," or, "They do that, but they really do this, and this, and this, and this." . . . I mean, you're just constantly dealing with this, and if you want to help them, and make it work, you need everyone to be flexible to come up with the right structure that falls into place for this particular type of visa (#4).

There was variation in how far lawyers were willing to depart from the truth, but it was not possible to generalize about the variations in this sample. The constant need to navigate the job description problem engendered some lawyer cynicism about the system and their obligation to the truth.

Factors Affecting Lawyers' Responses to the Lying Client

How do lawyers determine how to handle the lying client? Although the lawyers rarely mentioned the professional rules, the prohibition against *knowingly* assisting a client in criminal or fraudulent conduct or using false evidence (N.Y. Lawyers' Code 7-102) seemed to mark the outer boundary of the behavior in which most were willing to engage.[6] Lawyers occasionally reported that their families, their personal upbringing, or (very rarely) their religious beliefs taught them how to deal with lying clients. Yet religion and ordinary notions of morality do not clearly answer the question of how to respond to the desperate client who is or may be lying to obtain legal immigration status in a legal regime that lawyers viewed as arbitrary or unfair.

Indeed, the lawyers' responses to the lying client suggest that their behavior is also influenced by what they learn from other lawyers. Lawyers sometimes described the office "rule" or "policy" that guided their behavior. Lessons

---

6. The New York Lawyers' Code in effect at the time of the study was almost identical in this respect to the formulation in the ABA Model Rules of Professional Conduct.

learned early in practice can be especially powerful. One lawyer, who had been practicing for more than 25 years, recalled the lesson he had learned from his first employer:

> Well, he says, "You don't cross the line, and . . . if you do something unlawful or irregular, once your reputation is damaged, you're finished, forever! You have to appear in front of any agency, or multiple agencies: Department of Labor, Immigration Service, Department of State. And once your reputation is damaged, it's damaged permanently" (#40).

Likewise, a lawyer recalled that his mentor in his first job taught him "that the minute that fraud comes up, you show people the door" (#12). Another veteran lawyer, who started in practice with a more experienced attorney, recalled the first matter on which she worked:

> This company that we were talking about was extremely well-known, and had been involved in very serious scandals, some of them touching immigration. And they had hired him before I joined them to clean up their act. So his mission, which then became my mission, was to stick to the straight and narrow. And I think that that, at some level or another, has always impacted on the way I practice, and has brought me clients with similar circumstances (#41).

Several lawyers also mentioned that they learned how to resolve a variety of ethical issues by observing negative behavior as young lawyers. A few had had early experiences with employers who were suspended or disbarred, and quickly learned to avoid certain conduct. Of course, not all lawyers were able to resist some of the negative examples they observed, at least while they remained in the same firm. One young lawyer admitted that sometimes she told her clients to lie in order to obtain a green card. When asked how she learned that approach she replied, "By watching other people—my boss" (#66).

The sometimes long-lasting effects of early experiences in practice may be explained by psychological processes. Once a decision has been made about how to address an issue, people often use schemas or "scripts" to help them organize their thinking and determine how to address a similar issue in the future (Nisbett and Ross 1980; Singer and Salovey 1991). This obviates the need to constantly rethink decisions. Once lawyers decided how to respond to the lying client, the response often became routinized. Some lawyers referred to their "mantra" or their "rule of thumb" when describing their standard response to a lying client.

Concerns about maintaining their reputations with decision makers also affected how immigration lawyers responded to lying clients. One lawyer explained: "You don't want to be targeted as the person that brings in these fraudulent marriages. And I think, based on conversations with some of the Immigration officers, they know what attorneys come in with these fraudulent cases, and they know what attorneys don't" (#36). Another lawyer, when asked how he learned to respond to clients who asked him what they should say in immigration proceedings, responded, "I think I knew that right away. I'm very paranoid about getting in trouble, and I'm not going to. I've seen—there are a lot of immigration lawyers who get in trouble, and it's always for this kind of thing. It's manufactured stories, using these travel agents as their source of business. . . . But I can't have that. I don't have that reputation. I'm happy to say that I have a very good reputation with the immigration judges" (#16).

For some lawyers, concerns about criminal sanctions also influence their approach to lying clients. Lawyers described other attorneys who had been arrested for their involvement with fake marriages. Two lawyers had been asked to engage in misconduct by investigators involved in sting operations. As one business immigration lawyer noted, "So never mind ethical issues. Do you want to go to jail for somebody? How far are you willing to extend yourself, for that matter? So no, you have to be very careful" (#43). Some lawyers described themselves as cautious and "suspicious" (Levin 2011). One lawyer explained, "The old adage is that any time people talk to you, always pretend that they have a microphone—not sitting on the desk like that, but hidden, because you never know when the government might be running a scam. That's the way all immigration lawyers are taught" (#12).

Lawyer discipline was a significant concern for some lawyers. A few years before the study, a New York immigration lawyer had been disbarred (Abel 2008). Some of the lawyers had received discipline complaints that they attributed to In re Lozada (1988), which requires an immigrant to file a discipline complaint against a former lawyer in order to show ineffective assistance of counsel when trying to reopen a case. They also mentioned discipline imposed on other immigration lawyers, either because they had heard about it indirectly or because they had worked with a lawyer who was disciplined. As one lawyer observed, "People, clients, pull all kinds of stunts, and I was always like, 'No way!' I value my license tremendously. It took me a very long time to get it. If I get disbarred, my career as a lawyer is over. Nobody, or nothing, is worth it for me; not at all!" (#25). Another lawyer explained his thought process when a client wanted to lie: "My litmus test was always 'what would I say before an ethics tribunal?'" (#2).

On the other side of the equation, economic concerns and competition negatively affect how some lawyers respond to lying clients. One lawyer, when asked what he did when he was suspicious but was not sure that a marriage was a sham replied "sometimes you have to give the benefit of the doubt. And yes, of course there is a personal, egotistical reason for this, because if I don't give them the benefit of the doubt, they're not going to pay me; they're not going to continue with me" (#35). Another lawyer recalled that early in his career he would take "shabby" cases and "do whatever we needed to get the client out of proceedings," but said he no longer did so. When asked why, he explained: "You know, it may just be the people around me, and their own attitude. Like at the first firm I was at, you know, we would [do] almost anything. And at the second firm, I don't know—it might have been as I got more into the business end of things, which in a way is a little cleaner. . . . I have all this business work to do; I'm doing well. What do I need to take on a crummy marriage case for?" (#15).

But even some business immigration lawyers feel competitive or financial pressure to assist lying clients. A solo business immigration lawyer admitted that she essentially wrote whatever was needed to get an H-1B visa application approved. She explained, "Because guess what—if I don't [represent that the educational degree is related to the job], another lawyer will" (#60). Large firm lawyers may feel less financial pressure to do this or may have office colleagues who discourage this approach. One large firm lawyer, who had previously worked in a small firm, noted that "with a small firm I think there's perhaps less of a concern with blurring the lines—here you know, we're very careful [to] say, 'Look, it's got to be accurate or we can't sign off on it . . . and you shouldn't be either'" (#62).

Finally, the perception that the immigration system is not fair may affect some lawyers' responses to the lying client. Immigration lawyers want to help their clients, and they often feel that the immigration system is neither substantively nor procedurally fair. People's views about the legitimacy of laws and legal decision makers are linked to their assessments of the procedural justice of their experiences (Tyler and Huo 2002). Procedural justice includes the perceived fairness of the decision-making procedures and their interpersonal treatment by authorities (Tyler and Blader 2003). If people feel unfairly treated by legal authorities, they view the authorities as less legitimate and they obey the law less frequently (Tyler 2006).

Do lawyers, like laypeople, comply less with the law when they view the legal system as unfair? There is some evidence that attorneys and lay litigants use the same criteria and apply them in similar ways to generate their procedural justice judgments (Lind et al. 1990). Not surprisingly, lawyers tend to perceive greater process fairness than their clients (MacCoun et al. 1988). Lawyers are socialized in law school to respect the US legal system, even though they quickly learn that the adversary system is not always fair. Some immigration lawyers in the study noted, however, that the US immigration system is even less consistent and fair than the legal system that they learned about in law school.

One lawyer who viewed the immigration system as unfair felt that it "clearly" affected the way he dealt with government personnel. As he noted, "I have a cynical view of them." He continued:

A lot of times, the whole system is really not a fair system, and it's premised on things that—for example, labor certifications. The whole process bothers the heck out of me, because I will never be convinced that an employer can't really find somebody locally for 90% of the jobs that they're seeking to fill! But they make them go through this whole process where they set up an ad, so of course they're not going to find somebody, because it's so specialized. I mean, they don't just call it what it is, and let people hire who they need to hire. So I mean, you're always constantly in this fictional world, dealing with these fictional sections, and going through these motions. . . . You know that these employers really are crafting these things to meet the requirements, as opposed to it really being a reality. And Immigration, they play the same game. "Okay, you met these requirements; we'll give you the benefit" (#32).

The lack of consistency in US immigration adjudication and enforcement may also lead to disregard for the law. Consistency is the major criterion used to assess procedural justice (Tyler 2006), and the perceived inconsistency in the immigration system may negatively affect compliance. For example, when asked why large law firm partners would lie on their personal immigration forms, one experienced business immigration lawyer said:

I think part of it is that the Immigration Service itself is held in very low esteem. I think the system is visibly corrupt. I mean, you work at 26 Federal Plaza; you deport people all day long, and then you take the number 7 train home to your house in Queens, and there isn't a single person on the train who isn't deportable! What does it mean? . . . The whole thing is crazy! And so the system, I think, is so rotten, that it just breeds, sort of, contempt (#41).

Not only are the law and procedures viewed as unfair, but the quality of interpersonal treatment—of lawyers and clients—is sometimes poor. As noted, interpersonal treatment also affects procedural justice judgments. A few lawyers who said they would not engage in outright fraud suggested that the perceived unfairness of the immigration system more subtly affected their conduct. Further study would be needed to determine whether—and how—lawyers' responses to the lying client are affected by their perceptions that the immigration system is unfair.

Conclusion

The moral terrain of the immigration lawyer is hazardous. Many are drawn to their work because of their desire to help others (Levin 2009). They often have close connections to the immigrant experience and great sympathy for their clients' plights. As one lawyer noted, it is tempting to "manipulate something. . . . [Y]ou have to overcome this feeling that you want to help everybody" (#67).

The immigration lawyer's decision about how to respond to the lying client is typically made in the lawyer's office, beyond the view of government officials and the larger immigration bar. Since these lawyers do not advocate or negotiate against one another, they do not have the same opportunities for direct collegial control as has been reported within other segments of the bar, such as the criminal court workgroup (Eisenstein and Jacob 1977) or the divorce bar (Mather, McEwen, and Maiman 2001). But this is not to say that immigration lawyers do not influence one another. Lawyers' early experiences at work affect their responses. Firm office policies and expectations guide conduct, as does competition from other lawyers and nonlawyers, and knowledge gained through their personal networks and their specialty bar (Levin 2011).

Even within the immigration bar, context affects lawyers' responses to the lying client. Lawyers who perform different types of immigration work confront different types of lies. Some lawyers confront outright fabrications (for example, forged documents), while others confront more subtle lies. The resources of the lawyers' clients (e.g., individual versus small company versus large organization) affect lawyers' incomes and have implications for their ability to resist the lies. Differences in enforcement efforts with respect to different types of fraud may also affect lawyers' responses. For example, lawyers expressed more concern about marriage fraud than about lies in connection with H-1B visa applications, where enforcement was relatively rare.

Additional research is needed to determine whether and how the desperation of the client's situation or the perceived unfairness of the immigration system affects lawyers' willingness to accommodate the lying client. Susan Coutin's research suggests that public interest lawyers who represent Salvadoran immigrants were not willing to represent clients who fabricated the circumstances of persecution, but would "manipulate" narratives for those who seemed to have more legitimate asylum claims (2000, 91–94). Is this manipulation justified—psychologically or normatively—as a corrective to a legal system that appears unfair? This raises the issue posed by Elizabeth Chambliss (chapter 3) of the benchmark problem when discussing lawyers' ethical conduct: By what measure should immigration lawyers' response to the lying client be judged when the system itself may be fundamentally unfair?

The challenges immigration lawyers face are not altogether unique. Indeed, in many respects, immigration lawyers resemble tax lawyers and criminal defense lawyers, who do not advocate against one another. Instead, their adversary is the government. Like tax lawyers, business immigration lawyers work within a regulatory regime where intent is malleable and where compliance may be more fictional than real. And immigration lawyers, like criminal defense lawyers, often view the legal system in which they operate or the players within it as unfair (Van Cleve, chapter 14). Both immigration lawyers and criminal defense lawyers may deliberately avoid learning the "truth" so they can freely advocate for their clients (Mann 1985). These similarities raise the question of whether lawyers' responses to ethical challenges in different practice areas may be explained by the perceived fairness or logic of the legal regimes within which they operate. A deeper understanding of how these perceptions may affect lawyers' compliance with the law is especially important, not only to understand the conduct of immigration lawyers, but because lawyers in other specialties also encounter lying clients in legal regimes they view at best, as unreal, and at worst, as unfair.

References

Abel, Richard L. 2008. *Lawyers in the Dock: Learning from Attorney Disciplinary Proceedings.* New York: Oxford University Press.

Carlin, Jerome E. 1966. *Lawyers' Ethics: A Survey of the New York City Bar.* New York: Russell Sage Foundation.

Coutin, Susan Bibler. 2000. *Legalizing Moves: Salvadoran Immigrants' Struggle for US Residency.* Ann Arbor: University of Michigan Press.

Eisenstein, James, and Herbert Jacob. 1977. *Felony Justice: An Organizational Analysis of Criminal Courts.* Boston: Little, Brown.

Kalin, Walter. 1986. "Troubled Communication: Cross-Cultural Misunderstandings in the Asylum Hearing." *International Migration Review* 20:230–241.

Langevoort, Donald C. 2000. "Taking Myths Seriously: An Essay for Lawyers." *Chicago-Kent Law Review* 74:1569–1597.

Levin, Leslie C. 2009. "Guardians at the Gate: The Backgrounds, Career Paths, and Professional Development of Private US Immigration Lawyers." *Law & Social Inquiry* 34:399–436.

———. 2011. "Specialty Bars as a Site of Professionalism: The Immigration Bar Example." *St. Thomas Law Journal* 8:194–225.

Lind, E. Allan, Maureen Ambrose, Maria de Vera Park, and Carol T. Kulik. 1990. "Perspective and Procedural Justice: Attorney and Litigant Evaluations of Court Procedures." *Social Justice Research* 4:325–336.

Lustig, Stuart L., Niranjan Karnik, Kevin Delucchi, Lashika Tennakoon, Brent Kaul, Dana Leigh Marks, and Denise Slavin. 2008. "Inside the Judges' Chambers: Narrative Responses from the National Association of Immigration Judges Stress and Burnout Survey." *Georgetown Immigration Law Journal* 23:57–83.

MacCoun, Robert J., E. Allan Lind, Deborah R. Hensler, David L. Bryant, and Patricia A. Ebener. 1988. *Alternative Adjudication: An Evaluation of the New Jersey Automobile Arbitration Program.* Santa Monica, CA: Rand.

Mann, Kenneth. 1985. *Defending White-Collar Crime: A Portrait of Attorneys at Work.* New Haven, CT: Yale University Press.

Mather, Lynn, Craig A. McEwen, and Richard J. Maiman. 2001. *Divorce Lawyers at Work: Varieties of Professionalism in Practice.* New York: Oxford University Press.

Morando, Sarah. 2010. "Law in Action: How Immigration Attorneys Manage Legal Uncertainty." Paper presented at the annual meeting of the Law and Society Association, Chicago, IL, May 27–30.

National Conference of Bar Examiners (NCBE) and American Bar Association (ABA) Section of Legal Education and Admissions to the Bar. 2011. *Comprehensive Guide to Bar Admission Requirements 2011,* edited by Erica Moeser and Claire Huismann. Madison, WI: NCBE.

Nisbett, Richard, and Lee Ross. 1980. *Human Inference: Strategies and Shortcomings of Social Judgment.* Englewood Cliffs, NJ: Prentice Hall.

Ramji-Nogales, Jaya, Andrew Schoenholtz, and Philip G. Schrag. 2007. "Refugee Roulette: Disparities in Asylum Adjudication." *Stanford Law Review* 60:295–411.

Rivlin, Gary. 2006. "Dollars and Dreams: Immigrants as Prey." *New York Times,* June 11, C1.

Singer, Jerome L., and Peter Salovey. 1991. "Organized Knowledge Structures and Personality: Person Schemas, Self Schemas, Prototypes, and Scripts." In *Person Schemas and Maladaptive Interpersonal Patterns,* edited by Mardi J. Horowitz, 33–79. Chicago: University of Chicago Press.

Spragens, John. 2005. "Notorious Notarios: When Illegal Immigrants Need Legal Help, Illegal 'Lawyers' Exploit Them." *Nashville Scene,* June 9. http://www.nashvillescene.com/nashville/notorious-notarios/Content?oid=1191771.

Tyler, Tom R. 2006. *Why People Obey the Law.* Princeton, NJ: Princeton University Press.

Tyler, Tom R., and Stephen L. Blader. 2003. "The Group Engagement Model: Procedural Justice, Social Identity and Cooperative Behavior." *Personality and Social Psychology Review* 7:349–361.

Tyler, Tom R., and Yuen J. Huo. 2002. *Trust in the Law: Encouraging Public Cooperation with the Police and Courts.* New York: Russell Sage Foundation.

US Citizenship and Immigration Services. 2008. *H-1B Benefit Fraud & Compliance Assessment.* http://imminfo.com/Library/employer_issues/Benefit%20Fraud%20Assessement%20Report.pdf.

———. "H-1B Fiscal Year (FY) 2012 Cap Season." 2011. http://www.uscis.gov/portal/site/uscis/.

Wasem, Ruth Ellen. 2006. Memorandum. "H1-B Visas: Legislative History, Trends Over Time, and Pathways to Permanent Residence." Congressional Research Service: Washington, DC. http://www.aila.org/content/default.aspx?docid=18974.

Wilkins, David B. 1998. "Fragmenting Professionalism: Racial Identity and the Ideology of 'Bleached Out' Lawyering." *International Journal of the Legal Profession* 5:141–173.

Cases, Statutes, and Rules

Benslimane v. Gonzales, 430 F.3d 828 (7th Cir. 2005).

In re Lozada, 19 I. & N. Dec. 637, 638–639 (BIA), *aff'd,* 857 F.2d 10 (1st Cir. 1988).

Illegal Immigration Reform and Immigration Responsibility Act of 1996, Pub. L. No. 104-208, 110 Stat. 3009.

New York Lawyers' Code of Professional Responsibility DR 7-102 (2006).

Plaintiffs' Lawyers and the Tension between Professional Norms and the Need to Generate Business

Stephen Daniels and Joanne Martin

"As long as the phones are ringing, we're OK. If the phones stop ringing, I may as well turn out the lights." So said a plaintiffs' lawyer in Texas we interviewed in 2006.[1] He was talking about *the* challenge facing plaintiffs' lawyers—maintaining a steady stream of clients with injuries the legal system will compensate adequately (sufficient for the client's compensation, the lawyer's fee, and reimbursement for the costs incurred by the lawyer in representing the client). If this challenge is not met, the lawyer goes out of business. Our interest is in the ethical dimensions of this challenge.

Plaintiffs' lawyers are not unique—getting clients is a challenge for all lawyers, especially those working in the personal services sector. This challenge is particularly acute and the ethical stakes involved are heightened for plaintiffs' lawyers because their practices rely on a contingency fee–based compensation model. These lawyers must stay in business, and hopefully make a profit, while not running afoul of the formal rules governing client acquisition (the disciplinary code) or the informal norms within the plaintiffs' lawyers' practice community (the norms that help define that community's view of itself and its notions of acceptable behavior). Violating the former can lead to various levels of sanction by a governing professional board, including disbarment. Violating the

Research funded by the American Bar Foundation. The views expressed are those of the authors, not the Foundation.

1. As a part of a multiyear study, we conducted 151 in-depth interviews with Texas plaintiffs' lawyers—100 in the late 1990s and another 51 in 2005–2006. All interviews elicited information on lawyers' practices. All lawyers quoted in this chapter are among those interviewed. To strengthen our research and because we did not want to rely on interviews alone (which may give an incomplete picture), we also conducted two mail surveys of Texas plaintiffs' lawyers.

latter carries additional sanctions, the most serious of which is being ostracized or functionally shunned within the community of plaintiffs' lawyers.

This ethical challenge has long concerned the legal profession. After the US Supreme Court's decision in *Bates v. State Bar of Arizona* (1977), that concern deepened because *Bates* struck down long-standing bans on lawyer advertising. In commenting on the impact of *Bates*, William Hornsby (2005, 255) noted that the decision meant the "ethics rule governing the conduct of lawyers in every state became unconstitutional. In the blink of an eye, lawyers had the right to advertise their service—a right that had been suppressed for nearly seventy years. . . . [*Bates*] is no doubt the most significant milestone in the evolution of client development." Hornsby sees the decision in terms of a long-term struggle that goes to the very heart of the concern about professionalism and dignity. This ethical concern, perhaps more than any other, cuts to the core of the profession's sense of itself as something different than a business. Rather than a business, the legal profession is about public service. Says Hornsby (2005, 257):

> To understand how client development threatens professionalism and dignity, we must look to the work of Dean Roscoe Pound. In 1953, Dean Pound defined professionalism as "a group of men pursuing a learned art as a common calling in the spirit of public service." Providing legal services may result in financial compensation, but according to those advancing this notion of professionalism, that compensation cannot be the motivation for a lawyer to provide those services. That motivation must be the pursuit of public service.

Plaintiffs' lawyers and their client acquisition techniques have long been seen as one of the major threats to professionalism and lawyer dignity.

All lawyers, of course, work in a world in which professionalism and economic interest necessarily coexist. This is seen in the way one of the most respected Texas plaintiffs' lawyers of the mid-twentieth century, Otto Mullinax, described the ethos of his firm, Mullinax, Wells. The firm justified its existence by adhering to three simple objectives:

> First, to earn a good living for its members and staff;
> Second, to make that living representing unions and working people, if possible; and,
> Third, to use those resources, produced above the need to serve the first two objectives, in advancing liberal political processes in government and society. (Mullinax 1986, 1)

Pound may disagree with the order of Mullinax's priorities since the economic aspect came first, and one may also disagree with Mullinax's particular idea of public service, but there is no doubt that the practice of law was about more than just making a good living. The issue is how lawyers navigate the coexistence of goals that pull in different directions. We hope to show that plaintiffs' lawyers' own normative values are a key element in that process.

To set the context, we need to do two things. The next section addresses the first by briefly describing the Texas plaintiffs' lawyers who interest us and providing basic information on the plaintiffs' bar more generally. The following section addresses the second by exploring the scant information available on formal disciplinary actions involving these lawyers in Texas. Of particular interest are violations related to client acquisition. The third section explores the broader ethical decision making of plaintiffs' lawyers surrounding the challenge of generating a steady stream of clients. It emphasizes the importance of the practice community's informal norms as they are balanced against the practical necessities of staying in business.

Texas Plaintiffs' Lawyers and Practices

The few systematic studies of the plaintiffs' bar share some key findings (Daniels and Martin 2002; Van Hoy 1999; Kritzer 2004; Parikh 2006–2007). Most important, plaintiffs' lawyers typically represent individuals rather than large corporations and work in the personal plight sector (Heinz and Laumann 1982). They rely primarily on contingency fees rather than hourly or flat fees. Their firms are small, with most lawyers working as solo practitioners or in firms of five or fewer lawyers and having very small staffs. Caseloads tend to be moderate and typically dominated by automobile accident cases. Case values are modest, and most lawyers make a comfortable but not substantial income. The plaintiffs' bar is largely white, male, middle-aged, and educated at local or regional law schools. Finally, the plaintiffs' bar has its own hierarchy with lawyers specializing in various kinds of cases. At the top of this bar are those who specialize in high-stakes, high-value cases like medical malpractice. At the other end are lawyers whose practices focus on low-complexity, low-value cases like minor auto accident cases.

The findings of a 2006 survey of Texas plaintiffs' lawyers we conducted fit well within this set of characteristics.[2] The respondents are lawyers whose practices

---

2. This is the second of two such surveys; the first was fielded in 2000. A description of the 2000 survey is found in Daniels and Martin (2002, 1826–1828). The methodology for the 2006

focus on plaintiffs' cases taken on a contingency fee basis, rather than lawyers who occasionally take such cases. Similar to the findings of Mather, McEwen, and Maiman (2001) on divorce lawyers, plaintiffs' lawyers constitute a distinct practice community in Texas and elsewhere. The best evidence of this is their participation in specialized professional organizations: 60% of our respondents belong to the American Association for Justice (formerly Association of Trial Lawyers of America); 68% belong to the Texas Trial Lawyers Association (TTLA); and 61% belong to a local plaintiffs' lawyers' organization.

Consistent with this, these lawyers are specialists. The median percent of caseload made up of plaintiffs' cases taken on a contingency fee basis among our respondents is 75%, and the mean is 95%. In contrast, the comparable figures for all private practice lawyers in Texas are 2% and 19% (State Bar of Texas 2004).[3] As further evidence of specialization, over one-third of the respondents are board certified in personal injury trial law and/or civil trial law. The Texas Board of Legal Specialization currently certifies lawyers in 20 practice areas and enforces substantial requirements for certification. In contrast, only 4% of all Texas lawyers are certified in personal injury trial law and/or civil trial law (State Bar of Texas 2009).

For most of our respondents, automobile accident cases account for the largest percentage of their caseloads, followed by medical malpractice, commercial litigation, and products liability. Most do not handle high-value cases—the typical case value is modest ($38,000 in 2006 dollars). In addition, the size of their practices is small. Thirty-seven percent of our respondents are solo practitioners, and another 48% work in firms of 2 to 5 lawyers. This means that 85% work in very small firms or as solos. The comparable figure for Texas lawyers generally is 60% (State Bar of Texas 2009). With the exception of the visible lawyers with high-volume or mass tort practices (Engstrom 2009), Texas plaintiffs' lawyers also tend to have small staffs. This would be expected for practices relying on the contingency fee, which must keep overhead as low as possible.

Turning to how lawyers get clients, the predominant source of clients for the respondents to our 2006 survey and for private practitioners in Texas generally is some form of referral. For each group, just under three-quarters of their caseloads comes from referrals (73% for plaintiffs' lawyers and 74% for

---

survey was the same except it used a current list of plaintiffs' lawyers, and it included new questions asking about reforms enacted since 2000. The 2000 survey had 552 respondents and a response rate of 29.1%, and the 2006 survey had 460 respondents and a response rate of 25.7%.

3. All statistics for lawyers generally come from the State Bar of Texas Referral Practices Survey (2004).

lawyers generally). Referrals from other lawyers are much more important for plaintiffs' lawyers than for lawyers generally, and this may reflect their status as specialists and their willingness to pay referral fees to the lawyers who refer cases to them. Referrals from clients are the most important source of business for lawyers generally, and they are the second-most important for plaintiffs' lawyers.

Advertising, despite the attention it gets as an ethical issue, is not a substantial source of clients (15% for plaintiffs' lawyers and 7% for lawyers generally). The most frequently used forms of advertising are basically the same for both sets of lawyers, with the Yellow Pages being the most often used (by 49% of plaintiffs' lawyers and 21% of lawyers generally). Although most lawyers do not invest in television advertising, a higher percentage of plaintiffs' lawyers do so (13% versus 4%). Reflecting the importance of lawyer referrals as a source of business, a higher percentage of plaintiffs' lawyers use direct mail to other lawyers than is the case for lawyers generally (15% versus 3%).

Finally, plaintiffs' lawyers have a much more prominent presence on the Internet, with more than half of our respondents reporting that they have a firm website, compared to less than one-fifth of all lawyers. Still, on average, firm websites account for just 4% of business for the 264 respondents in the 2006 survey who reported having a firm website. The use of firm websites by Texas plaintiffs' lawyers has continued to grow since the time of that survey. Of the 196 respondents who did not have a firm website in 2006, 181 were still in private practice in Texas in April 2011. Internet searches and State Bar of Texas information show that over half (96) of those lawyers did have a firm website in April 2011. Thus, in just five years, advertising by firm websites increased from 57% to 78% by the original 460 respondents to the 2006 survey.

Formal Lawyer Discipline in Texas

Overview
The second matter to address in providing a context for our exploration of ethical decision making by plaintiffs' lawyers is the formal disciplinary process. In Texas, the State Bar's Commission for Lawyer Discipline oversees professional discipline. During the June 1, 2008, to May 31, 2009, reporting period it received 7,108 grievances, 73% of which were dismissed as not involving professional misconduct. The remaining matters were classified as complaints receiving further inquiry, and most of these involved the areas of criminal, family, and personal injury law. The most common allegations were neglect,

failure to communicate, and complaints about the termination or withdrawal of representation. Only 335 complaints were resolved with the imposition of some form of sanction—the largest proportion involved suspensions (38%), and only 10% resulted in disbarment (State Bar of Texas Commission for Lawyer Discipline 2009, 15–18).

The only publicly available information on individual disciplinary matters is found in the reports of the Commission's public decisions in the *Texas Bar Journal* (*TBJ*). This includes all sanctions imposed except private reprimands. We examined two years of public reports of disciplinary actions that appeared in the *TBJ*—2008 and 2009—and the statistics discussed in this section come from that examination. We found 362 reported disciplinary actions in which sanctions were imposed between September 2007 and October 2009. The practice area involved was reported for 180 of the 362 disciplinary actions. The largest proportion of the 180 involved divorce and other family matters, 24%; followed by personal injury matters, 22%; and criminal matters, 18%. No other practice area accounted for more than 7% of the 180 matters.

A total of 1,260 specific violations were reported during the time period covered. Two-thirds involved "Client-Lawyer Relationship" (Texas Disciplinary Rules of Professional Conduct 1.01–1.15) and another 23% involved "Maintaining the Integrity of the Profession." The area most germane to how lawyers get clients is "Information about Legal Services." It deals with advertising and other forms of solicitation, with the goal being to protect consumers from false, misleading, and deceptive practices (7.01–7.05). Among other things, this set of rules governs the nature of advertising a lawyer may do (for instance, actors cannot be used in advertisements) and even prohibits certain kinds of solicitation (such as in-person or telephonic/electronic solicitation of accident victims or paying nonlawyers to solicit clients). There were only 24 violations of the rules in this area, comprising 2% of all violations. In short, client acquisition techniques do not appear to be a major disciplinary issue as far as public sanctions are concerned.

Professional Lawyer Discipline: Plaintiffs' Lawyers

Given that personal injury is one of the most prevalent practice areas involved with the disciplinary process, we might expect that plaintiffs' lawyers would be among the most often disciplined attorneys. We used three approaches to determine which of the lawyers who appeared in the two years of reported disciplinary actions in the *TBJ* are in fact plaintiffs' lawyers. First, we matched the names of disciplined lawyers with the master list we used to draw the sample for our 2006 survey. That master list, provided by TTLA, contained 11,565 names including TTLA members as of 2005, former members going back at least to 1990, and prospects (lawyers who were never members but who TTLA thought may be regularly handling plaintiffs' work). Second, we looked at the profile of each lawyer on the disciplinary list on the Texas State Bar website. Finally, we did web searches for each disciplined lawyer to look for evidence of a practice centering on plaintiffs' work. Based on these searches, we are relatively certain that 39 lawyers on the disciplinary list are plaintiffs' lawyers—or 11% of the 362 total. The actual percentage of the Texas bar made up of plaintiffs' lawyers is unknown, but in a 2002 article we roughly estimated that in 2000 no more than 11% of the lawyers licensed in Texas were plaintiffs' lawyers (Daniels and Martin 2002, 1784).

Using the roster of 39 lawyers, what can we learn about plaintiffs' lawyers and professional discipline? Unfortunately, the published reports provide the area of practice involved in the disciplinary matter for only 16 of these lawyers, with personal injury–related matters accounting for 9 and family matters accounting for another 4. No other area accounted for more than 1. For 3 of the 39 plaintiffs' lawyers, criminal activity of some kind was alleged (22 of the 362 lawyers [6%] were involved in criminal activity). Three of the 39 were disbarred, and another 7 resigned. Eighteen received some sort of suspension, and 11 received a public reprimand. The 39 lawyers were responsible for a total of 131 violations—about 10% of the total 1,260 violations. As with lawyers generally, most of these violations involved "Client-Lawyer Relationship" (73%) and "Maintaining the Integrity of the Profession" (21%). There were no plaintiffs' lawyer violations of the rules dealing with "Information about Legal Services," which cover advertising and other forms of solicitation.

While this brief empirical analysis is very tentative and exploratory, it suggests that plaintiffs' lawyers are publicly disciplined for violations not all that different from those for lawyers overall. One reason for the basic similarity may have to do with a broader finding regarding who is publicly disciplined. As noted earlier, the vast majority of Texas plaintiffs' lawyers work in very small firms or as solo practitioners, as do most lawyers generally. Firm size is available for 313 of the lawyers in the disciplinary list, and almost all of these lawyers work as solos or small firm practitioners (70% are solos and 22% are in 2–5 lawyer firms). Firm size is available for all 39 of the plaintiffs' lawyers, and their practice demographics mirror those of the other lawyers in the disciplinary list—72% are solos and 15% are in 2–5 lawyer firms. This rather lopsided pattern for disciplined lawyers is consistent with what little we know about public disciplinary actions in other states (e.g., Levin 2004, 310–316). It suggests that plaintiffs' lawyers may be publicly disciplined for reasons related to small firm practice generally, rather than something unique to their area of practice.

Navigating the Challenge: Do Ethical Considerations Matter?

Perhaps the reason few lawyers are formally disciplined for matters related to client acquisition is that getting clients is easy, and consequently lawyers have few ethical issues to confront. Reality, of course, is quite different. Almost all plaintiffs' lawyers see their environment as a highly competitive one. Some complain that disciplinary enforcement by the state bar is not vigilant enough. These complaints focus on major television advertisers, direct mail solicitors, and those using "runners" (nonlawyers who are paid to sign up accident victims as clients for lawyers). The implication is that much unethical behavior in this area goes unchecked. Even if this is presumed to be true, few plaintiffs' lawyers we interviewed seemed interested in joining the crowd of ethical scofflaws in light of lax enforcement. According to one San Antonio lawyer, "Some of these guys have gotten so large and so powerful that whenever the state bar has tried to actually enforce the regulations and the rules, these attorneys are able to outspend the state bar. . . . Usually the state bar either backs down or accepts a lesser fine. You see so much blatant solicitation just going on and nothing is being done about it." When it came to the question of his own behavior, he said, "There is a large group of us that . . . I am always afraid. I know if I did something like that, they'd make an example of me." Regardless of the level of enforcement, most lawyers do not cross the formal ethical boundaries in their client acquisition practices.

Still, as the comment above suggests, there are lawyers for whom the normative values embodied in the formal rules of professional conduct are of little concern. Their business model—whether successful or not—relies on practices that are explicitly not allowed by the formal rules. Of course, no lawyer we interviewed admitted to currently using such practices. However, one lawyer did offer the following: "When I started doing it [personal injury work], comp [workers' compensation] was the thing that ran most personal injury businesses in Texas, and in order to have a big comp business you had to pay runners to bring the cases into you. Now that's illegal and unethical but no one ever got prosecuted for it . . . now since I've had my own office I didn't do that. But I will say that I am familiar with the practice, let's put it like that."

Another group of plaintiffs' lawyers appears to view ethical rules as simply being boundaries on their business practices—ones they must operate within. For them, not operating within those boundaries places the business at risk. There is little concern with the normative side of professionalism and its ideals—it is just about business. One heavy advertiser with a high-volume business explained his view as follows:

> Sometimes I think I really would like to get into the courthouse and try a lot of cases, because I think I'd be pretty good at it. But then again more important to me, to be perfectly frank with you, is to make money. I don't mean to sound crass about it, but, you know, heck if I've got an opportunity to be liquid for a few million dollars by the time I'm 35 or so . . . I'd rather do that than, you know, become Perry Mason.

He needs to pay attention to the rules, or he won't have a shot at making the money that he wants.

Lawyers like this one will do whatever the rules allow and will try any number of things that the rules do not explicitly prohibit. If the rules change, they adjust accordingly. One lawyer said the following with regard to a form of direct mail solicitation that was allowed at one time: "Frankly, they [a competitor] were making a fortune out of it. . . . Our feeling was that if anybody else was going to do it, they're taking cases away from us and so what are we going to do? Are we going to let them take away from us and do nothing? So we did it too and [it] was very effective." When the disciplinary rules changed, he stopped using direct mail. Such lawyers are businesspeople, and they approach things much as any other business would—it just happens that law is their business. They seem little interested in the professional aspects of lawyering. For instance, when asked if he participated in the organized bar to any extent, the lawyer quoted above said, "No, no, not at all. I never go to the meetings."

Ethical Considerations Do Matter for Many Lawyers

The normative aspects of professionalism are important for a substantial number of plaintiffs' lawyers and for their professional organizations as well, especially TTLA. Many of the lawyers we interviewed expressed serious concerns about aggressive techniques for getting clients. Among their comments:

> It makes me sick . . . I mean they're tasteless, horrible ads . . . advertising demeans a profession.

> I don't like TV advertising; I'll make no bones about. I think it's bad. I think it's bad for the profession and I think it's bad for the system.

> I think it's been demeaning, undignified, harmful, crass, grotesque. I hate it.

> It ain't fittin' you know. I don't think it looks professional is all I can say. It's just an intuitive, sort of gut feeling.

Clearly, these lawyers believe aggressive techniques for getting clients undermine the profession in the eyes of the public.

Worse, the increasing use of advertising in the late 1980s into the early 1990s occurred as the tort reform debate in Texas was developing into a major political issue. Texas experienced a series of intense political battles over tort reform with substantial reforms enacted in 1987, 1995, and 2003 (Sanders and Joyce 1990; Calve 1996; Swartz 2005). The reform effort included an aggressive public relations campaign featuring allegations of frivolous lawsuits, runaway juries, greedy plaintiffs' lawyers, and the like. All too often, the image of plaintiffs' lawyers one could take away from many television advertisements or direct mail solicitations fit neatly into the tort reformers' critique of the civil justice system (Daniels and Martin 1995).

The strong language many plaintiffs' lawyers use to criticize those using aggressive techniques is meant to label them as miscreants or outsiders to be shunned, and it says much about this practice community's sense of itself as a profession. One lawyer recounted a heated discussion he had with another lawyer working for one of Texas' prolific advertisers:

> I was in a meeting with one of X's lawyers on this topic [aggressive television advertising]. . . . "Well," he said, "we're in the same business. I don't know why you're against us." I said, "No, we're not in the same business." I said, "I know every one of my clients. Most of the time, I've been to their home, I've met their children." I said, "If one of your clients walked in the door right now, would you know 'em?" I said, "Don't tell me we're in the same area of practice."

Another lawyer's characterization, although somewhat extreme, literally paints aggressive advertisers as outsiders:

> I don't see them; I don't interact with them; I don't touch them; I don't fool with them. . . . I know some of them send us cases [refer cases with the expectation of a fee] when I don't know they're aggressive advertisers . . . if I find out, I send the case back. I just . . . there's something about that I find repulsive.

It is almost as if those outsiders, and even their cases, are literally diseased and the community needs to protect itself from them. This elite lawyer's remarks also suggest, as Parikh (2006–2007) has argued, that referral relationships can function as an important means of social control within the plaintiffs' bar.

Consistent with such views, a few lawyers adamantly refuse to advertise or solicit business in any way, even though their practices are suffering as a result. An East Texas lawyer provides an example: "I'm a solo practitioner. I like the freedom of being solo. . . . I just want to help people on a one-on-one basis with car wreck and workers comp and, you know, premises liability. And I enjoy doing that." He built his practice on referrals. "Over the years I've tried to develop a good referral network of other lawyers who send business . . . there's been a very steady stream of them for 15, 20 years now and that's . . . how my practice has grown. . . . It's just been word of mouth." A previously successful lawyer, he is facing intense competition from heavy television advertisers for cases. As he put it, "my practice has collapsed. I made $23,000 last year."

Trying desperately to find ways of staying in business without resorting to advertising or other forms of direct solicitation for clients, the East Texas lawyer above has depleted his retirement savings to keep his practice afloat. Nonetheless, he cannot bring himself to advertise. He finds it, especially television, abhorrent. As he put it:

> A guy comes home from work, gets his beer, sits in front of the TV and hears this lawyer, this smarmy looking lawyer telling him, "If you get hurt, I'll make you rich." . . . And I know how I personally respond to lawyer advertising in a very negative way . . . you know, when somebody looks at that, the average person, they see graft. They see fraud. They see corruption.

Such lawyers reflect the community's values in their purest form—they are the true believers.

While the dislike of aggressive techniques is widely shared, the approach of most lawyers to getting clients in a competitive environment is more pragmatic. For these lawyers, three factors are important in their approach to how they get clients, reflecting the basic balance between business and professionalism seen in Otto Mullinax's comments. They are the professional community's normative values, necessity, and cost. In our interviews, we found that issues involving normative standards and professionalism were intertwined with concerns about economic necessity and costs. We deal with these three factors next.

The Community's Normative Values

Three elements appear important in understanding the community's normative values, and they appear most clearly in the criticisms of the miscreants
in which much of the community indulges. First is the commitment to public
service or the public good—as the plaintiffs' lawyers define it. Related is the
idea of actually trying cases. Last is the nature and substance of the solicitation
techniques used.

COMMITMENT TO THE PUBLIC GOOD. In explaining what they find objectionable in the practices of the miscreants, lawyers often point to the goals of those
they criticize in contrast to what they view as a more appropriate set of professional goals. The criticized lawyers are *only* interested in making money or
building their practices—it's just a business. One lawyer neatly summarized this
view: "You know, those characters are obviously making money. If you speak to
them of the profession or the culture of the profession or the traditions, they
would look at you like you're from Mars. They're in it for a buck." Such lawyers
are not concerned with their clients' best interests. Their practices are derisively
called "mills," and the lawyers themselves are referred to as "bottom feeders" or
"scumbags." One highly respected plaintiffs' lawyer simply said that the heavy
television advertisers "are not competent to handle business. . . . They make a fee
on it [but] their client is not very well served. . . . I view those people as bottom
feeders." Another lawyer said, "They don't give a damn. They got into it for no
worthy cause."

What is missing in the practices of these "bottom feeders" (allowing, of
course, for making a decent living) is the "worthy cause" that helps to define for
the critics what lies at the heart of their profession. It is the sentiment underlying the second of the guiding principles for Otto Mullinax's firm and is seen in
the remarks of a younger lawyer in Houston:

> Amongst plaintiffs' lawyers . . . you have two categories of lawyers. You have
> true believers who are doing this because they really care, they love people,
> they want to work for people, they want to help people and that's why they
> got into this business in the first place. It wasn't just driving fees and mak-
> ing money. . . . What has appealed to me is a family with kids whose life gets
> turned upside down because someone in the family gets seriously hurt or
> killed and they're facing a greater than David and Goliath battle and they
> need someone to fight for them. Guys like me, we can go do the commercial
> litigation and make money. . . . If you are a true believer, then what's the

point of that? So you make money and you are not doing something you believe in. You're not helping people.

A lawyer in Austin who said, "I'd still rather be a lawyer doing what I do for individuals than represent the bank or the insurance company or Pa Bell," also articulates this view.

TRYING CASES.   Actually trying cases is fundamentally important to plaintiffs' lawyers' sense of themselves as professionals. It is not that one must always be in the courtroom. Rather, it is whether you ever try cases or at least want to. The heavy advertisers and others who are openly aggressive in getting clients are seen as never trying cases, and this helps in characterizing them as outsiders. As one Houston lawyer said, "Most of those people . . . have never seen the inside of a courtroom and don't intend to ever see the inside of a courtroom, consider it a complete waste of time." The idea is that you cannot be serving your clients well if you're not willing or able to litigate. The clients will not get the settlement they deserve because the insurance companies will not pay an appropriate case value if you are unwilling to litigate. In discussing some of the television advertisers, a Fort Worth lawyer remarked, "The ones I knew . . . never tried any cases . . . my impression of [a local advertiser] was that he used to settle for whatever he could get. He told the client he had to take it."

Over and over we heard the complaint that certain lawyers are never seen at the courthouse or that their names do not appear in the local jury verdict reporters. In short, the major advertisers have no professional reputation—they are not really seen as lawyers. A San Antonio lawyer simply said, "You get the reputation over at the courthouse." This can be seen in the comments of an established Austin lawyer in talking about a younger lawyer who was originally looked at with a jaundiced eye. He said, "They made their practice around chiropractic referrals. They've done a lot of aggressive marketing. . . . Two years ago they were really just thought of as having a chiropractor running cases for them." However, some successful medical malpractice cases changed things: "On the other hand, [name omitted] has had a couple of outstanding results . . . his results have started to at least confer something of a reputation on him."

THE NATURE AND SUBSTANCE OF ADVERTISING AND OTHER CLIENT ACQUISITION TECHNIQUES.   What is it about the nature and substance of advertising and direct solicitation that is so troubling? In terms of its nature, at the extreme some activities actually violate the formal rules, such as the rule against paying nonlawyer "runners." Needless to say, there is no tolerance in the community if a lawyer uses techniques that violate the formal rules—even if the violator is a prominent member of the community. Perhaps *the* example is the late John O'Quinn of Houston—a highly successful plaintiffs' lawyer with a formidable reputation. The Texas Commission for Lawyer Discipline twice tried to disbar O'Quinn, both times based on allegations of case running in the aftermath of airplane crashes. The first attempt in the 1980s eventually led to only a public reprimand, a fine, and community service. In the second, in 1998, one of the most respected members of the Texas plaintiffs' bar, Broadus Spivey of Austin (TTLA president, 1981–1982; state bar president, 2001–2002; International Academy of Trial Lawyers president, 2002–2003 [Spivey & Grigg, LLP 2010]), took a substantial amount of time out of his own practice to act as the lead attorney for the Commission in the disbarment proceedings. A lawyer knowledgeable about disciplinary matters remarked that not even O'Quinn's level of success means a free pass: "You know, somebody's got to . . . if you think something's not right, then you've got to go in there and take it to the mat. And that's what Broadus did."

The criticism also extends to the substance of activities that are within the formal rules. The critics share the legal profession's traditional dislike of advertising and direct solicitation (of recent accident victims or their families) because they believe such practices erode the profession's legitimacy. The constant complaint is that the activities are somehow tasteless or tacky or even cheesy. But there is more behind the criticism—the fact that much of the substance of the objectionable activities dovetails with the aggressive tort reform public relations campaign. It is like a one-two punch.

Lawyers are quite specific in talking about the consequences of tasteless advertisements even if they are within the formal rules. The most concrete indicator of the effects of advertising for plaintiffs' lawyers is what they see when they go to the courthouse and choose a jury. A Fort Worth lawyer's comments are typical of what many others said:

> I think advertising is bad. It greatly contributed to the public cynicism towards lawyers and personal injury lawyers. I think it's been a very major factor. Every time I go down to the courthouse for a trial, I ask this because this is a question that will always get you a response—have they seen the ads for lawyers advertising for clients? At a minimum, two-thirds have seen them, usually more than that. Then if you say how many of you formed a bad impression about a personal injury lawyer or personal injury cases

because of those television ads, the vast majority of them raise their hand. The case I tried in Dallas, there were eight jurors disqualified for cause on that issue alone.

A Houston lawyer said:

I think advertising has been an engine that helped drive tort reform . . . so many attorneys, particularly the less experienced and less capable, did an overwhelming amount of poor taste advertising that just gave the appearance of the worst. . . . I think it gave people the impression that we are all a bunch of used car salesmen, and I hate that. Does that answer your question!?

In short, the advertisers have helped "poison" the jury pool. A San Antonio lawyer said, "There is so much solicitation going on, the public is getting such a bad taste in their mouth for personal injury litigation in general—it's reflected in the jury verdicts." Almost all plaintiffs' lawyers would agree with this assessment. In other words, the concern over aggressive techniques for getting clients is not merely a matter of traditional professionalism. There is also the pragmatic assessment that such activities are bad for business in the long run.

Despite the community's general dislike of advertising and solicitation, some lawyers who share that dislike still feel they must advertise to stay in business. Their situation offers additional insight into the decisions lawyers make in meeting the challenge of getting that steady stream of clients they need to survive. They must find ways of attracting clients without offending their peers, especially the established lawyers who are the opinion leaders and the influential members of the plaintiffs' lawyers' professional organizations. From them we can get a better sense of the how the community's normative values influence what they do when necessity looms.

Necessity and Community Norms

Some, but not all, lawyers recognize that a certain amount of advertising may be necessary—especially for younger lawyers trying to build their practices in a highly competitive environment. The competitiveness has intensified because of tort reform and its supporters' aggressive public relations campaigns, and because of the aggressive advertisers who have siphoned off a significant portion of the automobile accident market. These cases, especially the numerous small to modest ones, are the bread and butter cases a younger lawyer can handle successfully, build a reputation on, and use to grow a client base for future referrals. Many younger lawyers say they must advertise to develop their practices, and some established lawyers recognize this. One such lawyer said, "There is a group like our firm that doesn't believe in it [advertising]. There are a lot of other younger lawyers who do. They say, 'how else am I going to get business? I'm not established and I've got to do this.' I don't argue with that."

Reflecting this idea, a younger lawyer said, "I don't like lawyer advertising, but I think—I realize that it's a necessary evil, to some extent, in order to maintain your business." He is not alone. Another said, "I've been in the Yellow Pages for five years, just pretty much out of necessity." He emphasized the idea of advertising tastefully and that he doesn't object even to television advertising, "as long as it's done tastefully." Another younger lawyer defended his firm's Yellow Pages ad (its only advertising), saying, "I think ours is fairly innocuous. If you looked at ours versus other people's, I mean we don't have any dogs foaming at the mouth. . . . Ours says that we're clearly in the personal injury business." He went on to say: "I don't think we're offending anybody with our ad. We may be. Some lawyers don't like any advertising. They say that it is unprofessional . . . but it is a necessary part of our practice, particularly for those of us trying to build a client base. We may not get the greatest cases in the world through our Yellow Pages ad, but if we get cases that we're able to take, eventually those will result in referrals from our former clients."

A younger lawyer in Houston, who had just aired his first television ad, talked about the problem of juries with regard to advertising. In a changing, competitive market, he was not getting enough cases relying on lawyer referrals. He faced a dilemma because he was beginning to get a reputation as someone who tries cases and wins. As he put it, his television ad "was the best that I could come up with to balance the need to get business and the need not to hurt my ability to represent my clients." He described his ad as follows:

People tell me that they really appreciated my ad because it's just me in a courtroom in a suit. I say, "My name is [omitted], if you are injured by another's negligence, please contact me. I will fight for you." There's no lightening bolts, there's no car wrecks, there's no graphics. It's just me saying, "If you're hurt, I will fight for you. I will try to do the right thing. Come hire me." . . . The people that were producing the ad were saying, "This isn't going to work." They wanted to do all these things that were embarrassing. They wanted to put in music, I said, "No." They wanted to put in waving flags, I said, "No." They wanted to put in car wrecks, no. They wanted to have a car wreck flash on the screen, I said, "No." Because I have to try cases.

> I can't beat [name omitted, a prolific television advertiser based in Houston] and try cases. I can't have the car wrecks and the fist pumping.

This lawyer knew he would be risking his developing reputation as a plaintiffs' lawyer if his ad was seen as problematic in the eyes of jurors or of his peers.

It is not just younger lawyers who face the necessary evil. A midcareer lawyer in Austin said, "I don't like to advertise, but I've had to do television advertising from time to time." A Fort Worth lawyer was blunt in his statement, even though he recognized the potential downside: "I did it when I had to do it . . . ten years ago I had billboards . . . I don't need to do it now, and if I needed to do it I would." The potential downside comes when a juror asks if a lawyer advertises. "They look at you with less suspicion when you tell them no, I don't advertise."

We also found lawyers who took a longer-term view of necessity and a very different—but quite pragmatic—approach to advertising. For instance, a midcareer West Texas lawyer said, "We didn't want to advertise and don't like to advertise, but we do because other people are advertising and we want to get our name out there as well." His approach is more of a preemptive strategy than a reactive one. While some lawyers may advertise, even though they dislike the idea, because their businesses are already suffering, this lawyer wanted to advertise before his business was in trouble. It is a longer-term strategy related to his business *and* to the profession more generally. As he said, "We do a different type of advertising than most people probably do . . . ours is an image-type advertising." We found a number of lawyers doing roughly the same kind of public relations advertising. Like them, this lawyer is very much an insider with an excellent reputation.

In explaining his advertising strategy, he said, "One of the ads that we run is if you were going to see a doctor . . . you'd want to see a board certified doctor and all the lawyers in our law firm are board certified in personal injury trial law. That's basically it." It is a 30-second television spot. Another one of his ads is an informational one about the jury system, and there is one "about trial lawyers—trial lawyers basically defend principles of who's right and personal injury and fairness." He readily admitted, "It's not a get business type of deal." Its purpose is directed elsewhere. "We have gotten a lot of positive comments from people talking about our ads. They like our ads and they say, you know, we like yours and, boy, the other guy's ad, I can't stand it." Rather than get business in the short run, he said, "I think it's helped our public image a lot, which is what we wanted to do."

This approach not only helps his public image, but also hopefully enhances the public image of plaintiffs' lawyers more generally. It presents the public with a positive image of a plaintiffs' lawyer—one much more professional and serious, and not one simply looking for business. Protecting the image of the profession motivated another firm to become local underwriters of the *NewsHour* on PBS. One firm member noted some initial disagreement within the firm about this investment:

> They thought that you wouldn't get any business whatsoever for doing that, and it's probably true . . . but that wasn't the reason for doing it. The reason was to show that you had the public interest at heart and it was a good will type thing—a true good will type thing. Because we could say then, when we went over to select a jury, that we don't advertise except we do sponsor a program on public television. There's more to it than just being a mercenary interest.

Necessity drives some lawyers to advertise, albeit reluctantly, because of the immediate need to get clients, but the community's normative values shape what they do and how they do it. Necessity drives other lawyers to advertise as a long-term strategy to further and protect the community and its normative values.

The Problem of Cost

While the community's normative values have an important influence on the decisions lawyers make in meeting the challenge of getting a steady stream of clients, they are not the only factor to be considered. There is also the very practical issue of cost. While advertising or other forms of client acquisition may bring in potential clients, these techniques can be expensive. A lawyer must balance the cost of the advertising against the possible return. In our interviews, lawyers regularly raised the cost issue. As one lawyer said of his Yellow Pages ad, "We ran a full-page ad this year; cost us $3000 a month to run that. We're making $2000 a month off it, so we're running a $1000 a month shortfall." Another said, "The Yellow Pages, of course, cost us a fortune . . . it just makes me sick to write those checks. It's $20,000 to $25,000 we're spending on it." That is a per month expense because this lawyer was advertising in five different telephone books in his metropolitan area; but he believes it brings in enough business—direct business from people who call based on the ads and indirect business from other people those clients may refer to this lawyer in the future. Back covers of telephone books cost well over $100,000. Television advertising, of course, is the most expensive, with the most prolific advertisers spending over $1 million a year just for the airtime. More than anything, this may explain why so few lawyers use television advertising to any extent.

Mass advertisers have additional costs, such as marketing firms to oversee much of the advertising process. For instance, one television advertiser tried doing things on his own, but quickly realized he could not. "So I got an expert. He tracks the trims. He's in Nashville. He gives me a sheet every month that tells me who's calling, what programs, where I get the calls . . . [he does] it more scientifically as to what times to put advertising; what times not to put advertising; what times of the year are better than other times of the year; when can you get the best TV buys for the time." The marketing firm also works on the content of the ads and on targeting them for a particular clientele or a particular type of case.

For any lawyer who advertises to any degree, there are still more expenses— the costs of the personnel and infrastructure needed to handle the calls coming into the practice as a result of that advertising and screening those calls. A Dallas lawyer who advertises said:

> Advertising is an expensive proposition. These guys that are running spots on TV, they are spending some big bucks. And when you spend that kind of money in the type of advertising, you gather up every kook in town; a lot of them with their shopping bags full of papers. A "shopping bag" case, [as] we refer to them. . . . How much are you going to have to pay someone to go through that shopping bag and determine that the statute [of limitations] ran ten years ago and they're still shopping it around?

One television advertiser averaged about 1,000 calls a month from his ads and was carrying $100,000 a month in overhead to process those calls.

For many plaintiffs' lawyers, the costs involved are enough to deter them from advertising—or advertising to any great degree. Cost together with the potential damage to one's reputation among other plaintiffs' lawyers and the response of jurors provide a formidable barrier to advertising, especially on television. The fact that some lawyers still advertise to get clients and face the potential censure of their peers is an indication of just how precarious their situations may be.

Conclusion

In this chapter we set out to explore the ethical dimensions plaintiffs' lawyers face in addressing the challenge of maintaining a steady stream of clients with injuries that the legal system will adequately compensate. Despite the widespread traditional concern over advertising and aggressive client acquisition, we found very few formal disciplinary actions in Texas for violations of the rules of professional conduct governing client acquisition—not just for plaintiffs' lawyers, but for lawyers generally. While some lawyers would say this is a result of lax enforcement by the state disciplinary authorities, our evidence suggests that most plaintiffs' lawyers do little direct solicitation for clients or advertising regardless of concerns about or actual enforcement activity by the disciplinary agency—even eschewing techniques clearly allowed by the rules of professional conduct.

Plaintiffs' lawyers make up a distinct professional community with its own normative values that help define it as a professional community. These normative values discourage advertising and the solicitation of clients, and they clearly shape what plaintiffs' lawyers do when it comes to getting clients. The community's approach to those norms, however, is decidedly pragmatic, and only a few lawyers will strictly adhere to them. Necessity tempers those norms because most plaintiffs' lawyers, like Otto Mullinax, want to make a good living as well as serve the professional goals that motivate them. This means that some lawyers will advertise because they have to if they want to stay in business. As a number of these lawyers said, it is a necessary evil. The community may tolerate some advertising activity in the name of necessity, but there will be limits.

We also found that the community's normative values regarding advertising and solicitation are themselves pragmatic. While not eschewing a commitment to traditional ideas of professionalism, there is recognition that maintaining and enforcing the community's values is good for business. In the eyes of most plaintiffs' lawyers, very real and very negative consequences result from the aggressive pursuit of clients. They believe they see the effects in the jury box when they try cases—juries are poisoned against plaintiffs and their lawyers by the antics of a few lawyers who aggressively advertise for clients. This concern serves as an effective deterrent for many lawyers when they consider various ways of getting business. As if to provide further proof of this pragmatism, we also found some lawyers—among them respected leaders of the plaintiffs' lawyers' community—who now advertise strategically. They hope to burnish the public perception of plaintiffs' lawyers with ads not immediately geared to getting business, but rather to serve some broader public service. No one seems to object to advertising in the community's interest.

Finally, there is cost. Advertising and direct solicitation of clients costs money—a lot of money to make it worthwhile. This in itself is enough to keep many lawyers from doing much advertising and so helps to reinforce the community's norms.

References

Calve, Joseph. 1996. "Poured Out." *Texas Lawyer,* December 16.

Daniels, Stephen, and Joanne Martin. 1995. *Civil Juries and the Politics of Reform.* Evanston, IL: Northwestern University Press.

———. 2002. "It Was the Best of Times, It Was the Worst of Times: The Precarious Nature of Plaintiffs' Practice in Texas." *Texas Law Review* 80:1781–1828.

Engstrom, Nora Freeman. 2009. "Run-of-the-Mill Justice." *Georgetown Journal of Legal Ethics* 22:1485–1548.

Heinz, John P., and Edward O. Laumann. 1982. *Chicago Lawyers: The Social Structure of the Bar.* New York: Russell Sage Foundation.

Hornsby, William. 2005. "Clashes of Class and Cash: Battles from the 150 Years War to Govern Client Development." *Arizona State Law Journal* 37:255–305.

Kritzer, Herbert M. 2004. *Risks, Reputations, and Rewards: Contingency Fee Legal Practice in the United States.* Palo Alto: Stanford University Press.

Levin, Leslie C. 2004. "The Ethical World of Solo and Small Law Firm Practitioners." *Houston Law Review* 41:310–392.

Mather, Lynn, Craig McEwen, and Richard Maiman. 2001. *Divorce Lawyers at Work: Varieties of Professionalism in Practice.* New York: Oxford University Press.

Mullinax, Otto. 1986. "Introducing the Honorable Oscar Mauzy as the Newly Elected Member of the Texas Supreme Court." Unpublished manuscript, on file with the authors, January 3.

Parikh, Sara. 2006–2007. "How the Spider Catches the Fly: Referral Networks in the Plaintiffs' Personal Injury Bar." *New York Law School Law Review* 51:243–283.

Sanders, Joseph, and Craig Joyce. 1990. "Off to the Races: The 1980s Tort Crisis and the Law Reform Process." *Houston Law Review* 27:207–295.

Spivey & Grigg, LLP. 2010. "Broadus Spivey." http://www.spiveygrigg.com/broadus.htm.

State Bar of Texas. 2004. "Referral Practices Survey." Data on file with the authors.

———. 2009. "Statistical Profile of the State Bar of Texas Membership, 2008–2009." http://www.texasbar.com/AM/Template.cfm?Section=Demographic_and_Economic_Trends&Template=/CM/ContentDisplay.cfm&ContentID=8792.

State Bar of Texas Commission for Lawyer Discipline. 2009. "Annual Report, 2008–2009." http://www.texasbar.com/Content/NavigationMenu/ForThePublic/FilingaComplaint/ContactaDisciplinaryCounselOffice/CommissionforLawyerDiscipline2009Annual Report.pdf.

Swartz, Mimi. 2005. "Hurt? Injured? Need a Lawyer? Too Bad!" *Texas Monthly,* November. http://www.texasmonthly.com/preview/2005-11-01/feature4.

Texas Bar Journal. 2008, 2009. "Disciplinary Actions." Vols. 71 and 72, nos. 1–11 for each vol., pages vary by issue.

Van Hoy, Jerry. 1999. "Markets and Contingency: How Client Markets Influence the Work of Plaintiffs' Personal Injury Lawyers." *International Journal of the Legal Profession* 6: 345–366.

Cases and Rules

Bates v. State Bar of Arizona, 433 U.S. 350 (1977).

Texas Disciplinary Rules of Professional Conduct 1.01–1.15, 7.01–7.05 (2010).

Betwixt and Between

The Ethical Dilemmas of Insurance Defense

Herbert M. Kritzer

A central driving force for many of the ethical dilemmas lawyers encounter is the tension between professional norms and the business realities of private legal practice. Lawyers frequently complain that legal practice today has become a business in contrast to some idealized golden age when lawyers could concentrate on being professionals and providing a professional service to their clients. Whether there ever was such a golden age is dubious; laments about legal practice becoming more of a business are by no means a recent development. This long-standing tension between the profession of practicing law and the business of practicing law provides the source for the central ethical dilemmas confronting lawyers retained by insurance companies ("insurers") to represent policyholders ("insureds").

Lawyers hired by insurers to defend claims that would be paid by the insurer constitute a subgroup of the "defense bar," lawyers who defend civil lawsuits. The defense bar includes both lawyers hired directly by defendants and lawyers hired by an insurer to represent insureds,[1] with some lawyers handling both cases received via insurers and cases coming directly from defendants.[2]

I would like to thank Dan Schwarcz, Lynn Mather, and Leslie Levin for extremely helpful comments on earlier drafts of this chapter. I would like to thank George Brown and Alex Zelenski at the State Bar of Wisconsin for making available data from the 2008 Economics of Law Practice in Wisconsin survey. I would also like to thank Emily Adams for assistance with legal research.

1. The defense bar has both national organizations, such as DRI (originally the Defense Research Institute) and state-level organizations, such as the Minnesota Defense Lawyers Association; there are no organizations that I have been able to identify specifically devoted to lawyers doing insurance defense.

2. Some insurance defense lawyers also do "coverage work," in which the insurance company retains the lawyer to either give an opinion as to whether the insured's loss is covered by

In addition to representing insureds, insurance defense lawyers may represent insurance companies when an insured seeks compensation from her own insurance company under a no-fault policy or uninsured/underinsured motorist (UM/UIM) clause of a liability policy.

The first image that many people have of insurance defense work is the lawyer who represents an insured individual sued in connection with injuries someone suffered in an automobile accident or on the insured's property (e.g., slipping and falling on a stairway). In fact, these lawyers handle a wide range of cases, many of which involve insureds that are organizations rather than individuals. Some of the more prominent types of cases include workers' compensation, premises liability of businesses (e.g., a slip and fall in a commercial establishment), motor vehicle liability of businesses, construction defect cases, environmental harms, and professional negligence (medical, legal, accounting, etc.). In all of these cases, the insurer retains a lawyer to represent the insured.

This representation arises because of the contractual relationship between the insurer and the insured defined by the insurance policy. The policy normally provides that the insurer takes on the responsibility of defending the insured, and this typically includes hiring and directing any legal counsel that is needed. In return, the insured grants the insurer the right to direct the defense and to settle the matter at the insurer's discretion;[3] the insured also agrees to assist and cooperate in the defense. In some types of policies (e.g., medical malpractice), the insured may have the right to approve any settlement the insurer might propose to make. As Silver and Syverud point out (1995, 264–268), this contractual relationship is between the insurer and the insured; the

---

the policy or to actually contest the question of whether the loss is covered. I am not considering this kind of work in this chapter.

3. In essence, the insurance contract addresses the issue raised by the American Bar Association (ABA) Model Rule of Professional Conduct 1.8(f):

A lawyer shall not accept compensation for representing a client from one other than the client unless:

(1) the client gives informed consent;
(2) there is no interference with the lawyer's independence of professional judgment or with the client-lawyer relationship. . . .

Presumably, the letter (discussed below) that a defense lawyer sends to an insured upon receiving the file from the insurer serves to meet the informed consent requirement in that the lawyer presumes consent is given unless the client/insured notifies the lawyer of a lack of consent. Alternatively, by entering into the insurance contract, the insured may be presumed to have consented in advance. The insured is always free to decline the defense offered by the insurer and retain and direct counsel at his own expense.

lawyer is herself not a party to that contract. It is important to keep in mind that an insurance defense lawyer typically becomes involved only after a lawsuit is filed, and the majority of cases involving claims covered by insurance are settled without the filing of a suit.[4] In those cases, the insured has little or no involvement in the claims handling beyond providing his version of what happened; the insurer will most likely notify the insured that a claim has been filed and then notify the insured when the claim is resolved, perhaps providing information on the resolution. This is probably what the typical insured wants because most people purchase liability insurance with the intent of both covering any losses and avoiding, as much as possible, having to deal with any claims filed against them.

Betwixt and Between I: The Eternal Triangle

The central ethical dilemmas that are specific to insurance defense practice arise because of the tension that exists between the lawyer's need to maintain an ongoing (business) relationship with the insurer, and the lawyer's professional obligation to the insured whom the insurer retains the lawyer to represent. This tripartite relationship has frequently been characterized as a triangle, sometimes as the "eternal triangle" (Silver and Syverud 1995, 269–270; Wunnicke 1989).[5] It is helpful to represent the relationship graphically.

As figure 7.1 shows, the relationship and the resulting obligations between the insured and the insurer are contractual (i.e., defined by the insurance policy). Between the insured and the lawyer, the relationship is "professional" (i.e., governed by the rules of professional responsibility and related law). The situation for the relationship between the insurer and the lawyer is more complex, and a subject of some debate among experts on legal ethics. In many states, both the insured and the insurer are deemed to be clients; however, when a lawyer is retained to represent an insured, the relationship between the insurer and the lawyer is probably best thought of as essentially a business relationship (i.e., governed largely by the market). Even when the lawyer/insurer relationship is

---

4. A study of paid auto accident tort claims filed against individuals and settled in 2002 found that 87% were settled without the filing of a lawsuit (Insurance Research Council 2003, 104). Even for larger commercial claims (payments in excess of $10,000) something less than half of paid claims lead to the filing of lawsuits, although for some areas, such as medical malpractice, a much larger percentage of paid claims involve a lawsuit (Texas Department of Insurance 2009).

5. Baker (1997) has extended the triangle relating lawyer, insured, and insurer to three dimensions by adding the claimant/plaintiff (treating the claimant and her lawyer as a unit), which produces a tetrahedron (a four-sided solid shape formed by triangles on each side).

Figure 7.1. The Enhanced Lawyer-Insured-Insurer Triangle

deemed to be that of a lawyer and client, the relationship involves both professional and business dimensions (Kritzer 1984), and arguably the business dimension is likely to be dominant for many, if not most, lawyers who specialize in insurance defense work because of the dependence most such lawyers have on a small number of insurers for an ongoing flow of cases. The business pressures of maintaining a successful insurance defense practice can, under some circumstances, be in tension with rules of professional conduct.

Insurance Defense Practice: Between the Two Hemispheres

The Two Hemispheres of the Legal Profession

As discussed in chapter 1, one of the most widely used metaphors in the study of the legal profession is the idea that the profession (or at least the roughly 80% of the profession engaged in private practice) has "two hemispheres" defined by clientele, with one hemisphere serving corporations and large organizations and the other serving individuals and their small businesses. There are major differences in legal practice tied to the hemisphere in which a lawyer works. Practice in the corporate hemisphere tends to be in large firms, with a relatively small set of recurring clients; fees are mostly hourly, with relatively high hourly rates. Contact between the lawyers in the firm and the corporation is often through in-house legal staffs such as those discussed by Sung Hui Kim (chapter 10). Practice in the personal services hemisphere tends to be in small firms or as solo practitioners. Clients are transient, and fees from any one client tend to be relatively modest. Charging may be on a contingency basis, on a flat fee basis, or by the hour (with hourly rates typically well below those charged by lawyers working in the corporate hemisphere). One of the more interesting implications of this analysis is that lawyers serving individuals and small businesses tend to have more professional autonomy than those working on behalf of corporations (Heinz and Laumann 1982, 360–365). That is, in the personal services sector such as divorce (Mather and McEwen, chapter 4) or immigration (Levin, chapter 5), lawyers tend to call the shots, at least with regard to how to proceed on a legal matter if not with regard to the goals being sought; in the corporate sector (Kirkland, chapter 8; Flood, chapter 9) the clients tend to call the shots. Moreover, while lawyers for individuals or small businesses often will say no to client requests that the lawyer sees as problematic, lawyers working in the corporate sector will typically find ways to accede to what the client wants to avoid having the client seek counsel elsewhere (Heinz 1983, 899–903).

Betwixt and Between II: Where Lies Insurance Defense Practice?

Insurance defense is an area of practice that falls into the category of corporate services, but it has characteristics of both corporate services and personal services. The cases that insurance defense lawyers often deal with involve personal plight matters, but the lawyers depend not on individuals but on corporations—insurance companies—for their work and their livelihood. That is, like other lawyers providing services to corporations, insurance defense firms rely on repeat business from a relatively small number of sources. However, as discussed below, the fees that the insurance defense lawyers can charge tend to be relatively low, and the firms in which they work tend to be small. Given the low rates insurers are willing to pay, large corporate firms do not find it profitable to handle insurance defense work because of income expectations and the firms' overhead structure (i.e., the costs of maintaining fancy offices in high-rise buildings). Mixing insurance defense work with other types of corporate work can be problematic because the difference in the fees that can be obtained may lead to undesirable tensions in the firm.

In the discussion that follows, I draw in part on my previous work on insurance defense practice (Kritzer 2006). That research involved about three and one-half months of observation during the fall of 2004 in a firm, which I call Etling, Burke & Howe (EBH), where much of the practice was insurance defense. In addition to the observation, I conducted a series of 17 semistructured interviews with insurance defense practitioners in other firms; the interviews were designed to assess the generalizability of what I observed at EBH. EBH was somewhat unusual for insurance defense firms because at the time of my observation about 30 lawyers in the firm (which totaled about 60) did insurance defense work. In preparing this chapter, I had some additional conversations with the lawyers at EBH and with lawyers previously interviewed; I also spoke with some former colleagues with experience as either defense or plaintiffs' lawyers, as well as a small number of other knowledgeable informants who were recommended to me.[6] To help draw a statistical portrait of insurance defense practice, I obtained some data from 2007 for lawyers in Wisconsin who do "personal injury defense" work.[7]

Characteristics of Insurance Defense Practice

As noted above, insurance defense firms tend to be small to moderate in size. No firm doing significant insurance defense work in the Twin Cities has more than 50 lawyers, and most such firms are under 20 lawyers. Lawyers' hourly rates tend to be low relative to other areas of corporate representation; circa 2004, the average rate was about $130 per hour, and few lawyers, even quite senior partners, were able to charge more than $150 for work they received from insurance companies. Billing expectations for insurance defense lawyers working full time tend to be in the range of 1700–1900 billable hours per year. For 43 Wisconsin lawyers doing "personal injury defense" in 2007, the median hourly rate charged was $139 (mean $151); the median firm size was 7 lawyers with the 75th percentile at 16 lawyers (only 1 of the 43 lawyers was a solo practitioner). The Wisconsin lawyers had been in practice for an average of 20 years. Only 6 of the 43 (14%) of the lawyers were female, a figure that I suspect is a bit low; it is likely that something on the order of 20 to 25% of insurance defense practitioners are female. Lawyers handling insurance defense work tend to be drawn from local and regional law schools. For example, at one larger insurance defense firm in the Twin Cities area, well over 80% of the lawyers obtained their JD degrees from one of the local law schools, and only two lawyers obtained their JDs from schools outside the Midwest.

While most insurance defense lawyers work in private firms, some are salaried employees of the insurers. The formal arrangements vary for this group. Some work in "staff counsel" offices. For others, a semblance of distance is cre-

6. The quotations from my own work below are either taken from transcripts of interviews or were reconstructed from notes of observations, interviews, or conversations.

7. The Wisconsin data are from the 2008 Economics of Law Practice in Wisconsin survey conducted for the State Bar of Wisconsin covering practice in 2007. A variety of states conduct such studies, but none that I have found has a specific category for "insurance defense practice." Most do not separate out personal injury plaintiffs from personal injury defense or workers' compensation claimants from workers' compensation defense (and none provide information that allows one to consider other areas of insurance defense practice such as property damage or construction claims); none of the reports I have found break out much detail by areas of practice.

ated by presenting the lawyers as working in a firm or as solo practitioners (e.g., "The Law Offices of Jane Doe and Associates"), but these are "captive firms" that work only for the specific insurer. In the discussion that follows, I refer to all such lawyers as "staff counsel" regardless of the formal arrangement.

The Central Ethical Dilemma of Insurance Defense: Loyalty

Insurer and Insured in Conflict: Where Goes the Lawyer?
The most prominent ethical issues in insurance defense practice arise when a lawyer is retained to represent an insured and there is a conflict between the insured and the insurer. Most common among these conflicts are situations where the potential damages may exceed the policy limit or when there may be some question whether part or all of the claim against the insured is covered by the policy. Both of these situations are discussed below.

Before turning to issues posed by limits and coverage problems, we need to consider some of the broad issues insurance defense lawyers encounter in their daily work. Most prominent is the need to maintain a flow of work from a small number of insurers. Moreover, in some of that work the lawyer represents the insurer in opposition to an insured (i.e., in no-fault cases or UM/UIM cases where there is a conflict over what compensation the insurer owes to the insured). Notwithstanding the case-to-case variation in the insurance defense lawyer's formal relationships with the insurers, it is those insurers that the lawyer must keep happy if she is to receive future cases.

Insurance defense lawyers are well aware of the dilemma presented by the need to keep the insurer sending cases and their professional duty to the insured. One lawyer commented to me: "You want to keep the insurance company as a *client* [emphasis added] because they pay your bills and there is not so many of them . . . there is always a temptation to [let that loyalty supplant your obligation to the insured]." Susan Shapiro (2002, 123) quotes one of the respondents in her study of conflicts of interest as follows:

> We make it clear to the insured: "Hey, look it. I'm your lawyer. My primary obligation is to you. But let's not lose sight of the fact that I'm going to represent you in one case, but I've got a hundred cases for that insurance company. You can certainly feel uneasy and say, 'Why is this lawyer really serving me? When I'm long gone, he's got to make the insurance company happy.'" I said, "I feel strongly about my obligation to you. But it's more important how you perceive it. And, therefore, if you are uneasy at all, you

should seek separate counsel—at your own expense—and talk it out with him and have that lawyer call me to express your views, if you feel that those views need to be expressed."

Lawyers do differ in how they see their obligation to the insurer. One lawyer bluntly stated, "The insured is my client; what I owe the insurance company is an honest bill." It is worth noting that the lawyer who made this comment is quite senior and is not dependent on a small set of insurance companies for a majority of his cases. I suspect that the degree to which a lawyer feels dependent on a small set of sources for clients will influence the lawyer's ability to act independently of what the lawyer sees as the desires of the insurer.

In the vast majority of cases, particularly those cases involving individuals as insureds in routine tort cases (e.g., auto accidents, premises liability, animal bites), the insurer's and the insured's interests coincide. The claim is clearly covered by the insurance policy, the amount of damages is clearly less than the policy limit, the insured wants the claim to go away with as little hassle and involvement as possible, and the insurer wants to resolve the claim with as little cost as possible. In these cases, the goals of the insured and the insurer will almost always coincide: resolve the matter in a favorable manner, preferably with as little cost and hassle as possible (although the insurer may have reputational concerns that go beyond any one case, which could lead the insurer to play hardball with plaintiff's counsel).

In fact, in these kinds of cases the lawyer retained by the insurer to represent the insured may have very little contact with the insured. One lawyer described his interaction with the typical insured in the following way:

> When I receive the file, I send a letter to the insured telling him that I've been retained to represent him and that the case is now in suit. My paralegal will work with the client to prepare responses to discovery requests. If the case gets to the point of a deposition, I will meet the client an hour or two before the deposition to prep him. When the case settles, I will send a letter to the client notifying him that the settlement has occurred.

This lawyer went on to report that he did not normally copy the insured on routine status reports to the insurer or other routine communications, although he noted that other lawyers in his firm did routinely "cc" the insured on more or less everything that went out. If a case gets close to actually going to trial, the communication between the lawyer and the insured becomes much more common regardless of the amount of communication during the early pretrial phases. Arguably, the level of communication described by the lawyer above is inconsistent with Model Rules 1.2 and 1.4. Rule 1.2(a) provides that "a lawyer shall abide by a client's decisions concerning the objectives of representation and, as required by Rule 1.4, shall consult with the client as to the means by which they are to be pursued. . . . [A] lawyer shall abide by a client's decision whether to settle a matter." Rule 1.4(a) states that a lawyer shall

(1) promptly inform the client of any decision or circumstance with respect to which the client's informed consent . . . is required by these Rules;
(2) reasonably consult with the client about the means by which the client's objectives are to be accomplished;
(3) keep the client reasonably informed about the status of the matter;
(4) promptly comply with reasonable requests for information.

However, it is important to consider the purpose behind these rules, which is to allow the client to make the decisions necessary to control the litigation. Under the insurance contract, the insured has assigned the responsibility for defending and settling the case to the insurer, and if the claim is clearly covered by the policy and the damages are clearly within the policy limits, the insured's desire is likely to be to have as little to do with the matter as possible. In such cases, the lawyer's duty does not require routine communication with the insured in the absence of special circumstances or a specific request from the insured. This approach is approved by ABA Standing Committee on Ethics and Professional Responsibility Formal Opinion 96-403 (1996), which counsels insurance defense lawyers to "apprise the insured of the limited nature of his representation as well as the insurer's right to control the defense in accordance with the terms of the insurance contract." The Formal Opinion then notes that "once the lawyer has apprised the insured of the limited nature of his representation and that he intends to proceed in accordance with the directions of the insurer, he has satisfied the requirements of Rule 1.2(c)."

Even when there is no issue of coverage and the potential damages are clearly within the policy limit, cases do arise where an insured really wants to go to trial in order to be vindicated. While the lawyers I observed or interviewed described such occurrences as extremely rare, Shapiro (2002, 126) quoted one insurance defense lawyer she interviewed:

> We get a lot of situations where the people we represent as defendants will find out [that] a case is settled. And they call up and they are boiling mad.

They can't believe the insurance company paid any money. They don't want the case settled; they want to go to trial. . . . [They think the settlement is] an admission—of some type—that they're at fault, even though the releases specifically say that it is not an admission.

This situation would seem to facially violate Rules 1.2 and 1.4(a) quoted above because the lawyer clearly neither consulted with the insured regarding the insured's view of settlement nor informed the insured that a settlement had been agreed to by the insurer. However, by contract the insured had assigned the authority to settle the matter to the insurer and therefore is essentially powerless to veto a settlement within policy limits that fully releases the insured (unless, as in many medical malpractice policies, there is a "consent to settle" clause). In all of my observations, both in defense offices and in plaintiffs' offices, I have never seen a situation in which the defense-side representative indicated a need to check with an insured to get approval for a proposed settlement. This approach is consistent with ABA Standing Committee on Ethics and Professional Responsibility Formal Opinion 96-403 (1996), which provides that so long as the lawyer has apprised the insured of the limits on the representation and the insurer's right to settle the matter under the policy, "the lawyer may follow the directions of the insurer to settle, without further communication with the insured."

In rare cases, the insured might inform both the insurer and the lawyer retained by the insurer to represent the insured that he does not want the case settled, and that it must go to trial so he can be vindicated. One might ask whether this is a reasonable demand on the part of the insured. Imagine an insurance policy that covered the damages paid out but left the insured himself to pay any legal expenses. How many insureds would insist on going to trial in that situation? Moreover, such an instruction would not be binding on the insurer because the insured has already contracted away his right to control settlement.[8] This still creates a potential dilemma for the lawyer retained to defend the insured. The lawyer in such a situation might remind the client of the contractual power of the insurer, and possibly suggest that the insured consult

---

8. As noted previously, some medical malpractice policies contain a "consent to settle" clause that permits the insured to veto any proposed settlement. Some policies containing such a clause also contain a "hammer" or "suicide" clause that would require the insured to personally pay any difference between the proposed settlement and an eventual damage award. While there is no systematic evidence on how insureds respond when informed of the hammer clause, anecdotal evidence suggests that few insureds insist on going to trial once made aware of the risk they will face.

with another lawyer about the implications of his demand to go to trial (because the insured would be violating the insurance contract's provision granting control to the insurer, the insurer could be within its rights to withdraw its defense). In any case, the insured is always free to reject the defense offered by the insurer and to retain his own counsel at his own expense. Even in this situation, there is nothing to stop the insurer from negotiating a settlement with the plaintiff and securing a full release for the insured. One might speculate about how a court would respond to an objection from the defendant to a stipulation of dismissal by a plaintiff who has accepted a settlement offered by the insurer and provided a full release for the defendant-insured.

As noted above, there are two primary situations in which conflicts between the interests of the insured and the insurer can arise that create potential ethical quandaries for the insurance defense lawyer. The first is when there is a claim that potentially exceeds the limit of the policy. In this case, particularly if there is any doubt about liability, the insurer as a repeat player (Galanter 1974) might from a business perspective want to play the odds and go to trial, figuring its liability cannot exceed the limit and that it is worth the additional costs of trial for the chance of paying considerably less or possibly nothing at all. In contrast, the insured—a one-shot player—has a lot to lose in this situation and would normally want the insurer to agree to a settlement within the policy limit. The insurance defense lawyer is supposed to represent the insured's interest but has no power to force the insurer to agree to a settlement. However, the threat of bad-faith claims against the insurer combined with state laws imposing a "duty to settle" on the insurer have mitigated this issue in important ways (Pryor and Silver 2001a, 623–624).[9]

The second conflict occurs when there is the possibility that the policy does not cover part or all of the claim. This can arise for two reasons: The insured may have failed to provide (or misrepresented) information related to the original issuance (or subsequent renewal) of the policy and hence the policy may be deemed invalid, or the incident leading to the claim may not be covered due to the terms of the policy. A standard example of the latter arises when the underlying behavior constituted an intentional tort (e.g., a battery). The following sections consider in more detail the issues in limits cases and in cases

---

9. All but two states (Nevada and West Virginia) have imposed a duty to settle on insurers (Hyman, Black, and Silver 2011, 52n7); this duty makes the insurer potentially liable for any judgment in excess of the limits if an insurer declines a plaintiff's offer to settle at or below the policy limits. States vary as to the strictness of the duty to settle, with some states imposing what amounts to strict liability and others using more of a negligence standard.

involving issues related to coverage, and how insurance defense lawyers deal with those issues when they arise.

Limits Cases

Despite some perceptions that "excess [above limits] claims arise infrequently" (Pryor and Silver 2001a, 632), limits cases occur with a surprising degree of regularity. Using data on personal auto insurance claims closed in 2002 (collected by the Insurance Research Council), I estimate that in about 5% of the claims the insurer paid the policy limit;[10] in about one-half of 1%, the insurer paid *more* than the policy limit. While limits cases are less common in commercial insurance claims, they do occur with at least some regularity. Drawing on data collected by the Texas Department of Insurance and work by Hyman, Black, and Silver (2011), I estimate that policy limits or more were paid in about 1% of commercial auto claims in Texas, perhaps 15% of medical malpractice claims, and about one-half of 1% of other types of commercial liability claims. One study of California cases that got to a jury verdict found that 20% of personal injury cases had at least a risk of an excess verdict, as did about 60% of nonpersonal injury torts (calculated from Gross and Syverud 1996, 22).

What happens when an insurance defense lawyer is faced with a case in which more than the policy limit is at stake? First, it is a fairly standard procedure for the insurance defense lawyer to send a letter advising the insured that she might find it desirable to retain another lawyer to deal with issues related to excess exposure such as the insurer balking at paying the policy limit because the insurer prefers to take its chances at trial (Shapiro 2002, 126–127). One lawyer told me that he went beyond this and informed the insured that he would defend the insured on the question of liability and damages but could only negotiate settlement amounts on behalf of the insurance company. When there is little or no doubt concerning the insured's negligence or about causation, and when damages clearly exceed the policy limit, the insurer is very likely to tender its policy limit and seek to obtain a full release of the insured. Problems arise when the plaintiff makes a facially reasonable limits demand, but the insurer balks at accepting that demand. Two lawyers described to me the "hammer letter": a letter from the insured (or separate counsel retained by the insured) to the insurer demanding that the insurer settle the claim within the policy limit

10. As one might expect, the probability that the insurer paid the policy limit (or more) decreases as the limit increases: 20% for policies with a limit of $25,000 or less, 9% for $25,001–$50,000, 4% for $50,001–$100,000, 2% for $100,001–$500,000, and about 1% for policies over $500,000.

(Quinley 2009); the letter may reference the insurer's duty to settle, and/or it may explicitly threaten a bad-faith claim if the insurer fails to settle within the policy limit and an excess verdict results. As one lawyer explained:

> Whenever there is a possibility that a claim will exceed the policy limits, the client is sent a letter advising that he might want to retain private counsel to represent his interests vis-à-vis the insurer. If the insurer seems reluctant to settle for the policy limits, I will tell the client [the insured] to have *another* [emphasis added] lawyer send the insurer a hammer letter. If the client hasn't retained private counsel, I may go so far as to suggest someone who could send the hammer letter on behalf of the client.

What happens if the plaintiff refuses to give a full release in return for receiving the policy limit? It may be that the nature of the tortfeasor's behavior was so egregious that the plaintiff wants the tortfeasor to personally feel some financial pain by demanding what Baker (2001) described as "blood money." It may be that the plaintiff wants some contribution from the tortfeasor because the tortfeasor was intentionally underinsured (Baker 2001, 296–298) and hence will not provide a release for the insured without such a contribution. An insurance company representative described the problem vis-à-vis obtaining a release for the insured as arising when

> there was some grossly improper behavior on the part of our insured such as driving while intoxicated. In those kinds of cases, we want the attorney we retain to try to work with the insured to find a way to resolve the case. Maybe the attorney can convince the plaintiff to provide a full release if our insured will agree to put up some relatively small amount of his own money.

The scenario outlined above is one where the insurance defense lawyer would be seeking to serve the interests of the insured. There are two factors that can complicate this type of situation: (1) "pay-and-walk" provisions that allow an insurer to discharge its duty to defend by paying (or possibly even by offering) the policy limit without regard to whether the plaintiff will provide a full release for the defendant-insured, and (2) arrangements between the insurer and the lawyer concerning how the lawyer is to be paid.

Standard insurance policies often contain a provision along the lines of, "Our duty to settle or defend ends when our limit of liability for this coverage has been exhausted by payment of judgments or settlements." States vary considerably, either by statute or by case law, on whether and when an insurer can act on such a pay-and-walk provision to discharge its duty to defend by paying the policy limit. In states that allow pay-and-walk, the lawyer's professional duty to the insured can come into tension with the insurer's desire to get out of the case by paying the policy limit. Specifically, can the defense lawyer negotiate a settlement that will allow the insurer to terminate its defense of her client? In practical terms, the insurer can ameliorate this problem for the defense lawyer by retaining the lawyer to defend only on liability and to have either its adjuster or a lawyer retained specifically to represent the insurer's interests negotiate the limits settlement (Pryor and Silver 2001a, 613, 628). If the insurer terminates its defense after paying the policy limit without the involvement of the lawyer retained to represent the insured, it is not an issue between the insured and the defense lawyer, but rather between the insurer and the insured as to whether the insurer has met its contractual duty to defend. The question between the insured and the defense lawyer is what, if any, continuing duty the defense lawyer has to the insured once the insurer discontinues paying the lawyer. In theory, the insured could take over paying the lawyer or the lawyer could continue representation on an unpaid basis (although there is no obligation for the lawyer to do so), but I am unaware of any examples where either of these situations actually occurred.

How might the fee arrangement between the insurer and the insured create problems in a limits case? While most insurance defense lawyers bill insurers on an hourly basis, many firms and insurers have tried alternative billing methods, often involving fixed fees (Kritzer 2006, 2060–2068). If a case is resolved within the policy limits with a full release of liability for the insured, the insured is unlikely to care how the lawyer was being paid. However, if the case goes to trial and a verdict in excess of the policy limits is returned that is not covered by the insurer, the method of compensation for the lawyer could raise issues. One lawyer used this problem to explain why he did not take cases on a fixed fee basis:

> To me, there is an inherent conflict; an immediate and apparent conflict on the flat fee basis. You can imagine this scenario. Insured has a $50,000 limit, and you've agreed to a $5,000 flat fee. You're now at $4,995; you propose to take some depositions, and some other things. The insurer is all for it because now you are on your own nickel. Let's say the case comes back with a verdict of $125,000. The insured, your client, to whom you owe due diligence, fealty, and loyalty, now says,
>
> "What happened?"
> "We got a bad result."

"How come you didn't do any discovery after May 16?"

"I didn't think it was necessary."

"What billing rate did you have?"

"I had a flat fee."

"When did you hit the flat fee cap?"

"May 14."

And so what it creates is an immediate conflict, because the age old conundrum for insurance lawyers has been the proscription against, in the rules of ethics [Model Rule 1.8(f)], of being paid by someone other than your client.

The comment above describes a hypothetical problem. Another lawyer described an actual case in which the possible linkage between a verdict above the policy limit and fee arrangement arose:

> Several years ago, I defended a client [an insured] who while drunk drove the wrong way down a divided expressway and crashed head on into [an] oncoming car. The driver of the other car suffered serious injuries requiring lifetime medical care. My client had a $100,000 limit policy, but plaintiff refused to settle for the policy limit because she wanted a judgment reflecting the actual amount of damages even if it was uncollectible. The case went to trial, and the jury returned an award for multiple millions.
>
> A couple of years later, my client turned around and sued me for failing to provide a vigorous representation. He claimed that I should have argued that the design of the expressway entrance was defective—if the entrance had been properly designed, it would not have been possible to get on the highway going the wrong way, and thus the government was at fault for defectively designing the expressway. During discovery, the former client's lawyer found something in my file that suggested I had handled the case on a flat fee basis; the lawyer advanced the argument that this was evidence that I had failed to provide zealous representation. Fortunately, as it turned out, I had in fact told the insurer that the case was too big and complex to handle on a fixed base and it was actually handled on an hourly basis.

Threats to Coverage

While most of the time the insurer and the insured have a common interest in resolving a tort claim with minimum cost and effort, this assumes that there is no doubt that the claim is covered by the insurance policy. Insurance policies exclude certain types of claims, such as injuries that were intentionally inflicted. Moreover, the pricing of insurance policies is based on information provided by the insured, and the failure to provide certain kinds of information or providing false information could be the basis for the insurer disclaiming coverage under its policy. In some circumstances the insurer has questions about whether part or all of the claim is in fact covered by the insurance policy. In those circumstances the insurer will undertake the defense while notifying the insured that it is unsure of the coverage question and reserving the right to disclaim coverage (and to hence discontinue its defense) if it becomes clear that the policy does not cover the claim; that is, the insurer is defending with a "reservations of rights" (ROR).

Two kinds of problems can arise in such cases. First, the lawyer knows that there is an issue of coverage and that the investigation required to defend the claim could lead to information resulting in the withdrawal of the defense. In some cases, advancing the best defense to the insured's liability could also put coverage at risk. For example, if an insured is sued for wounding someone with a gun, the insured might want to argue that he was acting in self-defense. However, acting in self-defense would constitute an intentional act, and the insurance policy might specifically exclude from coverage injuries resulting from an intentional act. The second issue the lawyer faces in an ROR case is that the insurer may want to limit expenditures on the defense in the anticipation of possible withdrawal or possibly direct the defense in a way that is likely to reveal information to the insurer that would negate coverage. When a case is defended under a reservations of rights, some states require that the insurer pay for independent counsel for the insured and not direct the defense; other states allow more insurer control when there has been a reservation of rights but less than would be the case if there was not a reservation of rights (Baker 2008, 544). If the insurer is at most minimally directing independent counsel, and independent counsel does not have a continuing business relationship with the insurer, a question may still arise as to what information counsel may be obligated to share with the insurer given the insurer's continuing authority to settle the claim. However, the lawyer, while paid by the insurer, usually does not depend on that insurer (or possibly any insurer) for future cases and hence does not experience the conflict between professional loyalty and business imperatives that exist for lawyers who regularly receive cases from the insurer.

In cases without a reservation of rights, a conflict for the insurance defense lawyer can arise if the lawyer becomes aware of information that puts coverage in doubt. What factors influence how the lawyer deals with the question of whether to withhold information from the insurer? How should the lawyer deal with a situation in which the insured specifically asks the lawyer to withhold that information? On one side is the insured, who is clearly the client of the lawyer. On the other side is the insurer with which the lawyer has an ongoing business relationship (and which may be deemed to be a client, depending on the state). Professional rules and norms concerning client confidences require lawyers to protect the confidential information of their clients except in very rare circumstances (Model Rule 1.6). From the business perspective, the lawyer faces concerns about how the insurer might respond if it learns the lawyer withheld information that would have negated coverage. While the insurer should recognize that the lawyer is constrained by her duties to the insured, the insurer may decide not to refer cases to the lawyer in the future.

It is important to draw two distinctions. First, there are two kinds of information of which the lawyer might become aware. One type relates only to coverage (e.g., the insured's failure to reveal information when the policy was issued, such as use of the car for business purposes or the presence in the insured's household of an unrelated person who had a number of traffic violations and who had regularly operated one of the insured's vehicles). The other type of information relates directly to the incident giving rise to the claim and could be significant for the insurer's decision about the insured's liability. Given that the defense counsel is retained to investigate the factual issues related to the claim, the lawyer would normally expect to share such information with the insurer so that the insurer who is directing the defense can provide appropriate direction to the lawyer and make decisions concerning settlement (Silver and Syverud 1995; Pryor and Silver 2001b, 65–67). If the information does not relate to the incident leading to the claim, and hence is not relevant for assessing liability or damages, the lawyer should withhold it from the insurer on the grounds that it is protected by attorney-client confidentiality and is not relevant to the insurer's right to direct the defense of the claim. Even if the information does relate to the claim, it may relate more to coverage issues than to issues related to defending or valuing the claim, and at least some courts have determined that revealing such information, which furthers only the insurer's interests and not the insured's, is a violation of the attorney's duties to the insured (*Parsons v. Continental National American Group* 1976; Shapiro 2002, 124–125).

All of the defense lawyers I have spoken with are adamant that it would be unethical to inform the insurer that they had become aware of a coverage problem (that was not directly related to the claim being defended). At the same time, I picked up hints of concern should such a situation arise. After all, as

I previously quoted one lawyer, "You want to keep the insurance company as a client . . . they pay your bills and there is not so many of them." A lawyer is likely to have at least some concern that if the insurer, who provides a significant portion of the lawyer's work, becomes aware that the lawyer withheld information about a coverage issue, the insurer might look elsewhere for lawyers to handle cases in the future. In this situation, insurance company staff counsel lawyers may be in a safer position than are lawyers in outside firms (Silver 1997, 249–250). One lawyer in private practice who had previously worked for many years in a staff counsel office insisted that he and his colleagues were extremely careful with regard to revealing coverage issues to adjusters or others within the insurance company. He explained, "Our duty is to the insured. Moreover, if I revealed this kind of information it would put the company at risk of a bad-faith claim." The lawyer went on to observe that even if this were not the case, he was not concerned that he would have been penalized in any way by the company for failing to reveal such information:

> Actually, the situation is harder for a lawyer in a private firm. A firm lawyer might be worried that if he didn't reveal coverage-related information and the company eventually became aware of the information and that the lawyer had the information, the company would stop sending him cases. I didn't have to worry about being punished because if the company did something punitive to me, it risked opening itself up to all sorts of legal problems.[11]

It is important to note that in situations in which a claim is being defended under a reservation of rights, defense by staff counsel would not be appropriate given the clear conflict between the insurer and the insured, just as is the case for an outside lawyer who is directed by the insurer (Silver 1997, 247).

This still leaves the situation in which the lawyer becomes aware of information clearly relevant for the defense of the claim and the insured explicitly tells the lawyer not to reveal it to the insurer. What should the lawyer do in that situation? None of the lawyers I spoke with described a situation of this type,

11. The former staff counsel lawyer may have underestimated the company's ability to impose penalties, such as reduced raises or prospects for promotion. However, a second lawyer with extensive experience as a staff counsel lawyer strongly expressed the view that the insurer would not be able to impose disciplinary consequences in this type of situation, even asserting that he would feel obligated to withhold information given to him in confidence by the insured that raised coverage issues *and* related specifically to the claim at hand (e.g., that the act leading to the plaintiff's injury had been intentional), a kind of situation in which Pryor and Silver assert that the lawyer would be obligated to terminate representation (2001, 86–89).

but the answer provided in a discussion for insurance defense practitioners (Pryor, Silver, and Syverud 2003, 9) was quite clear:

> Generally speaking, a defense lawyer cannot withhold from [the insurer] information relating to the investigation, defense or settlement of a liability claim, regardless of the source from which the information is received. Explain this to the [insured], ask for permission to disclose the information, and tell the [insured] that you will have to withdraw if your request is refused. If the [insured] insists on secrecy, withdraw.

This advice is consistent with ABA Formal Opinion 01-421, which includes the statement, "In those relatively rare situations when the lawyer reasonably believes that disclosure of confidential information to the insurer will affect a material interest of the client-insured adversely, the lawyer may not disclose such confidential information without first obtaining the informed consent of the client-insured" (ABA Standing Committee 2001). Note that while withdrawing would solve the lawyer's ethical problem vis-à-vis client confidentiality conflicting with her duties to the insurer, the simple fact of withdrawing, even though the lawyer could not then reveal the information, would "signal to the [insurer] something is amiss" (Pryor, Silver, and Syverud 2003, 38) and would undoubtedly trigger an intense investigation by the insurer to determine if there was a coverage issue of which it was not aware.

Conclusion

The insurance defense lawyer stands at the intersection of the corporate and personal sectors of legal practice. Much of the insurance defense lawyer's work deals with personal plight issues and often involves representing individuals or small businesses. At the same time, the lawyer looks to insurance companies as the source of her work. The resulting triangular relationship creates the potential for a wide variety of ethical dilemmas, many turning on the tension between her professional duty toward the insured she has been retained to represent and the insurance company that retains her, reviews her bills, and pays her.

Over time, practitioners have developed a variety of standard procedures for dealing with the ethical issues that arise in the triangular relationship. These include being very clear about the limits of the representation they are providing, advising insureds when they should consider retaining their own counsel at their own expense (possibly even directing the insured to particular lawyers), identifying boundaries on the information they can share with the insurer, and reminding insurers of their duty to settle. Most insurers have also become conscious of the risks of bad-faith litigation they face if they fail to meet their duty to defend or their duty to settle. While the lawyers continue to struggle, at least to some degree, to balance the loyalty they owe to the insureds they are retained to represent with the business imperative of maintaining their ongoing relationship with the insurers they depend on for cases, these standard procedures go a long way to ameliorating the inevitable conflicts that will occur. However, the market pressures on insurance defense firms mean that practitioners need to stay attentive to the potential for conflicts lest those pressures rise to the level that the temptation to prioritize their business needs over their ethical duties to the insureds who are their clients becomes too strong to resist.

References

American Bar Association (ABA) Standing Committee on Ethics and Professional Responsibility. 1996. "Obligations of a Lawyer Representing an Insured Who Objects to a Proposed Settlement within Policy Limits." Formal Opinion 96-403, August 2.
———. 2001. "Ethical Obligations of a Lawyer Working Under Insurance Company Guidelines and Other Restrictions." Formal Opinion 01-421, February 16.
Baker, Tom. 1997. "Liability Insurance Conflicts and Defense Lawyers: From Triangles to Tetrahedrons." *Connecticut Insurance Law Journal* 4:101–151.
———. 2001. "Blood Money, New Money, and the Moral Economy of Tort Law in Action." *Law & Society Review* 33:275–319.
———. 2008. *Insurance Law and Policy: Cases, Materials, and Problems.* 2nd ed. New York: Aspen.
Galanter, Marc. 1974. "Why the 'Haves' Come Out Ahead: Speculations on the Limits of Legal Change." *Law & Society Review* 9:95–160.
Gross, Samuel R., and Kent D. Syverud. 1996. "Don't Try: Civil Jury Verdicts in a System Geared to Settlement." *UCLA Law Review* 44:1–64.
Heinz, John P. 1983. "The Power of Lawyers." *Georgia Law Review* 17:891–911.
Heinz, John P., and Edward O. Laumann. 1982. *Chicago Lawyers: The Social Structure of the Bar.* New York: Russell Sage Foundation and American Bar Foundation.
Hyman, David A., Bernard Black, and Charles Silver. 2011. "Settlement at Policy Limits and the Duty to Settle: Evidence from Texas." *Journal of Empirical Legal Studies* 8:48–84.
Insurance Research Council. 2003. *Auto Injury Insurance Claims: Countrywide Patterns in Treatment, Cost, and Compensation.* Malvern, PA: Insurance Research Council.
Kritzer, Herbert M. 1984. "The Dimensions of Lawyer-Client Relations: Notes Toward a Theory and a Field Study." *American Bar Foundation Research Journal* 1984:409–428.
———. 2006. "The Commodification of Insurance Defense Practice." *Vanderbilt Law Review* 59:2053–2094.
Pryor, Ellen S., and Charles Silver. 2001a. "Defense Lawyers' Professional Responsibilities: Part I—Excess Exposure Cases." *Texas Law Review* 78:599–678.

———. 2001b. "Defense Lawyers' Professional Responsibilities: Part II—Contested Coverage Cases." *Georgetown Journal of Legal Ethics* 15:29–94.

Pryor, Ellen Smith, Charles Silver, and Kent D. Syverud. 2003. "Practical Guide for Insurance Defense Lawyers." *Defense Counsel Journal* 70 [supplement].

Quinley, Kevin M. 2009. "Decoding Hammer Letters: Adjusters Must Know When to Settle." *Claims* 57:14–17. http://www.propertycasualty360.com/2009/09/01/decoding-hammer-letters.

Shapiro, Susan P. 2002. *Tangled Loyalties: Conflict of Interest in Legal Practice.* Ann Arbor: University of Michigan Press.

Silver, Charles. 1997. "Flat Fees and Staff Attorneys: Unnecessary Casualties in the Continuing Battle over the Law Governing Insurance Defense Lawyers." *Connecticut Insurance Law Journal* 4:205–257.

Silver, Charles, and Kent Syverud. 1995. "The Professional Responsibilities of Insurance Defense Lawyers." *Duke Law Journal* 45:255–363.

Texas Department of Insurance. 2009. *The 2008 Texas Liability Closed Claim Annual Report.* Austin: Texas Department of Insurance. http://www.tdi.state.tx.us/reports/pc/documents/taccar2008.pdf.

Wunnicke, Brooke. 1989. "The Eternal Triangle: Standards of Ethical Representation by the Insurance Defense Lawyer." *For the Defense* 31:7–16.

Cases

Parsons v. Continental National American Group, 550 P.2d 94 (Ariz. 1976).

The Ethics of Constructing Truth

The Corporate Litigator's Approach

Kimberly Kirkland

Truth is both a goal of the adversary system and a value that pervades it. The system is designed to uncover and determine the truth of legal disputes. Although the truth derived through this process is understood to be imperfect, the search for an authoritative and accepted truth for purposes of resolving the dispute is central to the notion of the just resolution of legal controversies. The system relies on the various players within it to engage with, and to exhibit due respect for, the process of discerning this authoritative and accepted truth.

Corporate litigators are one such group of players in the adversary system. Corporate litigators work in large law firms and represent corporate clients. Their job is to make factual and legal cases for their corporate clients—to tell stories.[1] To do so, they must reconcile multiple, competing accounts of the dispute in a way that will achieve the client's ends, without obstructing the process or thwarting the goals of the system.[2] They have limited guidance from the rules of procedure and professional responsibility since those rules only address conduct at the margins, providing, for example, that litigators must not tell their clients to lie or to hide or destroy documents. Accordingly, corporate litigators must navigate grey areas on their own. Throughout discovery, they regularly make decisions that call into question what is true and who

---

1. All litigators construct factual and legal cases for their clients. This chapter focuses on the ways litigators in large law firms (generally firms of 200 or more lawyers) think about creating and telling those stories.

2. This is the normative reference point, or what Elizabeth Chambliss (chapter 3) refers to as the normative benchmark, from which I begin my examination of lawyers' ethical decision making.

will have access to information that might shed light on the truth. A layperson would likely view the discretionary decisions in these grey areas as an ethical minefield, but corporate litigators do not. In this chapter, I explore how and why this is the case.

I begin by examining the empirical data on corporate litigators' approaches to three common ethical issues in discovery. Corporate litigators' approaches to discovery are important because discovery is where corporate litigators spend the majority of their time. Wayne Brazil's (1980) seminal study of civil discovery indicated that in contrast to smaller-scale litigation, discovery is a very substantial part of the complex and/or high-stakes litigation that constitutes a mainstay of the corporate litigators' work. Moreover, Brazil found that in large-case litigation, as opposed to smaller-scale litigation, "tactical maneuvering is likely to play a substantially larger role in the discovery process, [and] discovery is less likely to be successful in the sense that the parties' discovery efforts often fail to dislodge all the significant information from their opponents" (230).

I examine litigators' approaches to three particular aspects of discovery—educating witnesses, speaking objections, and responding to discovery requests—because each of these tasks has the potential to create tension between the corporate litigator's role as her client's advocate and her obligation to refrain from thwarting the truth-seeking function of the adversary system. I seek to understand these approaches by reference to the context of corporate litigators' work—examining first, the nature of the litigator's task in the adversarial system, and second, the experience of work in corporate law firms. I describe how the context of their work shapes litigators' ethical consciousness in ways that prepare and allow them to regularly make difficult decisions, which potentially influence the adversary system's ability to uncover an authoritative and accepted truth without experiencing those decisions as ethically challenging.

Corporate Litigators' Ethics in Discovery

The civil discovery process is designed to facilitate the exchange of information between opposing parties, allowing them equal access to information that may shed light on the truth of the dispute. Civil discovery rules provide mechanisms for discovering information in opponents' files and witnesses' memories. This process creates a fundamental tension for the litigator. On the one hand, the litigator eagerly makes use of discovery to benefit her client's case. Through document requests, interrogatories, and depositions, the corporate litigator susses out the parties' often varying versions of the facts and the legal significance of one another's conduct. The litigator uses this information to construct and refine the factual and legal story she will tell to make her client's case.

On the other hand, the litigator is wary of opposing counsel's use of the discovery process. For instance, when a corporate litigator prepares a witness for his deposition, she is acutely aware that the deposition may limit her ability to craft a story because opposing counsel will use the deposition to try to commit the witness to a certain version of events. The procedural rules require that a party be forthcoming with information the other side requests in discovery unless some legitimate ground for objecting applies. As an advocate in an adversary system, however, the corporate litigator has an incentive to be only as forthcoming as required by the rules or as is helpful to her own cause. Because these rules are open to interpretation, the corporate litigator's understanding of what it means to be ethical comes into play every time she determines what is a "legitimate" ground for objecting.

For this reason, corporate litigators' approaches to preparing for and defending depositions and responding to document requests provide insight into their ethical consciousness. However, it has proven difficult to get an empirical "fix" on the ethical norms corporate litigators employ in the discovery process. In a seminal study initiated by the Litigation Section of the American Bar Association (ABA), a team of legal scholars and social scientists investigated corporate litigators' ethics (Frenkel et al. 1998).[3] The study, which is commonly referred to as *Ethics: Beyond the Rules* (EBR), involved extensive individual and group interviews with partners and, separately, with associates working in five large law firms in each of two cities. The researchers interviewed 19 corporate litigators in an effort to understand their working ethics.[4] The researchers found corporate litigators' answer to most questions about what they believed was appropriate and inappropriate conduct in discovery was "it depends" (Suchman 1998, 870). This response is telling. It suggests that outside the extremes where there is broad consensus (e.g., it is unethical to advise a client to lie), corporate litigators generally do not bring a fixed set of ethical norms to

3. The six researchers (Douglas Frenkel, Robert Gordon, Carla Messikomer, Robert Nelson, Austin Sarat, and Mark Suchman) each wrote an article on the data collected. They are published under the general title *Ethics: Beyond the Rules* in an issue of the *Fordham Law Review* cited above.

4. The researchers also interviewed plaintiffs' lawyers, judges, and in-house counsel from the same cities.

their decision making in discovery. Instead, they place the possible discovery tactics along a spectrum—ranging from the most aggressive stance (meaning the least forthcoming and most obstructionist) to the most conciliatory stance (meaning the most forthcoming and cooperative) (851). What is proper and improper is determined situationally. That said, there are several situations in which corporate litigators employ tactics that they view as generally legitimate, in other words, as normatively appropriate. Below I explore corporate litigators' views about what is appropriate conduct in three distinct contexts.

Educating Witnesses

In civil litigation, each side is permitted to depose the opposing party and other witnesses. When preparing a witness for a deposition, a litigator confronts the question of whether and how to tell the witness what facts the law requires each party to establish to prevail on its claims or defenses. The litigator must also decide whether and when to tell the witness the "story" she hopes to tell based on the information she has pieced together from documents and other witnesses. Does the lawyer tell the witness what she understands happened before asking the witness what he remembers? Or does the lawyer ask the witness what he remembers and then inform him of what other witnesses and documents suggest happened? The ethical issue is, of course, that hearing either what the law requires or the lawyer's reconstruction of the story might influence the witness's recollection, consciously or unconsciously. The rules of professional conduct, the criminal law, and basic notions of procedural fairness prohibit a lawyer from telling a witness to lie and from knowingly allowing a witness to lie under oath (ABA Model Rules of Professional Conduct 3.3, 8.4). The EBR study found that corporate litigators have accepted this prohibition as a norm: They believe it is unethical to tell a witness to lie (Suchman 1998). Beyond these prohibitions, however, the rules provide little guidance for a litigator about what is appropriate conduct when preparing a witness for a deposition. Because witness preparation occurs behind closed doors, it rarely comes under scrutiny. As a result, litigators have little guidance from courts or disciplinary authorities about what might constitute "going too far" in witness preparation.

So what do corporate litigators believe is ethical conduct in this grey zone? Although giving a witness information before asking what he remembers may color the witness's memory and might even cause him, consciously or unconsciously, to change his story, most corporate litigators believe it is appropriate to "educate" the witness to some degree (Suchman 1998, 867). What corporate litigators considered appropriate education, however, was by no means consistent. Asked what they do—what conversation they have with a client to determine whether they had facts sufficient to support a claim that a document was protected from discovery by a recognized privilege (e.g., the attorney-client privilege)—corporate litigators described a variety of tactics:

1. Ask the client open ended questions without suggesting the answer that will favor the claim of privilege;
2. Ask . . . leading questions . . . designed to produce the favorable response;
3. Explain the legal consequences . . . and advise the client to tell the truth, whatever the consequences;
4. Explain the legal consequences . . . and leave entirely to the client the decision about whether to tell the truth;
5. Explain the legal consequences . . . and advise the client to tell the truth [with a warning explaining why he's likely to be discovered if he lies];
6. Explain the legal consequences . . . and try to establish whether the answer, true or false, is likely to be contradicted by anyone . . . or
7. [Characterize the decision as a strategic one to be made by the lawyer, and then ask questions about how the document was prepared that are designed to elicit support for the chosen end.] (Gordon 1998, 713–714)

Thus, most corporate litigators believe it is appropriate to provide a witness with some of the story of the case, although their approaches to educating witnesses vary. A partner explained, "It is important to remove as much doubt as you can [including] what the case is about [and] the contentions of the other party . . . to make sure that the witness understands the theory of the case on both sides" (Messikomer 1998, 744). What this partner "termed 'the incidental psychological effect' of hearing the defense's position, in his mind, was not a question of ethics" (744). These comments suggest corporate litigators do not identify witness preparation as an activity fraught with challenges. Why not?

Making Speaking Objections

Having prepared her witness for his deposition, the corporate litigator will then defend the deposition. Court rules in many jurisdictions prohibit a lawyer from making "speaking objections" during a deposition (Federal Rule of Civil Procedure 30(d)(1); Texas Rule of Civil Procedure 199(5)(e)). A speaking objection is often designed to communicate information to the witness about how he should answer the question. For instance, the opposing lawyer might ask the witness, "What was your understanding about the nature of Ms. West's complaints about her supervisor's conduct?" The corporate litigator might respond: "Objection, the question is vague. Are you asking about the witness's understanding before or after the meeting on March 2?" The objection communicates to the witness that his understanding may have been different before than it was after the meeting and that he should distinguish between the two in answering the question. Speaking objections are also used to remind a witness about something he appears to have forgotten, to clear up confusion, or to keep errant witnesses on message. Most corporate litigators view speaking objections as appropriate and necessary and make them regularly, even when court rules in their jurisdictions explicitly prohibit them (Suchman 1998). As one litigator explained, "An attorney isn't expected to stay away from these lines [between ethical and unethical conduct] and leave the witness out there alone. . . . You don't feel you're doing your job without speaking objections" (854). When litigators overstep the line, the rules prohibiting speaking objections are rarely enforced (Gordon 1998; Nelson 1998). As with their decisions relating to witness preparation, corporate litigators do not see the decision to use speaking objections, notwithstanding rules prohibiting them, as ethically charged. Again, the question is why not?

Responding to Document Requests

The rules of civil procedure and rules of professional conduct provide little specific guidance for lawyers responding to opposing parties' requests for production of documents. Rules of civil procedure allow a party to request that the opposing party produce documents in its possession. (For example, Federal Rule of Civil Procedure 26(b) is representative.) Once a request has been made, the responding party is usually obligated to produce documents responsive to the request unless (1) a privilege applies; (2) the request calls for irrelevant material; or (3) the request is duplicative, calls for the production of publicly available information, or compliance would be unreasonably burdensome. The rules of professional conduct prohibit a lawyer from "failing to make a reasonably diligent effort to comply with a legally proper discovery request from an opposing party" (Model Rule 3.4(d)).

Most corporate litigators report that they generally read discovery requests narrowly, thereby reducing the universe of "responsive" documents (Suchman 1998; Gallagher 2011). For instance, a document request might ask for all "correspondence relating to the development of product X." Reading the request narrowly, the corporate litigator might decline to produce internal company memoranda about the development of product X on the ground that internal memoranda are not "correspondence." An associate describes his experience as follows: "You're taught these things when you walk into the firm. You're taught to be aggressive and not just hand things over. The attitude is almost that they have to rip it out of your hands otherwise we're going to build up all sorts of roadblocks" (Suchman 1998, 863). William Gallagher's study of patent litigators (a specialized subset of litigators who often work in large law firms) reaffirms these findings. One of Gallagher's interviewees noted:

> I interpret requests as narrowly as possible. I see what they want but I'm not going to do his work for him. Make him be a good lawyer. They have to work to figure out what I'm objecting to, what I'm producing, whether my objections and interpretations are legitimate. That's being a good lawyer. If the other side is good, they'll figure it out. (Gallagher 2011, 321)

Further, most corporate litigators report that they believe it is ethically appropriate to withhold responsive documents as long as they assert an objection that signals to the opposing party that it is not receiving all of the documents requested (Suchman 1998). The litigator might do this by objecting to the request in its entirety on the grounds that it is overly broad and unduly burdensome and refusing to produce any documents. Alternatively, the litigator might object on the ground that the request is overly broad because it seeks documents created over a 10-year period and then, subject to that objection, produce only responsive documents created in the last two years, a period the lawyer has deemed reasonable. Most corporate litigators believe that withholding potentially relevant documents in this manner is perfectly appropriate because the objection signals to opposing counsel that relevant documents may have been withheld (Suchman 1998).

Thus, corporate litigators view their duty as a duty to send the right signals; they do not understand their duty as an obligation to be forthcoming with the information sought (Suchman 1998). Withholding without signaling would be unfair. But as long as the litigator sends an "honest" signal that she is withholding—e.g., "The defendant objects on the ground that the document request is overly broad"—she is acting ethically because she is not hiding the fact that she is not being forthcoming (Suchman 1998). One might expect that determining what constitutes an honest signal raises ethical issues for the corporate litigator: Does she explain that she is only producing documents about product X sold under a specific name? But corporate litigators do not tend to identify the task of deciding what signal to send as involving difficult ethical issues.

Corporate litigators believe that once they have sent the appropriate signal, it is up to opposing counsel to make a motion to compel (Suchman 1998). They cite the adversarial system as justification for this approach: It is not my responsibility to do the work of opposing counsel (870–871). In the corporate litigator's mind, having "tee[d] up" the issue with her signal, it is the opposing lawyer's responsibility to understand the rules of the discovery game and respond accordingly (871). He, in turn, must review the responses attentive to any such signals and, if necessary, pursue any information withheld through a motion to compel.

Opposing counsel may not pursue a motion to compel for a variety of reasons. He might decide not to pursue the information because he knows corporate litigators tend to withhold information almost reflexively, regardless of whether the information is helpful to the other side. Sometimes opposing counsel is too busy or lazy or does not have the resources to pursue the issue. Or, opposing counsel may not understand the signals being sent. In the latter instance, the ethical issue in the corporate litigator's mind is not that she failed to produce the requested information. Rather, it is her opponent's failure to understand the language of the discovery game (Suchman 1998, 867). An associate's remarks typify this view: "The lack of reaction by the plaintiff's attorneys to these responses borders on negligence. To just take these responses and see where they are going with this—I mean there are a lot of red flags that need responses" (866–867). In the corporate litigator's mind, having sent a signal, she has put the ball squarely in opposing counsel's court, and opposing counsel has an ethical duty to understand and respond zealously to that signal (Suchman 1998).

Thus, just as basketball players view fouling a player to prevent him from scoring a basket or to stop the clock as an acceptable tactical rules violation, corporate litigators view evasive responses to discovery requests as acceptable tactical lawyering. In basketball, the pervasive use of tactical fouling is seen as merely a part of the game, albeit a tool that changes the nature of the game—from one that is won or lost on a team's field goal scoring and defense to one that is often decided by a team's ability to master the tactical foul and foul shot. Likewise, corporate litigators view evasive responses to document requests as acceptable—as merely part of the "game" of complex and high-stakes litigation. As a result, corporate litigation risks becoming in both the corporate litigator's mind and in the end result a test of the corporate litigator's ability to craft evasive responses and her opponent's ability to detect the signs of evasion, rather than a test of the merits of the claims and defenses based on all of the relevant information.

Why is this conduct viewed as ethically uncontroversial in the corporate litigator's mind? Corporate litigators' notions of what it means to be ethical are shaped both by the nature of litigation and their role in that process and by their careers in their corporate firms. To understand the corporate litigator's ethical consciousness, we must explore both.

The Lessons Learned from Litigation Practice in Large Corporate Law Firms

The corporate litigator's approach to the discovery process is shaped by her experience and role as an advocate in the adversary system. In the common law system, litigators make arguments about how the law should be remade to resolve new factual issues that test and shape the law. Indeed, chief among the litigators' tasks is the job of making arguments about how the law should be remade and persuading judges to do so in ways that benefit their clients (Llewellyn 1930). In an elegant empirical study, Duffy Graham (2005) explores how litigators make sense of this work. Graham conducted in-depth interviews with eight litigators about how they see the world and the lessons they learned from litigation.[5] Graham's study indicates that litigators are acutely aware that the law is not fixed. They understand and embrace their roles as adversarial architects in the construction and deconstruction of the law's meaning (Graham 2005). From their first days in law school, litigators learn to argue both sides of a case (Llewellyn 1930). Throughout their careers, litigators come up with arguments that the courts should remake the law in ways that benefit their clients, and they anticipate and prepare to attack their opponents' counterarguments. The litigator's job is to exploit the law's lack of fixedness.

Testing Appearances Because Truth Is Ambiguous

Another core task that is particularly relevant to a litigator's understanding of her responsibility to truth is the litigator's role in constructing factual stories. From her earliest days in practice, a litigator is in the business of telling stories. As a litigator prepares a case, she begins to piece together the factual and legal

---

5. Throughout this section, I cite quotes from Graham's interviews to Graham as the source.

story she will tell. That story is constructed from documents created at the time of the events at issue and from the stories told by the client, the opposing party, and any witnesses. Through their experiences piecing together the story of what happened, litigators learn to be skeptical (Graham 2005). They learn that clients' claims to legal right or to the moral high ground are often over-stated and sometimes flat-out wrong. Further, clients' and witnesses' memories of the facts are often inconsistent. Sometimes clients or witnesses lie, but often they are not intentionally untruthful. Human memory is faulty, and litigators learn that what we see and how we make sense of what we see is shaped by our biases and self-interest. A litigator explains:

> You and I can stand at the intersection and watch a car wreck and your description could be completely different than mine, even if we're both impartial observers. So, you become used to the fact that there is surprisingly little that is completely, clearly, and unambiguously true. Or that you can establish as that. . . . [I]t's partly because it's a human process. Different people perceive things in different ways, colored by their self interest and their experiences . . . and so it can be surprisingly difficult to determine what the truth is and to get evidence and people agreeing on what the truth is. (Graham 2005, 110)

Another notes:

> From having taken hundreds of depositions and reviewed endless boxes of documents, I realize that memory is fallible and plastic. Most of us have the conceit that what we remember is accurate. Often it isn't, especially when there are strong incentives—generally money—or emotions tugging the recollections one way or another. (110–111)

Thus, the litigator learns that appearances are often deceiving, and it is her job to test appearances. Just as she does not accept her client's or the opposing party's version of events at face value, the litigator is skeptical of both sides' claims of legal right and wrong (Graham 2005). A client may have breached a contract, but the breach may not have caused the damages the plaintiff claims. The client's statements to the plaintiff at the time they negotiated the contract may suggest that an ambiguous term means something different than what the client now contends it means. Rather than accept either party's version of the facts or of legal and moral right and wrong on its face, the litigator delves into the messy complexities of human interactions (Graham 2005).

With her client's desired outcome in mind, the litigator reconstructs events. The story is not fiction, but rarely is it the precise story her client tells. Rarely does any client or witness know the entire truth. In fact, the litigator is acutely aware that we often cannot know the whole and precise truth about past events (Graham 2005). So the litigator constructs a story based on the best approximation of the events she can discern that will support her client's desired outcome. This may mean that a litigator defending an employer in a sexual harassment case elects not to focus her defense on her client's belief that the actions of the alleged perpetrator were welcomed. Instead, she may focus on the plaintiff-victim's failure to report the harassment to a supervisor who could have put an end to it. The litigation process teaches the litigator to be comfortable with a lack of complete certainty about the truth of what occurred, with ambiguity about legal fault, and with the task of constructing stories and explaining their meanings in the face of this uncertainty (Graham 2005).

This work encourages distinctive habits of mind. Because litigators generally assume that appearances belie the complexity of the interactions and situations underneath them, they develop the habit of testing appearances. Litigators do not appear to draw harsh judgments from this reality (Graham 2005). They recognize that (1) people see and understand situations through their own lenses, (2) the law is not fixed, and (3) rarely is a party entirely in the right or wrong (Graham 2005). This understanding allows the litigator to find arguments and stories she can believe in, even when her client appears, on the surface, to be in the wrong.

Embracing Moral Dissonance

Because they repeatedly encounter situations in which who is right and who is wrong is complicated and ambiguous, corporate litigators become comfortable with "moral dissonance"—an understanding that although a client may be in the legal or moral wrong in some respects, the other side rarely has an exclusive claim to the legal and moral high ground (Graham 2005, 83–107).[6] A litigator explains:

> I don't think I have ever, and maybe ever is a strong word, but nothing comes to mind where I ever thought a case I was involved in was that unambiguous. The importance of that, I think, is, for me at least . . . there has always been something that I can believe in about a client's case. . . . There's very

6. Graham notes that there are some exceptions whom his subjects refer to as "true believers" (106–107).

little that I've seen that I'd call black and white. . . . I haven't been able to find a situation where there wasn't something that I could fight for. (85)

Another litigator gives an example of the way in which the fact that right and wrong are often ambiguous gives him space to find arguments he can believe in:

> For example, in the environmental context, sometimes you have to represent the bad guy, the guy who caused the pollution. And what I've learned is that particularly in the environmental context, in many cases the regulators are taking such a strict position, such a stringent interpretation of a rule, that, in fact, yes, the client did do x, but, number one, it's clear that it wasn't intentional, number two, it's clear they did everything they could to prevent it, and number three, it's clear nobody got hurt. . . . So is it really appropriate to hit them with penalties that are going to cripple the company? . . . I guess all of this is a very long-winded way of saying it's a rare day that you can't find some moral ground that's worth defending for a client. (87–88)

The litigator's experience that truth and right and wrong are rarely unambiguous shapes her ethical consciousness. As one noted, "Being a litigator has taught me something about seeing both sides of an issue, even if I'm paid to argue only one. So I think a spirit of humility and skepticism is as close as I would come to a creed" (Graham 2005, 115). The habits of testing appearances and embracing moral dissonance evolve in conjunction with habits of mind that corporate litigators learn as they navigate their careers in their firms—identifying and following situation-appropriate norms and managing perceptions.

The Habits of Mind Encouraged by Work in Corporate Law Firms

My own study of lawyers working in today's corporate law firms reveals that to succeed and advance in those firms, lawyers must hone several essential skills (Kirkland 2005). I conducted confidential interviews with 22 corporate lawyers from 10 law firms ranging from 160 to over 1,000 lawyers.[7] Through these interviews, I explored whether and how work in large corporate law firms shapes lawyers' ethical consciousness.

---

7. These interviews were conducted between 2003 and 2005. I describe my methodology in detail in Kirkland (2005). The quotations from my interviews included here were originally published in that article.

My interviews revealed that corporate lawyers learn to identify and follow relevant "practice norms." Practice norms are the unwritten rules that govern their approaches to litigation: For instance, does the litigator adopt a cooperative, reasoned approach or an aggressive, no-holds-barred, take-no-prisoners approach to dealing with the other side and the court? The practice norms in use within corporate firms often vary across the firm, so corporate litigators must be able to identify the appropriate norms to follow in any given situation. In addition, corporate litigators must respond to the firm's management norms—the stated and unstated rules about lawyers' roles in the management of the firm. For example, management norms govern how much time lawyers devote to administrative tasks and whether lawyers need to be concerned with generating business. Management norms in corporate law firms can change frequently. As a result, corporate lawyers must learn to identify and respond to those changes.

Second, corporate lawyers must learn how to successfully manage the perceptions they create. Appearances have particular salience in the contemporary corporate law firm, where many lawyers do not know one another personally. For instance, in some situations a young lawyer might be expected to project an image of confidence and independence when doing something for the first time, while in others she might be expected to project a cautious and deferential image when facing a novel situation. As a result, understanding how one must be perceived in a given situation and being able to create that perception are crucial to advancement in today's corporate law firms. The habits of mind and skills corporate lawyers develop to navigate their careers in firms along with those they adopt in litigation shape their approaches to the ethical dilemmas they encounter in practice.

Identifying and Following Situation-Appropriate Norms

The business and structure of contemporary corporate law firms play a role in shaping corporate litigators' normative landscapes. Practice norms are, in part, a reflection of the way litigation work is organized and carried out in large firms. Litigation work in corporate law firms is organized hierarchically around cases, with a team made up of senior and junior lawyers assigned to each case. Work on a case is managed either by the equity partner who brought the work into the firm (sometimes referred to as the "finder") or by one of the finder's trusted colleagues, typically an equity or nonequity partner (the "binder"). The finder or binder overseeing the litigation (the "case manager") typically acts as the primary contact for the client and directs and supervises the work of the lawyers assigned to the case. A "minder," a senior associate or nonequity partner assigned to work for the case manager, does the bulk of the more complex work on the case (communicating with opposing counsel, taking and defending depositions, drafting pleadings, and often arguing motions), and one or more junior associates are usually assigned to work under the minder. That group makes up the "case team." Until these more junior lawyers can develop their own clients (a difficult task in a corporate law firm where the fee structure is prohibitive for all but the most successful corporations), they are entirely dependent on the finders and binders for work. For this reason, it is essential that junior corporate litigators build relationships with successful finders and binders so they will continue to invite them to work on their case teams. They do this by understanding and meeting their superiors' expectations. The first and most important expectation in most corporate firms is that corporate litigators "be available" to their superiors and to clients. A senior associate explained:

> Some associates don't understand or don't care what is expected. I leave my Blackberry on vibrate at night. One time I was working with [a partner] on a matter. At 2:00 a.m. I'm asleep . . . and my Blackberry goes off. It was this partner emailing me from the office. I got up and emailed a response. This went on for several nights. James [this associate's equity partner mentor] never asks for this explicitly but I know he wants it too. . . . [H]e wants me to return his emails over the weekend. He tells me he likes it that I have never turned him down when he asks for something" (#3).[8]

The pressure to be available does not necessarily end when a lawyer makes partner. Partners who do not generate their own work must be available to the finders who keep them busy. As one nonequity partner explained, "If you are not responsive to [the partners you service,] you are at risk. If you are not there, partners and clients find someone else and you are out" (#6).

A lawyer must also make sure the content of his response conforms to the norms the case manager employs. In the fluid environment of the contemporary corporate law firm, practice norms can be quite variable. Today, lawyers are unlikely to practice at one corporate law firm for their entire careers. Turnover among young associates is particularly high, but partners come and

---

8. Quotes from my interviews are demarcated with the number I assigned to the subject.

go as well. A partner with a profitable book of business is marketable and may be lured to a new firm by the promise that the new firm will value his practice more highly and compensate him more generously than his current firm does. Thus, partnerships in today's corporate firms include lawyers who have practiced at the firm for their entire careers, lawyers hired into the firm as lateral associates or partners, and lawyers who became part of the firm as a result of a merger with or acquisition of another firm. Because many partners in a firm will have "grown up" in other firms, they bring to the firm their own practice norms. Moreover, the sheer size of these firms ensures that the norms followed by numerous lawyers in offices spread across the globe will vary.

Young lawyers learn this from their earliest days at the firm. A former summer associate explained:

> The summer associates were assigned to work with a primary and secondary lawyer. The primary lawyer was a partner; the secondary lawyer was a more senior associate. The better associates would tell you, "this partner wants X, Y, and Z." For instance, there was a standard interoffice memo form, but you always had to check with the associate to make sure this partner wasn't looking for something different. Or the associate might tell you that although the partner said he wanted something back . . . in two weeks, he really wants it in two days (#13).

In addition to variations in expectations about written work, norms relating to interactions with opposing counsel may vary from partner to partner within a department or practice group. One litigation partner may be very aggressive with opposing counsel, refusing to agree to continuances or to schedule depositions cooperatively, while another may be more conciliatory. The same summer associate reported, "I watched associates take more aggressive stances with opponents [on certain cases] because that's what the partner on the case would do" (#13).

Being able to identify and follow superiors' practice norms continues to be important as a corporate litigator moves up the ladder. As lawyers become more experienced, they are expected to make decisions about strategy and tactics on their own. A senior litigation partner described the skills required of the lawyers working for her:

> For litigators the most difficult position is being in the middle between the senior partner and the associate. The associate just does what he or she is told. The minder is supposed to take part of the load off the senior person.

This means making some calls. [They] need to try to figure out what the senior partner would do and hope [they] were right (#18).

A senior associate observed, "A downstream lawyer may vary style depending on who he's working for: When working for a take-no-prisoners partner, err on the side of being more aggressive. . . . [E]ven the lawyers at the top of the food chain have to do this. If they have a really aggressive client, they adjust" (#8).

Changes in corporate law firms' relationships with their clients over the last 30 years increase the incentives for lawyers to "adjust" to their clients' expectations. In recent years, corporations have become far less loyal to corporate law firms (Nelson 1988; Galanter and Palay 1991). With the exception of highly specialized "bet the company" litigation and transactions, clients consider one corporate law firm's services to be as good as the next's (Nelson 1988; Galanter and Palay 1991). Consequently, in many cases, the most important factors in a client's decision about which firm to hire are price and the partner's relationship with in-house counsel (Kirkland 2005). Because in most firms an equity partner's compensation is tied closely to the profitability of her client relationships, having strong client relationships is essential (Nelson 1998). Profitable client relationships also make the partner attractive to other firms and thus marketable. Partners are acutely aware of clients' expectations with regard to practice norms and have strong incentives to adopt them (Sarat 1998, 828–829). The client may want the lawyer to be an "attack dog" or "hardball" litigator, meaning the client expects the litigator to be uncooperative and even contentious with opposing counsel (Nelson 1998, 778–779). Another client may expect the litigator to avoid unnecessary contentiousness to keep costs down.

As a result, it is imperative that corporate litigators working their way up the case team hierarchy develop the skill of identifying the appropriate practice norms to follow in any given situation (i.e., the norms of the superiors and clients they are working for and with at the time) (Kirkland 2005; Gallagher 2011). At the same time, corporate litigators must attend and respond to their firms' management norms.

The time and personnel required to manage today's corporate law firms is substantial. Layers of lawyer and nonlawyer managers are required to run the business of corporate firms. At the top are the firm's leaders (usually known as "managing partners" or "chairmen") who often give up their practices to become full-time managers. They set the direction of the firm—formulating the strategic plan that determines whether the firm will merge with or acquire other firms and whether to emphasize particular practice areas and deemphasize others. Corporate firms are organized by practice area into "practice groups." For instance, the firm's litigation department might include intellectual property litigation, securities litigation, and general business litigation practice groups.

Under the managing partners and department heads are lawyers who manage the practice groups (the practice group leaders or "PGLs"). PGLs must compete for a place in management's strategic plan. Decisions about which practice groups to emphasize are based on predictions about the future market for and likely profitability of those practices and the reputation and image management hopes to create for the firm. Practice groups that are highly valued in the firm's planning receive more of the firm's resources. Firm management is more likely to permit a practice group to hire lawyers and paralegals, to devote resources toward the group's marketing efforts, and to promote the group's associates and nonequity partners if the group is profitable and has a prominent place in the firm's strategic plan. This means PGLs must ensure that their groups are profitable and otherwise meet the management norms established by the firm's leaders.

Management norms, however, are not static. Expectations and priorities shift as management positions change hands and when those in power revise the plan. To maintain support for their practices, all firm lawyers must recognize when management's expectations are changing and respond to those new norms. A nonequity partner describes the "paradigm shifts" in his firm's management norms that have complicated his quest for equity partnership:

> During my first four years at the firm, there were two categories of lawyers . . . the people who brought in the work and the people who did the work. There was a paradigm shift [somewhere between] my five to ten year mark. Then the idea du jour was "everyone needs to bring in business." . . . "Everyone needs to become a rainmaker." If you didn't you were looked on negatively or forced out. I focused on rainmaking. I'm a good schmoozer. I brought in $400k as a [young] associate one year. . . . [Firm management] would ask me to be on panels for seminars for associates about rainmaking. I was . . . well regarded.
>
> In the last two to three years the idea du jour has been "driving work." Litigators are supposed to expand the business coming from existing clients (usually clients of other departments). Now we are being told "don't waste time rainmaking; litigators can't generate business." Now you need to be

the "go to guy" for a corporate guy who needs a litigator. [This puts me in a difficult position.] I haven't worked on establishing relationships within the firm and I don't want to be working for [a corporate partner]. I like autonomy. Every time the paradigm shifts it sends me into a tailspin (#9).

As they develop the skill of identifying and responding to varying practice and management norms, corporate litigators come to experience norms as mutable. They are not focused on judging the content of norms followed by the various senior lawyers in the firm or trying to harmonize them. Rather, the corporate litigator's habit of mind is to focus on whose norms to apply at any given time.

Managing Perceptions

Because markets for legal services can change radically and a lawyer's or practice group's likelihood of generating business is uncertain, many judgments in corporate firms are based on a mix of historical data, predictions about markets for legal services, and perceptions about the future profitability of individual lawyers and practice groups. As a result, corporate litigators become accustomed to being judged and judging one another on the basis of appearances and perceptions. To succeed, they must become skilled at discerning what appearances they need to project in a situation and in creating those perceptions.

Perceptions play a central role in decisions about who makes partner. Both the candidate for partnership and her practice group must create the appropriate perceptions for a candidate to be promoted. Most large corporate law firms are structured as two-tiered partnerships: a large group of nonequity partners and a smaller group of equity partners who share in the firm's profits (Galanter and Henderson 2008). It is very difficult to make equity partner in today's corporate firm. The ranks of the equity partnership are kept relatively small to maximize each partner's share. Firm managers worry that if they do not distribute sufficient profits to equity partners each year, they may lose profitable partners to other firms (Galanter and Henderson 2008). Thus, only candidates who have a powerful partner or practice group championing their cause will be promoted to equity partner. If a lawyer's practice group is not one that firm management is aiming to grow, it is unlikely that the firm will allocate coveted equity partnership seats to that group (Kirkland 2005). This means that PGLs must understand what perceptions they need to create to win a prominent place for the group in management's strategic plan, allowing them to garner resources and to advance their candidates for partnership. This also means luck is a significant factor in the quest for partnership. What is "hot" when a young lawyer entered the firm may well have lost favor in management's strategic plan 10 years later when the lawyer is being considered for partner.

Like the PGLs, candidates for partnership must create the right perceptions to be viable candidates for promotion. Most firms task committees with evaluating the candidates for partnership, and most members of the committee are unlikely to know candidates' work personally, given that lawyers working in corporate firms are often spread across offices around the world. A candidate must therefore create the perception that she is equity partner material. For instance, an equity partner described meetings with a number of nonequity partners about their objection to being paid less than several recent lateral hires. The equity partner noted that one of the nonequity partner's comments made him stand out as partnership material. The lawyer recalled that the other nonequity partners "whined" about the pay differential, but "[he] says to me, 'I'm upset and you can write down that I'm upset, but tell the guys at the top, I'll take a $50,000 pay cut if they will give me first chair in a trial for a Fortune 50 client. I can make a career out of that'" (#1).What indicated that this nonequity partner was equity partner material was not that he was any more qualified to first-chair a case involving a Fortune 50 client than the other nonequity partners—he was not. It was that he understood that it was appropriate in response to the pay discrepancy issue to project confidence and eagerness. He knew what perception he needed to create in the situation.

As corporate litigators attend to and manage the perceptions they create, they become accustomed to judging others on appearances, notwithstanding their knowledge that the other lawyers in the firm are managing perceptions as well. In the corporate litigator's mind, the fact that both in litigation and in their firms, decisions are made on the basis of perceptions and not on objective truth is accepted and unremarkable. In litigation, corporate litigators learn to view the truth as ambiguous. That ambiguity requires them to reconstruct the truth and permits them to offer a version of truth that puts their clients' claims in a favorable light that makes those claims appear meritorious. In their firms, corporate litigators rely on advantageous appearances as well. They learn to assert versions of themselves that will lead to favorable career advancement, and they evaluate those around them on similar grounds. In both cases, they accept that judgments are made on the basis of appearances, but they frame the appearances they construct as claims of truth.

To laypeople, asserting claims of truth while disbelieving the existence of truth—or that the truth can be accurately ascertained—might seem problematic. But corporate litigators are comfortable with this task. Recognizing the truth as ambiguous, they see no ethical tension in relying on those aspects of possible truth that are most favorable to their clients. Perceptions and reconstructed truths are the currency of their world: They operate in a legal system that is admittedly imperfect but that succeeds in accomplishing necessary tasks, including resolving disputes through corporate litigation and facilitating career development within corporate firms.

In addition, the task of litigating leads corporate litigators to view claims to legal and moral right with skepticism. At the same time, they learn that within their firms, norms are mutable. The fact that one partner sitting atop one case hierarchy believes it is entirely appropriate and perhaps imperative to take an aggressive stance with opposing counsel, while the partner sitting atop another might see that approach as improper, is less likely to be disconcerting to a corporate litigator who views right and wrong as complex, often ambiguous notions, and who has learned to exercise restraint in judgment about who is right and who is wrong. The corporate litigator's willingness to embrace moral dissonance likely makes a world in which norms are viewed as mutable less remarkable. These habits of mind shape the corporate litigator's ethical consciousness; that consciousness then frames her approach to ethical decision making in discovery.

Conclusion

The corporate litigator sees herself as the architect of the story of her client's case. It is her job to know all the versions of the facts and all of the arguments about the law. It is also her job to resist accepting anyone's version of the facts or the law or legal right and wrong—even her client's—at face value. She collects information and makes judgments about what happened and how best to interpret the meaning of events to meet her client's ends. Eventually, she will know the "story" better and have a better read on its legal meaning than her client and any of the witnesses.

Reconstructing a credible version of events and, from that, crafting a story that achieves a client's legal ends is an active and messy pursuit. It requires the corporate litigator to make calls about what is true and what is not, and what is credible and what is not. In this context, deciding whether and when to tell one's client some or all of what others have said before asking what the client remembers is not likely to have the same ethical significance as it might to someone not accustomed to taking charge of reconstructing truth on a daily basis. Even if the corporate litigator appreciates the potential ethical pitfalls of telling a witness what other witnesses or documents say about a topic before asking what he remembers, she is likely to view doing so as a necessary method of reconciling disparate versions of truth coming from a number of sources. An outsider might see this as an effort to manipulate the truth or as a tactic so impossibly fraught with the danger of influencing the witness's story as to make it illegitimate. But corporate litigators are not trained to attend to an obligation to abstract notions of truth as they reconstruct stories advantageous to their clients. Recalling an earlier stage in her career as a large firm litigator, a federal judge interviewed in the EBR study explained, "I never learned or believed that my role [as a defense litigator] was to find the truth and provide complete disclosure" (Messikomer 1998, 762).

The practice of making speaking objections is also consistent with the lessons the litigator derives from litigating. Witnesses can forget important, even crucial facts under the pressure of opposing counsel's questions at a deposition. A clever opposing counsel may word a question in such a way that the witness ends up testifying to something he does not mean to say or believe. Opposing counsel may rattle the witness causing him to answer carelessly. Speaking objections allow the corporate litigator to protect the client from some factors that might impair his ability to testify consistent with the story the litigator has reconstructed. As a result, some corporate litigators violate rules that forbid the use of speaking objections with a clear conscience. This approach is notable for two reasons. First, while the use of speaking objections might be justified to help an embattled witness remember the facts, using speaking objections to encourage a witness to testify on message, contrary to his own memory, violates the notion that an advocate has a responsibility to the truth of the dispute. That said, litigators do not appear to focus on discerning the former situation from the latter when deciding whether to make a speaking objection. Rather, the corporate litigator approaches these decisions with a sense that truth is ambiguous and a view that her primary obligation is to zealously represent and protect her client. Second, corporate litigators' approaches indicate that they see the court rules prohibiting speaking objections, which are rarely enforced, as guidelines, not as articulations of right and wrong, ethical and unethical conduct. This is not surprising given that corporate litigators must regularly identify and follow varying practice norms and changing management norms in order to please their superiors and, as a result, are accustomed to viewing norms as elastic.

Corporate litigators generally believe that when responding to document requests, their ethical responsibility is to send the appropriate signals to the other side, rather than to be forthcoming. Mark Suchman, one of the EBR researchers, characterized the corporate litigator's guiding professional ideal as residing in a notion of a "ritualized adversary contest . . . [and] the nobility of a game well played" (1998, 870–871). This view is consonant with both (1) the premium placed on creating the right perceptions within corporate firms and (2) the view that norms are mutable. Thus, the ability to determine what norm is appropriate to follow is paramount. Judging the content of norms is not.

As discussed above, corporate litigators deal in perceptions in their firms every day. They know that those who are unable to discern the appropriate appearance to project in a given situation will not succeed. Likewise, litigators engaged in discovery are expected to be adept at reading and understanding the significance of signals. In this context it is also unsurprising that when asked about the ethics of responding to document requests, corporate litigators focus on whether they signal that they are not producing all documents rather than the "content" of their action: an evasive response. Thus, the habits of mind corporate litigators adopt in their firms are as evident in their approaches to document requests as they are in their approaches to preparing witnesses for and defending depositions.

Notably, corporate litigators' approaches to discovery may vary with their seniority. Several associates interviewed in the EBR study agreed, "It is the younger partners . . . who tend to be the most aggressive in the discovery process, and who are most prone to engage in the calculated withholding of documents and in fierce discovery fights" (Suchman 1998, 747). This suggests that when she draws lines within the discretionary grey zone of ethical decision making in discovery, the corporate litigator's ethical consciousness leaves room for the influence of other factors. Midlevel partners came of age in their firms at a time when clients were becoming increasingly less loyal to corporate firms and the pressure for partners to generate business was increasing. Gallagher (2011, 331) notes that the patent litigators he interviewed reported that their clients "exert a great deal of influence over how discovery is done."

Corporate litigators see their tactics—even those that violate court rules—as legitimate because they believe they are consistent with their duty to protect their clients and they conform to their ideal of an adversarial game well played. And although, or perhaps because, corporate litigators know that "truth" in litigation is necessarily an imperfect, constructed truth, corporate litigators do not appear to regularly engage in a conscious balancing of their roles as advocates with their obligations to refrain from obstructing or impeding the truth-seeking function of the adversary system. Corporate litigators do not regularly ask themselves or discuss with one another, "How do I pursue and protect my client's interests when responding to this document request without obstructing the process or the truth-seeking goals of the system?" They are not taught to do so. Rather, they are focused on and rewarded for successfully discerning and employing the practice norms of the partner in charge of the case team and the client. They do so in a world where the incentives for partners to please clients and to win are greater than ever.

Thus, corporate litigators do not routinely question and test the stories they tell themselves and others about their conduct, cognizant of the incentives and pressures that are likely to influence their ethical decisions. In other words, while corporate litigators approach the stories their clients and others tell and the claims they make with skepticism, they do not bring the same skepticism to their own conduct when educating witnesses, making speaking objections, and responding to document requests.

References

Brazil, Wayne. 1980. "Views from the Front Lines: Observations by Chicago Lawyers about the System of Civil Discovery." *American Bar Foundation Research Journal* 1980:217–251.

Frenkel, Douglas N., Robert W. Gordon, Carla Messikomer, Robert L. Nelson, Austin Sarat, and Mark C. Suchman. 1998. "Report: Ethics: Beyond the Rules." *Fordham Law Review* 67:691–895.

Galanter, Marc, and William D. Henderson. 2008. "The Elastic Tournament: A Second Transformation of the Big Law Firm." *Stanford Law Review* 60:1867–1929.

Galanter, Marc, and Thomas Palay. 1991. *Tournament of Lawyers: The Transformation of the Big Law Firm*. Chicago: University of Chicago Press.

Gallagher, William T. 2011. "IP Legal Ethics in the Everyday Practice of Law: An Empirical Perspective on Patent Litigators." *John Marshall Review of Intellectual Property Law* 10:309–364.

Graham, Duffy. 2005. *The Consciousness of the Litigator*. Ann Arbor: University of Michigan Press.

Gordon, Robert W. 1998. "The Ethical Worlds of Large Firm Litigators: Preliminary Observations." *Fordham Law Review* 67:709–738.

Kirkland, Kimberly. 2005. "Ethics in Large Law Firms: The Principle of Pragmatism." *University of Memphis Law Review* 35:631–730.

Llewellyn, Karl. 1930. *The Bramble Bush*. New York: Columbia University School of Law.

Messikomer, Carla. 1998. "Ambivalence, Contradiction, and Ambiguity: The Everyday Ethics of Defense Litigators." *Fordham Law Review* 67:739–770.

Nelson, Robert L. 1988. *Partners with Power: The Social Transformation of the Large Law Firm*. Berkeley: University of California Press.

———. 1998. "The Discovery Process as a Circle of Blame: Institutional, Professional and Socio-economic Factors That Contribute to Unreasonable, Inefficient, and Amoral Behavior in Corporate Litigation." *Fordham Law Review* 67:773–808.

Sarat, Austin. 1998. "Enactments of Professionalism: A Study of Lawyers' and Judges' Accounts of Ethics and Civility in Litigation." *Fordham Law Review* 67:809–836.

Suchman, Mark C. 1998. "Working Without a Net: The Sociology of Legal Ethics in Corporate Litigation." *Fordham Law Review* 67:837–874.

Rules

Federal Rules of Civil Procedure 26(b), 30(d)(1) (2010).

Texas Rules of Civil Procedure 199(5)(e) (2010).

Transnational Lawyering

Clients, Ethics, and Regulation

John Flood

Transnational lawyering is a field dominated by the large law firms and their lawyers. With transactions measured in the billions of dollars, these deals often fall into the "bet the house" category, which means it is not the occasion to try out a new law firm. The risk of experimentation comes at too high a cost. Transnational lawyering does not fit the normal categories of lawyering. The following is typical. Santander, a Spanish bank, listed its Brazilian subsidiary on the Sao Paulo stock exchange for $8 billion (McLeod-Roberts 2009). The New York law firm of Shearman & Sterling acted for the syndicate banks leading the deal (Santander Investment, Credit Suisse, BoA Merrill Lynch, UBS, and BTG Pactual). Davis Polk & Wardwell, another New York law firm, advised Santander in Spain. Even though Shearman had acted for Santander in Brazil for a number of years, the bank wanted its Spanish advisers to work with it, so Shearman switched sides in the deal. Two Brazilian firms advised on local law; and the in-house lawyers at Santander also worked on the deal. What is worth noting here is that this deal, picked at random, is not unusual. The law firms are essentially New York firms with international practices: Davis Polk has a Madrid office, and Shearman has one in Sao Paulo; and the lawyers are a mix of local and American. The local law firms in Brazil and the in-house lawyers in Santander were used for minor matters. These types of transactions commonly use large law firms from New York or London, or possibly from one of the other major world metropolises.

It is difficult to isolate the economic contribution of transnational law practice, but since it is primarily the realm of the large law firms, we can examine their contributions. In the United States, net legal exports amounted to $5.4 billion (US Bureau of Economic Analysis 2009). The largest US law firms earned

$65 billion in 2009 (Press and Mulligan 2010). In the UK, law firm exports totaled $463.7 million, and the largest 100 law firms generated fee income of $22 billion in 2007–2008 (IFSL Research 2009, 2).[1] When taken to the global level, the Global 50 law firms earned revenues of over $86 billion in 2007–2008 (2). Of this, UK law firms generated 20% of the Global 50 revenues while US firms brought in nearly 60% (2). Nearly 40% of this revenue came from corporate and finance work, and dispute resolution produced 28% (5).

The scale and size of these international law firms outstrips their predecessors. The largest global law firm, Baker & McKenzie, has 3,750 lawyers with offices in 69 countries (Baker & McKenzie 2011). Clifford Chance has 3,200 lawyers with 33 offices in 23 countries (Clifford Chance 2011). And the next 15 firms have over 1,400 lawyers each, and their revenues are each in excess of $1.6 billion (IFSL Research 2009, 5). However, even the largest law firms pale in comparison with the scale of the accounting firms. For example, PricewaterhouseCoopers has approximately 163,500 professionals in over 750 offices in 151 countries (PricewaterhouseCoopers 2009).

This chapter is presented in three sections. The first lays out the theoretical issues involved in analyzing transnational law and law firms. The second sets out examples where the culture of transnational lawyering can be seen more closely. In the third, I focus on two ethical issues. Case study 1 concerns conflicts of interest, but in a different way than is normally presented in professional responsibility texts. Case study 2 deals with the problem of lawyers' truth telling. While there is no explicit rule that says a lawyer must tell the truth, we have to consider to what extent the ethics of professionalism might impel lawyers toward appropriate behavior. And finally, I address whether we can expect a more rigorous form of ethical behavior from lawyers or whether we are being overly optimistic in our expectations.

It is important to explain my methodology. The world of large law firms has become increasingly popular among sociolegal scholars in recent years. This is matched by two other developments. One is a burgeoning legal trade press that reports on large firms, such as *American Lawyer, International Financial Law Review,* and *Legal Week.* These publications report on deals done, law firm

---

1. In describing the Lord Mayor of London, Sir David Lewis, Abramson (2008, 6) writes: "Crucially, being a lawyer has allowed David added facility in *selling English law* and our sophisticated dispute resolution regime to companies in other countries. . . . When travelling, he always sees the local Minister of Justice, a superb opportunity to discuss relevant legal issues of the day. *The English legal system therefore becomes one further exportable item,* an immediately apparent added benefit of having a solicitor in the Mansion House" (emphasis added).

mergers, partners' remuneration, and partners' defections from firms. They are a mine of information. The second development is that large law firms have opened up to allow themselves to become sites of research. Some scholars have been able to observe the workings of large law firms; others have interviewed law firm partners. In my research, I have done both. The data in this chapter's case studies are based on interviews with three law firm partners who were actively involved in the cases. The background for the chapter depends on interviews I have carried out with hundreds of lawyers over a number of years. I selected these cases because they are more or less typical of the work being done by transnational lawyers and are rarely viewed by these lawyers as ethically problematic. It is in the ordinary course of work that we perceive how "good people can do dirty work" (Hughes 1958, 49–50).

Background to Transnational Lawyering

Jonathan Goldsmith, secretary general of the Council of Bars and Law Societies of Europe (CCBE), provides a telling anecdote of meeting a Flemish large law firm lawyer in Brussels who said, "There is no more idea of service to a client. It is all just billable hours. We are machines for making money. We use [forms] that have been agreed at head office. . . . The values have gone out of our lives" (Goldsmith 2008, 445). The quotation is important for a number of reasons that are relevant to this chapter. It tells us how law firms function; it tells us about the autonomy of professionals; it tells us about lawyer-client relationships; and it tells us about values and ethics. Let me deconstruct this.

Before transnational lawyering became an established field with the rise of globalization in the late twentieth century, it had an important role in world commerce. The mid-nineteenth century gave rise to the railroads that were being constructed in all parts of the world—the United Kingdom, Canada, Mexico, the United States, Argentina, South Africa, and India, to name just a few locations. Much of the financing came from the major capital markets, of which London was the prime (Cassis 2006). Corporate lawyers were intimately involved in the promotion of the companies that built the railroads and with the banks that were financing them (Flood 2011a). As the focus of capital markets oscillated between London and New York, the legal industries that serviced them grew and spread as their clients demanded.

A few law firms started with an international dimension to their characters. The late Coudert Brothers originated in Paris and New York in the 1850s, specializing in international law. The most distinctive approach to international law practice was that taken by Russell Baker with the formation of Baker & McKenzie in 1949 (Bauman 1999). Baker was taken with the internationalist viewpoint of his professors at the University of Chicago in the 1920s. The Chicago-based law firm was predicated on a deliberate internationalist model backed up by a profitable domestic insurance practice. Baker realized he could exploit certain provisions of the US Tax Code designed to assist trade with Latin America. By establishing foreign subsidiaries, US companies could make considerable savings. Baker actively marketed this legal "knowledge" to his clients, which led to the establishment of Baker & McKenzie offices in Latin America and later elsewhere (Bauman 1999).

Most other law firms that expanded overseas were less calculating and let circumstance dictate their moves. Some notable law firms—for example, Wachtell, Lipton, Rosen & Katz (New York), Cravath, Swaine & Moore (New York), and Slaughter & May (London)—refused to open overseas offices or did so only in limited circumstances. Yet all major law firms engage in transnational lawyering regardless of their office locations. Those with no or few offices outside their parent countries use networks or "best friends" where they ally with foreign firms on a repeat basis to obtain local capabilities (Morgan and Quack 2005).

Carole Silver (2002) has further shown a marked reluctance by US lawyers to move overseas, unless for a fixed term, although the credit crisis is changing attitudes toward working outside the United States (Bringardner 2008). While it is necessary for US law firms to export some lawyers to head a foreign office, the majority of the firms' employees tend to be locally trained lawyers (Faulconbridge and Muzio 2008). Here there is a distinct difference between the legal professions of the United Kingdom and the United States. The United Kingdom has a long tradition of exporting lawyers overseas, partly because of the empire's needs and partly because of globalization (Flood 2011b). It is estimated that there are in excess of 6,000 UK solicitors in practice overseas (Law Society 2011).

What underlies the law firms' success? As the investment banks sought new markets, they relied on the law they were used to: New York and English law. For finance, therefore, these two forms of law became dominant, the new *lex mercatoria* (Flood 2007). To be somewhat skeptical, it is reasonable to say that institutional laziness (or path dependency) impelled these legal systems to the top rather than any inherent legal superiority. It enabled a global reach across multiple legal jurisdictions at relatively low cost. The problem of the local jurisdiction was not totally removed, but at least it was contained. Perhaps this is best summarized rather whimsically by one in-house counsel who said, "Like all good professionals we make it up as we go along and hide our copy of *Libyan Law for Dummies* under a pile of learned papers" (Smith 2009, 16).

The Anglo-American hegemony is reinforced by the use of standardized documentation in transactions, either of a particular firm or of the organizations that promote standardized documents, such as the Loan Market Association (LMA), which is a European trade association for syndicated loan markets. Its membership includes banks, investors, law firms, and rating agencies, among others (Loan Market Association 2011). Another key organization is the International Swaps and Derivatives Association (ISDA), which has 820 institutional members around the world including corporations, government bodies, and professional service firms who subscribe to a master agreement and other documentation originated by the ISDA (ISDA 2011). Certain law firms such as Allen & Overy and Cravath, Swaine & Moore have formed close links with the ISDA and are intricately involved in the drafting of its documents. We can even portray the product of organizations like the LMA and ISDA as a new form of internationally accepted law or regulation by best practice, given their almost universal adoption. But what is critical for the discussion here is that this new law has been created by the US and UK large law firms that practice it. This gives them a powerful advantage in global law beyond most others.

Large law firms have become institutions riven by their success. Not many international law firms would be able to fit their partners in one room. The traditional notions of collegial partnerships have transformed into a form now referred to as the MPB, the managed professional bureaucracy (Hinings, Greenwood, and Cooper 1999). This is a structured, hierarchical organization that depends less on external inputs and more on its own modes of production. With the introduction of finance management, IT and human resources departments, law firms place more emphasis on their own in-house training and value creation as in the cases of continuing legal education and preliminary training of associates. They even train lawyers how to become and behave as partners as they approach the partnership decision. Emmanuel Lazega (2001), in his study of a New England corporate law firm, showed how law firms were internally competitive institutions in which niche groups of partners competed with each other over scarce resources such as associates and clients. Associates are assigned to partners who are busiest; conflicts involving different partners' clients would be resolved in favor of rainmakers. These struggles enable the firm to hold onto its members but also force them to defect if necessary. With increasing bureaucratic control, however, comes greater internal regulation of action and behavior. The effect of the growth of the law firm is to diminish professional autonomy while instead permitting only degrees of discretion in behavior, as Goldsmith's Flemish lawyer suggests. Business targets, billable hours, and so forth become determinants of a continuing career for corporate lawyers.

Perhaps the most contentious part of corporate lawyers' existence is their relationship to the client. Most professional rules of conduct depict the relationship as dyadic, one on one, and most are presented that way, especially in the media. Yet, in corporate law it is not so straightforward. In chapter 7, Herbert Kritzer refers to Heinz and Laumann's (1982) two hemispheres of the legal profession and notes that the corporate part is more prone to client pressures than the individual one. Then in his analysis of insurance lawyers and their clients, he introduces new dimensions of an "in between" sort: in his case, the role of the insurer and the conflicts that portends because of business tensions. With transactional and transnational lawyers, similar tensions and conflicts exist. The example of a transaction I gave at the beginning of the chapter is typical in that capital markets revolve around a set of enduring relationships between lawyers and investment banks. If clients are borrowers or developers, then we are in a similar relationship to Kritzer's insurance clients. In this case, the relationship is tripartite between bank-lawyer-client (Flood 2009). But the question remains: Who is the client?

Let me provide one example in which the relationship becomes confounded. A large law firm banking lawyer told me that a corporate client was introduced to his London firm by an investment bank that the client had asked for funding. The bank had told the client, who was borrowing to finance a business expansion, that the client's usual law firm was too small to work with the bank and that the bank's usual law firm had more experience with this type of transaction. The lawyer told the "new" client that since more funding would inevitably be needed as his business grew, he might as well transfer all his company's legal business from its normal law firm so as to save time and effort in the future. The implication was that to continue to obtain funding, this new lawyer-client relationship would have to continue. It was a classic "bait and switch" operation for the benefit of the bank and the new law firm, which gained a potential raft of new business at the expense of the client's prior lawyer-client relationship.

The Ethics and Regulation of Transnational Practice

The transnationalization of law and legal practice now appears on the syllabus in law schools. While both US and UK legal education have regulated curricula, they have significant degrees of freedom in how their courses are delivered and what they contain (Silver 2006). Their freedom has been particularly exploited at the master's level where myriad LLM programs have flourished to tap into the perceived need for specialist expertise or knowledge of other legal systems (Silver 2006). These programs have attracted large numbers of civil law–trained lawyers to UK and US law schools as their own civil law schools have traditionally not been able to offer courses on, for example, the globalization of law (Silver 2006). Observation of European law firms now shows that as many as a third of the junior lawyers have such LLMs (Muzio, Faulconbridge, and Cook, forthcoming).[2]

One essential component of legal education is the teaching of professional responsibility or legal ethics. Such teaching varies enormously from country to country with different principles imparted to students (Moore 2007). Moore argues that US lawyers are caught in the double deontological trap[3]: Their home rules and their host rules are often quite different. For example, conflicts of interest rules in the United Kingdom are more relaxed than in the United States (see case study 1 below); in-house counsel privilege is not the same in Europe as in the United States (*Akzo Nobel Chemicals Ltd. v. Commission*, 2010); unauthorized practice of law rules vary widely from country to country (in the United Kingdom they hardly exist). To which rules does the lawyer adhere? If they are contradictory, the lawyer is in a Catch-22 situation, with no escape.[4] Legal education reflects those differences. In Europe, professional responsibility is not given the same attention as in the US classroom. For example, in the United Kingdom, legal ethics is "taught" during the Legal Practice Course (a one-year postgraduate vocational course for aspiring solicitors). It is, however, a "pervasive" topic, one that arises from time to time during the year's teaching in whatever subject is being studied at the time. It has no defined identity in the curriculum as in US professional responsibility courses and has only a

2. Many of these previously conservative countries' law schools (e.g., China, Germany, and Italy) are now offering their own LLM programs in English (Vanistendael 2004).

3. See Nagel (2007) for an explanation of how this affects US and UK lawyers in the European context.

4. For an attempt at providing guidelines, see, e.g., IBA Conflicts of Interest Subcommittee (2010).

small examination, but nothing on the scale found in the United States (SRA 2009, 20). We should also note, however, that professional responsibility is not a compulsory course for LLM students in either country.

The formal professional rules do not provide much guidance to lawyers. Most of the English rules under the Solicitors' Code of Conduct apply to overseas practice without setting up any arduous requirements (Rule 15). Likewise, Rule 5.5 of the American Bar Association (ABA) Model Rules of Professional Conduct simply states, "A lawyer shall not practice law in a jurisdiction in violation of the regulation of the legal profession in that jurisdiction, or assist another in doing so." Essentially, the core of the English and American rules applies to law firms wherever they practice. However, if a US lawyer practices US law in the United Kingdom without becoming a registered foreign lawyer or becoming a solicitor, then he or she is not subject to English disciplinary rules or regulation. The United States takes a different view: For example, New York State subjects foreign legal consultants working in New York to state discipline, even though they are not practicing New York law.[5]

The English and American jurisdictions introduced their professional codes at different times. The ABA adopted its first canons in 1908, but the Law Society did not acquire rulemaking powers until 1933, and its first code did not appear until the 1960s. Its first complete professional code only appeared in 2007 and will soon be superseded by a new one that acknowledges the challenges of international practice (Boon and Levin 2008). The prospect of being a transnational lawyer or a global lawyer is a daunting one as lawyers wend their ways through the maze of conflicting rules that govern their working lives. This comes about because of the nascent state of global law and its regulation, which has not yet reached maturity so the necessary institutions are still to be created (Goff 2007). Nevertheless, the major Anglo-American law firms have begun to navigate their way in global practice. The result, perhaps a perverse one, is that lawyers inside these firms *do not think* about cross-border ethical issues because of their intrinsic complexity and the pressures of work: This has instead become the responsibility of firms' own general counsel. For example, London's Allen & Overy has 15 general in-house counsel who deal with rules and general compliance (Denyer 2010; Parker 1999, 184).

The next section examines examples of the intricacies of transnational lawyering and some of the ethical concerns that arise, looking at what happens

5. McKinney's New York Rules of Court, Rules of the Court of Appeals for the Licensing of Legal Consultants, pt. 521 (2011).

inside these deals. The first two occurred inside UK law firms, but the problems and difficulties they illustrate are not unique to that country. I make reference to US and English rules where appropriate.

Case Studies of Transnational Lawyering

Is There Such a Thing as a Conflict of Interest?
In 2005 Celtel, a Dutch telecommunications company with 5.3 million cellphone subscribers in Africa, sold 85% of its company to one of the Middle East's largest telecoms companies, MTC of Kuwait. The key lawyers in the transaction were the international law firms of Clifford Chance, which acted for MTC, and Linklaters, which acted for Celtel, but as we shall see from the discussion below, these lawyer-client relationships are not always fixed. As previously noted, Clifford Chance has 3,200 lawyers operating in 33 offices across 23 countries (Clifford Chance 2010). Linklaters has 2,200 lawyers with 26 offices in 19 countries (Linklaters 2010). Given the size of these global law firms, it is no surprise that lawyer mobility is high and that transfers between firms of this scale are frequent and common, and therefore the potential for conflicts of interest is wide open.

As the *Lawyer* reported (O'Connor 2005), Celtel was "Sub-Saharan Africa's largest mobile provider, with coverage in 13 countries and more than five million subscribers." MTC, the buyer, had operations in Kuwait, Iraq, Jordan, and Lebanon. Tim Schwarz of Linklaters said:

> MTC has what it calls its "three-by-three-by-three strategy." During the first three years—from 2002 to 2005—it invested in its home region. In the second three years it began to invest in its surrounding neighbourhood, buying Celtel. It's the third three years that will be the most interesting. That's when it plans to go global. It will be very interesting to see whether it makes it. (Byrne 2006)

This deal was occurring in the second phase of MTC's strategy. MTC approached Clifford Chance's Dubai office, which worked on the deal in conjunction with the firm's London office. In this deal, Celtel asked an investment bank, Goldman Sachs, to run a controlled auction. According to MTC's lawyer, a partner in a large London law firm whom I interviewed, the bank sent letters "to anyone they could think of who might be interested in buying this business. Any mobile operator, any telecoms company, and private equity houses as well." The MTC lawyer explained further: "You start by getting the investment banks running the deals from London. And because they are based in London they will turn to the English firms because we have some of the biggest firms in the world and that means with size comes depth of experience. Sophistication naturally resides here."

In the first stage, the investment bank, on behalf of Celtel, approached around 100 companies with a rough outline of the deal. The next stage was for the sellers to select, out of a field of 10 to 20, four who would submit binding offers. This would go to a final stage in which two bidders would negotiate the final terms. The final sale price was $3.4 billion. There is always a possibility that this kind of deal could turn sour and fail to complete. In part this is due to the complexity of the funding arrangements required to be in place for this size of transaction to go through. These transactions usually involve leverage, that is, other people's money or debt, and therefore all types of guarantees have to be arranged, default conditions prepared for, and more. This particular transaction was being funded by loans from four banks in the Middle East, the United Kingdom, Switzerland, and the United States, namely, National Bank of Kuwait, UBS, Credit Suisse First Boston, and Barclays, all of which were represented by a single law firm in London, Allen & Overy. Allen & Overy would have to ensure that the banks' interests were protected under English law. If the sale were to fail, the vendor's lawyers were running a parallel track with the sale to place an initial public offering in the market. The hope was that the IPO would be unnecessary.

Although the operations were based in Africa, Celtel was headquartered in the Netherlands. No African country had the scale or sophistication in its legal market to handle such a large transaction. However, some local African law firms were used during the due diligence process to monitor minor regulatory matters. One UK lawyer stated that "it used to be the case that there was little or no in-house regulatory capacity at many of the telecoms companies. Increasingly they've skilled up" (Byrne 2006). Local contracts would be investigated by the UK lawyers, however, on the basis that the content would be the issue—and not the law—and that the content would be too complex for local lawyers. Moreover, as English lawyers, they naturally used English law. But as the MTC lawyer remarked in our interview:

> We need a lingua franca and that's English law. The governing law of a transaction—a share acquisition—doesn't really matter that much. The

terms and mechanisms are pretty much identical regardless of whether it's English, German, French or Dutch law. Obviously you take account of the peculiarities of national law but the agreements will look the same and they will all be in the English language, even in France where it's technically illegal. But people pay the 300 euro fine and don't mind.

In this transaction, even though Celtel had 16 operating subsidiaries, what was actually bought was a single block of shares in a Dutch company. The share purchase agreement was done under English law while various minor ancillary elements, such as the transfer documents which were Dutch shares, had to be done under Dutch law. The MTC lawyer said that usually share purchase agreements would be done under local law, but this was an exception because although Celtel was Dutch, the business was pan-African and there were more than 100 shareholders who came from a variety of locations. And the purchasers came from different places, so English law provided a common locus. In this respect, the varieties of laws in play were significant as far as the regulatory issues were concerned, but to the overall structure of the transaction they were relatively insignificant.

The transaction therefore was a combination of relatively simple corporate law issues, complex regulatory matters, and complicated financing and tax issues. The lawyers' tasks were to bring these together into a set of coherent structures, which enabled the parties to complete their transactions under a range of headings that included private and state concerns. It helped that the lawyers from the different law firms were used to working with one another and that they were used to working with the investment banks. The enduring institutional relationships and networks were a vital key to the success of the transaction.

Yet these relationships were not quite as straightforward as they appeared. Clifford Chance had a long-standing relationship with the acquirer, MTC, which is not unusual, but it had also advised Celtel some years previously on its plans to go public (O'Connor 2005). On the other side of the table was Linklaters for Celtel, with whom Linklaters had an established relationship. And, as mentioned, the four banks were all represented by Allen & Overy. Shortly after concluding this deal, the Clifford Chance Dubai partner, who brought in the deal to Clifford Chance, moved to head Linklaters' Dubai office. As O'Connor (2005) puts it, "A canny bit of talent spotting . . . that." Linklaters continued to act for MTC (now acquired by another telecom, Zain) on subsequent acquisitions, thereby ousting Clifford Chance as the MTC's counsel.

English lawyers tend to be relaxed about these kinds of actual and potential conflicts,[6] and they argue that sophisticated corporate clients understand these relationships and do not use them to conflict out lawyers. Moreover, the clients' economic power allows them to assert authority in situations if their interests are threatened. US lawyers are more concerned about conflicts because their professional rules are more restrictive with respect to conflicts involving current and former clients. Joe Flom, senior partner of Skadden, Arps, Slate, Meagher & Flom in New York, predicted more than 25 years ago that large law firms would begin to find themselves harboring extensive conflicts as they grew in size and as lawyers circulated from firm to firm (Federal Bar Council 1984, 126). As Wald (2007) notes, these relationships bring the ABA Model Rules 1.6 (concerning confidentiality) and 1.7 (concerning conflicts of interest) into tension with each other, especially in the light of increased lawyer mobility. Yet English lawyers have not succumbed to the rigors of such rules.

Griffiths-Baker (2002) discovered that although official Solicitors Regulation Authority (SRA) rules forbade solicitors acting for both sides in transactions, large law firms regularly ignored them. And large solicitors' firms developed screening procedures to protect clients' interests when a firm is acting on both sides of a transaction. To resolve the conflicts problem, the City of London Law Society (CLLS), the large law firms' lobby group, led an intensive lobbying campaign to revise the conflicts rules so that they would permit "sophisticated" corporate clients to agree to their lawyers acting for both sides in noncontentious matters (Dean 2010). In 2009, the SRA agreed to change Rule 3 on conflicts of interest to allow clients to consent to additional conflicts. Rule 3.02(2)(a) now states: "Your firm may act for two or more clients in relation to a matter in situations of conflict or possible conflict if: the clients are competing for the same asset which, if attained by one client, will make that asset unattainable to the other client(s)." Furthermore, the CLLS has been lobbying the New York Bar to permit New York lawyers practicing abroad—who at present follow New York rules—to be

---

6. The English rules on conflicts of interest currently state, in part:

You or your firm may act for two or more clients in relation to a matter in situations of conflict or possible conflict if:

    (a) the different clients have a substantially common interest in relation to that matter or a particular aspect of it; and
    (b) all the clients have given in writing their informed consent to you or your firm acting.

Solicitors' Code of Conduct Rule 3.02(1).

able to choose which jurisdiction's rules they will follow (e.g., United Kingdom or France). The agenda of the CLLS is to have the same rule adopted in *all* jurisdictions throughout the world, so as to benefit global law firms.

Despite these moves and shared understandings, which are deeply entrenched in London law firms, lawyers still make seemingly incomprehensible and elementary mistakes. In another example of conflict of interest in a complex transaction, Philip Green, a fashion retailer, attempted to acquire the department store Marks & Spencer in a hostile takeover in 2004. Green was assisted in this $14 billion acquisition by Barry O'Brien, the corporate finance head of Freshfields, a big London law firm (Herman 2007).[7] The problem was that Freshfields had a long-standing relationship with Marks & Spencer, the target. Freshfields undertook a conflicts check and found that although it had done work previously for Marks & Spencer on restructuring and litigation, the firm's chief executive decided these were not material to the bid and the firm set up a series of "Chinese Walls"— information barriers to prevent the flow of information between certain lawyers in a firm (O'Connor and Jordan 2004).

O'Brien worked with 50 staff on the matter for months before Green went public with his bid. Marks & Spencer immediately obtained an injunction from a judge who had been a large law firm partner before joining the bench. O'Brien and Freshfields immediately appealed, but the Court of Appeal affirmed, forcing O'Brien and Freshfields to cease working for Green (Nisse 2004). Although the firm was dropped, it still billed Green over $1.5 million in fees. In addition, it had to pay over $400,000 in costs to Marks & Spencer's law firm for the injunction. The conflict could not be any clearer, under either UK or US rules. Interestingly, Marks & Spencer decided it would not make a formal complaint having obtained its desired result, so the Law Society (the professional body), which had decided not to investigate the matter, then came under pressure from its governing members to initiate a complaints procedure. The judge who had granted the injunction questioned the effectiveness of Chinese Walls as screening devices. Freshfields attempted to claim the moral high ground by saying it would never reveal any confidential information, a maneuver that singularly failed to impress the Law Society.

O'Brien was disciplined and fined $14,000 by the Solicitors Disciplinary Tribunal in 2007 and ordered to pay costs of $78,000. He also paid another $78,000 to the Law Society for bringing the complaint (Aldridge 2009). O'Brien

---

7. Freshfields Bruckhaus Deringer is a law firm with more than 2,400 lawyers with 27 offices in 15 countries (Freshfields Bruckhaus Deringer 2011).

was forced to resign his partnership, yet Freshfields retained him as of counsel (i.e., neither partner nor associate). At the tribunal, his counsel argued his error of judgment was a one-time blip on an otherwise distinguished career that included masterminding a rescue plan for Lloyd's of London, the insurer, which was said to have saved the insurance market from collapse. The tribunal further heard excerpts from *The Legal 500* and *Chambers Directory* that described him, with no hint of irony, as "the first choice, every time, for complex advice," a "robust heavyweight," and "first class adviser" (Herman 2007). Despite his conviction and the imposition of discipline, he continued to work for his regular clients. Although he was not an official partner, he behaved as such. No client left the firm as a result of his actions: Indeed, O'Brien worked on several multibillion dollar takeovers during this period. His expulsion from the Eden of his law firm was rescinded in 2010 when Freshfields made him a partner and head of corporate finance for the second time (Freshfields Bruckhaus Deringer 2011b; Aldridge 2009).

What these stories tell us is that the very notion of conflicts of interest is fluid rather than rigid. It is open to interpretation. In some contexts, as in the Freshfields case, it cannot be explained away as a "blip" since, as Griffiths-Baker would suggest, conflicts are not uncommon. But in most large-scale business transactions, business and legal relationships are complex and varied. A strict interpretation of conflicts rules would effectively halt a considerable amount of business or perhaps otherwise deflect it to other firms. So, in the United Kingdom at least, the situation has been revised by the regulator to permit what has been taking place informally for many years. It can also be argued that in transnational business, the ability to raise conflicts issues is diminished because there are relatively few law firms that engage in this work; partners are constantly moving between firms; and it is difficult for dispersed clients to bring complaints and actions in different jurisdictions. And given the relatively small number of actors who engage in this work, it contains the elements of a club that should not have its "dirty laundry" washed in public. Informal sanctions such as criticism and taking business elsewhere are more powerful than the formal regulatory process.

So, What Is Truth?

According to the preamble of the ABA Model Rules of Professional Conduct, a lawyer is obligated to "conform to the requirements of the law" and is urged to "demonstrate respect for the legal system." Moreover, a lawyer shall not knowingly make a false statement to a tribunal or third party (Rules 3.3, 4.1, 8.4). But nowhere do the Model Rules say that a lawyer has to tell the truth. Similarly, the Solicitors' Code of Conduct in Rule 1 talks about a lawyer acting with integrity, upholding the rule of law, and not diminishing the trust of the public, but it too fails to mention the role of truth.

The second case study concerns the sale of a large office building in London by a joint venture of Japanese banks to an offshore British Virgin Islands–based company involving a number of different jurisdictions. The building was worth £343 million, and the purchaser was a UK public limited property company, Delancey (Delancey 2011), a former PLC that had gone private and established a series of offshore investment vehicles in the British Virgin Islands (BVI), a well-known tax haven. It is one of the most sophisticated players in the property market dealing in hedging and property derivatives. The purchase was a joint venture between Delancey and an Australian pension fund. Delancey wanted the deal done in a combination of English, as the lead law, BVI, Australian, Jersey, and Japanese law. The lawyer for Delancey at the London firm of Olswang LLP took the lead in drafting the documentation used.[8] Initially she expected the transaction to take several weeks, but the complexity of it combined with tax difficulties and the respective needs of local laws meant that ultimately it took six months to complete.

To make the joint venture work, the lawyers used BVI law to set up a special purpose vehicle to hold the assets of the transaction, but the actual sale would occur under English law. The key element in these types of transactions is minimizing the tax burdens that arise. Since Delancey is offshore, it is usually protected from UK Revenue and Customs, though not always. The transaction was complex, and as the lead UK lawyer said:

> The problem was that for the Revenue, tax domicile is a question of *fact.* Although Delancey is offshore in the BVI where "management and control" are based, it also has a large office in central London, which clouds the issue. All my emails to Delancey *had* to appear to go to the BVI even though a number of important decisions were being made in the London office. The email trail had to be kept clear and direct so the Revenue wouldn't query anything.

8. Olswang ranks number 32 on the *Lawyer UK 200* with 321 lawyers and offices in the United Kingdom, Germany, and Belgium. It also has a "best friends" relationship with a US law firm, Cooley LLP, a San Francisco firm (*Lawyer* 2010).

The Olswang lawyer unpacked the role of the transnational transaction lawyer as one in which the attorney concentrates primarily on the deal yet may do many transactions for particular clients, rather than act as a continuing adviser. She put it this way:

There's a problem for transaction lawyers around risk management. Transactions *are* individual items, but if you do a series of them for the same client, then do you become an adviser as well? How much do you have to recall about past deals? I always send an email to the client near the end of the deal to say that you must check these representations to ensure everything is covered. There is a strong possibility that the client's lawyers could be held to know about things and so not be able to state, "Oh, that was just a single deal."

Corporate clients, as Heinz and Laumann (1982) describe them, do not sit in the traditional professional-client relationship that Carr-Saunders and Wilson (1933) analyzed where the professional is the dominant member of the professional-client relationship. To them the relationship was an inversion characterized by patronage (Johnson 1972) where the lawyer did not so much exercise autonomy but rather discretion (Evetts 2002). It is apparent in the Delancey example the lawyer had very little autonomy. Her instructions were clear and to the point: Tax liabilities were to be minimized. This involved some sleight of hand so that the e-mails had to be routed to appear to go from London to the BVI rather than from Olswang to Delancey's London headquarters. The key decisions had to appear to be made in the Caribbean, not in London where they were actually made. The construction of the deal had to follow a prescribed course that would satisfy both legal rules and the tax authorities. Some may see the lawyer's behavior as fraudulent, but she and the clients saw it as normal. She remarked that many of her deals with this client followed a similar pattern and so had now become normalized for her and therefore contained no anomalies.

Was she being untruthful? In a strict sense, she was. As part of the course of business, these actions were ordinary. She could claim that as far as she was concerned, Delancey's decisions were made in the BVI and not London. The trail of the e-mails backed this up. And as long as she did not allow her tiredness to make her careless, the performance could be maintained. The tax authorities could mount an investigation, and the lawyer (and client) could potentially face sanctions for fraud from them and the Solicitors Regulation Authority, yet this was considered highly unlikely. The main point here is that although the

attorney saw her actions as somewhat underhanded, the behavior was not perceived by either lawyer or client as dishonest or even *unethical* (cf. Kirkland,
chapter 8). Elizabeth Chambliss (chapter 3) describes this behavior as "ethical
fading," the loss of ordinary morality as expertise develops. If ethical fading
is characteristic of development through the large law firm (Kirkland 2005),
then it could result from the psychological pressure on actors to conform to
group norms (Levin 2009).

We can also ask, was she a bad lawyer? From the client's perspective, she was
a good lawyer. If she had refused to do the deal in the way the client demanded,
she would have lost the business and the client. It is significant that Delancey
was a repeat player that generated significant billings for the firm. Even if the
lawyer refused to do as told, the firm probably would have continued to act for
the client with another lawyer. Goffman (1961) describes institutionalization—
how people adapt to the mores of the situation they find themselves in. This is a
capacity that law firms possess: They incubate their lawyers to act in particular
ways with respect to clients and other lawyers. Delancey's lawyer might have
understood the moral ambiguity of her situation, but she did not let it trouble
her as long as it continued with a semblance of normality. Corporate lawyers
are put in this position all the time; they are subject to demands made by clients and senior partners (Kirkland, chapter 8). Their career paths depend on
how well they carry out the demands. The pressures of work, clients, and billing do not give them much respite to reflect on what they do.

Conclusion

Transnational lawyering, especially of the transactional kind, exists in an ambiguous world of shades and shadows where nothing seems fixed. Clients take
on new organizational forms. Lawyers move around from firm to firm, raising
the specter of conflicts wherever they stop (Wald 2007). Transnational lawyering is the remit of a relatively small number of law firms which, by the nature
of transactional work, are frequently working for the same range of clients.
Clients demand tenders and estimates for work, and they are prepared to live
with lawyers' ethical conundrums as long as they don't stop the flow of business. Moreover, in this area of legal practice, the client rules and the lawyer
serves. Perhaps Goldsmith's Brussels lawyer friend was not overly cynical in
his description of practice as being all about billable hours and not service. I
referred to Hughes's conception of dirty work in my introduction, and here
we can describe the lawyer as doing the dirty work of the client. The lawyer has

developed a carapace that removes the need to deliberate over moral ambiguity and instead accepts rule infringement as normal.

Kritzer (chapter 7) argues that the difficulty of understanding which of the many characters is the main client puts the lawyer in a position of continuing tension and conflict. If this is so, then how is a lawyer supposed to behave in an ethical manner? There is no easy answer. On the one hand, a lawyer should act with integrity as the rules state. But on the other, client demands can override the lawyer's sensibilities. In most situations, the problems fail to arise because they are not brought to the attention of regulators except in exceptional situations as with Barry O'Brien. But even O'Brien and his firm, Freshfields, ultimately believed they had done nothing blameworthy, to the extent that O'Brien was rehired as a partner after a few years.

It may be that the perceptions of clients and lawyers are too far apart. Lawyers engage in a profession in which ethical responsibility is supposed to be taken seriously; however, clients demand total commitment from their advisers to their business ends. Here we see a double shift. The lawyer, to succeed in the corporate world, takes on the persona of business both in her own organization in maximizing her returns and as her guiding principle in serving her clients' business. Does this mean business is amoral and that lawyers are prevented from acting ethically with corporate clients? Not necessarily. Even Adam Smith was aware of the role of morality in the marketplace when he wrote *The Theory of Moral Sentiments* (1759). And in the last few years, there has been a movement in business schools to introduce an MBA oath to "create value responsibly and ethically" (MBA Oath 2011).

Law firms are highly aware of the growing impact of the regulatory state on their practice, as repeated scandals like the US savings and loans debacle and the collapse of Enron graphically demonstrate. But what these appear to be telling us is what Simon (1998, 115) refers to as "another dimension of the loss of agency [which] is the lawyer's insensitivity to the underlying moral stakes of his work." Corporate practice is intensifying the moral anxieties of professionalism and will increase the pressures for external regulation over self-regulation. What these instances tell us is that socialization, conformity, and ethical fading are so prevalent, so deeply embedded into professionals' lives, that there is no escape. These ways are the norm. Is it feasible to conceive of an alternative that could exist in the pressured world of the corporate law firm? I leave this open as I am convinced no quick fix is available; nor am I able to see how regulation would alter the situation. We may have to live with it.

References

Abramson, John. 2008. "Interview with Rt. Hon. the Lord Mayor of London, Alderman David Lewis." *City Solicitor*, Autumn, 6–7.

Aldridge, Alex. 2009. "Life of O'Brien." *Legal Week*, July 16. http://www.legalweek .com/legal-week/analysis/1433519/the-life-o-brien.

Baker & McKenzie. 2011. "About Us." http://www.bakermckenzie.com/aboutus.

Bauman, Jon R. 1999. *Pioneering a Global Vision: The Story of Baker & McKenzie*. New York: Harcourt Brace.

Boon, Andrew, and Jennifer Levin. 2008. *The Ethics and Conduct of Lawyers in England and Wales*. Oxford: Hart.

Bringardner, John. 2008. "Lawyers Wanted: Abroad, That Is." *New York Times*, November 23, BU1.

Byrne, Matt. 2006. "Telecoms Specialists Look East for the Hottest M&A Action." *Lawyer*, March 13. http://www.thelawyer.com/telecoms-specialists-look-east-for-the-hottest-ma-action/119160.article.

Carr-Saunders, Alexander, and Paul A. Wilson. 1933. *The Professions*. Oxford: Clarendon Press.

Cassis, Youssef. 2006. *Capitals of Capital: A History of International Financial Centres, 1780–2005*. Cambridge: Cambridge University Press.

Clifford Chance. 2010. *Annual Review 2010*. http://www.cliffordchance.com/content/dam/ cliffordchance/AR2010/Reports/AR10_web.pdf.

———. 2011. "About Us." http://www.cliffordchance.com/about_us.html.

Dean, James. 2010. "SRA Poised to Relax Conflict of Interest Rules." *Law Society Gazette*, January 21. http://www.lawgazette.co.uk/news/sra-poised-relax-conflict-interest-rules.

Delancey. 2011. "About: Overview." http://www.delancey.com/about.html.

Denyer, Stephen. 2010. Paper presented at the International Legal Ethics Conference IV, Stanford Law School, Stanford, CA, July 15–17.

Evetts, Julia. 2002. "New Directions in State and International Professional Occupations: Discretionary Decision-making and Acquired Regulation." *Work, Employment & Society* 16:341–353.

Faulconbridge, James, and Daniel Muzio. 2008. "Organizational Professionalism in Globalizing Law Firms." *Work, Employment & Society* 22:7–25.

Federal Bar Council. 1984. "The Changing Nature of the Practice of Law." In *Federal Bar Council 1984 Bench & Bar, Conference Proceedings*. 84–127. New York: Goldner Press.

Flood, John. 2007. "Lawyers as Sanctifiers of Value Creation." *Indiana Journal of Global Legal Studies* 14:35–66.

———. 2009. "Ambiguous Allegiances in the Lawyer-Client Relationship: The Case of Bankers and Lawyers." Working paper, available on the Social Science Research Network. http://papers.ssrn.com/s013/papers.cfm?abstract_id=962725.

———. 2011a. "From Ethics to Regulation: The Re-Organization and Re-Professionalization of Large Law Firms in the 21st Century." *Current Sociology* 59:1–23.

———. 2011b. *Legal Education in the Global Context: Challenges from Globalization, Technology and Changes in Government Regulation*. London: Legal Services Board.

Freshfields Bruckhaus Deringer. 2011a. "Our Firm." http://careers.freshfields.com/our-firm .aspx.

———. 2011b. "People, Barry O'Brien." http://www.freshfields.com/people/profile/11/ 2623.

Goffman, Erving. 1961. *Asylums: Essays on the Social Situation of Mental Patients and Other Inmates*. Garden City, NJ: Doubleday Anchor.

Goldsmith, Jonathan. 2008. "The Core Values of the Legal Profession for Lawyers Today and Tomorrow." *Northwestern Journal of International Law & Business* 28:441–454.

Griffiths-Baker, Janine. 2002. *Serving Two Masters: Conflicts of Interest in the Modern Law Firm*. Oxford: Hart.

Heinz, John P., and Edward O. Laumann. 1982. *Chicago Lawyers: The Social Structure of the Bar*. New York: Russell Sage Foundation.

Herman, Michael. 2007. "Conflict of Interest Costs Freshfields Lawyer £59,000." *Times*, August 2. http://business.timesonline.co.uk/tol/business/law/article2188167.ece.

Hinings, Christopher R., Royston Greenwood, and David Cooper. 1999. "The Dynamics of Change in Large Accounting Firms." In *Restructuring the Professional Organization: Accounting, Health Care and Law*, edited by David M. Brock, Michael J. Powell and Christopher R. Hinings, 131–153. London: Routledge.

Hughes, Everett C. 1958. "Work and the Self." In *Men and Their Work*, edited by Everett C. Hughes, 42–55. Glencoe, IL: Free Press.

IBA Conflicts of Interest Subcommittee. 2010. "The IBA Guidelines on Conflicts of Interest in International Arbitration: The First Five Years 2004–2009." *Journal of Dispute Resolution International* 4:5–53.

IFSL Research. 2009. *Legal Services 2009*. http://www.thecityuk.com/assets/Uploads/Legal-Services-2009.pdf.

ISDA. 2011. "About ISDA." http://www2.isda.org/about-isda/.

Johnson, Terrence J. 1972. *Professions and Power*. London: Macmillan.

Kirkland, Kimberly. 2005. "Ethics in Large Law Firms: The Principle of Pragmatism." *University of Memphis Law Review* 4:631–730.

Lawyer. 2010. *UK 200 Annual Report 2010: The Cost of Cutting*. http://www.centaur2.co.uk/emags/thelawyer/uk200_2010.

Law Society. 2011. *Trends in the Solicitors' Profession: Annual Statistical Report 2010*. London: Law Society.

Lazega, Emmanuel. 2001. *The Collegial Phenomenon: The Social Mechanisms of Cooperation Among Peers in a Corporate Law Partnership*. New York: Oxford University Press.

Le Goff, Pierrick. 2007 "Global Law: A Legal Phenomenon Emerging from the Process of Globalization." *Indiana Journal of Global Legal Studies* 14:119–145.

Levin, Leslie C. 2009. "Bad Apples, Bad Lawyers or Bad Decisionmaking: Lessons from Psychology and from *Lawyers in the Dock*." *Georgetown Journal of Legal Ethics* 22: 1549–1594.

Linklaters. 2010. *Corporate Responsibility Executive Summary 2010*. http://www.linklaters.com/pdfs/mkt/london/CR_Executive_Summary_2010.PDF.

Loan Market Association. 2011. "LMA Members." http://www.lma.eu.com/institution.aspx.

MBA Oath. 2011. "Welcome." http://mbaoath.org.

McLeod-Roberts, Luke. 2009. "Davis Polk, Shearman Advise on £5bn Brazilian IPO." *Lawyer*, October 7. http://www.thelawyer.com/davis-polk-shearman-advise-on-%C2%A35bn-brazilian-ipo/1002221.article.

Moore, Nancy J. 2007. "Ethical Issues in Transnational Legal Practice: The US Lawyer Goes Abroad." *Bar Examiner*, August 29, 29–32.

Morgan, Glenn, and Sigrid Quack. 2005. "Institutional Legacies and Firm Dynamics: The

Growth and Internationalization of UK and German Law Firms." *Organization Studies* 26:1765–1785.

Muzio, Daniel, James Faulconbridge, and Andrew Cook. Forthcoming. "Learning to be a Lawyer in Transnational Law Firms: Communities of Practice, Institutions and Identity Regulation." *Global Networks.*

Nagel, Matthew T. 2007. "Double Deontology and the CCBE: Harmonizing the Double Trouble in Europe." *Washington University Global Studies Law Review* 6:455–482.

Nisse, Jason. 2004. "Law Society Probes Freshfields over M&S Bid Work for Green." *Independent*, July 25. http://www.independent.co.uk/news/business/news/law-society-probes-freshfields-over-mamps-bid-work-for-green-554317.html.

O'Connor, Joanne. 2005. "CC and Linklaters Steer Celtel and MTC Through Acquisition." *Lawyer*, April 4. http://www.thelawyer.com/cc-and-linklaters-steer-celtel-and-mtc-through-acquisition/114625.article.

O'Connor, Joanne, and Dearbail Jordan. 2004. "Freshfields, the £9bn M&S Bid and Just a Touch of Hubris." *Lawyer*, June 7. http://www.thelawyer.com/freshfields-the-%C2%A39bn-ms-bid-and-just-a-touch-of-hubris/110367.article.

Parker, Christine. 1999. "Lawyer Deregulation via Business Deregulation: Compliance Professionalism and Legal Professionalism." *International Journal of the Legal Profession* 6:175–196.

Press, Aric, and Greg Mulligan. 2010. "Lessons of the Am Law 100." *American Lawyer*, May 1. http://www.law.com/jsp/tal/PubArticleTAL.jsp?id=1202448340864.

PricewaterhouseCoopers. 2009. *Global Annual Review 2009.* http://www.pwc.com/annual review.

Silver, Carole. 2002 "The Case of the Foreign Lawyer: Internationalizing the U.S. Legal Profession." *Fordham Journal of International Law* 25:1039–1084.

———. 2006. "Internationalizing U.S. Legal Education: A Report on the Education of Transnational Lawyers." *Cardozo Journal of International & Comparative Law* 14:143–175.

Simon, William. 1998. *The Practice of Justice: A Theory of Lawyers' Ethics.* Cambridge, MA: Harvard University Press.

Smith, Adam. 1759. *The Theory of Moral Sentiments.* London: A. Millar.

Smith, Adam. 2009. "Local Laws—Global Clients." *Legal Week*, June 11, 16.

SRA. 2009. *Information for Providers of Legal Practice Courses.* http://www.sra.org.uk/documents/students/lpc/info-pack.pdf.

US Bureau of Economic Analysis. 2009. "Business, Professional and Technical Services." Table 7. http://www.bea.gov/international/xls/tab7a.xls.

Vanistendael, Frans. 2004. "Curricular Changes in Europe Law Schools." *Penn State International Law Review* 22:455–458.

Wald, Eli. 2007. "Lawyer Mobility and Legal Ethics: Resolving the Tension between Confidentiality Requirements and Contemporary Lawyers' Career Paths." *Journal of the Legal Profession* 31:199–278.

Cases and Rules

Case C-550/07, *Akzo Nobel Chemicals Ltd. v. Commission*, Judgment of September 14, 2010, European Court of Justice.

McKinney's New York Rules of Court, Rules of the Court of Appeals for the Licensing of Legal Consultants, pt. 521 (2011).

Solicitors' Code of Conduct Rules 1, 3.02, 15 (2010).

The Ethics of In-House Practice

Sung Hui Kim

For nine years, Oliver Budde served as an associate general counsel at Lehman Brothers, a venerable investment bank. As is typical of many lawyers employed in corporations ("inside counsel" or "inside lawyers"),[1] Budde first served six grueling years as an associate in a prestigious law firm before joining the bank. Initially, he enjoyed the work at Lehman Brothers. Budde recalled, "It was a job I was proud of. There was no 'ick' factor, at least at first" (Sterngold 2010). But things got more "icky" after just a few years. On one occasion, Lehman's outside accounting firm had proposed to lower medical insurance costs through the use of a questionable tax transaction. Budde openly objected. He noted, "My gut feeling was that this was just reshuffling some papers to get an expense off the balance sheet. . . . It was not the right thing, and I told them." But Budde's superiors in Lehman's general counsel's office disagreed, and the deal went through.

Worse, Budde noticed that Lehman was not transparently reporting its executive compensation in its filings with the Securities and Exchange Commission (SEC). Budde thought that Lehman's disclosure strategy, while not clearly prohibited, was too aggressive and misled public investors about how much Lehman was paying its senior executives. Budde complained to his superiors but was told that the bank's outside attorneys at the law firm of Simpson, Thacher & Bartlett had blessed the strategy.

Exasperated by Lehman's grudging attitude toward compliance, Budde eventually quit in 2006. Later, Budde discovered that Lehman continued with

I thank Jerry Kang, Robert Rosen, Tanina Rostain, and the editors, Leslie Levin and Lynn Mather, for helpful comments.

1. Inside lawyers are also commonly referred to as in-house or corporate counsel.

its disclosure approach even after SEC releases made clear that doing so would be improper. Of course, we now know that securities compliance was just one of a myriad of problems afflicting Lehman at that time. In 2008, Lehman Brothers collapsed in the largest bankruptcy in US history.

The tensions that Budde faced should ring familiar to many inside lawyers working in legal departments throughout corporate America. Once viewed as the quality-of-life refuge from private practice, the in-house position is now recognized as "among the most complex and difficult of those functions performed by lawyers" (Hazard 1997, 1011). One reason why the position is so complex and difficult is the ambiguity and internal contradiction in inside counsel's job description. On the one hand, inside counsel are intentionally carved into the corporate decision-making process to constrain managerial discretion and safeguard the company from legal trouble. Accordingly, inside counsel often have direct responsibility over compliance and are expected to intervene when significant legal risks are at stake. On the other hand, inside counsel are often regarded as mere "advisers" and thus remain subordinate to managerial prerogatives—even with respect to serious legal risks. On this view, inside counsel are expected to defer to business management at whose pleasure they serve.[2] This latter view is consistent with the conventional skepticism about inside counsel's willingness to check corporate misconduct (DeMott 2005, 967). This chapter explores how inside counsel negotiate these dueling job descriptions by analyzing the existing empirical literature.

Before examining how inside counsel perform their jobs, we need a basic understanding about who these lawyers are. There are approximately 65,000 inside counsel in the United States, working in about 21,000 non- and for-profit organizations, reflecting approximately 8 to 10% of the bar (Carson 2004; Hackett 2002, 610, 618). Most inside counsel work not in large, but small, corporate legal departments or as sole inside counsel for their companies.[3] One large-scale survey reported that the median and the mean of inside attorneys employed in corporate legal departments were just ten and six, respectively (Hackett 2002, 610). Most inside counsel moved in-house after working in private law firms for (on average) six years (618). The most common industries in

---

2. Most in-house general counsel (61.4%) report to their companies' chief executive officer. A minority report to another senior executive (e.g., the president or chief financial officer). Most inside counsel are physically stationed together in the corporation's central office, reporting up the ladder to the general counsel, as opposed to being stationed in various operating divisions and reporting directly to the head of the local operating unit (Hackett 2002, 612).

3. Many Fortune 500 companies have small law departments (defined as being less than 15 persons) but very large legal budgets (Hackett 2002, 613).

which inside counsel work are manufacturing (27.0%), finance and insurance (19.3%), and information (7.5%) (619). The most common areas of practice are general corporate transactions, general matters, general commercial law, intellectual property, and employment/human resources (611).

Since the 1970s, inside counsel have enjoyed increased visibility and stature (Liggio 1997). Due to the increase in business-to-business litigation, the proliferation of administrative regulations, and the exponential growth in legal costs (1203–1204), CEOs have grown to rely more on their in-house legal staffs and less on outside law firms for corporate legal advice. Accordingly, the balance of power has shifted from outside to inside counsel. To be sure, outside law firms remain important and perform the bulk of the litigation for companies in litigious industries (Hackett 2002, 613). Their influence is filtered, however, through inside counsel who monitor their performance and actively manage law firms' delivery of legal services to corporations.

But it is not just the increased stature of in-house legal staffs that justify the study of inside counsel. Inside lawyers' acts and omissions are often critical components of corporate misbehavior. What's more, inside lawyers are in many ways better situated than outside lawyers to prevent corporate malfeasance. This is true for at least two reasons. First, inside counsel are more likely to confront potential corporate misconduct. In their "preventive law" role (Brown 1950; Gruner 1997), inside counsel ordinarily manage corporate compliance programs to ensure that the company minimizes the risk of legal liability. In a recent survey of general counsel of Standard & Poor's 500 companies, 81% indicated that they oversaw compliance (Beardslee et al. 2010). In performing this formal role, they are likely to learn of instances of intentional or negligent noncompliance. Also, due to their physical proximity to those who hold information about misconduct (i.e., coworkers), inside lawyers normally have access to informal, back-channel information (Hazard 1997) that may contain the critical indicators of incipient, ongoing, or completed corporate misconduct.

Second, inside counsel are better situated to interpret the information they receive. Inside counsel understand what Robert Rosen (2010, 59) has described as the "bureaucratic pathologies [that] are commonplace in corporate legal practice": for example, why this manager insists that his project go through, why that manager favors the instant customer at corporate expense, and why business units obsess about their short-term balance sheets at the expense of the long-term business (59–60). In short, inside counsel have a better developed "spider sense," as cultivated by an intimate familiarity with the political landscape of the firm and well-practiced situational judgment (Kim 2008). By contrast, outside counsel are often privy to only filtered fragments of larger problems and are thus inherently limited in their ability to detect potential malfeasance. In sum, inside counsel play a crucial role in facilitating or preventing corporate misbehavior—which makes them significant targets of research and inquiry (Kim 2005).

What, then, do we know about how these lawyers actually play this role? How do inside lawyers approach their dueling job descriptions? Do they merely offer legal advice and punt the final decision to the business manager, as the conventional wisdom suggests? Or do they more proactively use their powers of persuasion to steer the company's agenda? Do they intervene in purely business matters, or do they keep it "strictly legal"? What do inside counsel do when they observe a fellow employee engaged in improper conduct that might harm the corporation? Do they intervene, or do they turn a blind eye and "see no evil, hear no evil"?

To organize these inquiries, I draw on the American Bar Association's (ABA) Model Rules of Professional Conduct. The Model Rules provide a baseline framework for what constitutes appropriate lawyer conduct (at least according to the ABA). Although Model Rule compliance hardly guarantees "ethical" behavior from any or all moral foundations, such compliance provides a useful benchmark of behavior deemed "ethical" according to the positive law. In addition, using the Model Rules as a reference point facilitates an understanding of how lawyers themselves define what is an appropriate professional response. This is not to say that lawyers have internalized (let alone, even recall) the specific disciplinary rules (Abel 1989, 143). But without the use of a uniform benchmark, it would be extremely difficult to compare the findings generated from the various empirical studies (Chambliss, chapter 3).

I rely primarily on Model Rule 1.13 (Organization as Client) to develop an analytical framework with which to evaluate the empirical research. Although the rule applies to both inside and outside lawyers representing organizations, it provides especially important guidance for lawyers working in-house, who, for the reasons described above, are more likely to encounter the situations contemplated by the rule. After explaining Model Rule 1.13 and my theoretical framework, I review the existing empirical research on inside counsel[4] to

---

4. The main studies focusing on inside counsel that I draw on are (1) John Donnell's study (1970) of 16 counsel and 18 client representatives of three large companies from three different

determine whether and to what degree inside counsel's behavior conforms to the Model Rules.

Model Rules of Professional Conduct: Organization as Client

Clarifying the Client

Inside counsel faced with managers who want to break the law must remind themselves who the client is. Model Rule 1.13(a) makes the crucial threshold clarification—that "a lawyer employed or retained by an organization represents the organization acting through its duly authorized constituents." Thus, the client is the *organization*, a term that includes corporations and other business associations. Accordingly, the in-house lawyer for an organization does not represent the organization's *constituents*, who include corporate officers, directors, employees, and shareholders.

Of course, the "organization" is a legal fiction that functions only through flesh-and-blood actors. Therefore, in practice, lawyers psychologically suspend this fiction and interact with the organization's "duly authorized constituents," *as if* they were the clients. For inside lawyers, these constituents are the senior corporate officials (the corporate directors and officers) and their delegatees, typically mid- to high-level business managers. Normally, these businesspersons are vested with the authority to act as the client's mouthpiece for purposes of soliciting corporate legal advice.

Reporting Up the Ladder

But these constituents do not enjoy limitless authority. Those limits are suggested by Model Rule 1.13(b), which addresses cases in which an officer, employee, or other constituent violates "a legal obligation to the organization, or [violates] law that reasonably might be imputed to the organization, and that

---

industries; (2) Robert Rosen's study (2010) (conducted in the 1970s) of 77 informants (comprising inside counsel, business managers, and outside counsel) from six manufacturing firms; (3) Eve Spangler's study (1986) on the role of inside counsel in her larger study of salaried lawyers; (4) Robert Nelson and Laura Beth Nielsen's study (2000) of 86 informants (comprising inside counsel, legally trained executives, and nonlawyer executives) from 46 large corporations and financial institutions; (5) Hugh Gunz and Sally Gunz's questionnaire survey (2002) of 484 Canadian inside counsel; (6) Sally Gunz and Hugh Gunz's study (2008) of 25 Canadian inside counsel; (7) Tanina Rostain's pilot study (2008) of 10 general counsel at Fortune 1000 companies; and (8) Michele DeStefano Beardslee's study (2009) of inside counsel's role in public relations, surveying 125 general counsels, 8 external and internal public relations executives, and 10 law firm partners.

is likely to result in substantial injury to the organization." Examples include securities fraud or the marketing of dangerous products, which could lead to civil or criminal liability for the corporation (Hazard and Hodes 2005). When the lawyer for the organization "knows" about such a serious infraction and the matter is "related to the representation," then she must "proceed as is reasonably necessary in the best interest of the organization" (Model Rule 1.13(b)). The rule establishes a presumption that in such cases the lawyer "shall" report the matter to higher organizational authorities, including, "if warranted by the circumstances, to the highest authority that can act on behalf of the organization" (Model Rule 1.13(b)).

This internal reporting protocol is similar to the reporting rules applicable to counsel for public companies as a result of the Sarbanes-Oxley Act of 2002 (Sarbanes-Oxley). Those rules, codified at 17 C.F.R. pt. 205 (2010), require any lawyer "appearing and practicing before the [SEC] in the representation of the issuer" (including inside lawyers handling securities matters) to report any "evidence of material violation" of law to certain designated organizational officials and potentially to the board of directors, if necessary to ensure that appropriate measures are taken. Unlike the Model Rules, however, the lawyer is not invited to make any independent calculation regarding the best interest of the organization. In other words, the SEC has already determined that it is in the organization's best interest to report up any material law violations.

Reporting Out

What if the lawyer reports up to the board of directors, which then turns a blind eye? Model Rule 1.13(c) provides that when the board acquiesces in a "clear . . . violation of law" and "the lawyer reasonably believes that the violation is reasonably certain to result in substantial injury"—then the lawyer *may* report even confidential information *outside* of the organization "to the extent the lawyer reasonably believes necessary to prevent substantial injury to the organization." The reporting *out* standard is more stringent than the reporting *up* standard: There must "clearly" be a violation of law, and the lawyer must be "reasonably certain" (as opposed to merely believing it "likely") that the organization will suffer substantial injury.

By vesting lawyers with the discretion to escalate matters not only up to but even outside the board, the Model Rules formally recognize that lawyers must sometime play the role of "gatekeeper"—an intermediary who prevents harm to the corporation by disrupting the misconduct of client representatives (Kim 2008).

Four Quadrants

Model Rule 1.13 is significant not only in its formal, literal application but also in its articulation, together with the comments, of a broader ethical roadmap. Comment 3 to Rule 1.13 provides important guidance:

> When constituents of the organization make decisions for it, the decisions ordinarily must be accepted by the lawyer even if their utility or prudence is doubtful. Decisions concerning *policy and operations*, including ones entailing *serious* risk, are not as such in the lawyer's *province*. Paragraph (b) makes clear, however, that when the lawyer knows that the organization is *likely* to be *substantially injured* by action of an officer or other constituent that *violates a legal obligation* to the organization or is in *violation of law* that might be imputed to the organization, the lawyer must proceed as is reasonably necessary in the best interest of the organization. (Emphasis added.)

Both the text of the rule and this comment highlight the relevance of two variables. First, violations of "law" and "legal obligation" are within the lawyer's "province"; by contrast, "policy and operations" are not. Accordingly, the Model Rules distinguish between legal and nonlegal (or business) domains or, more specifically, between unlawful and lawful (or at least not unlawful) actions. Second, Rule 1.13's various qualifiers about magnitude of harm (e.g., "substantial," "serious"), probability of occurrence (e.g., "likely"), and epistemological certitude (e.g., "reasonably certain") distinguish between what might be called material versus nonmaterial risks. If we intersect these two variables, we produce the four quadrants shown in table 10.1. These quadrants roughly categorize the situations that counsel to the organization are likely to face.

Quadrant I (Lawful Action; Immaterial Risk of Harm)

As a matter of common sense, courses of action falling under Quadrant I should pose the least concern for counsel. The Model Rules agree. As noted above, Comment 3 to Rule 1.13 makes clear that "decisions concerning policy and operations . . . are not as such in the lawyer's province." So long as the

Table 10.1. The Quadrants of Corporate Counseling

	Lawful Action	Unlawful Action
Immaterial Risk of Harm	Quadrant I	Quadrant III
Material Risk of Harm	Quadrant II	Quadrant IV

decision is not unlawful, the matter does not fall within the lawyer's decisional domain, and the lawyer must ultimately leave the matter for the businessperson to decide. For instance, if PepsiCo decides to phase out the Watermelon Ice flavor of its Gatorade line of sports drinks due to lagging sales, the legal department has no grounds to object.

To be sure, the Model Rules elsewhere point out that lawyers are not proscribed from giving advice beyond the legal domain. Indeed, Rule 2.1 states that a lawyer may also refer "to other considerations such as moral, economic, social and political factors that may be relevant to the client's situation." But this sentiment is hedged by the reminder that "a lawyer is not a moral advisor" (cmt. 2). Moreover, Comment 3 to Rule 2.1 indicates that a more deferential posture may be warranted when sophisticated clients are concerned: "A client may expressly or impliedly ask the lawyer for purely technical advice. When such a request is made by a client experienced in legal matters, the lawyer may accept it at face value."

Accordingly, the Model Rules permit lawyers to stick to "strictly legal" advice and leave the matter for the client (or client representative) to decide. This deference is reiterated in Rule 1.2's prescription that "a lawyer shall abide by a client's decisions concerning the objectives of representation" and the attendant observation that "lawyers usually defer to the client regarding . . . concern for third persons who might be adversely affected" by the legal representation (cmt. 2). Lest the lawyer harbor doubts about whether she, as a matter of professional ethics, may assist immoral (but not unlawful) conduct, Model Rule 1.2(b) clarifies that a lawyer's representation of a client "does not constitute an endorsement of the client's political, economic, social or moral views or activities." In sum, then, for Quadrant I matters, the Model Rules envision lawyers yielding to their clients in matters concededly lawful.

Quadrant II (Lawful Action; Material Risk of Harm)

What if the action is lawful, but the risk of harm is higher? Comment 3 to Rule 1.13 sticks to the same position: "Decisions concerning policy and operations, *including ones entailing serious risk*, are not as such in the lawyer's province" (emphasis added). As such, plans that are lawful even if they might financially ruin the company are classified by the Model Rules as *business* decisions. For example, if the Coca-Cola Company decides to change again its formula for Coke, its lawyer may advise against it, but then should defer to the company's business managers for the final decision.

Quadrant III (Unlawful Action; Immaterial Risk of Harm)

If the first two quadrants are deemed to be business decisions outside the lawyer's purview, one might assume that the next two (Quadrants III and IV)—because they both involve unlawful actions—would fall squarely within the lawyer's prerogative to stop. However, the Model Rules state otherwise for Quadrant III. Although counsel is free to try to dissuade an errant manager, the Model Rules require up-the-ladder reporting *only* when illegal conduct poses a risk of *substantial* harm to the corporation. By negative implication, illegal conduct posing an insubstantial risk of harm is excluded from the lawyer's formal gatekeeping jurisdiction. For example, underenforced regulatory violations or violations that risk nominal civil fines or agency warning letters (e.g., form violations of state bottled water labeling regulations) may fall in Quadrant III. Notwithstanding a lawyer's status as "officer of the court," the Model Rules have embedded within them thoroughly pragmatic accommodations. As such, a Quadrant III matter remains a business decision. That said, the Model Rules also clarify that any accommodation of the client must not transgress the norms against assisting a client's crime or fraud (Model Rule 1.2(d)).

Quadrant IV (Unlawful Action; Material Risk of Harm)

That leaves Quadrant IV, which encompasses unlawful actions that pose very serious risks to the organization. In this domain, the Model Rules grant the lawyer specific legal authority, indeed responsibility, to report up the ladder and, in narrow circumstances, to report out to law enforcement. For instance, if the CEO announced his intention to market defective kidney dialyzers, thus endangering the lives of nephrology patients (*Balla v. Gambro, Inc.*, 1991), counsel must report the matter to the board and *may* report out to enforcement agencies. Under the Model Rules, this would not be a mere business decision.

To recap, the Model Rules use two variables—lawfulness and materiality—to categorize the situations that might confront lawyers representing organizations. The Rules identify a single quadrant, Quadrant IV (unlawful action; material risk of harm), in which counsel must act as gatekeeper. If read less as positive law and more as normative pronouncements, the Rules sketch out a rough vision about the proper role for lawyers, including the appropriate zones of their activity and influence. Business matters (even those that might involve immoral but legally permissible conduct) are not "in the lawyer's province"; as such, lawyers may stick to the law and questions of legality (especially when dealing with sophisticated clients). Should the organization's actions potentially harm third-party interests, the Rules do not object to lawyers deferring to their clients. Even when faced with legal transgressions, counsel should ultimately defer to clients unless the risks are truly great. Arguably, the Rules subtly advocate a deferential posture as long as crimes or frauds are not abetted.

Seen in this way, the Model Rules accord with what has been called the "principle of nonaccountability" (Schwartz 1978, 674), the "principle of neutrality" (Simon 1978, 36), and the theory of "moral independence" (Painter 1994, 557–560)—the view, long espoused by the American bar, that so long as lawyers are not abetting illegality, they are not morally responsible for their clients' ends, even if such ends are immoral or unjust. This disclaimer of lawyer accountability for the morality of clients' actions is one critical component of what has been called the "standard conception of the lawyer's role" (Postema 1980, 73). The "standard conception" excuses lawyers' aggressive pursuit of clients' ends, even if morally problematic, so long as such ends are not unlawful.

Empirical Findings

Of course, what the Model Rules say may have little bearing on what lawyers actually do. The empirical research on inside counsel shows the extent to which their self-reported behavior conforms with the Model Rules' vision of lawyering. Although critical questions remain unresolved, the research reveals general confirmation of the Model Rules' baseline.

Quadrants I and II: Empirical Confirmation

Matters falling in Quadrant I (lawful action; immaterial risk of harm) and Quadrant II (lawful action; material risk of harm) do not raise questions of legality. As such, whatever risks they pose, they are not legal risks. For such matters, the Model Rules require the lawyer to let the client decide. The empirical literature suggests that inside lawyers generally follow this instruction. Indeed, the inside counsel respondents in all the studies rarely challenged business managers' final authority to decide matters falling squarely within the business domain.

For example, in her pilot study of general counsel of Fortune 1000 companies, Tanina Rostain (2008) recounted how one general counsel described "the occasional request from managers to include provisions to indemnify particu-

lar customers in connection with certain sales" (475), a matter that is ordinarily viewed as a business decision.[5] Although this general counsel disagreed, as a
matter of policy, with the decision to create a contractual obligation in favor of
certain customers, "he often deferred to managers on this issue" (475).

But despite this general confirmation of the Model Rules's approach, the
studies also reveal that many inside counsel do not confine their involvement
to matters that are "strictly legal," as the Rules permit. Indeed, many inside
counsel participate actively in both Quadrant I and II decisions even though
they pose no legal risk to the corporation. Even more interesting, these lawyers
fall into two very different camps.

Entrepreneurs. In their study of inside counsel's lawyering styles conducted
in the 1990s, Robert Nelson and Laura Beth Nielsen classified 33% of the 42 inside lawyers in their sample as "Entrepreneurs." Entrepreneurs embraced the
business values in their work and, like the businesspeople, were motivated by
financial gain and not just potential legal loss. They were proud of their ability
to go beyond giving just legal advice. One general counsel of a holding company exemplified the typical entrepreneur:

> The chairman and chief financial officer consult me, as part of the strategic
> planning process that we go on. On matters outside of the legal function, I
> think probably because of the credibility I've gained in representing them
> over the last ten years in a variety of contexts, they've never expected, and
> we don't expect, our attorneys to limit their advice and input to pure legal
> advice. The client here has never found that to be the most valuable type
> of relationship. There are some clients that certainly expect the lawyers to
> limit their input to legal advice, but those folks have not succeeded well and
> don't represent the mainstream of our business management. (Nelson and
> Nielsen 2000, 466)

Nelson and Nielsen also observed that Entrepreneurs seemed to have greater
influence on corporate activities than those lawyers who tended to narrow
their concerns to strictly legal matters. In their case study of a major financial
institution ("Alphacorp"), a separate component of their larger project, the authors observed that "the higher-ranked lawyers [were] more entrepreneurial
than their subordinates" (2000, 481).

---

5. Ordinarily, including an indemnification provision in a contract is a legally unobjection-
able course of action. As a result, the decision to add an indemnification obligation is normally
viewed as a business decision to be finally decided by business managers.

Robert Rosen (2010) made similar observations in his study of inside counsel in six manufacturing firms in the 1970s. Rosen identified a group of inside counsel ("decision consultants") who often ventured into managerial domains and mixed business and legal advice (116). He noticed that these decision consultants exercised greater influence over corporate conduct than the other group of inside counsel ("risk analysts"), who confined themselves to legal risk analysis and played no meaningful part in corporate decision making (90).

Interestingly, Nelson and Nielsen (2000) observed that the entrepreneurial orientation of certain inside counsel influenced their approach to ethical issues. Instead of viewing the law as a constraint, Entrepreneurs saw the law as "a source of profits, an instrument to be used aggressively in the marketplace" to gain competitive advantages for their companies. As such, some "push[ed] the envelope in grey areas of the law," while others sought to legitimate their function by reference to economic values, "portray[ing] the law [to business executives] as adding value to the business, rather than only cost" (487). On the whole, Entrepreneurs discounted their role in policing management and emphasized their role in facilitating business deals and plans. In other words, Entrepreneurs who were active in Quadrant I and II matters displayed a tendency to minimize their gatekeeping role.

Counsel. As distinguished from Entrepreneurs, Nelson and Nielsen identified approximately 50% of the inside counsel sampled as "Counsel." These lawyers occasionally ventured beyond issues of legality to influence the outcome of business decisions. But their motivations differed from Entrepreneurs who emphasized business values. Instead, Counsel would pursue a particular course of action either because it was the morally right thing to do or it protected the company from reputational harm. Similarly, Canadian researchers Sally Gunz and Hugh Gunz (2008) identified a breed of inside counsel who "handle[d] decisions . . . by using his or her professional social capital to try to influence the behaviour of senior non-legal colleagues without playing the role of 'cop'" (930). Other researchers also described individual inside lawyers who exhibited characteristics resembling those of Counsel.[6]

One respondent classified as Counsel in Nelson and Nielsen's study (2000) described how he actively influenced certain decisions, including the proverbial "legal but stupid" decisions. This inside counsel clearly viewed his role as much more expansive than the conventional legal adviser:

---

6. For example, Donnell (1970) found inside lawyers' roles varied from "policeman" to "advisor," the latter being more similar to Nelson and Nielsen's Counsel.

I believe that it's my role to make the decision and to make sure the business person goes along with it. Now that's contrary to everything I'd say on the outside or any general counsel would say, because we'd say, "It's not our role to make business decisions." We lay out the risks and the alternatives to our clients and then they make an informed business decision. Well, if they are making an informed business decision, in my mind there is only one decision they can make, the one I want them to make or I think they ought to make—because that's my job. I don't conceive it to be just laying out the risks, but I have to know enough about the company and enough about the situations and circumstances to weigh those risks. . . . [I]f I think they are doing something that is legal, that is stupid, it's my job to say to them, "That's stupid," or to convince them in such a way that they come around to my point of view, thinking it's their point of view. (465)

The mechanisms by which Counsel (or lawyers similar to Counsel) would intervene in Quadrants I and II varied. Sometimes, they directly employed moral suasion to influence business decisions. For example, one outside lawyer described an inside lawyer's superior ability to raise fairness concerns in a situation where no legal obligation had existed:

The client wanted to know if he had to pay the debt. I found that the statute of limitations had run and that there was no legal requirement. I had known the client for a while and we talked about what was fair. He left wondering whether it was a waste of corporate resources to pay. The inside counsel then talked to him about just what the debtee had done for the company. He was needed to convince the client that in light of all the circumstances, it was proper to pay. I just couldn't do that. (Rosen 2010, 127)

More often, Counsel would raise ethical issues indirectly, by appealing to the firm's long term or reputational interests. For example, they may refer to potential jury reaction as a proxy for ethical concerns. Although Eve Spangler (1986, 92–93) did not classify the lawyers she interviewed for her study, she described how one inside counsel for an insurance company deployed predictable jury reaction and financial impact to great effect:

My observation after fifteen years here [is that] if I said to a claims person, "As a legal matter you can raise the defense that you want to raise. But as a practical matter, if you go before a jury with that technical type defense [against] a poor disabled guy, out of work, with a family to support, they're not going to listen. You're going to lose. It's probably going to cost you penalties. It might cost you punitive damages. It's also going to cost about $50,000 to try the damn thing." If I say that to them, I have never in my life seen an instance where they pursued the legal [claim].

Rostain (2008, 474) recounted how one general counsel handled managerial conduct that was legal but risked tarnishing the company's image:

He described a recent incident where employees had been interested in trading in company stock. Although he and other managers were confident that the trading was not suspect, he believed that from outside the company the conduct might look like insider trading. On the recommendation of the GC, the CEO issued instructions to stop the trading.

For companies marketing products to consumers, reputational concerns dominated strictly legal ones. As Rostain (2008, 477) reported:

According to this GC [of a food processing company], he instructed [the lawyers] to ask themselves three questions, starting with whether the conduct was ethical. His test was whether he wanted it to appear in the *Wall Street Journal*— and then whether it was consistent with the company's core values. If action passed these two tests, then the last question was whether it was legal.

As evidenced above, inside counsel can sometimes draw on their knowledge of the company's "core values"—its corporate culture—to influence business decisions. Because inside counsel interface with different constituents and handle many aspects of the company's operations, inside counsel may better grasp the company's culture and acceptable risk levels. And because corporate law departments are often responsible for housing important corporate documents, inside counsel sometimes function as de facto company historians. Inside counsel can draw on this background in articulating the corporate culture to business managers and, as a result, exert persuasive influence (Rosen 2010, 130).

In sum, the empirical literature confirms behavior in accordance with the Model Rules. Inside counsel ultimately defer to businesspersons' authority on Quadrant I and II matters—where the proposed course of action is not unlawful but may generate some business risks. However, the findings also show that a significant number of inside counsel—whether they be classified as Entrepreneurs or Counsel—participate actively in such business decisions, acting more like participants with a vested interest in the outcome rather than mere advisers. More specifically, Entrepreneurs emulate their business colleagues. Indeed, many inside counsel consider the opportunity to participate in business decisions to be one of the chief advantages of working in-house

(Weaver 1997). By contrast, Counsel appear to be motivated by ethical concerns and long-term reputational consequences. As such, they act as a more corporate version of the lawyer-statesman (Kronman 1993), navigating a broad terrain that extends beyond questions of mere legality.

Quadrant III: Empirical Confirmation

Recall what the Model Rules say about Quadrant III matters (unlawful action; immaterial risk of harm). Although lawyers are free to give advice against taking unlawful action that poses little risk of harm, they must, in the end, defer to the manager's decision even if it is to ignore the lawyer's advice. (To be clear, the lawyer may not knowingly assist criminal or fraudulent conduct (Model Rule 1.2(d)).) The Rules do not require lawyers to report up the corporate ladder when the risk of harm is immaterial. Comment 3 to Rule 1.13 specifically suggests a general duty of deference: "When constituents of the organization make decisions for it, the decisions ordinarily must be accepted by the lawyer even if their utility or prudence is doubtful." Do inside counsel act consistently with this prescription? Here, we run into some methodological complications within the empirical research. Because most studies failed to distinguish systematically between immaterial and material legal risks, it was frequently unclear whether inside counsel were reporting about Quadrant III or Quadrant IV matters. That said, to the extent that the matter clearly fell in Quadrant III, the empirical research seems to confirm that inside lawyers behave in accordance with the Model Rules' guidance.

Rostain (2008, 475) reported that an important function for general counsel was line drawing—"distinguishing more significant legal risks, which fell within their decisional purview, and less important legal risks that they left to managers to decide." This suggests that general counsel typically defer on Quadrant III matters but do not defer on Quadrant IV matters. For example, in one situation, a manager urged the company to save on significant compliance costs by ignoring the state advertising laws, which the company's competitors were ignoring. The general counsel noted that in such circumstances "he might leave it to the manager to decide" (476).

Another general counsel of a computer parts wholesaler stressed the importance of inside lawyers acting as team players for all but the most serious of legal risks:

> Our mission here as a legal team is to provide practical solutions to the highest priority problems in the business, so we view ourselves as having to provide solutions. Now, that doesn't mean that we're absolutely "yes men" and

that they can do anything. Because we're not a highly regulated industry, there are very few things that we wind up doing that are going to be serious violations of a criminal or legal stature. If that's not the case, then all we're trying to do is help the team negotiate a business deal. (475)

Of course, as with all the quadrants, what falls in Quadrant III will not always be crystal clear. For example, the legality of a proposed course of action may be ambiguous. Perhaps the relevant facts are unique or uncertain and do not fit neatly within existing legal precedent. Or perhaps the facts are clear but the law is clumsily worded and subject to multiple interpretations. In such cases, absent overriding reputational concerns, inside counsel are likely to treat the matter as a business decision. As one general counsel explained:

> If the law is less than clear, or if the fact pattern isn't clear, then it is a matter of risk assessment. And one of the things that—and I am a firm believer—if it is a matter of assessing the risk, the lawyer's job is to give the best description or explanation of the risk and how it might impact the company and then ultimately it is a business decision. (Rostain 2008, 477)

In sum, for Quadrant III matters, the self-reported behavior of inside counsel generally conforms to the ethical floor of the Model Rules. Inside counsel cede to managers the right to determine ultimately Quadrant III matters—actions that may run afoul of some minor rule or regulation but are immaterial in terms of the risk of harm to the corporate entity. The lawyer may offer advice, but the manager makes the final call.

Quadrant IV: Empirical Uncertainty

Given the stakes, we would expect inside counsel to act most aggressively in Quadrant IV (unlawful action; material risk of harm). In addition, the Model Rules grant counsel the authority to escalate matters up the corporate ladder or even outside the organization, effectively vesting counsel with a powerful "trump." How do inside counsel approach Quadrant IV matters? Do they throw their weight around, even threatening to use their trump card? Or do they subordinate themselves to managers and leave it to them, again, to make the final call?

As mentioned above, since most researchers did not systematically distinguish the seriousness of legal risks, it was often unclear from respondents' remarks whether they were discussing Quadrant III or Quadrant IV matters. Moreover, it was unclear whether some of the respondents ever encountered a

Quadrant IV matter (Nelson and Nielson 2000, 471), which presumably occurs less frequently. Despite these complications, however, one can reasonably conclude from the studies that at least *some* inside counsel do escalate and assert their professional authority in Quadrant IV circumstances.

In particular, one breed of inside counsel, classified as "Cops" by Nelson and Nielsen, exhibited characteristics suggesting a willingness to interpose themselves in Quadrant IV matters. These Cops, comprising 17% of their respondents, identified most strongly with their status as lawyers and understood their primary job as policing the conduct of management. They performed an active gatekeeping role, "marked by an affirmative obligation to monitor compliance, the ability to say no to business clients, and the ability to go over the head of management" (2000, 468). Of all of Nelson and Nielsen's ideal types, Cops were most reluctant to tread outside of their expertise and offer nonlegal advice. They were also less likely than the others to soft-pedal their legal advice to minimize conflicts with the business folk. Perhaps for these reasons, there were significantly fewer Cops than Entrepreneurs in Nelson and Nielsen's study (487).

Similarly, the general counsel in Rostain's study "articulated a robust account of their jurisdiction over questions of legal risk" (2008, 473). They professed the willingness to say "no" in situations that appear to fall in Quadrant IV (i.e., situations implicating significant civil or criminal liability). Rostain (2008, 476) reported:

> With other legal risks, this GC was clear that his department's role was to say "no." [An example] came from the antitrust context: A manager who was quoted a competitor's price by a buyer wanted to contact the competitor to verify it. This lawyer was clear that in these situations, which were apparently not uncommon, he was firm that the conduct violated the law. As he put it, "When I make those statements that's pretty much [it]. People move on."

Another general counsel recounted how merely "issuing a threat (implicitly or explicitly) was sufficient to deter managers from such [risky] conduct" (474). According to him, typically, the manager would respond by loudly complaining "about the excesses of regulators or Congress," and then "the issue would then be dropped" (474). Yet another general counsel described how he occasionally displayed handcuffs in a board meeting to "get attention" (489).

Of course, not all inside counsel arrive at a board meeting, props in hand. Others just check in with the manager's boss, ultimately deferring the final decision to *a* business manager but policing the issue of who gets to decide. As one inside lawyer put it:

> Our job is to assess risks, and it's the business person's job to make decisions
> about risks, what risks they are willing to assume. Now, having said that,
> I also think of it as my job to make sure that the decision about what risks
> to assume is being made at the appropriate level. So, if somebody was pre-
> pared to assume a risk which I felt was inappropriate, I would say, "I don't
> think this is a decision for you to make. I need to talk to your boss." (Nelson
> and Nielson 2000, 473)

Escalating a matter to a manager's boss is not a decision made lightly. Like any
corporate employee, inside counsel must be selective about which matters to
take up to higher authorities. Otherwise, they run the risk of being tagged as
"rigid" and being circumvented by "forum-shopping" managers who will turn
to more pliable lawyers for advice (Nelson and Nielsen 2000; Gunz and Gunz
2008).

While inside counsel's power is constrained by pragmatic considerations,
they still may exercise more influence than outside counsel. One inside lawyer,
who formerly represented the company as its outside lawyer, remarked:

> I have to decide when legal issues should prevail. On the outside, I used
> to say, "Here is my opinion and the risks. It is up to you to decide whether
> you want to assume the risk." On the inside, it is the same principle, but if
> we put up enough of an argument against something, chances are it won't
> go through. You have to pick and choose when to do that. It requires some
> judgment about how strongly to say no. (Rosen 2010, 100)

This statement is consistent with anecdotes in other studies and, contrary to
the conventional wisdom, suggests that inside counsel may be *more* likely than
outside counsel to intervene in situations entailing serious legal risk.

Generally speaking, we see evidence that some inside counsel readily assert
their professional authority when faced with serious legal risks. But should we
infer that this is common behavior? As it turns out, the empirical literature
seems deeply conflicted. According to Nelson and Nielsen, although, "when
questioned, almost every attorney could imagine a situation in which he or she
would go over the head of management to become a deal stopper" (2000, 471),
only 17% of respondents (the Cops) exhibited strong gatekeeping proclivities.
Indeed, the authors found that their respondents "typically leave the final call
on acceptable levels of legal risk to the businesspersons involved" (2000, 486).
Similarly, Rosen found that most inside lawyers were generally reluctant to
challenge a manager's decision about legal risk (2010).

In contrast, Gunz and Gunz (2008) found that 59% of inside counsel's responses reflected some degree of willingness to challenge managerial decisions. Also, Gunz and Gunz found that a significant number of inside counsel, although never specifically quantified, reported being willing to "raise their heads above the parapet" (940), including resigning or reporting the matter to governmental authorities. Although difficult to know for sure (given that the authors reported the number of responses and not the number of inside counsel), it seems that Gunz and Gunz's inside counsel were (at least when responding to hypothetical questions) more willing to assert their authority to stop unlawful conduct than Rosen's or Nelson and Nielsen's lawyers.

Finally, Rostain provides the most robust account of inside counsel's willingness to interpose themselves in matters implicating legal risks. Contrary to Rosen's and Nelson and Nielsen's findings, Rostain's general counsel were not resigned to acting as mere advisers. Instead, her respondents "were unanimous in insisting that responsibility for determining the appropriate level of risk to be undertaken by their companies lay with them" (Rostain 2008, 473). They characterized their gatekeeping functions "in very strong terms" and were all "confident of their capacity to stop deals that they believed posed significant legal risks to the company" (Quadrant IV matters) (473–474). Although they occasionally found reason to cede the final call on low-level risks to managers (Quadrant III), these general counsel "were the ultimate arbiters of which risks were negotiable and which were not" (479).

How might these disparate empirical findings be reconciled? First, we should be cautious about what can be inferred from small samples. As Rostain readily acknowledged, hers was a pilot study of only 10 lawyers. Gunz and Gunz interviewed 25 inside counsel, Nelson and Nielsen drew on interviews with 42 lawyers (and 12 managers), and Rosen interviewed 77 people (including inside counsel, outside counsel, and business managers). Moreover, Rostain acknowledged the possibility of a biased sample (2008, 479): Most of her general counsel respondents "worked for traditional blue chip companies, none of which had a known history of legal problems or significant risk taking," and some described their companies as having a "deep culture of compliance" (474).

Second, the different findings may be explained by the type of respondents interviewed. Both Rosen and Nelson and Nielsen interviewed not only inside counsel but also their business colleagues. By contrast, Gunz and Gunz and Rostain confined their structured interviews to inside counsel. As a result, the latter studies, which are based solely on lawyers' self-reported behavior, may reflect a more self-serving account of inside counsel's power and willingness to police management. That said, Gunz and Gunz were the only researchers who employed vignettes, or "short cases describing hypothetical situations involving ethical dilemmas" (2002, 259), for their discussions with inside counsel. As they noted, "Vignettes have been described as particularly suitable for reducing social desirability bias, and indeed there is evidence that people are more likely to describe their real reaction to ethical dilemmas if presented with vignettes" (259).

Third, the various studies were conducted at different times and under different regulatory environments. The Rosen and Nelson and Nielsen studies were conducted prior to the enactment of Sarbanes-Oxley and the 2003 amendments to Model Rule 1.13. These events ushered in a period of enhanced criminal penalties and greater enforcement activity by regulatory agencies. By contrast, Gunz and Gunz and Rostain conducted their studies *after* Sarbanes-Oxley and the Model Rules amendments. (It is not clear whether or how Canadian counsel in the Gunz and Gunz study would be affected by these US events except indirectly.) Therefore, it is plausible that the findings of the latter studies (particularly Rostain's) reflected the enhanced power of general counsel as a consequence of an increased corporate commitment to compliance and risk management. While a majority of Rostain's general counsel insisted that their "gate-keeping role long predated the corporate scandals" (Rostain 2008, 479), most seemed to suggest that "the statute has had a subtle and wide spread influence on directors' approach to serving on boards and serves as resource for general counsel to draw on to assert their authority within the corporation" (489).

Fourth, the researchers interviewed lawyers with very different levels of seniority, which may have affected their willingness to assert their gatekeeping authority. Almost all of the lawyers in the Gunz and Gunz study were relatively senior in rank, with an average tenure of 22 years. Rostain's study was similarly confined to the most senior inside lawyers—general counsel. By contrast, Nelson and Nielsen culled from a wider pool of lawyers. In their sample, 10 of 11 (or 91%) of the respondents working in corporate or divisional management indicated that they made the final decision about whether to incur a legal risk. But only 35% of other (more junior) lawyers claimed to make that final call. As one general counsel in the Gunz and Gunz study explained, "Just sort of letting senior management handle it, that may work fine for more junior lawyers in a legal department and in fact that it may be asking too much of them to do anything more than that. But general counsel can't stop here" (2008, 936). This explanation is also consistent with theories of "ethical learning," whereby "lawyers gradually acquire specialized ethical expertise" (Chambliss, chapter 3, 48; Chambliss and Wilkins 2002).

Seniority may also play an indirect role in the fifth explanation, which focuses on how legal matters are distributed among various lawyers within a single legal department as determined by the particular lawyer's seniority level. Since different types of matters may be routinely handled by different lawyers, respondents may have been approaching the same key question ("Who makes the final call on acceptable levels of legal risk?") from very different vantage points. Since, for many companies, the general counsel cannot personally evaluate every single legal risk facing the company, the legal risks that are likely to percolate to the general counsel are precisely those that pose the gravest threat to the company. And those legal risks are likely to be the ones that come to mind when general counsel report in surveys whether they had the right to make the final call. If true, it should not be surprising that Rostain's general counsel—the highest-ranking lawyers in their respective companies—insisted that they had the final authority to decide whether to assume a particular legal risk. For the same reason, it should not be surprising that only half of Nelson and Nielsen's inside counsel, which included both senior and less experienced lawyers, said they made the final call on legal risks.

The fifth explanation is consistent with Gunz and Gunz's observation that the closer the lawyers were to "the top management team . . . the more often they encountered ethical dilemmas" (2008, 930). This explanation is also consistent with anecdotal evidence suggesting a division of labor between senior inside counsel and subordinate inside counsel based roughly on the seriousness of the legal risks posed. For example, John Donnell (1970) found that one general counsel handled antitrust matters (which could implicate criminal liability) while his subordinate inside counsel handled more routine contracts matters (which normally pose, at most, contractual liability). Accordingly, it may be that when answering survey questions, the more senior lawyers were considering a pool of matters with higher concentrations of Quadrant IV risks than the pool of matters considered by the more junior lawyers.

In sum, it seems clear that some inside counsel do assert their gatekeeping authority for matters potentially falling in Quadrant IV. Where the empirical literature is inconclusive is the extent to which inside counsel make the final call on legal risks. Further research that more carefully distinguishes between Quadrant III and Quadrant IV legal risks and accounts for seniority status would illuminate how robustly inside counsel exercise their gatekeeping authority.

Conclusion

Inside counsel's role demands the complex balancing of colliding norms and competing interests. Lawyers working in-house feel considerable pressure to accede to management's demands and to search for creative legal means of achieving business objectives. Instead of hindering business by throwing up roadblocks, inside counsel are pressured to "Be the Solution," as the conference title of the Association of Corporate Counsel's 2010 annual meeting exhorts. The discretion of inside counsel is thus constrained by business ends.

At the same time, inside counsel must also play a gatekeeping role and protect the company from more serious legal risks. The empirical research is still inconclusive as to what extent inside counsel assert their authority to make the final call on acceptable levels of legal risks. Generalizations are difficult because of the tremendous complexity and variability in approaches both across different contexts and among the various inside lawyers. As the researchers acknowledged, efforts to classify lawyers according to their most typical counseling approach may obscure important variations in their individual approaches to different problems. Nelson and Nielsen observed that "inside counsel play different roles in different circumstances" and that the interviews "are full of seemingly contradictory statements, until one realizes that the lawyers are describing a repertoire of responses to different situations" (2000, 463). Hence, they wisely caution against a reductionist interpretation of inside counsel's identities and strategies.

Building and expanding on the analytical framework developed in this chapter, the next generation of research on inside counsel should concentrate on isolating the sources of these observed variations, such as the nature of the risk (e.g., business, legal, public relations, material, immaterial); companies' risk tolerance levels/risk culture; the individual characteristics of inside counsel (e.g., personality, seniority, or tenure at the firm); the organizational structure and size of the corporate law department; the nature of the industry and the competitive position of the firm within the industry; and the extent to which globalization has changed inside counsel's practices. Inside counsel are crucially important intermediaries between law and economic power. We need to gain a better understanding of their behavior.

References

Abel, Richard L. 1989. *American Lawyers*. New York: Oxford University Press.

Beardslee, Michele DeStefano. 2009. "Advocacy in the Court of Public Opinion, Installment One: Broadening the Role of Corporate Attorneys." *Georgetown Journal of Legal Ethics* 22:1259–1333.

Beardslee, Michele DeStefano, John C. Coates IV, Ashish Nanda, and David B. Wilkins. 2010. "Hiring Teams from Rivals: Theory and Evidence on the Evolving Relationships in the Corporate Legal Market." http://papers.ssrn.com/sol3/papers.cfm?abstract_id=1442066.

Brown, Louis M. 1950. *Preventive Law*. New York: Prentice-Hall.

Carson, Clara N. 2004. *The Lawyer Statistical Report: The U.S. Legal Profession in 2000*. Chicago: American Bar Foundation.

Chambliss, Elizabeth, and David B. Wilkins. 2002. "The Emerging Role of Ethics Advisors, General Counsel, and Other Compliance Specialists in Large Law Firms." *Arizona Law Review* 44:559–592.

DeMott, Deborah A. 2005. "The Discrete Roles of General Counsel." *Fordham Law Review* 74:955–981.

Donnell, John D. 1970. *The Corporate Counsel: A Role Study*. Bloomington: Indiana University Press.

Gruner, Richard S. 1997. "General Counsel in an Era of Compliance Programs and Corporate Self-Policing." *Emory Law Journal* 46:1113–1196.

Gunz, Hugh P., and Sally P. Gunz. 2002. "The Lawyer's Response to Organizational Professional Conflict: An Empirical Study of the Ethical Decision Making of In-House Counsel." *American Business Law Journal* 39:241–287.

———. 2008. "Ethical Decision Making and the Employed Lawyer." *Journal of Business Ethics* 81:927–944.

Hackett, Susan. 2002. "Inside Out: An Examination of Demographic Trends in the In-House Profession." *Arizona Law Review* 44:609–619.

Hazard, Geoffrey C., Jr. 1997. "Ethical Dilemmas of Corporate Counsel." *Emory Law Journal* 46:1011–1022.

Hazard, Geoffrey C., Jr., and W. William Hodes. 2005. *The Law of Lawyering*. 3rd ed., vol. 1. New York: Aspen.

Kim, Sung Hui. 2005. "The Banality of Fraud: Re-Situating the Inside Counsel as Gatekeeper." *Fordham Law Review* 74:983–1077.

———. 2008. "Gatekeepers Inside Out." *Georgetown Journal of Legal Ethics* 21:411–463.

Kronman, Anthony T. 1993. *The Lost Lawyer: Failing Ideals of the Legal Profession*. Cambridge, MA: Harvard University Press.

Liggio, Carl D. 1997. "The Changing Role of Corporate Counsel." *Emory Law Journal* 46:1201–1222.

Nelson, Robert L., and Laura Beth Nielsen. 2000. "Cops, Counsel, and Entrepreneurs: Constructing the Role of Inside Counsel in Large Corporations." *Law & Society Review* 34:457–494.

Painter, Richard W. 1994. "The Moral Interdependence of Corporate Lawyers and Their Clients." *Southern California Law Review* 67:507–584.

Postema, Gerald J. 1980. "Moral Responsibility in Professional Ethics." *New York University Law Review* 55:63–89.

Rosen, Robert Eli. 2010. *Lawyers in Corporate Decision-Making*. New Orleans: Quid Pro.

Rostain, Tanina. 2008. "General Counsel in the Age of Compliance: Preliminary Findings and New Research Questions." *Georgetown Journal of Legal Ethics* 21:465–490.

Schwartz, Murray L. 1978. "The Professionalism and Accountability of Lawyers." *California Law Review* 66:669–697.

Simon, William H. 1978. "The Ideology of Advocacy: Procedural Justice and Professional Ethics." *Wisconsin Law Review* 1978:29–144.

Spangler, Eve. 1986. "Company Men Through and Through: Corporate Staff Counsel." In *Lawyers for Hire: Salaried Professionals at Work*, 70–106. New Haven, CT: Yale University Press.

Sterngold, James. 2010. "Who Cares About Another $200 Million?" *Bloomberg Businessweek*, May 3–9, 56–59.

Weaver, Sally R. 1997. "Ethical Dilemmas of Corporate Counsel: A Structural and Contextual Analysis." *Emory Law Journal* 46:1023–1051.

Cases, Statutes, and Regulations

Balla v. Gambro, Inc., 584 N.E.2d 104 (Ill. 1991).

Sarbanes-Oxley Act of 2002, Pub. L. No. 107-204, 116 Stat. 745, 784.

17 C.F.R. §§ 205.1–205.7 (2010).

The Ethical Lives of Securities Lawyers

Patrick Schmidt

Crises of confidence in markets have accompanied every era, not as aberrations but as regular—not to say routine—elements of capitalism. Little surprise should accompany this observation; sociologists since Emile Durkheim have observed that scandal and deviance are not failures of law but integral parts of constructing the community's (legal) norms. It was from the crisis of 1929 that the US Securities and Exchange Commission (SEC) was born, and if the desire to bring stability to the financial sector seems unfulfilled, it may be less enervating to approach securities regulation from an assumption that crisis is a constitutive part of the system.

For securities lawyers, the past decade has renewed discussion of ethics as a significant feature of their corner of the realm of capital markets policy. This is not new. Since the 1970s in particular, an important feature of the cat and mouse game between the state and the markets has been the effort to align securities lawyers with state power, to enlist them as agents of the public interest in their representation of corporate clients—a game in which the Sarbanes-Oxley Act of 2002 provided the key move. Whether or not one takes seriously the ambition of using policy reforms to stop the cycle of scandals in a capitalist economy, the desire to see ethics as a vital policy instrument begs the question: What effect do ethical considerations have on the work lives and work product of securities lawyers? Separating work lives from work product helps to focus our attention on both what lawyers consciously say about their work and what goes into their work when they do it. That dual interest means that

I thank Caroline Ettinger for her assistance with the quantitative data reported here, and Cali Cope-Kasten and Simeng Han for their work with the qualitative data. The survey data reported here were made possible by a grant from the National Science Foundation (SES-0001773).

I treat ethics with a partial skepticism, seeing it as a constructed conversation that serves the needs and interests of the profession while I also assume that it is something "real"—a form of norms that does work against other considerations in the lives of lawyers. In short, we can take ethics seriously for what it does—with a concern for the effects of ethics—while also thinking critically about why we might imagine that ethics matter at all.

I explore the tensions produced by our conversation on securities ethics by drawing on a range of empirical materials, including both qualitative interviews and a survey of securities lawyers. The first section of this chapter establishes the basic context of securities law practice and rehearses the ongoing dialogue about securities lawyers' ethics in the United States. Then, after a brief section detailing the research supporting the analysis, I turn in two sections to the day-to-day experiences that bring ethical considerations to the foreground of lawyers' work and to the dynamics of ethics in this field when viewed from a long-term perspective that puts "crises" into relief. The two halves of the analysis do not remain divided: In conclusion, I argue that the disruptions of economic crises and subsequent calls for a "return to ethical standards" struggle to overcome the forces, inherent and inertial, that threaten to reduce ethics to mere background noise in securities law.

The Setting for Securities Law Practice

The ethics of securities lawyers is a secondary concern for the financial markets as a whole, but it is more than a tempest in a teapot. A thumbnail sketch first offers an explanation of the essential context for securities law disclosure.

The Disclosure-Enforcement System

Though widely seen as the "cop on the beat," US securities law does not make the SEC the ultimate authority for regulating financial markets. The core mandate of the SEC, established as a New Deal response to the loss of market confidence and the Great Crash of 1929, was to ensure that complete information about companies and financial markets would be available to investors, who in turn would assess and "regulate" corporate management and performance. This exemplar of a transparency-based system gave the SEC a secondary role in "disclosure-enforcement," one of overseeing the distribution of information by companies and prosecuting failures by corporate officials to make broad disclosure of all facts thought necessary to investors making investment decisions (Khademian 1992). In theory, then, the marketplace produces a private ordering of informed judgments about the soundness and anticipated profitability of firms, rewards those companies with good business practices, and increases the confidence of all investors that public companies are not fraudulent enterprises.

Assuming that sunlight is the best disinfectant, this system, established by the Securities Act of 1933 and the Securities Exchange Act of 1934, governs numerous parties, including fund managers, broker-dealers, and stock exchanges. But the centerpiece is disclosure by public companies engaged in the sale of securities. For a company to sell new securities—either in an initial public offering (IPO) or as an established company seeking to raise money by issuing a new round or class of securities—it must register the securities with the SEC and provide information about the company. Some kinds of information are common to most enterprises, such as information about company leadership, basic financial data, and known risks to a company; more generally, companies must present all considerations that would be "material" to an investor wishing to make an informed decision. A "cooling-off" period between the submission of registration statements and the sale allows the SEC time to halt the sale if its oversight reveals that the registration submissions are "incomplete or inaccurate in any material respect" (15 U.S.C. § 77h(b)). Publicly traded companies have continuing obligations to disclose material information, including through quarterly and annual reports filed with the SEC.

The system has evolved steadily, particularly in the wake of financial crises, with increasing attention to oversight of financial accounting and the clarity of disclosure documents (Fung, Graham, and Weil 2007, 108–109). Though scandalous revelations may betray the trust of investors, and compliance with securities disclosure imposes costs on firms, strong support for the principles of the system has endured. The tensions have been deflected to the bedeviling details of what must be disclosed and whether consumers of information actually make decisions based on available information. The dot-com bubble of the late 1990s, followed by the collapse of Enron and WorldCom, illustrated the hazard of trusting information about firms or, even with information, understanding it in the appropriate light (Benston et al. 2003).

But the central problem is that transparency systems such as the one developed for securities markets play a great game of "trust but verify": A regulator asks for the production of information because it cannot be observed directly, at least at the time that the information is desired. The SEC's enforcement process, much maligned in the past decade, provides one kind of ex post punishment that is thought to create incentives for full disclosure. Private shareholder litigation likewise operates far later in the process, when a company has had a bad turn of fortune and the plaintiffs assert that the company withheld material information or made false statements.

Lawyers as Gatekeepers of Finance

To further protect the public, securities lawyers have been elevated to the role of gatekeepers for disclosure. In one articulation of it, securities lawyers serve as reputational intermediaries, repeat players whose own reputations speak on behalf of corporations, allowing investors to trust that representations made by the companies are trustworthy (Coffee 2006, 2). The use of lawyers as third-party enforcers can be thought essential because if ex post penalties are the only incentives for transparency, the likelihood of enforcement may seem too weak or too distant (Kraakman 1984, 881; Kraakman 1986; Gilboy 1998).

From the founding of the SEC, lawyers have been closely linked to its mission, with a tone set by some of its early chairmen, including James Landis, William O. Douglas, and Jerome Frank (Seligman 2003). Since then, it has been highly lawyered, from the Commission through its full ranks of professional staff. A revolving door for young lawyers leads many to go from law school to one of the regulator's divisions, conducting reviews of corporate disclosure documents or leading enforcement actions, before taking that expertise into private practice. The very active Association of Securities and Exchange Commission Alumni claims nearly 1,000 members, who join an organization founded "to continue the camaraderie" that they shared when they worked at the SEC (Association of SEC Alumni 2007). Many thousands more practice securities law without prior experience at the SEC.

In the fullest expression of the vision of corporate regulation, lawyers would be the ideal choice to serve as gatekeepers. A senior SEC official who spoke to me in the 1990s and claimed that "the vast majority who practice before the agency have a respect for the system, and they do the right thing," explained this was a "culture" that had evolved. He echoed a famous statement by the Commission in a 1973 decision that looked to "our bar" to live by "appropriately rigorous standards of professional honor" (*In re Emanuel Fields*, 1973). Unpacked a bit further, here lay the basic issue of ethics for securities lawyers: the extent to which their advice and actions bring the public value of transparent corporate finance and capital markets to bear on their clients' decision making and legal compliance. The professional rhetoric holds that a rich ethical vision is not only useful but necessary to the health of securities law. The Commission itself famously observed:

Members of this Commission have pointed out time and time again that the task of enforcing the securities laws rests in overwhelming measure on the bar's shoulders. . . . Very little of a securities lawyer's work is adversary in character. . . . He works in his office where he prepares prospectuses, proxy statements, opinions of counsel, and other documents that we, our staff, the financial community, and the investing public must take on faith. This is a field where unscrupulous lawyers can inflict irreparable harm on those who rely on the disclosure documents that they produce. (*In re Emanuel Fields*, 1973, 83,175n20)

This decision was issued a year after the SEC had begun a significant effort to pursue lawyers when enforcing securities laws. That securities lawyers may be subject to legal action when they actively participate in securities fraud has not been in question. The more difficult question concerned the liability of attorneys who had urged their clients to comply with the law but, when the client failed to comply, had not taken further steps with the board of directors or others.

The long-standing authority for SEC regulation of professionals appearing before it is known today as Rule 102(e) of its Rules of Practice, which includes authority to bar an attorney from the practice of securities law if the attorney has "willfully violated, or willfully aided and abetted" a breach in federal securities law or has "engaged in unethical or improper professional conduct." Like most ethics rules, Rule 102(e) lacks detailed definition, including the meaning of the key phrase "unethical or improper professional conduct." The meaning has been established by practice. After decades with just a handful of disciplinary hearings targeting lawyers, the SEC held 85 hearings involving lawyers in the 1970s. The profession closely watched both the SEC's enforcement policy and the subsequent decisions in leading cases, as the SEC challenged experienced members of the bar for their decisions and failure to speak up when the lawyers knew of problematic situations (*SEC v. National Student Marketing Corp.*, 1978; *In re Carter and Johnson*, 1981). Among the greatest fears for the securities bar was the suggestion that the SEC was heading toward an ethical order in which attorneys could voluntarily disclose client fraud to protect the public, a position that would have violated the understood boundaries of attorney-client confidentiality and could have had a significant chilling effect on the cooperation given to attorneys by their clients.

The SEC's attacks against the lawyers of this earlier generation were largely halted in the 1980s after serious and sustained protest by the bar, but that cycle repeated itself and resulted in the passage of the Sarbanes-Oxley Act of 2002. This landmark, multifaceted legislation sought to enhance corporate responsibility through additional requirements and penalties, increase disclosure and oversight, and ensure the independence of securities analysts and auditors. Fresh on the heels of Enron's death spiral, in which its outside counsel were among those implicated, Congress also included in the Act Section 307, which directed the SEC to issue new "minimum standards of professional conduct for attorneys," to include "up-the-ladder" rules. These rules require counsel to take evidence of securities law violations to company executives and then to the board of directors if the problem is not properly addressed. The SEC's proposed Rule 205 also included a provision requiring attorneys to make a "noisy withdrawal"—to withdraw from representation and inform the SEC accordingly—if going up the ladder yielded no results. The American Bar Association's vigorous opposition played a role in winning an about-face from the SEC, which refrained from implementing that requirement in the version of Sarbanes-Oxley that became effective in 2003 (Harrington 2009, 895). Instead of a "noisy withdrawal" requirement, lawyers were given permission under Sarbanes-Oxley to voluntarily report confidential information to the SEC if justified by the need to prevent financial injury or illegalities.

The terms of this cyclical discussion have been rehearsed now for more than 40 years, in a voluminous professional literature (Kim 2010). Should securities attorneys be regarded as different from the "zealous advocates" of adversarial litigation? If so, what do they owe to their clients, and what do they owe to the public interest? What is the balance between the public interest and effective client representation, which itself serves a social good? These are the clashes of values that occur in and around a debate that presumes the importance of ethics to the work of securities lawyers. The bar's objections recognize that these rules create uncertainty for lawyers; the SEC maintains a stance that makes ethics a legal command.

Researching Securities Lawyers

This chapter draws on research I have conducted with securities lawyers over the past 15 years. The largest component of the research has been over 100 semistructured, qualitative interviews with securities lawyers, primarily in law firms. Interviews have proceeded in stages, beginning with 45 interviews in Washington, DC, in 1997, in a sample that included SEC officials and two distinct subpopulations of law firm–based lawyers: corporate securities defense attorneys who represent clients under investigation by the SEC and securities counsel who advise companies in all stages of public financing and disclosure. I conducted a roughly similar number of interviews between 2001 and 2003 in New York and London, during the aftermath of the WorldCom and Enron collapses.[1] The interviewing there emphasized securities lawyers who counsel clients in corporate disclosure and transactions involving due diligence related to securities laws, and also included in-house counsel and counsel for leading underwriters. Further interviewing of a more limited sample of about a dozen attorneys in law firm–based securities law practice, drawn from Silicon Valley and Minneapolis, continued in 2009 and 2010.

Additionally, I conducted an anonymous written survey of the securities bar in late 2004, some results of which are reported here. Although interviews pointed to the potential importance of in-house counsel in securities law practice, since I seek to explore the belief that law firm lawyers possess a particular independence from their clients, here, too, my focus and the data center on law firm-based attorneys. As Sung Hui Kim (chapter 10) observes, in-house counsel operate under different legal and organizational constraints. Finding elite transaction-focused securities lawyers for interviews is relatively simple, but surveying based on the notion of a securities bar—an identifiable group of securities lawyers as a subject of systematic research—needs caveats. Whatever concentrations and strata of securities lawyers are found in major commercial centers, such attorneys can be found across the whole of the United States, anywhere they can access their client base of public companies and private firms that seek money from capital markets. The notion of a "community of practice" as an underlying framework for examining the salient elements of lawyers' work lives (ethics, client relationships, etc.) is a powerful and useful one, and the fact that the "securities lawyer" is a salient concept in discourse may be enough to justify a survey based on that idea.

Yet, the community defined by that label is underspecified and overinclusive. It is underspecified in that a sharp cleavage divides securities litigators (either enforcement defense or shareholder defense, along with the further separate shareholder plaintiffs' counsel) from specialists in transactional work, including public offerings and mergers/acquisitions. Respondents to the survey overwhelmingly self-identified as practitioners of corporate securities

---

1. The emphasis in London remained on US attorneys, but included some English lawyers in analogous legal contexts in foreign law.

228 • PATRICK SCHMIDT

advising, and the survey further allowed litigators to opt out of questions per-
taining to transactional work. A third, more specialized group includes those
who assist the industry (e.g., stock exchanges, broker-dealers) with regulatory
compliance. The term "securities lawyer" is such a big tent that many lawyers
may fail to see themselves as part of an identifiable group at all. For purposes of
a survey, the overinclusiveness of the label creates a severe sampling problem.
The available commercial databases include thousands of attorneys who claim
"securities law" as a specialization, though this is often a weak designation
placed alongside many others when positioning one's practice in a commercial
directory. Ultimately, I defaulted to a broad target audience for receiving the
survey but emphasize self-selection in being identified as a securities lawyer.
In prior research, I demonstrated that use of directories, while sometimes necessary, suppresses apparent response rates and reaches lawyers who are less
likely to be specialists in that area of the law—but positively, in that the respondents are more likely to self-select according to whether the survey is relevant
to their work.[2]

Legal Ethics in Securities Disclosure Practice

The need for disclosure dominates the framework for thinking about capital
markets and corporate regulation. Officials in corporations, confronted by
calls to consider not only their profits and shareholders but also their social
responsibilities, and concerned about external threats ranging from state
regulation to consumer boycotts, every day consider what to disclose, in what
manner, to whom, and when. Meaningful transparency hangs in the balance.
One commentator flagged the "tragedy" of how companies approach much
disclosure, blaming "a confluence of factors that create incentives for corporations to dissemble, or to embrace a kind of strategic ambiguity in their public

2. Schmidt 2005, 227. Unlike the survey of Occupational Safety and Health Administration
(OSHA) lawyers reported in that book, this survey of securities lawyers relied on just one source,
the *Martindale-Hubbell Legal Directory,* from which I purchased a comprehensive list of all lawyers claiming to work in the area of securities law. This totaled 3,986 individuals, of whom approximately 50 individuals were identified as not being lawyers at all. A mail survey sent out in
2004—before e-mail surveys were considered reliable or standard—yielded a net response rate
of 12.3%, with 470 valid responses. Based on the pattern observed in the OSHA survey using
Martindale-Hubbell, it is reasonable to conclude that the effective response rate from securities
law specialists is higher than that figure. Comparing the initial distribution of self-identified
securities lawyers and the corresponding distribution in response, I concluded that the survey
was broadly representative.

communications" (Siebecker 2009, 122). For the task of meeting the SEC's disclosure requirements, lawyers play a particularly important, institutionalized role. What are the consequences of what lawyers bring to the table—their cultures, logic, incentives, and, of course, their ethics?

In the black box of human behavior, it is difficult to know how ethics actually affects lawyers' behavior—material considerations always present a reductive explanation for one's motivations. But bracketing the question of the ultimate motivations for lawyers' actions, it is possible to open a window on the ways that notions of the public interest operate in the work of securities lawyers. This section begins with the observation that lawyers do disagree with clients about disclosure requirements, in an attempt to develop a richer portrait of when and how ethical considerations play a part in the work of lawyers.

Disagreeing about Disclosure

A basic question is to ask whether attorneys ever experience a conflict between the public and corporate interests. If so, do lawyers actively disagree with their clients about these judgments? There must be disagreement if ethics is to have space in which to operate, though scholars have not assumed that lawyers and clients conflict. Coffee (2006) describes the contemporary failure of gatekeeping as a product of changed forces that marginalize the input of lawyer counselors. In-house counsel have risen in prominence while the environment for outside counsel has become more competitive, lowering lawyers' ability to resist client demands for facilitative legal assistance. Further, social scientific research shows that lawyers tend to align themselves with the views of their clients (Nelson 1988).

In the securities field, meaningful conflicts do emerge between lawyers and their clients in the course of legal representation. Though much securities law practice involves cooperative teamwork between companies and their outside counsel, differences emerge around the necessary or wisest course in judgments tinged with both legal and economic considerations. Much of the explanation can be reduced to the incentives that drive corporate behavior. A wide range of commentators argue that corporate behavior is opportunistic and profit-driven, as we should expect given the imperative on corporations to maximize shareholder value. Perhaps in the camp of "confirming the obvious," recent work by economists has demonstrated that even firms with nothing to hide can rationally perceive value in secrecy, a condition that drives mandatory disclosure systems in the first place (Fishman and Hagerty 2003). Attorneys are well aware in practice that clients experience disclosure requirements—in

Table 11.1. Beliefs and Reported Behaviors of Securities Lawyers

	Strongly Disagree	Disagree	Agree	Strongly Agree
Public disclosure documents (such as listing documents and regular reporting) do not communicate enough useful information to justify the time and money spent producing them. (N = 370)	10.8	53.0	29.5	6.5
I would rather that clients disclose more than is strictly necessary as "insurance." (N = 376)	1.9	18.1	56.9	23.1
I prefer that clients disclose more than might be necessary, so as to avoid a "gray area" of the law. (N = 369)	1.4	15.2	68.6	14.1
I have encountered some securities lawyers whom I believed were too cautious or too deferential to securities regulators. (N = 357)	3.6	48.2	41.5	6.7
My work involves mostly "boilerplate" with little scope for creativity. (N = 384)	44.3	49.7	4.2	1.8
I have encountered problems of legal compliance that required me to withdraw from representation of a client. (N = 359)	44.3	28.7	22.8	4.2
One can always find ways of stating or packaging items for disclosure so as to satisfy client objections or concerns. (N = 361)	6.1	41.6	45.7	5.3

a wide range of contexts, from mergers, to efforts to secure financing, to regular reporting—as a direct and indirect cost. Disclosure is a direct cost in terms of time and money, sometimes interfering when firms are under pressure to raise money in the capital markets. Disclosure is also an indirect burden on the company, requiring company discussion of issues and risk factors that are negative, when the desire of a forward-looking businessperson may be more optimistic or at least focused on the potential rather than the downsides.

The ground for disagreement is plain. Results of my survey of securities lawyers found a clear agreement with the proposition that public disclosure is cost-beneficial (see table 11.1). As one interviewed lawyer stated, "Businessmen don't instinctively understand that disclosure is not a negative thing." Yet the visceral "I don't want to disclose it" attitude is only one form of resistance to transparency, and possibly not the most vexing in securities practice. More problematic are the many ways in which vagueness and uncertainty enter into the discussion. One such area is defining what must be disclosed to the public, for which the key standard is "materiality": Would a reasonable shareholder consider a piece of information important in making a decision about the company? Corporate executives can have a distorted vision of their companies, emphasizing the favorable and discounting the negative, finding it easy to dismiss something as a nonmaterial consideration. "I don't think you know it when you see it," one attorney mentioned in an interview, invoking the famous line of Justice Potter Stewart about how one defines pornography.

But from my interviews with lawyers it appears that professional socialization and position shape the way lawyers and clients disagree. One kind of uncertainty faced by lawyers and clients involves the kind of risk that a company would face if a material fact is omitted and only comes to light down the road if the company hits a rough patch. Then the issue becomes one of assessing the amount of legal exposure to the company if it fails to disclose. Asked to assess their approach to risk, only slightly more than half (52%) reported that they were more risk-averse than their clients (see table 11.2). Some attorneys broadly speak of legal education as training into skepticism, and as Kimberly Kirkland (chapter 8) observes, they may become accustomed to seeing risk around every corner. But lawyers themselves vary, as do their clients, with

Table 11.2. Client Behaviors Reported by Securities Lawyers

	Strongly Disagree	Disagree	Agree	Strongly Agree
Most of my clients commit sufficient resources and attention to securities compliance matters. (N = 370)	4.1	30.8	56.8	10.3
In-house counsel with whom I work are not always influential in their companies' decision making. (N = 351)	8.3	42.7	45.9	3.1
My clients are usually less risk-averse than I am about operating in the "gray areas" of the law. (N = 373)	7.5	40.5	47.2	4.8
My clients sometimes make choices about legal issues against my recommendations. (N = 394)	2.8	34.5	59.4	3.3
I have encountered clients whom I believed were not being completely forthcoming with all material disclosures. (N = 375)	4.3	22.1	62.1	11.5

industry type and size mattering. A Fortune 500 company and a Silicon Valley start-up experience radically different pressures, and when the very survival of the company is subject to year-to-year doubt, the enthusiasm for disclosure will vary. Especially when the law is complex, lawyers adopt norms that may appear—to them—highly contextualized, echoing Elizabeth Chambliss's wider observation about lawyers (chapter 3).

More generally, differences in perspective between lawyers and nonlawyers are reflected in the concern securities lawyers have with the ways in which clients may not appreciate the magnitude of legal problems. Approximately one-third of the attorneys were not satisfied with the commitment of resources and attention to securities compliance by most of their clients, and about half believed that in-house legal counsel are marginalized within company decision making. Law firm lawyers take the role of their in-house comrades as a measure of how much their clients value legal advice and perspectives. These contributing factors boil down to the report made by a clear majority of attorneys (62.7%) that their clients have made decisions on legal issues against their recommendations. In sum, securities lawyers see the environment for practice as offering plenty of opportunity for conflict between the values of law (as they understand it) and the priorities of their clients.

Doing Due Diligence

As securities law has evolved, due diligence—making a reasonable investigation before making disclosures—has emerged as a key portion of lawyers' work. Disentangling the ethical considerations wrapped up in due diligence from the lawyers' own liability is difficult. Securities lawyers, when interviewed, frequently have no difficulty pointing to exceptional cases of corporate fraud and concluding that the attorneys involved either "knew or should have known" that wrongdoing was going on. In the traditional ideal of lawyers with longstanding relationships with their clients, the task of due diligence is easier. But client relationships vary. As one Minneapolis attorney said:

> I have some clients that, their management teams are pretty open and I've gotten to know the businesses pretty well. I have a . . . pretty good idea of where the dead bodies lie, or whatever the case is. I have other clients that are more interested in, "tell me what it is I need to say and we'll do a draft internally here of what it is and present it to you to review." There is a definite difference being outside counsel as compared to if you're inside the company as their general counsel.

The ethical problem for securities lawyers begins with the lack of information. The obligation of attorneys, and the basis for their central role in the SEC's approach to regulation, is that attorneys know what is happening "on the inside" that concerns the public interest. How do lawyers enact that in practice? It involves building relationships, as one described:

> As lawyers we're pressing clients to make full disclosure, if only at least the initial level to us so that we can make the decision or work with them on how to disclose things. . . . But getting them to make that initial disclosure to us could be very awkward and very sensitive and create a lot of tension. . . . [F]ortunately to this point we've been able to satisfactorily deal with all [of our clients], but I think that quite a lot of it might be dealt with by the fact that we don't know everything. Even though we're their lawyers we can't just walk into the company and start perusing through their files. If they choose not to tell us something, and we don't know about it, what can we do? Getting them comfortable with the idea that disclosing to us isn't disclosing to the world at large is the first step.

The experience is widely shared. Nearly three-quarters of surveyed securities lawyers (73.6%) reported having encountered clients whom they believed were not completely forthcoming to them with all material disclosures. This may be natural given the difficulties in building a culture of compliance and a system of control across a large organization. The emerging role of ethics officers, internal to companies, as one tool in promoting strong corporate governance has been a response to the need for someone in upper management to build trust with a firm and develop a wide knowledge of the organization (Llopis, Gonzalez, and Gasco 2007, 99). Whether motivated by the need to avoid liability or by the sense of duty articulated for the special role of securities lawyers, the often mundane work of due diligence is laced with significance to the public interest beyond the interest of the client.

Culture and Difference in Sharper Relief

The problem behind due diligence is winning cooperation from the client. A common strategy attorneys claim is education: preparing a client for the process by setting expectations and attempting to win buy-in by clients to the larger mission of securities regulation. Few attorneys interviewed either before or after Sarbanes-Oxley have reported ever needing to fire a client for failure to give access to needed records. But that basic level of trust is aided in the United States by the shared cultural understanding provided by the SEC's long-standing framework itself. One of the most common refrains among securities lawyers interviewed in this research has been the shared belief in disclosure as the foundation for healthy capital markets. Many securities lawyers begin work with new clients by giving them written materials or through a spoken message—some even say "the speech"—that establishes the shared understandings about the role of the lawyer and the regulations, so that if a client finds discomfort later in the process, reference can be made to the "insurance" from later legal difficulties provided by disclosure. The difficulty in so educating a client may be most challenging when taking a private company public. A family firm or closely held company may experience some shock at the breadth of the requirements as well as the extent to which past ways of operating (such as decision making) are exposed to scrutiny. Investors can and will insist on scrutinizing details. As a company decides to go public, it must come to terms with these changes.

Qualitatively, a commonly expressed view among securities lawyers, particularly among Washington and New York interviewees, holds that SEC alumni (that is, lawyers who once worked at the SEC) are more strident in their belief in disclosure and are less likely to advise clients to "sail close to the wind" in gray areas. Such a relationship is plausible; career experiences in a variety of ways shape the work of lawyers. But significant differences between SEC alums and those without SEC experience failed to appear in the quantitative data about reported behaviors and perspectives. Given the strong direction of the qualitative evidence, further research may be necessary to see whether the absence of a relationship in the quantitative data is a spurious result.

The cultural differences that most explicitly raise ethical concerns that rise to the level where Sarbanes-Oxley-type rules must kick in arise with the increasing globalization of capital markets and corporate structures. Cross-border mergers bring lawyers into contact with clients (business executives) from different countries, meaning they may not share the narrative that lawyers tell about disclosure as the source of strength of confidence in US financial markets. Indeed, the nexus that is required to bring a firm within the scope of US securities law is not very large. To begin the process of educating foreign clients, one London-based US attorney sits down with her "culturally sophisticated" clients and "we will make sort of a joke about how the securities laws technically sort of apply to every transaction everywhere in the world. . . . Some people just sort of roll their eyes and often times they will just joke, but most of the time they just sort of nod and listen."

Lawyers can effectively act as gatekeepers of US markets, then, playing an intermediary role in ensuring that clients comply with at least a minimal vi-sion of the public good when foreign clients seek entry to US markets or must make some form of disclosure filing to the SEC. Many attorneys report that the economic realities make their work especially easy. Foreign executives readily mention litigation as a prevailing feature of American society, and that impression "really focuses everybody's attention on disclosing properly" said one London attorney, because the penalties are easily communicated to com-panies. He continued, "Notwithstanding all the scandals . . . the fundamen-tal approach has been a far harsher standard of disclosure because there are people out there that can sue you if you get it wrong."

The differences between US and European regulation can be overstated. There are differences to be sure, and in the whole panoply of regulation there are significant complications to cross-border finance, but disclosure issues are not usually among them. Foreign corporations must be educated about the specific implications of US securities laws—for example, when a company can use a newspaper advertisement to promote an upcoming share offering—but in principle they are comfortable with the notion of disclosure. Foreign firms want access to US capital and so agree to US terms that are different in degree rather than kind.

Of two particular problems that emerge in cross-national contexts, the problem of language is the lesser but still deserves mention. Due diligence—the ability of lawyers to learn about and state potential material concerns—is hampered by language barriers. High-level business officials and local lawyers around the world may speak English, but the documentation that must be re-viewed remains in native languages. English-speaking attorneys report a loss of confidence in being able to always assess the workings of corporations when all of the contracts exist in Russian, Bulgarian, or even more exotic languages. Lawyers must give comfort letters, such as to a US parent company, and assist with disclosure without the usual level of confidence.

More important, the cross-national context puts into sharper relief the ex-tent to which securities attorneys see themselves as fighting corruption and serving as gatekeepers. Like a police investigator motivated by the horrors seen at the crime scene, the global context of securities law exposes the moral impulses behind lawyers' work. Interviewees volunteered their concerns with possible mafia involvement in Russian companies and bribery in Nigeria. A US attorney operating out of London described problems "you just can't imag-ine" with a transaction in the Ukraine. The company being acquired by a US firm was just riddled with corruption, so basically you have no idea who is behind some of your shareholders. . . . You have people who have been jailed for corruption at various points in time and you are trying to tackle that. Contracts that are with them, we have cleared contractual kickbacks sometimes. . . . Management contracts . . . with just million dollar bonuses that clearly have no relation to anything going on in the business. . . . You're not going to find that stuff in France and Germany.

The attorney in foreign transactions must pursue full disclosure more aggressively than in domestic transactions, and even then she may remain the eyes of investors that are otherwise half-blinded by the smokescreens of foreign economies. In a more limited sample of attorneys with cross-border experience, an overwhelming majority responded (20.4% "strongly agreed" and 60.8% "agreed") that due diligence in a cross-border environment is "substantially more difficult" (N = 245).

In interviews, the bias toward transparency and disclosure was the most pronounced when attorneys spoke of their work related to Asia. The illegalities of Eastern Europe or other developing markets pose challenges at a technical level but not a philosophical one. But the hope of forming a shared understanding with clients about the public interest in transparency—and the desirability of being cautious in gray areas—appears dimmest with Asia. With Asian companies, numerous attorneys reported "real resistance to honest, authentic compliance with US securities laws" with an emphasis on confidentiality and trade secrets. "You will get determined, very polite, usually totally nonconfrontational resistance to full and fair disclosure," the attorney continued. In one case, a company refused to provide details on the accounting of their employee benefit program, until the attorney successfully persuaded the executives to file two amendments to their SEC submissions.

A: It's very, very difficult to persuade your client that they have to play by the rules, and in fact they're quite savvy and they're very used to US lawyers talking like Boy Scouts and saying how important it is to be fully and accurately disclosed, but in fact just allowing things to go on which they know shouldn't go on.

Q: What ultimately allowed you to persuade them?

A: They wanted to raise money in the capital markets and it was a very good time to raise money in the capital markets. We told them unless they made these changes we'd just walk away.

Q: Have you ever walked away from clients before?

A: Well, no. In fact it's not even clear to me . . . if [my] firm would have walked away, but I said I would have walked away and I *would have* walked away personally from the deal, because it would have been just impractical for a US lawyer to go into that situation under those circumstances.

An ambivalence in this attorney's account makes the work of the gatekeeper appear noble but leaves between the lines a hint of the organizational and economic context in which professionals operate. Would a firm lose a valued client in an emerging market over such an issue? Even in this case, it is not clear that the firm was prepared to "fire the client," even though the spectre of malpractice or enforcement actions against the lawyers made the situation risky. The cross-border examples suggest how lawyers can be challenged in their work, but do not comfort those who want to trust lawyers to do the right thing. The limits of ethics—indeed, the very possibility of ethics—begs the question of what really motivates lawyers.

When Push Comes to Shove

The lawyer in the preceding quotation evoked one of the most drastic steps that might be taken by securities lawyers—withdrawing from representation. If US lawyers are perceived as "Boy Scouts," then perhaps the accumulated cultural environment from the SEC has indeed produced meaningful norms of behavior. Perhaps, too, the debt is owed to professionalization into a skeptical, risk-averse mindset. Coffee suggests that lawyers can be expected, on account of their professional training, to be aggressive advocates of full disclosure, acting more like auditors. His suggestion relies on a set of context-specific norms (2006, 198). Yet a dearth of empirical evidence hinders this discussion.

Survey data supports the notion that shared understandings of professional responsibility operate in the securities law field. In 2004, in the early days of Sarbanes-Oxley, 14.7% of attorneys reported having taken a problem up the ladder within the previous 12 months. With an unlimited time frame, a quarter of all securities attorneys (27%) reported that they had encountered a problem of legal compliance serious enough that it required them to withdraw from representation (see table 11.1).

This occurs at the extreme end, and lawyers often struggle to balance their risk aversion with their need to give clients realistic advice. The identity of lawyers as gatekeepers competes with their identity as creative professionals who can serve clients' needs. Creativity, inherent to the work of law, means the ability to frame problems in such a way so as to satisfy both the law (as understood by the lawyer) and the client. Interviewees regularly speak with pride of their ability to develop disclosure that fulfills the goal of lowering liability by providing sufficient disclosure.

In the survey data, lawyers appeared evenly split about the limits of this role, with about half (51%) agreeing that one can "always find ways of stating or packaging items for disclosure" to clients' satisfaction. Securities law, echoing research in other areas of legal practice, enables "nondisclosing disclosure" that is both "perfectly legal" and inconsistent with the fullest version of the public interest that regulators might wish (McBarnet 1991; McBarnet and Whelan 1999). Creative lawyering means, almost by definition, identifying a self-serving interpretation that appears to meet the terms of the law, even though the authors of the rule had not anticipated it being interpreted in that way. Creativity does not have to mean "minimal compliance," but it often provides a special version of it: Only a narrow or even tortured reading of the text, divorced from the norms, values, or interests behind the law, can justify the position the lawyer takes. Praise for creativity by lawyers thus reflects their desire for solutions in their daily work that allow them to avoid becoming the spokesperson for values, norms, or interests other than the self-interest of the client who faces the command of the law.

Other modes of control—the fear of liability—help support and overlap with ethical considerations. To one lawyer, liability was a complete explanation, supplanting the ethical "angel":

> During the height of the bubble in the tech sector it was very difficult to persuade people I think. And so just it's not so much sort of the avenging angel of goodness and right as it is in order to be a responsible lawyer your job is to make sure that your client doesn't get themselves into trouble any more than they have to. And even if you take the most aggressive sort of libertarian interpretation of how contract and regulatory law are supposed to work and . . . even in the most aggressive context, everyone does that sort of cost benefit analysis and decides whether to break the law or not. In the case of SEC fraud the cost benefit analysis is always "don't do it." And it's easy enough to say that because you're not the person responsible for managing the business and deciding whether or not you're going to do what WorldCom did in order to compete like WorldCom or not.

As detailed in table 11.1, overwhelming majorities of securities lawyers found agreement with the proposition that it is better to recommend to clients that they exceed a minimal understanding of disclosure laws to avoid legal gray areas and to provide clients greater "insurance" from liability. Legal ambiguity, and aggressive policing by shareholders' attorneys, serves the interest of the regulators by giving corporate gatekeepers a tool with which to advocate for greater disclosure. Liability insurance for law firms further supports this because the explosion of concern for liability (Morgan 2007, 376) has forced law firms to develop policies and practices. As with law firms, recent research among insurers has demonstrated their role in shaping corporate governance by transmitting securities law principles to corporate directors and officers as well (Baker and Griffith 2007). When insurers make determinations of the risks involved, the culture and character of firms—and their willingness to follow best practices—plays a part. Agreement with external goals, to the extent it has been developed by the SEC and other outside forces such as insurers, is consistent with ethical dialogue.

Boilerplate and Lawyers' Ethical Lives

Even if lawyers take ethics seriously, crises of the magnitude of Enron remain possible. Lawyers have limited control over clients, they may end up backing down in periods of excessive exuberance, or ethics may be unable to reach the kinds of problems that give rise to crisis. Still, what is the impact of legal ethics on the work that securities lawyers do? Why has a dialogue on ethics taken root in the past half century, such that the SEC and Congress have kept the heat on the bar? Is it a case of a few "bad apples"? Or perhaps is there a structural rot in the heart of securities ethics? I argue in this section that efforts to push ethics in securities law have resulted in patterns of work product that defeat any good intent behind them.

The evolving response to the Sarbanes-Oxley Act of 2002 from the securities bar provides the opportunity to see the cyclical nature of crisis and response. The law was a dramatic incursion into the securities field, with specific measures aimed at the behavior of lawyers, yet it may not have fundamentally changed some aspects of practice. Increased disclosure is not the same as improvement; new forms of action are not the same as more thoughtful behavior. To be sure, the specific content of disclosures has changed, such as the rise in salience of executive compensation.

Yet, while crises are moments of disruption in which new possibilities arise and old ways of acting are suppressed, legal practice in securities law is mediated by the convergence of practices around models and agreed practices—in a word, boilerplate (Kahan and Klausner 1997; Langevoort 2000). The need for greater attention to threats of enforcement or lawsuits may result in a state of concern by lawyers about their clients' risk profile, but that is not to say that that heightened interest leads to a state of reflection. One lawyer interviewed in 2010, critical of disclosure documents, tied overdisclosure to a certain thinness of transparency:

> It's funny, you know, there is no rule that specifies how long a paragraph has to be that discusses a certain thing. There's a list of things that have to be in a document. But very cursorily. But the custom that's developed is to over disclosure against all those things. And so you get this huge management discussion [and analysis], you know, and huge descriptions of business and . . . my view is that particularly in transactions I'm involved in, all of that is excessive.

The Sarbanes-Oxley initiatives compare to initiatives made in prior eras to change what and how corporations communicate with the public. For example, many interviewees mentioned the SEC's "Plain English" initiative, a 1998 amendment to its rules, requiring companies to avoid jargon, to streamline text, and to clarify graphics when preparing disclosure documents, so that they would be more understandable to investors. Many lawyers credit the initiative with changing the overall impression of disclosure documents. But for whose benefit? The public interest was not the beneficiary. Securities documents may be more understandable as lawyers conceive of "understandability" but still have an uncertain effect on "Main Street" investors. Even from the lawyer's perspective,

> although the plain language rule . . . has had some impact on the style of documents, in fact, it's just resulted in a new boilerplate. And the fact that it was boilerplate before and is boilerplate again means, you know, the whole point of boilerplate is that it's stuff that people don't read. I can't tell you how many prospectuses I get in the mail every week for stocks that I own that I throw out. And somebody's paying for that.

For lawyers to incorporate the public interest into corporate disclosures, they must be considering the needs of the public. But in changing times, with complex issues, lawyers were asked in 2004 where they went to keep up with the law. With extremely strong agreement (94.2%), the foremost answer was attorneys in their own law offices, followed by their personal or firm databank of precedents (71.6%) and attorneys in the firm's other offices (60.7%). The SEC staff was the least preferred source of information about regulations, with only

33.7% citing this as an approach they had taken (N = 298). Lawyers construct their work, most commonly, from within smaller rather than larger circles of practice.

Drawing on the work of Lauren Edelman and related work in organizational studies (Edelman 1992; Edelman, Uggen, and Erlanger 1999), boilerplate here refers to the manner in which lawyers responded to Sarbanes-Oxley by adopting shared approaches—texts and forms for documents—that were thought to be responsive to the requirements of regulators. Though it is an independent question whether new forms of providing disclosed information are substantively beneficial to those who consume the information, the notion of mimetic isomorphism leads us to suspect that some aspects of securities disclosure, both before and after Enron, are performative—things that must be seen to have been done and to have been done in ways that quickly take on the sense of being the "right way" to do it.[3] One attorney connected that sense of having settled into the requirements of Sarbanes-Oxley (in 2010, many years after the law was enacted) with the feeling that the disclosures do not serve a public purpose, noting that "where we took the time to create what we thought was the right disclosure at the time and it hardly ever gets looked at or thought about anymore, and everybody has kind of adopted it that way, and I think it gets glossed over, it doesn't add anything."

Put another way, ethics becomes recognized through its anthropological form, and in the disclosure environment, the real substance of information must be produced, but the communication of those pieces of information can be contained as much in the structure of the disclosures as in their explicit meaning (Riles 2000; Ben-Shahar 2007; Frohmann 2008). Legality is as much produced in observing the conventions of the practice—as understood and communicated by the lawyer—as in trying to represent the public interest by disclosing information outside of the expected form. One lawyer found that cautionary statements were such a vehicle where it is easy to appeal to the form:

> The Commission [SEC] did adopt a rule creating a safe harbor around disclosure for forward-looking statements as long as at the same time you

---

3. "Isomorphism," as used in the social sciences, refers to the tendency of organizations to conform in response to environmental conditions. Mimetic isomorphism is the mimicking behavior common to organizations experiencing uncertainty and ambiguity, conditions that make it appear that the safest course is to imitate what other, successful organizations have done.

accompany it with meaningful cautionary statements. Now, those meaningful cautionary statements have become boilerplate little mini-risk factors which we think about for a moment and [ask]: "[Are] there a few things that relate to what's up here that we could toss in?"

The ethics of disclosure, if understood to connect to the representation of the public interest, depends on understanding not just how lawyers aid illegality—the "bright-line" violations of the law exemplified by the most famous cases of lawyer-led fraud—but also how lawyers help produce "perfectly legal" results, results that create models that come to be understood as "plausible" within the legal field though they do not press the public goal of meaningful disclosure to the public. Put most succinctly by one interviewee, the starting point for disclosure in the present, "quite honestly, is last year's document."

Conclusion

In its vernacular usage, "ethics" conjures up an image of an internal value system. Yet values are constructed in a social context, and for that the SEC has done its part, first establishing a culture within the agency and then, since the 1970s, moving toward enforcing those values. As Wilkins (1992) suggests, government efforts to produce ethical compliance can undercut the internal production of those values. Now decades past the SEC's incursion into legal ethics, those values may not be spontaneously and internally generated, but instead spurred by external risks and enforcement; but even so, the work lives of securities lawyers offer evidence of how differences of opinion about compliance with securities regulations get played out with clients. Although the public often views lawyers somewhat cynically, an image that companies like Enron have only sharpened, in the lived experience there is reason to think that lawyers can and do play a role as gatekeeper to capital markets.

That conclusion should not be understood as altogether optimistic, however, because the evidence of successful gatekeeping appears so problematic. Scandals recur in cycles over the decades, each time revealing both exceptional bad apples and shared, almost ritualistic practices that limit the effective value of transparency. Ethical norms may flourish among some—in the lore of some securities lawyers, among SEC alumni in particular, though evidence for that remains thin at best—and creative lawyering is as central to lawyers' identities as the call of the public interest. Even when compliance is the goal, lawyers all too quickly fall into the boilerplate of the day. Like the ritual of doing the

Macarena at a wedding reception, securities lawyers learn to repeat gestures in a continuing pattern, turning in unison, with mistakes and missteps expected and tolerated. With everyone partaking in the gestures and nods, performing the dance reasonably close to its essential pattern, until they later see the video record of what transpired, no one needs to worry about just how silly they all might look.

References

Association of Securities and Exchange Commission (SEC) Alumni. 2007. "About Us." http://www.secalumni.org/content.asp?contentid=1.

Baker, Tom, and Sean J. Griffith. 2007. "Predicting Corporate Governance Risk: Evidence from the Directors' & Officers' Liability Insurance Market." *University of Chicago Law Review* 74:487–544.

Ben-Shahar, Omri, ed. 2007. *Boilerplate: The Foundation of Market Contracts.* New York: Cambridge University Press.

Benston, George, Michael Bromwich, Robert E. Litan, and Alfred Wagenhofer. 2003. *Following the Money: The Enron Failure and the State of Corporate Disclosure.* Washington, DC: AEI-Brookings Joint Center for Regulatory Studies.

Coffee, John C., Jr. 2006. *Gatekeepers: The Professions and Corporate Governance.* New York: Oxford University Press.

Edelman, Lauren B. 1992. "Legal Ambiguity and Symbolic Structures: Organizational Mediation of Civil Rights Law." *American Journal of Sociology* 97:1531–1576.

Edelman, Lauren B., Christopher Uggen, and Howard S. Erlanger. 1999. "The Endogeneity of Legal Regulation: Grievance Procedures as Rational Myth." *American Journal of Sociology* 105:406–454.

Fishman, Michael J., and Kathleen M. Hagerty. 2003. "Mandatory versus Voluntary Disclosure in Markets with Informed and Uninformed Customers." *Journal of Law, Economics & Organization* 19:45–63.

Frohmann, Bernd. 2008. "Documentary Ethics, Ontology, and Politics." *Archival Science* 8:165–180.

Fung, Archon, Mary Graham, and David Weil. 2007. *Full Disclosure: The Perils and Promise of Transparency.* New York: Cambridge University Press.

Gilboy, Janet A. 1998. "Compelled Third-Party Participation in the Regulatory Process: Legal Duties, Culture, and Noncompliance." *Law & Policy* 20:135–156.

Harrington, Caroline. 2009. "Attorney Gatekeeper Duties in an Increasingly Complex World: Revisiting the 'Noisy Withdrawal' Proposal of SEC Rule 205." *Georgetown Journal of Legal Ethics* 22:893–910.

Kahan, Marcel, and Michael Klausner. 1997. "Standardization and Innovation in Corporate Contracting (or 'The Economics of Boilerplate')." *Virginia Law Review* 83:713–770.

Khademian, Anne. 1992. *The SEC and Capital Market Regulation: The Politics of Expertise.* Pittsburgh: University of Pittsburgh Press.

Kim, Sung Hui. 2010. "Lawyer Exceptionalism in the Gatekeeping Wars." *Southern Methodist University Law Review* 63:73–136.

Kraakman, Reinier H. 1984. "Corporate Liability Strategies and the Costs of Legal Controls." *Yale Law Journal* 93:857–899.

———. 1986. "Gatekeepers: The Anatomy of a Third-Party Enforcement Strategy." *Journal of Law, Economics & Organization* 2:53–104.

Langevoort, Donald C. 2000. "Taking Myths Seriously: An Essay for Lawyers." *Chicago-Kent Law Review* 74:1569–1597.

Llopis, Juan, M. Reyes Gonzalez, and Jose L. Gasco. 2007. "Corporate Governance and Organisational Culture: The Role of Ethics Officers." *International Journal of Disclosure and Governance* 4:96–105.

McBarnet, Doreen 1991. "Whiter than White Collar Crime: Tax, Fraud Insurance and the Management of Stigma." *British Journal of Sociology* 42:323–344.

McBarnet, Doreen J., and Christopher Whelan. 1999. *Creative Accounting and the Cross-Eyed Javelin Thrower*. London: John Wiley.

Morgan, Thomas D. 2007. "The New Legal and Ethical Duties of Corporate Attorneys: Comment on Lawyers as Gatekeepers." *Case Western Reserve Law Review* 57:375–380.

Nelson, Robert L. 1988. *Partners with Power: The Social Transformation of the Large Law Firm*. Berkeley: University of California Press.

Riles, Annelise. 2000. *The Network Inside Out*. Ann Arbor: University of Michigan Press.

Schmidt, Patrick. 2005. *Lawyers and Regulation: The Politics of the Administrative Process*. New York: Cambridge University Press.

Seligman, Joel. 2003. *The Transformation of Wall Street: A History of the Securities and Exchange Commission and Modern Corporate Finance*. 3rd ed. New York: Aspen.

Siebecker, Michael R. 2009. "Trust & Transparency: Promoting Efficient Corporate Disclosure through Fiduciary–Based Discourse." *Washington University Law Review* 87:115–174.

Wilkins, David B. 1992. "Who Should Regulate Lawyers?" *Harvard Law Review* 105:799–887.

Cases, Statutes, and Rules

In re Carter and Johnson, [1981 Transfer Binder] Fed. Sec. L. Rep. (CCH) ¶ 82,847 (SEC Feb. 28, 1981).

In re Emanuel Fields, Securities Act Release No. 5404, Fed. Sec. L. Rep. (CCH) ¶ 79,407, at 83,175 (SEC June 18, 1973).

SEC v. National Student Marketing Corp., 457 F. Supp. 682 (D.D.C. 1978).

Sarbanes-Oxley Act of 2002, Pub. L. No. 107-204, 116 Stat. 745.

Securities Act of 1933, 15 U.S.C. §§ 77a et seq. (2011).

Securities Exchange Act of 1934, 15 U.S.C. §§ 78a et seq. (2011).

SEC Rules of Practice 102(e), 17 C.F.R. § 201.102(e) (2011).

Scientists at the Bar

The Professional World of Patent Lawyers

John M. Conley and Lynn Mather

Since the first patent statute was enacted in 1790, the United States has granted patents to inventors to provide exclusive rights to their inventions for a set period of years. Throughout the early years of the new republic, few patents were issued, and little was required of the applicant beyond registration. Congress created the precursor of the current US Patent and Trademark Office (PTO) in 1836, and it began the practice of scrutinizing patent applications for compliance with more rigorous standards of patentability. Patent lawyers emerged to help inventors navigate this increasingly complex patent system.

Today, with intellectual property rights having enormous economic significance, patent law has evolved from an obscure specialty into a highly lucrative area of legal practice. Yet patent lawyers, in part because their remote ancestors were moonlighting engineers and inventors, remain essentially scientific in their backgrounds and approaches. This chapter describes the patent bar and the nature of patent firms, and then addresses two ethical issues of particular importance for this legal community: avoidance of conflicts of interest and the duty of candor.

We draw on interviews with 22 lawyers engaged in various kinds of patent practice in the Northeast, the Southeast, and California. All of the lawyers we interviewed considered themselves to be patent specialists, and most of them were registered to practice before the PTO. Interviews with some of the lawyers were conducted over a period of several years. The firms ranged in size from regional boutiques of 3 to 30 intellectual property (IP)[1] lawyers to large

---

1. Intellectual property encompasses federal copyright, trademark, unfair competition, and patent law, as well as the state law of trade secrets and publicity. Many firms that practice

multi-office corporate law firms with more than 1,000 attorneys. One of the authors (Conley) also draws on his six years of full-time practice as an IP lawyer and 27 years of active counsel work.[2]

The Patent Bar

The History of the Patent Bar

The term "patent bar" can refer to the general community of patent attorneys and agents—nonlawyer practitioners who are licensed to "prosecute" (file and advocate for the allowance of) patent applications in the PTO and give ancillary advice. However, the "patent bar" also has a more specific meaning, referring to the examination given by the PTO to license attorneys and agents, as well as to the roster of those who have passed the exam, met the PTO's science education requirements (with experience sometimes allowed to substitute), and been registered. Patent law is the only legal specialty that has a separate barrier to entry. Other fields have voluntary board certification, widely respected LLM degrees, and other forms of endorsement, but these are add-on credentials, not requirements to enter the field.

Through the first half of the nineteenth century, anyone could prepare and prosecute a patent application on behalf of an inventor (Carlson, Migliorini, and Vacchiano 2005). The first patent-preparation firms in England emerged in the 1830s and 1840s—but they were formed and staffed by engineers, not lawyers (Dutton 1984; Van Zyl Smit 1985). In this country, the ancestor of the New York patent law firm Kenyon & Kenyon was founded in 1879, with much of its early work involving Thomas Edison, Nikola Tesla, and other pioneers of electrification. Fish & Richardson, now an international IP boutique, was founded in 1878 by Frederick Fish, whose early clients included Alexander Graham Bell and the Wright brothers.

Complaints about freelance patent practitioners caused the Commissioner of Patents to require, in 1869, the filing of a power of attorney before a person "of intelligence and good moral character" could represent another in a

---

patent law also practice the other branches of federal IP law. IP firms that primarily represent entertainment and literary clients, however, tend to focus on federal copyright and state publicity and licensing law, and rarely include patent lawyers. We use the term "IP boutique" to refer to a firm that specializes in IP law.

2. In addition, Mather draws on her observations and informal interviews from four professional meetings in 2008–2010 (three patent law institutes and a national meeting of the American Intellectual Property Law Association). For this preliminary study of patent lawyers, we selected attorneys nonsystematically, using informal contacts, including former students.

proceeding before the PTO (cited in *Sperry v. Florida*, 1963, 388). In 1899, the Commissioner required registration of patent agents and attorneys. The patent bar was established in 1922, and a specialized patent bar examination was created in 1938.

Currently, there are about 30,000 lawyers and 10,000 agents registered to practice before the PTO (US Patent and Trademark Office 2011b). To become registered, both patent attorneys and nonlawyer patent agents must pass the patent bar and demonstrate good moral character and sufficient "legal, scientific, and technical skill," as evidenced by education or experience (37 C.F.R. § 10.7). Whereas applicants formerly had to draft patent claims, the exam now consists of 100 multiple-choice questions to be answered over six hours. Recent pass rates have been in the 50% range (Crouch 2007).

Prosecutors and Litigators

Patent practice is divided into two broad categories, viewed increasingly as distinct specialties: prosecution and litigation. The division of labor and authority is complex. Only registered patent lawyers and agents can engage in patent prosecution: writing applications, appearing personally before the PTO on behalf of inventors, and filing other paperwork with the PTO in an effort to establish the patentability of their clients' inventions. However, agents cannot give clients legal advice on matters not strictly related to patentability (concerning licensing, for example), and only lawyers can write opinions about whether an invention is likely to infringe a third party's patent. Significantly, whereas agents cannot appear in court, *any* licensed lawyer can handle litigation brought to enforce or challenge a patent, whether or not the lawyer is registered to practice before the PTO. Another way to characterize the division of labor is to say that registered patent lawyers can do anything related to patents (prosecute, advise, opine, and litigate), agents can only prosecute, and lawyers not registered to practice before the PTO can litigate and offer legal advice (they are not ethically barred from writing opinion letters, but most do not because of concerns about competence).

Prosecutors typically begin the process of seeking a patent by working with the inventor to write a patent application, which describes the background and field of the invention, gives a highly detailed technical description of what it does and how it works, explains why the invention is distinguishable from existing technology ("the prior art"), and then sets out the "claims," which define exactly what will be protected. In over 95% of the cases, the PTO issues an initial rejection, usually based on similarities between the claimed invention and the prior art (Crouch 2009). There may then be multiple rounds of "office actions" in which the PTO states its objections and the patent prosecutor attempts to overcome them, often by narrowing or otherwise redrafting the claims to avoid the prior art. After what is often a period of two or three years of negotiation, the PTO allows the claims or issues a final rejection. In the latter case, the applicant can appeal both within the PTO and to the courts.

Litigation can ensue in several ways. Patent holders can sue infringers for damages and/or injunctions. The alleged infringer can defend by saying that its product or activity is not covered by the patent claims and thus is not infringing. But the defendant can also argue that the patent was improperly granted and is thus invalid—because, for example, the patented invention was anticipated by or obvious in view of the prior art. Alternatively, a party that believes it may be sued for infringement can launch a preemptive strike and sue first, seeking a declaratory judgment that the patent is invalid.

Patent lawsuits tend to be long, expert-heavy, and very expensive. Indeed, legal fees in high-stakes cases "now average $5 million per side" (Burk and Lemley 2009, 18). The conventional view is that 20 to 25 years ago, registered patent lawyers handled not only the prosecution of claims before the PTO but most of the litigation as well (though not litigation involving specific patents they have prosecuted since that would often require them to be witnesses, a violation of American Bar Association (ABA) Model Rule of Professional Conduct 3.7). But the situation has become more complex in recent years. As a consequence of the recent growth in patent litigation[3] and the economic opportunities that growth presents, a new group of lawyers coming from corporate litigation now handles a significant amount of patent litigation, and many of them are not registered with the PTO.[4] According to *Corporate Counsel* magazine's 2009 Patent Litigation Survey, the most active patent litigation firm was Fish & Richardson, a 350+ lawyer IP boutique (Mullin 2009). But joining it at the top of the rankings were not only peer boutiques Kenyon & Kenyon and

3. The number of patent cases filed in the US district courts roughly tripled between 1980 and 2006, and greatly exceeded growth in the number of patents issued (Kesan and Ball 2006; Bessen and Meurer 2008). In 2007, there were 3,017 patent lawsuits filed, but only 2,796 in 2008, a change related to the economic downturn (Marco and Sichelman 2010).

4. A recent study of 55 California patent litigators (defined as handling patent cases at least 50% of the time) found that about one-half of them were registered with the PTO (Gallagher 2011, 318).

Finnegan, Henderson, but also such general corporate megafirms as Kirkland & Ellis, Foley & Lardner, and Jones Day.

Some patent lawyers we interviewed attributed the migration of generalist corporate lawyers into the field to both the general increase in patent litigation and some huge and highly publicized damage awards. The trend began when Polaroid's lawsuit against Eastman Kodak in 1990 yielded a judgment of nearly $1 billion (Poss 1990). Since then, awards of hundreds of millions of dollars have been reported in numerous patent cases, including a $290 million jury verdict against Microsoft upheld by the US Supreme Court (*Microsoft Corp. v. i4i Ltd. Partnership*, 2011). Judgments such as these attracted litigators from large firms, some of whom began to specialize in patent litigation even though they lacked the science background of the traditional patent bar. This effort to get into patent litigation was reinforced by the behavior of large corporations: As they began to invest heavily in patent litigation because of the high stakes, they selected top litigators from the largest firms rather than the "no-name attorney" from smaller IP boutiques (Quinn 2010).

Not surprisingly, some patent lawyer litigators deride the lack of scientific and technical patent knowledge of the generalists, whereas the generalists complain of the patent lawyers' lack of basic litigation skills. Corporate clients seem to have bought both of these arguments, as big-case litigation teams typically include both patent lawyers and conventional corporate litigators. As one patent litigator explained:

> What we've done is we've tried to have a general commercial litigator who doesn't have a patent background work on each case with us. And that helps us, first of all, integrate with the firm a little bit more, because we're not just our own little group, and also I think there's an advantage to the client, to have someone who doesn't understand patent law, so they will ask some questions that perhaps are apparent to the patent litigators but wouldn't be apparent to a judge or jury (#22).[5]

The Backgrounds of Patent Lawyers

Patent lawyers registered with the PTO are required to have an undergraduate hard science degree or equivalent experience-based scientific background. The

5. All lawyers interviewed were promised anonymity. The numbers used throughout the chapter indicate the particular attorney quoted.

science backgrounds of members of the patent bar are about equally divided among the chemical disciplines, various forms of mechanical engineering, the biological sciences, and computer-related fields (Clifford, Field, and Cavicchi 2010). Undergraduate science degrees remain the norm in "traditional arts" such as electrical and mechanical engineering, but PhDs are becoming increasingly common—and even required by elite patent firms—in the growing field of biotechnology.

Significantly, the applicant's science degree and background are often more salient hiring credentials than the law school record—the direct opposite of the corporate legal market, where the law school record is all-important in getting one's foot in the door. Scientific background continues to be an important distinguishing characteristic throughout a patent lawyer's career. When asked to describe differences among patent prosecutors, one attorney responded, "There are the software guys, the hardware guys, the bio guys, the chem guys, and the business methods guys. Those are the Big Five" (#3). Similarly, a senior partner heading a patent prosecution firm said:

> There are three types: the electricals/electronics, the mechanicals, and the biochems. The electricals and biochems can do a mechanical patent—as a general rule of thumb, everyone here is expected to handle a simple mechanical thing—but an electrical can never do a biochem patent and a biochem cannot do an electrical (#5).

Seeking to have expertise on many fronts to appeal to a range of clients, some small and medium-sized patent law firms hire to fill scientific slots. Other firms stay focused on one particular area, like biochemistry or software.

Second-career patent lawyers are both common and successful. Those who have been engineers or scientists for a number of years may decide to go to law school to write patents in that area, sometimes after spending some time as a nonlawyer patent agent. In contrast to highly paid elite lawyers in some other segments of the bar, successful patent lawyers often come from night or lower-tier law schools. Law firms sometimes hire patent agents for their scientific expertise, and if they prove themselves capable and committed, the firm may send them to night law school to become patent lawyers. For young scientists, the starting pay at a law firm may be better and the work conditions easier than in a science lab. For example, one 30-year-old PhD in chemistry chose between a post-doc position at a $53,000 salary and a patent agent job at $103,000. After several years, she decided to accept her firm's offer to attend law school, a not uncommon career track. Indeed, a large recent study found that graduates of urban non-elite law schools were especially likely to be working in large law firms if they had undergraduate degrees in science, and those large firm lawyers were significantly more likely than elite law school graduates to be working on intellectual property matters (Wilkins, Dinovitzer, and Batra 2007).

What Patent Lawyers Think about Their Work

Patent lawyers work closely with clients who are scientists or engineers. Perhaps ironically, that which connects them with their clients disconnects them from other kinds of lawyers. What do patent prosecutors like about their work? According to one, "I enjoy working with the inventor. They're excited about their creation and, as a scientist, I get excited about that too" (#3). Another said, "I can be close to my clients [all scientists] but not get my hands dirty" (#4). An MIT graduate who had left a large litigation firm to join a patent prosecution boutique noted:

> I'd rather be dealing with the scientists and working on building portfolios that will ultimately be valuable to the company . . . we're more of an integral part of their team, building the IP strategy . . . that's where I draw satisfaction and that's where I want my practice to go (#11).

Patent lawyers also like their compensation and relatively manageable hours. A patent lawyer purporting to quote his wife said, "Patent lawyers are the dermatologists of the legal profession. They work 9-5. Make oodles of money. And no one calls them at home at night or on weekends" (#20). Echoing the point, a patent associate took exception when a senior partner in her firm called her during her Hawaiian vacation: "I hated that. It really messed up my vacation!" (#3). An associate in a corporate firm would have found such a call routine—if she had felt secure enough to take time off to go on a Hawaiian vacation in the first place. Hard data comparing associates' billable hours in patent firms and in general corporate firms tend to confirm these impressions (Kobylarz 2007).

But there are tensions as well. Interviews with patent prosecutors about their role in litigation suggested that some play an occasional advisory role to litigators, providing "support" and "patent knowledge," but it is the litigator who will plan the tactics, file motions, and argue the case. One prosecutor commented, "I am called in for advice and sit at the table with them, but don't argue the case" (#5). A senior prosecutor with a strong engineering background working at a medium-sized corporate firm explained his frustration with the lack of respect he got in an organization "dominated by the litigators. Litigators write briefs. And I write amendments [to applications]. They're the same thing as briefs. And I argue with the Patent Office. What's the difference?" (#7) But the patent prosecution activity that this attorney perceived as akin to litigation is in fact entirely different, according to a patent litigator with 12 years of experience: "There are completely different skill sets involved in prosecution and litigation. Hardly anyone does both. Prosecutors talk science and don't know how to talk law. They're the pocket protector crowd" (#6). This litigator added that prosecutors cannot litigate their own patents because of the ethical and strategic problem it presents: "The prosecutor might be deposed and asked, 'why didn't you disclose such and such prior art?'" (#6).

Unlike patent prosecutors, who interact almost exclusively with clients and the PTO, patent litigators—whether patent lawyers or generalists—deal with other lawyers, arguing motions, taking depositions, producing documents, and engaging in trial. (Litigators in IP boutiques typically do only patent and perhaps other IP litigation, whereas patent litigators in large corporate firms may work on other kinds of cases as well.) Litigators' work takes them all over the country, sometimes seeking out federal courts (such as the Eastern District of Texas) whose judges hold themselves out as interested and expert in patent cases. Infringement cases are complex, costly, and lengthy; one litigator described spending the last six years on the same case—motions, hearings, jury trial—"and it's still not done yet" (#1).

Patent litigators see themselves as a different breed from their prosecutor cousins. In the words of one litigator, "Prosecutors are science, nerd types. Litigators are big-time aggressive types. Litigators have higher pressure, travel a lot, make much more money" (#6). They also see attractions in *patent* litigation that extend beyond the remuneration that all litigators receive. As one of them said, "Unlike the rest of corporate litigation, it's not just about the money. There's a story there. And my job is to figure out the story" (#1). She added, "There's also a real intellectual challenge." Another patent litigator said he liked the respect he received from other lawyers at his corporate firm. As a fourth-year associate whose undergraduate degree was in politics—not science or engineering—he felt his peers were somewhat in awe that he could understand the technical and scientific details of his patent cases.

Changes in Patent Practice

The biggest changes for patent lawyers over the past 15 to 20 years have been in the nature and size of their practice organizations. In the 1970s and 1980s, before the patent litigation boom, patent law and specialized IP was "practiced in relatively small boutiques" (and often solo) for firms to avoid conflicts of interest in representing clients with interests adverse to one another (Shapiro 2002, 76). By about 1990, the boutique firms had begun to expand, and large corporate firms started acquiring them. Both of these trends were part of the general growth in firm size. By 1995, Heinz et al.'s (2005) survey of Chicago lawyers found that patent law was practiced primarily in middle-sized firms of 31 to 99 lawyers and that there were fewer small patent firms than there had been in 1975.

Patent boutiques were especially attractive acquisition targets for expanding corporate firms for several economic reasons. First, the general corporate firms could offer their business clients "one-stop shopping." More to the point, the business firms could now bring patent prosecution work in-house and capture some of the premium fees (that is, in excess of normal hourly charges) that patent lawyers would be able to charge because of growing demand and limited (by the patent bar requirements) supply. In addition, the acquisition of patent boutiques gave the corporate firms a stronger position in the lucrative business of patent litigation. The usual practice had long been for corporate law firms dabbling in patent litigation to associate a patent firm as co-counsel to handle or at least advise on the more technical patent issues. A corporate firm with a captive boutique can bring all aspects of the litigation under its own roof, with obvious marketing and billing advantages. Large firms also hoped for new revenue as patent prosecutors with long-term clients would bring these clients with them and attract others as well; the corporate firm could then "cross-sell" their other capabilities to these clients.

Notwithstanding what appear to be obvious economic advantages, the acquisition of a patent boutique presents economic, cultural, and ethical hurdles. Paul Goldstein, a Stanford Law School IP professor, describes the cultural challenge of moving patent work into large corporate firms in his recent novel about patent lawyers:

> Patent lawyers had only lately ascended to the aristocracy of the American bar. Trained not just as lawyers but as scientists or engineers, and working in small, specialized firms, they were at one time rudely dismissed by corporate lawyers as gearheads in green eyeshades, not good enough at science to be scientists, nor sufficiently talented at law to be real lawyers. Then came the intellectual property revolution of the 1990s, and these onetime outcasts found themselves ruling the last vibrant corner of the American economy. Suddenly every large corporate firm . . . had to have its own

patent department. But even as the corporate firms sought mergers with the few remaining intellectual property boutiques, the tensions between the two camps persisted. (Goldstein 2008, 67)

By their own account, patent lawyers are used to working fewer hours for more money. Also, disputes over billing rates emerged as clients who were used to the lower fees of their boutique lawyers balked at the higher fees of the corporate firm. For example, one experienced patent prosecutor in the biochemical field moved his 10-person practice to a nearby firm of more than 1,000 lawyers in 2004, but when the large firm raised its fees across the board a few years later, he left the firm. Rather than lose work from his longtime clients, he set up a new 5-person patent boutique with several of the attorneys from his original firm, reduced fees, and kept his clients (#4). A patent lawyer in a large corporate firm reinforced this point, commenting that prosecution work is increasingly subject to competitive discounting. Another patent practitioner said that the fixed fees that his firm typically charged for prosecution work did not "mesh very well" with the "billable hour, minimum number of hours billed" mentality of the large firm (#5).

Finally, the expectations of new clients for the large firm were not always met. While the former boutique lawyers, once acquired, could maintain their existing clients, they would lose referrals from all general corporate firms other than their own. No competing corporate firms will send their clients to an enterprise that will be all too eager to poach their nonpatent work. As one attorney (who moved from a small firm to a large firm and then back to a small firm) recalled:

> What I saw [after leaving a small firm] was, if referral work from other attorneys came out of a faucet, when I went into the big firm the faucet was turned off, and when I came out of the big firm the faucet was full open. Full throttle. By that, I mean that I had all these friends in the general bar who knew that I was a patent attorney and that was all I did. Patent and trademark work. I was a safe harbor for them to send their clients . . . and as soon as I went into the big firm . . . those calls stopped coming because they were afraid of cross selling (#5).

Besides billing and business issues, problems of "fit" have also disrupted some of the patent firm acquisitions by corporate firms. One patent lawyer who left a large firm for a boutique described patent prosecution as "an odd creature. It doesn't seem to fit very well in large law firms" (#11). Another interviewee commented, "I don't think the integrations into large firms go as well as anticipated or hoped" (#20). As discussed above, patent lawyers who work closely with inventors and the PTO have different educational backgrounds from their elite business-firm counterparts. As a partner in a still-independent patent boutique put it:

> The IP practice is a bit, is substantially different than most other practices in a general practice firm, and the IP folks themselves are historically technically-minded, my wife would say "nerdy," which doesn't always fit well with a general practice firm. So we have sort of a different mindset and culture that doesn't always blend well (#20).

Given these tensions, an obvious question is why patent firms want to be acquired. A generation ago the patent boutiques seemed to have an ideal niche. Because they controlled supply through the patent bar, patent lawyers could charge premium fees for their work. They had a steady supply of work since business firms sent their clients over without fear of poaching—patent boutiques were no threat to steal, say, securities work. And they had the autonomy to adapt to changing conditions and new expectations of clients. So why has acquisition been attractive for some small firms, especially when they confront the realities of dealing with nonscientists, losing their self-governing status, and perhaps working longer hours just to maintain the same income?

There are several possible answers. One boutique partner described the move "as an exit strategy for some of the controlling people." Specifically, in an acquisition the most senior people might receive substantial compensation—a control premium for their shares, as it were—which would enable them to move quickly into a very comfortable retirement. In such circumstances, those senior people—who also controlled the governance of the boutique—might make decisions that would not necessarily be in the long-term interests of the junior and mid-level people. In addition, it seems likely that the early waves of acquisitions might have created a domino effect. As more and more large corporate firms acquired captive patent practices, the remaining independents might have seen referrals from those firms drying up and felt some panic about finding a captive arrangement for themselves. A related possibility offered by a senior patent firm partner emphasized the business challenges of keeping a small firm in good financial health: "One reason for going into a bigger firm is you don't have to worry about the personnel issues, the administrative issues, the billing issues as much" (#5). He also mentioned the attraction of "security" that the big firms appear to offer.

Whatever the reasons, the current reality is that high-end patent litigation is increasingly dominated by the patent and litigation departments of large corporate firms, while patent application work is spread across large firms and small boutiques, brought in-house (especially in biotech),[6] and even out-sourced to India. An interesting question is whether some of the acquisitions of IP boutiques will be undone, as has been the case with many general practice firm mergers. Comments from our interviewees about patent prosecutors suggest that they might be among the first to leave. The head of the IP practice at the Silicon Valley office of a global law firm said that his firm had recently "spun off their patent prosecutors." He continued with a comment that seemed to contradict the expectation of premium fees that motivated some mergers: "Prosecution is a commodity. It can be done out of a small office or at home. It's not profitable to keep it within the firm. Their insurance is very high. They don't really fit well in the firm. And the clients don't care" (#8).

There has also been a sharp increase in legal outsourcing of patent work to India. Forty-six million dollars were paid to patent prosecutors in India in 2007, and patent outsourcing is expected to quadruple from that base by 2012 (*National Law Journal* 2008). But it is unclear how serious a threat outsourcing poses to US patent prosecutors. A New England patent lawyer said that his firm experimented with outsourcing at the request of a client but that they were unhappy with the inconsistent quality of the work:

> The problem is, you know, someone needs to review all of the work that comes back from India. Some of it's good, some of it's not good at all. . . . So it makes it difficult to do that work . . . when you send it over there you just don't who is going to be doing the work from one case to the next and what the quality will look like (#10).

Patent lawyers take pride in the efficiency of their operations. The lawyer quoted just above described his firm as "low overhead providers," a claim echoed by a partner in the Southeast who proudly reported providing his clients with "a high quality product at a reasonable price" (#20). Another boutique attorney described his surprise when a large corporate client flew to his

---

6. One lawyer we interviewed had worked in patent prosecution for 10 years at a large law firm, performing 80% of his work for a single client, a medical device company of more than 3,000 workers. When that company decided to bring its patent prosecution work in-house to cut costs, "I was the logical choice," the lawyer explained, and he left his firm to become its in-house patent counsel (#9).

firm's rural location just "to see the office. They wanted to see how we worked, they wanted to make sure that . . . they weren't paying for mahogany paneling and original Picassos on the wall and sculptures and stuff like that" (#7). Drawing on the cultural affinities of patent prosecutors for the scientists they work with, the stable client bases of many boutiques, their sensitivity to clients' concerns about pricing, and the conflicts of interest problems discussed below, we suspect that there will continue to be a place for small patent firms such as these.

The Ethical World of Patent Lawyers

In this section, we focus on patent lawyers and the ethical world in which they operate. After an introduction to the disciplinary regime that patent lawyers face, we discuss two common problems that arise in their daily practice: conflicts of interest in representing clients and the duty of candor to the PTO. All lawyers face conflicts issues, and all have some duty of candor to the tribunals before which they appear, but these issues take on particular meaning in patent law due to the ways that the lawyers' obligations are defined and regulated and—particularly in the case of candor—to the potentially severe consequences of a violation.

Ethical Regulation of Patent Lawyers, Formal and Informal

Patent lawyers enjoy a stellar reputation for ethical conduct, ranking second among 42 legal specialties studied by Heinz et al. (2005), a position that is substantially unchanged since 1975 (Heinz and Laumann 1982). Much of their reputation is due to the regulatory environment in which they work. Like all attorneys, patent lawyers are subject to discipline for violation of state bar rules, but even more important for registered patent lawyers are the disciplinary regulations of the patent bar and their enforcement by the PTO's Office of Enrollment and Discipline (OED). The OED can discipline patent lawyers with sanctions that range from a warning to suspension or exclusion from patent law practice. Results of proceedings against individual lawyers are regularly published at the PTO website (US Patent and Trademark Office 2011a). Lawyers disciplined by the OED must report it to their state authorities, and additional discipline might then be imposed. The possibility of bar discipline for misconduct was perhaps less salient for patent attorneys than discipline by the PTO. As one attorney said, "Bar discipline, we sort of joke that, boy, if something ever came up, we're not sure that the bar—you know, the panel that would look at an ethical issue—would understand the patent issues well enough to be able to really appreciate what the issue is" (#10).

The two most common complaints against registered patent practitioners before the PTO are neglect/incompetence and lack of candor (Moatz 2008). The risk of an accusation of neglect/incompetence as a result of missing a deadline is shared by all lawyers, but patent prosecutors are especially vulnerable because of the myriad deadlines set by statute and the huge ramifications for missing one. One lawyer explained:

> Right now in our small firm, 10 practitioners, . . . we're tracking about 100,000 due dates. One hundred thousand! Now, of those, you know, they're all spread out over time and some of them are 10 years into the future, but when you think—when you appreciate that a single patent application from beginning to end there are probably 15–20 actions and events, maybe 20, that you have to track and some of them are critical (#5).

"Critical" dates are those mandated by federal statute that cannot be altered: "You miss the date and you're done. It's over" (#5). These crucial deadlines lie not only within the United States but also for filing international patent applications. Another interviewee pointed out, "You miss the deadline and you potentially forfeit the client's worldwide patent rights outside of the US. . . . There are potentially hundreds of millions of dollars of royalties that are gone as the result of missing that deadline" (#10). Indeed, many highly publicized cases of malpractice, such as the $30 million damage award in *Kairos Scientific v. Fish & Richardson* (2003), involve overlooked deadlines.

In addition to possible PTO discipline or malpractice complaints, patent lawyers who take ethical risks face the potential loss of a client and harm to their firm's reputation. Contrary to the image of the lone garage inventor, patent seekers are typically large corporations, or at least medium-sized businesses. These business entities are often repeat players, dealing with the legal system in general, and the PTO in particular, for decades. By staying with the same lawyers, clients reduce their costs (since the lawyers already know their technology and product line) and can also gain long-term advantages in thinking about future markets and anticipating possible infringers.

All of the small firms where we conducted interviews described a stable client base, one they could ill afford to lose. As one said, "We have a broad base [of clients] . . . large clients who require a lot of resources, it's a fairly dependable work stream, so they end up becoming very important to your business" (#20).

Another lawyer commented that an angry client was even more worrisome to her than PTO sanctions: "You've got to keep them [clients] happy" (#11). Our patent prosecutor interviewees estimated that 50 to 70% of their revenue came from ongoing clients, including Fortune 500 businesses and global companies such as Siemens and Intel. Even a small mistake on an attorney's part could result in such clients taking their business elsewhere.

Unhappy clients can cause not only immediate loss of revenue to the firm but also long-lasting reputational damage. Since patent lawyers typically gain new clients through word-of-mouth referrals, they can easily lose clients that way as well. More than one lawyer commented on the small size of the patent bar and the importance of one's reputation. As one patent prosecutor said:

> There are relatively few patent attorneys. Everybody around here knows everybody . . . the word's going to get out pretty quickly . . . you just don't want to have a bad reputation. . . . When I took the state bar, there were, I think, 7,500 people throughout the entire state [New York] who were taking the bar the same day I did. When I took the patent bar, there were 3,500 people across the entire *country* taking it (#7).

Not surprisingly, then, patent prosecutors (but not the litigators) pointed to the small community of lawyers in which they worked and their ongoing relations with the PTO as informal influences that reinforced standards of ethical conduct.

Conflicts of Interest

One ethical issue that our patent lawyers report as a significant problem is the increased incidence of conflicts resulting from the merger of IP boutiques into large corporate firms. This problem is not unique to the patent context; indeed, it is endemic to law firm mergers and big firm practice in general. The relevant PTO rule (37 C.F.R. § 10.66) largely tracks most state bar provisions, prohibiting the representation of a client where the lawyer's independent professional judgment is likely to be "adversely affected by the practitioner's [a term that encompasses attorneys and agents] representation of another client." The PTO rule, like the state rules governing lawyers, permits a client to waive a conflict if it is obvious that the practitioner can adequately represent the interest of each client. The practitioner's duty to maintain the confidentiality of attorney-client communications and protect client secrets (37 C.F.R. §§ 10.56–10.57) can also be relevant in a conflict situation.

Recent cases illustrate how these rules can come into play in patent practice. For one thing, there may be an inherent conflict in representing competitors seeking patents in the same technological field. In *Tethys Bioscience, Inc. v. Mintz, Levin, Cohn, Ferris, Glovsky & Popeo* (2010), Tethys sued its patent law firm for breaching its duties of loyalty and confidentiality because the firm had also prosecuted a patent for a competitor in the field of identifying biological markers for diabetes. The loyalty claim was based on the adverse interests of the two clients, and the confidentiality claim on the law firm's use of information learned from Tethys in preparing the competitor's application. In denying a motion to dismiss, a federal trial judge cited both PTO and California rules of professional conduct in ruling that Tethys had stated a potentially valid claim on both counts and was entitled to seek damages.

In *Sunbeam Products Inc. v. Hamilton Beach Brands, Inc.* (2010), another federal district judge disqualified a large national law firm, Steptoe & Johnson, from representing a patent infringement plaintiff (Sunbeam) because one of its associates—even though he was not working on the infringement case—had previously done patent prosecution and litigation work for one of the defendants on a product that Sunbeam claimed was infringing its patent. The court cited Virginia Rules of Professional Conduct 1.9(a), which provides that "a lawyer who has formerly represented a client in a matter shall not thereafter represent another person in the same or a substantially related matter in which that person's interests are materially adverse to the interests of the former client." The court found that the present litigation and the former matters were "substantially related," and therefore disqualified the associate. Under Virginia Rule 1.10, the disqualification of any one lawyer required the disqualification of his entire firm.

It is not a coincidence that both of these cases involved large, multi-office national firms: The general rule (and it is a simple mathematical rule) is that the bigger the firm, the greater the exposure to conflicts. Big firm lawyers report giving conflicts careful attention and sometimes obtaining client waivers in instances of what seem to be purely technical conflicts. For example, assume that company X, a patent licensee of a law firm's existing client, asks the firm to represent it in litigation that is unrelated to the license. This would not constitute a conflict under state bar rules,[7] but in practice most big firm

---

7. For example, Virginia Rule of Professional Conduct 1.7(a) cmt. 6 states in part: "Simultaneous representation in unrelated matters of clients whose interests are only generally adverse, such as competing economic enterprises, does not require consent of the respective clients."

lawyers would treat it as such (or at least as a potential client relations problem) and seek a waiver from the existing client. The waiver is likely to be routinely granted as long as the licensing relationship is friendly.

Not all conflicts are so easily resolved, however, and conflicts rules can be applied especially strictly in the patent context. Consequently, we have heard comments about potential firm mergers being rejected because of concerns about attorneys being conflicted out of lucrative representations. In the patent boutique context, it might be the case that the acquiring firm has a major corporate client that is a direct competitor of the acquired boutique's patent client. The latter client might be uncomfortable having its most intimate technological secrets passed around the offices of its competitor's law firm. Here again, although this potential clash of economic interests might not rise to the level of a conflict under state bar rules, practicing lawyers would almost invariably treat it as such and seek a waiver. Promises of "firewalls" around its confidential information notwithstanding, the boutique's client might refuse to waive the conflict and might instead force the newly merged firm to choose between the two competitor clients. When asked how large firms avoid conflicts problems in the acquisition of IP boutiques, one large firm litigator answered, "They don't! It's a huge problem" (#1). When forced to choose, large firms with patent practices may choose to keep the more lucrative infringement litigation while farming out the prosecution.

Just as conflicts of interest helped to limit the size of IP firms before the merger mania, so have they continued to shape patent practice. A lawyer in a fairly new IP boutique described having just acquired a group of several biotechnology prosecutors who left a large firm because of this issue. The lawyer explained:

> One of their motivating reasons for splitting off and joining us was the fact that they were *completely locked up in terms of conflicts space* because they were at a firm with offices all around the country and they couldn't bring in a new client here in [city] in the biotech space because there was always some kind of direct conflict with maybe something at the Mayo Clinic or down in the Research Triangle (#11) (emphasis added).

Another attorney compared the ways conflicts were handled at his old large business law firm and at his new IP boutique:

> When I was at [name deleted] there was a conflicts search database and you'd run through the names of the adverse parties and it was all litigation based.

So you're really looking at, you know, if there's someone on the other side and is there some direct adversity? *Here it's more based on subject matter in the patent area* and so then it becomes—if another client comes in the door and they want us to draft a patent application and there might be some overlap in the technology area with another client, you know, how much overlap would result in a conflict? (#10) (emphasis added).

As the emerging case law suggests, and as this lawyer and others noted, determining exactly how much overlap would result in a "subject matter conflict" becomes a very difficult question. The lawyers we interviewed suggested no bright-line rules for resolving it. The problem is exacerbated by constantly changing technologies and by the complexity of patents:

We're talking about integrated circuits and we're talking about not one patent application, we're talking about 20 patent applications, each of them has 20 to 30 claims that cover various iterations of some type of integrated circuit that does some very complicated function. So as practical matter, you know, evaluating the conflict issue in that situation is not as simple [as some might think] (#10).

Thus, in patent practice—more so than in some other areas of law—the economic benefit of having a new client may be outweighed by the risk of that client's impact on existing clients.

Duty of Candor

Patent lawyers (and their inventor clients) bear a higher duty of disclosure than lawyers in almost any other litigation or administrative contexts (with securities law a possible exception, as discussed by Schmidt, chapter 11). The general requirements under the rules of professional responsibility are that a lawyer may not knowingly "make a false statement of law or fact to a tribunal" and must disclose to the tribunal any authority that is directly contrary to the client's position (Model Rule 3.3(a)(1), (2)),[8] but a lawyer prosecuting a patent has an even higher duty: The lawyer must disclose to the PTO all information that would be material to the examination of the patent. Failure to do so, or "inequitable conduct," can result in the patent being invalidated—in litigation long after the patent was issued—and in the lawyer being sanctioned.

---

8. ABA Model Rule 3.3(b) imposes a related duty on a lawyer to take reasonable measures to prevent or remedy the perpetration of a fraud on a tribunal by the client, including disclosure if necessary.

The duty of candor is stated in the PTO's Rules of Practice in Patent Cases and referred to informally as Rule 56 (37 C.F.R. § 1.56). Subsection (a) provides that "each individual associated with the filing and prosecution of a patent application"—including patent attorneys, agents, and clients—"has a duty of candor and good faith in dealing with the Office, which includes a duty to disclose to the office all information known to that individual to be material to patentability." Subsection (b) defines materiality as noncumulative information that "establishes, by itself or in combination with other information, a prima facie case of unpatentability," or refutes or is inconsistent with the applicant's position. All of the lawyers we interviewed stressed the importance of this ethical duty and noted that they routinely communicated the duty in writing to their clients, reminding them again and again of their obligation to reveal to the PTO any information relevant to patentability.

Two recent cases illustrate just how demanding and dangerous the duty of candor can be. The first, *Therasense v. Becton, Dickinson & Co.* (2011), was recently decided en banc by the Federal Circuit. Becton tried to prove that a patent held by Abbott, Therasense's parent company, was invalid because of inequitable conduct during prosecution of the application. The case involved Abbott's failure to disclose to the PTO a statement that its lawyer had previously made in briefs to the European Patent Office. The argument is highly technical, turning on the meaning of a phrase—"optionally, but preferably"—used to describe a membrane employed in a blood sugar test. If assigned a particular meaning, the phrase might have had an adverse effect on the success of the application. Abbott argued to the PTO that the language was "mere 'patent phraseology' that did not convey a clear meaning." But while prosecuting a similar patent before the European Patent Office, Abbott had contended that the same language was "unequivocally clear." A federal trial judge and a three-judge panel of the Federal Circuit held that the interpretation of "optionally, but preferably" was material to patentability, that Abbott's failure to disclose its prior inconsistent interpretation of the phrase was intentional, and that Abbott's patent was therefore invalid.

Sitting en banc, the full Federal Circuit reversed. The majority held that a party seeking to invalidate a patent for inequitable conduct must show that "but for" the misrepresentation or omission, the patent would not have been granted. A court can also find inequitable conduct if "affirmative egregious misconduct" is shown. The case was remanded to the trial court for reconsideration under the new stricter standard. The PTO has already begun the process of revising Rule 56 to reconcile its language with *Therasense*.

The Federal Circuit clearly viewed its decision as making it harder to prove inequitable conduct, which in turn is likely to reduce the frequency with which such charges are made. But even if inequitable conduct becomes harder to prove, violating the duty of candor will remain a concern. This is illustrated by a pre-*Therasense* failure-to-disclose case that would probably still come out the same way now: *Avid Identification Systems v. Crystal Import Corp.* (2010). There, a federal trial judge found inequitable conduct because Avid's founder had failed to disclose that he had demonstrated an early version of the patented technology at a trade show years before filing the patent application. The failure to disclose was material because a patent will not be granted if the invention was in public use (and a demonstration can constitute public use) more than one year prior to the application date. The judge found the nondisclosure to have been intentional and held the patent unenforceable. The Federal Circuit affirmed.

One of our interviewees (#11) brought up the original *Therasense* ruling to illustrate the difficulty of compliance with the duty of candor given the large amount of global patent prosecution—"where we have our applications pending in multiple jurisdictions around the world"—and the uncertain nature of the law in this area. She explained, "We're constantly making judgment calls about whether information would be considered material, whether it would be considered cumulative in view of what's already been submitted." When asked how she resolved issues like that, she replied simply, "Overinclusive." The risk of being underinclusive would be an inequitable conduct claim. She said that she is "always looking further down the road to the event of 'will this patent ultimately be litigated?' and 'what will the other side dig up in terms of how it was prosecuted?'"

In theory, a lawyer and inventor might be tempted to withhold adverse prior art if they thought they could get away with it—in other words, if they were convinced that neither the examiner nor a subsequent challenger (i.e., an infringement defendant or a prospective defendant seeking a declaratory judgment of invalidity) would be likely to find it independently. One might also envision a quiet conspiracy not to look too hard for bad prior art, hoping to fool the examiner while skating around failure to disclose. But that is not what we heard from our interviewees. The lawyers in our study see themselves as adhering to high ethical standards and claim not to observe unethical conduct among their peers, either. One put it bluntly: "I can't think of any patent lawyer that I've ever met that I thought was a shady character" (#22). A boutique partner, when asked whether the recession is causing patent lawyers to become "less professional in their conduct than they might have been in better times," responded:

> No—I don't pick up any of that. No. I'm excluding the, some of the troll litigators [individuals and companies that buy up cheap patents in volume in the hope of windfall damages or settlements], but other than that, no. That's what you would have expected of them always, so. But no, I mean, as far as patent prep for prosecution, I haven't seen a change in that (#20).

With respect to the duty of candor, there are—with a few notorious exceptions—reasons to accept this account at face value. First, it is probably hard to get away with withholding (or not looking for) material prior art. The PTO is woefully understaffed, but by most accounts individual patent examiners are smart and diligent, and, with the extensive search software now available, information is far easier to find than ever before. Also, the market provides an enormous help. If the patent has economic value—if there are competitors who will have to invent around or license it—those competitors will have an incentive to do their own research on patent validity. If the patentee sues one of them for infringement, that incentive will increase exponentially. So if a patent prosecutor foresees a possible infringement case—as a prosecutor must with every commercially valuable invention—it is reckless to take the risk of nondisclosure. Another lawyer described his firm's practice to "just cite everything . . . find anything and everything that potentially could be relevant and err on the side of disclosure," a practice that is "usually driven by this fear of not citing something and then being deposed again in litigation" (#10).

Once again, there is also a reputational element. The patent bar remains a relatively small community; word gets out. Reputation matters within this small bar, just like it does in other legal specialties where lawyers encounter each other on a regular basis, such as personal injury (Kritzer 2004) or divorce (Mather, McEwen, and Maiman 2001). Reputational risk taking is often driven by economics: Carlin (1966) found that ethical problems were most prevalent among the bar's most economically marginal practitioners, for reasons of desperation. But the patent bar, in addition to being small, is also a relatively prosperous community. A patent lawyer would have to have a very pessimistic view of future prospects to risk becoming known as the one who mishandled a prior art search.

Finally, several of the attorneys we spoke with referred to the overlap between the objective nature of science itself, the personality and practices of scientists, and the patent lawyer's strict duty to disclose. "We're all science nerds," noted one, "you don't mess with the data" (#3). Another noted that "a scientist is not someone who is trying to cut corners. . . . Reputation matters as much to these people as any kind of monetary compensation" (#22). The scientists and engineers who become patent lawyers, lawyers reported, are "more objective [than other people]" (#7), "detail-oriented and rule-following by personality" (#10), and "conservative by nature" (#5). Personal characteristics appear to reinforce institutional structures, such as malpractice suits, PTO sanctions, and the incentives for others to discover undisclosed prior art, in discouraging ethical risk taking.

Conclusion

Patent practice presents a range of interesting professionalism issues, some of which are shared with other branches of the profession and some of which are peculiar to patent lawyers. In the former category are the growth in firm size and the recent wave of mergers and acquisitions, as well as clients' increased attention to the cost of legal services. The ethical questions arising from patent law's broad definition of conflict of interest and the strict duty of candor that it imposes have few direct counterparts elsewhere. Moreover, the sanctions patent lawyers face for ethical misconduct are both more consequential and more likely to arise than in many other areas of legal practice. Besides possible bar or PTO discipline, patent lawyers face the threat of malpractice complaints (they pay especially high premiums for insurance) and the possibility of invalidity rulings that could be highly damaging to clients. These factors, in combination with the unusual culture of the patent bar and the unique supply and demand dynamics that result from the requirement of a scientific background, make patent practice an important ethical case study and a particularly useful one for comparative purposes.

References

Bessen, James, and Michael J. Meurer. 2008. *Patent Failure: How Judges, Bureaucrats, and Lawyers Put Innovators at Risk.* Princeton, NJ: Princeton University Press.

Burk, Dan L., and Mark A. Lemley. 2009. *The Patent Crisis and How the Courts Can Solve It.* Chicago: University of Chicago Press.

Carlin, Jerome E. 1966. *Lawyers Ethics: A Survey of the New York City Bar.* New York: Russell Sage Foundation.

Carlson, Dale L., Robert A. Migliorini, and Carolyn J. Vacchiano. 2005. "Re-Thinking

Patent Bar Admission: Which Bag of Tools Rules?" *Journal of the Patent and Trademark Office Society* 87:113–147.

Clifford, Ralph D., Thomas G. Field, and Jon R. Cavicchi. 2010. "A Statistical Analysis of the Patent Bar: Where Are the Software-Savvy Patent Attorneys?" *North Carolina Journal of Law & Technology* 11:223–268.

Crouch, Dennis. 2007. "Computer Based Patent Bar Exam Statistics." *Patently-O* (blog), December 30. http://www.patentlyo.com/patent/2007/12/computer-based.html.

———. 2009. "Percentage of Patents That Were Initially Rejected." *Patently-O* (blog), April 3. http://www.patentlyo.com/patent/2009/04/percentage-of-patents-that-were-initially-rejected.html.

Dutton, Harry I. 1984. *The Patent System and Inventive Activity During the Industrial Revolution, 1750–1852*. Dover, NH: Manchester University Press.

Gallagher, William T. 2011. "IP Legal Ethics in the Everyday Practice of Law: An Empirical Perspective on Patent Litigators." *John Marshall Review of Intellectual Property Law* 10:309–364.

Goldstein, Paul. 2008. *A Patent Lie*. New York: Random House.

Heinz, John P., and Edward O. Laumann. 1982. *Chicago Lawyers: The Social Structure of the Bar*. New York: Russell Sage Foundation and American Bar Foundation.

Heinz, John P., Robert L. Nelson, Rebecca L. Sandefur, and Edward O. Laumann. 2005. *Urban Lawyers: The New Social Structure of the Bar*. Chicago: University of Chicago Press.

Kesan, Jay P., and Gwendolyn G. Ball. 2006. "How Are Patent Cases Resolved? An Empirical Examination of the Adjudication and Settlement of Patent Disputes." *Washington University Law Review* 84:237–312.

Kobylarz, Xenia. 2007. "IP Boutiques: Keeping Up with the Joneses." *Law.com*, March 29. http://www.law.com/jsp/article.jsp?id=1175072639205.

Kritzer, Herbert M. 2004. *Risks, Reputations, and Rewards: Contingency Fee Legal Practice in the United States*. Palo Alto, CA: Stanford University Press.

Mather, Lynn, Craig A. McEwen, and Richard J. Maiman. 2001. *Divorce Lawyers at Work: Varieties of Professionalism in Practice*. New York: Oxford University Press.

Marco, Alan C., and Ted M. Sichelman. 2010. "Do Economic Downturns Dampen Patent Litigation?" http://ssrn.com/abstract=1641425.

Moatz, Harry. 2008. "Avoiding Misconduct Complaints in Patent Prosecution." Paper presented at the Advanced Patent Law Institute, Alexandria, VA, January 10–11.

Mullin, Joe. 2009. "Patent Litigation Survey 2009: A Little Less Buzz." *Law.com*, September 1. http://www.law.com/jsp/cc/PubArticleCC.jsp?id=1202433129756.

National Law Journal. 2008. "Patent Services Outsourcing to India Hits $46 million." November 24.

Poss, Jane. 1990. "Polaroid Wins $909 Million Award from Kodak." *Boston Globe*, October 13.

Quinn, Gene. 2010. "The Strange Case of the Vanishing Patent Boutiques." *IP Watchdog*, April 6. http://www.ipwatchdog.com/2010/04/06/the-strange-case-of-the-vanishing-patent-boutiques/id=9877/.

Shapiro, Susan P. 2002. *Tangled Loyalties: Conflict of Interest in Legal Practice*. Ann Arbor: University of Michigan Press.

US Patent and Trademark Office. 2011a. "Decisions of the Office of Enrollment and Discipline." http://des.uspto.gov/Foia/DispatchOEDServlet?RetrieveAll=true.

———. 2011b. "Patent Attorney/Agency Search." https://oedci.uspto.gov/OEDCI/query.jsp.

Van Zyl Smit, Dirk. 1985. "Professional Patent Agents and the Development of the English Patent System." *International Journal of the Sociology of Law* 13:79–105.

Wilkins, David, Ronit Dinovitzer, and Rishi Batra. 2007. "Urban Law School Graduates in Large Law Firms." *Southwestern University Law Review* 36:433–507.

Cases, Regulations, and Rules

Avid Identification Systems v. Crystal Import Corp., 603 F.3d 967 (Fed. Cir. 2010).

Kairos Scientific v. Fish & Richardson, No. 415736, 2003 WL 21960687 (Cal. Super. Ct. July 29, 2003).

Microsoft Corp. v. i4i Ltd. Partnership, 131 S. Ct. 2238 (2011).

Sperry v. Florida, 373 U.S. 379 (1963).

Sunbeam Products, Inc. v. Hamilton Beach Brands, Inc., 2010 U.S. Dist. LEXIS 74001 (E.D. Va. July 22, 2010).

Tethys Bioscience, Inc. v. Mintz, Levin, Cohn, Ferris, Glovsky & Popeo, 2010 U.S. Dist. LEXIS 55010 (N.D. Cal. June 4, 2010).

Therasense v. Becton, Dickinson & Co., No. 08-1151, 99 U.S.P.Q.2d 1065 (Fed. Cir. May 25, 2011).

37 C.F.R. §§ 1.56, 10.56–10.57, 10.66, 10.7 (2010).

Virginia Rules of Professional Conduct 1.7(a) cmt. 6, 1.9(a), 1.10 (2010).

Prosecutors' Ethics in Context

Influences on Prosecutorial Disclosure

Ellen Yaroshefsky and Bruce A. Green

Two recent high-profile cases called attention to prosecutors' professional conduct, and particularly, to prosecutors' failure to fulfill their legal obligation to disclose fundamental exculpatory evidence to the defense. In 2006, North Carolina District Attorney Michael Nifong vigorously prosecuted three white Duke University lacrosse players for sexually assaulting a young African American woman. Nifong's serious professional misconduct included suppressing DNA evidence strongly supporting the defendants' innocence. After Nifong's misconduct was exposed, the attorney general of North Carolina took over the prosecution, dropped all charges, and called Nifong a "rogue prosecutor" (Wilson and Barstow 2007). Nifong became one of the rare prosecutors to forfeit his law license for prosecutorial misconduct. Later, in the second case, a federal judge set aside the conviction of former US Senator Ted Stevens for lying on Senate ethics forms after an FBI whistleblower revealed that federal prosecutors had withheld crucial evidence, including notes of their interview with the key government witness that contradicted his trial testimony. The district judge observed that in almost 25 years on the bench, he had "'never seen mishandling and misconduct'" like that found in this case (Lewis 2009).

Prosecutors believe that intentional misconduct of this nature is highly unusual; many defense lawyers dispute their claim. In all likelihood, prosecutors' violations of their disclosure obligations are most often the result of negligence or innocent mistakes. Whatever the cause of such violations, prosecutors' lapses can result in wrongful convictions, as demonstrated by "exoneration cases" in which defendants convicted of serious crimes are later proven innocent. Prosecutorial misconduct—including, notably, failures to disclose evidence—was found to have contributed to the convictions in 45% of the Innocence Project's first 100 exoneration cases (Innocence Project 2011). In response, scholars and reform organizations have called for the systemic examination of prosecutors' disclosure practices (Terzano, McGee, and Holt 2009; Yaroshefsky 2010).

As the Duke lacrosse case and the Stevens prosecution illustrate, misconduct in the criminal "discovery" process can occur in both state and federal prosecutors' offices, and both systems should be studied. However, this chapter focuses exclusively on state prosecutors, drawing on a study of seven offices located in different parts of the United States. We chose to study state rather than federal prosecutors because of the wider variation of disclosure practices among state prosecutors and because state prosecutors were more open to being interviewed. We consider both (a) prosecutors' compliance with legal obligations to disclose evidence and information to the defense under the applicable constitutional case law, statutes and criminal procedure rules, and professional conduct rules; and (b) prosecutors' exercise of discretion to disclose additional information. This study identifies both environmental and organizational influences that shape individual prosecutors' decisions about the pretrial release of information to the defense. The environmental influences include the statutory and regulatory frameworks for disclosure obligations and for lawyer discipline, the role of judges, and the interactions with other actors in the criminal justice system and with the wider community. The organizational influences include office leadership; the offices' policies and structures for training, mentoring, and supervision of case management; and prosecutors' cultures of expectations about their jobs. These frame prosecutors' own accounts of their motivations and personal ethics. We chose to study prosecutorial disclosure because it is one of the most significant areas of contention between prosecutors, defense lawyers, and judges; it is rarely studied; and it is essential to the functioning of the criminal justice system.

We suggest that when it comes to pretrial disclosure, the principal influences on prosecutors' decision making are likely to be organizational factors. Whether and how junior or "line" prosecutors comply with rules and law, and especially whether they exercise discretion wisely and fairly, is likely to be determined by the complex interplay of internal and personal considerations such as office culture and policy, office regulatory and supervisory practices, and prosecutors' own professional values.

Our Data

Empirical studies of prosecutors are hard to conduct. Much of prosecutors' work is not transparent, and nowadays prosecutors generally decline, often for legitimate reasons, to open their offices and confidential work to scholarly scrutiny (Yaroshefsky 2010). Typically, there are no public data or reports that provide insight into decision making, nor are internal records maintained in a way that facilitates research. However, for this study we conducted 35 interviews with current and former state prosecutors who worked in seven offices located in the Northeast, Southeast, and Midwest of the United States. In each office, we talked to the chief prosecutor or another high-level member of the office, a supervisor with five to ten years' experience, a training coordinator, and other prosecutors with one to three years' experience. The chief prosecutor then selected about five to six prosecutors at different levels of experience within the office for our interviews. Some offices requested, and were given, the list of interview questions in advance. All participants were promised anonymity, both as offices and as individuals.

The size of the offices, and the communities they served, varied greatly. The smallest office had only 3 prosecutors, while the largest had more than 500 prosecutors and a total staff of more than 1,200. The communities served ranged from fewer than 50,000 to more than 2 million individuals. All prosecutors had heavy caseloads. In urban districts, one prosecutor may handle approximately 60 to 80 felony cases per year, and another may handle hundreds of misdemeanor cases. Prosecutors in a statewide prosecutor's office were responsible for approximately 8 to 15 cases per year, but these cases were generally complex and involved multiple defendants. Although this was not a large or random sample, it offered a reasonably varied perspective on prosecutors' offices around the county. Our study necessarily reflects the inherent bias of results based on self-reporting. Although we obtained limited information from judges and former prosecutors in these jurisdictions, most of our conclusions are drawn from our interviews with prosecutors as well as the literature in the field. Despite these limitations, our interviews provide a preliminary basis for some generalizations about the influences on prosecutors' pretrial disclosure practices.

Our objective was to explore the influence of the environment in which the prosecutors' offices operate; the internal structure and culture that prosecutors' offices develop in response to that context; and the nature and character of the personnel who prosecutors' offices recruit. In other words, we sought to discover the extent to which decisions are guided by and based on law, rules and ethics provisions, office policies, leadership, norms, and culture. We also sought to learn the extent to which decision making is based on the individual's ethical or moral values and guideposts beyond those imposed by existing laws, rules, or implicit norms.

Environmental Influences on Prosecutors' Disclosure

The Legal Governance of Prosecutorial Decision Making

Prosecutors' pretrial disclosure decisions are substantially influenced by the legal framework in which these decisions are made. In an adversarial system of justice like that of the United States, it is generally assumed that fair trials require both sides to present the evidence most helpful to their positions. Often, however, the criminal defense lawyer will not be aware of helpful evidence, such as exculpatory accounts given by eyewitnesses, unless the prosecution provides it. Additionally, unless prosecutors disclose some of their incriminating evidence in advance, defendants may be "ambushed" at trial because criminal defense lawyers cannot depose witnesses, make requests for admissions, make document demands, or conduct other discovery as parties do in civil cases. Disclosure requirements are said to "contribute . . . to the fair and efficient administration of criminal justice" by encouraging pleas, avoiding unfair surprise, and enabling "an accurate determination of the issue of guilt or innocence" (Federal Rule of Criminal Procedure 16). However, some question whether the implementation of the disclosure requirements adequately achieves these objectives (Galin 2000; Griffin 2001; Levine 2004).

Prosecutors' disclosure obligations are governed by constitutional law, rules of criminal procedure and statutes, and rules of professional conduct. Federal constitutional standards, known as *Brady* obligations after the Supreme Court decision in *Brady v. Maryland* (1963), require all prosecutors to disclose, in a timely fashion, evidence that is "material" to guilt or punishment including impeachment information.[1] These cases establish a constitutional minimum for federal and state prosecutors. State court rules and statutes variously sup-

---

1. Evidence is deemed to be material if there is a reasonable probability that the outcome would have been different had the evidence been disclosed (*United States v. Bagley*, 1985). The *Brady* rule was extended to require the disclosure of impeachment evidence including the disclosure of "an alleged promise to a government witness that he would not be prosecuted if he testified on behalf of the government" (*Giglio v. United States*, 1972, 153–155). Cases require

plement state prosecutors' constitutional obligations. These may call for the disclosure of specified documents, physical items, and other information such as the defendant's written and recorded statements, reports of the defendant's prior criminal convictions, physical evidence that the prosecution plans to use at trial, expert reports, witnesses' criminal records, and prosecution witnesses' relevant written and recorded statements. Unlike in the federal system, where prosecutors need not list their witnesses prior to trial, prosecutors in many states must make prompt and full disclosure of witnesses' names and statements (Blasser 2010).

In many respects, the legal standard for pretrial disclosure is ill defined and imprecise in application. Under *Brady*, courts do not overturn convictions unless the prosecutor failed to produce exculpatory evidence that was material. Prosecutors and defense lawyers disagree about what constitutes materiality, and appellate courts take differing views (Schwartz 2010). There are also questions about the timing of necessary disclosure. Many courts require prosecutors to disclose information well in advance of trial (Justice Project 2007). Others do not require production until the eve of trial or, in the case of information useful to impeach prosecution witnesses, after the relevant witness testifies on direct examination (Hooper, Marsh, and Yeh 2004).

Professional conduct rules adopted in most states recognize that prosecutors have a broad obligation to seek justice. These rules impose additional and more specific obligations beyond the constitutional and statutory obligations (Green 1999; Zacharias 2001). American Bar Association (ABA) Model Rule of Professional Conduct 3.8(d) requires the prosecution to

> make timely disclosure to the defense of all evidence or information known to the prosecutor that tends to negate the guilt of the accused or mitigates the offense, and in connection with sentencing, disclose to the defense and to the tribunal all unprivileged mitigating information known to the prosecutor, except when the prosecutor is relieved of this responsibility by a protective order of the tribunal.

An ABA advisory opinion interpreted this rule as requiring disclosure prior to the entry of a guilty plea and disclosure of broader categories of information than required by constitutional law. It also required disclosure regardless of

---

prosecutors to make a reasonable request of the police to obtain information from their files that is subject to disclosure (*Kyles v. Whitley*, 1995).

the evaluation of the potential effect of the information on the outcome of the case (ABA 2009). State courts do not necessarily agree with this analysis.

Prosecutors recognize the *Brady* line of cases and relevant state statutes and rules as sources of disclosure obligations, but are not generally aware of the relevant professional conduct rule or of the possibility that it establishes obligations beyond those of other law. Chief prosecutors, trainers, and supervisors discussed ethics rules generally during our interviews, but lower-level prosecutors seemed to be unfamiliar with their specific provisions. Some had only vague memories of those rules from professional responsibility classes in law school and the Multistate Professional Responsibility Examination.

Because the relevant constitutional law leaves substantial room for interpretation, and statutes and rules may do so as well, decisions about whether and when to disclose particular evidence or information may depend on the particular prosecutor's understanding of and attitude toward the law, including whether the prosecutor elects to act based on a broad or narrow reading of the law when the law's requirements are unclear. Prosecutors ordinarily make these decisions without the trial court's involvement; prosecutors rarely ask the judge whether evidence must be disclosed. As we discuss below in the section on organizational influences, some offices have a policy calling for liberal disclosure, which limits the need for line prosecutors to make hard legal judgments. Indeed, some disclosure policies are so expansive as to call for providing virtually the entire prosecution file ("open file discovery"). But other offices require prosecutors to comply only with their legal obligations and produce nothing or little more, or leave it to individual prosecutors to decide for themselves whether to disclose more than the law requires ("narrow compliance jurisdictions").

Although there are strategic benefits for prosecutors to limiting or delaying disclosure, our interviews suggest that prosecutors do not invariably interpret the law to minimize disclosures, and they may even disclose more than law or office policy requires. Some prosecutors said they were reluctant to take advantage of technicalities or uncertainties, and others claimed to have a personal practice, independent of office policy, of being more forthcoming than legally necessary. For example, although some said that they disclosed exculpatory evidence only if it was material, in the legal sense that it would affect the case's outcome, others said that they would disclose any evidence that was "favorable to the defense" or "relevant to the [defense] case." One prosecutor said that he asks himself whether "the information is important in some way to the defense's case. If yes, then I would disclose the information." Others thought that the legal standard of materiality did not go "far enough" for appropriate disclosure. A prosecutor said, "I do not think about what I am obligated to do; rather, I think about what I ought to do." Another said, "People can hide behind the rules. A rules-based system creates less disclosure because rules create exceptions," and took the view that prosecutors "should exercise their discretion in a manner that is ethical and that protects the community they serve."

We sought to determine what factors influence prosecutors to take liberal or narrow views of their legal obligations or to exercise their discretion generously or sparingly. Some individual prosecutors may act on understandings or philosophies that they brought to their offices, but in many cases they appear to have internalized understandings developed in the course of their work. Do these understandings result from office training or office culture or from elsewhere? We first consider the influence of the public, accountability mechanisms, judges, and prosecutors' peers.

Prosecutors and the Public

Prosecutors are buffered from market influences and client influences brought to bear on private lawyers. They do not have to answer to a client, concern themselves with obtaining and keeping clients, or worry about lawsuits brought by unsatisfied clients. The chief prosecutor may be accountable to the public in an abstract sense and, if elected rather than appointed, may have some concern about satisfying the electorate, but she does not take direction from the public or any of its members.

Public opinion is unlikely to have a major impact on disclosure policies of a prosecutor's office and certainly not on the conduct of junior or line prosecutors. The public is often only dimly aware of what prosecutors do. Policies and practices regarding pretrial disclosure are unlikely to come to the public's attention or directly to contribute to the public's perception of the office, except in the rarest of high-profile cases such as the Duke lacrosse case in which disclosure decisions become a matter of public controversy.

If chief prosecutors fear that liberal disclosure will reduce their offices' conviction rates, they may adopt restrictive policies on the theory that "aggressive non-disclosure" may help win cases (Wright 2010). High-profile criminal cases can increase the pressure on the prosecutor's office to win, translating into withholding of evidence "until the very last minute" (Findley and Scott 2006; Barkow 2010). However, whatever small improvement in conviction rates might result from restrictive disclosure policies will probably not matter in the polls. Bibas (2009) observes that the public has few means of evaluating the prosecutor's performance, particularly when conviction rates or crime rates are used to garner positive news coverage. Such numbers can be manipulated or result from influences beyond the prosecutor's control. Wright (2009, 582–583) notes that prosecutor elections are not usually strongly contested, the incumbent usually wins, and campaigns focus on a few high-visibility cases. The prosecutor's disclosure practices or the office's priorities are not ordinarily debated (Mosteller 2008).

Further, regard for the public perception may equally cut in favor of liberal disclosure policies. If chief prosecutors worry that line prosecutors' public failures to comply with the disclosure law will lead to public embarrassment, they may adopt open file policies or encourage line prosecutors to err on the side of disclosure. The motivation may be less to secure reelection than to promote public confidence necessary for the office's general success. One chief prosecutor said that he told his assistants: "If we don't do our jobs in a manner that is ethically appropriate, then the longer term consequence is that people don't trust you. If they don't trust you, then they won't tell you the things that you need to know in order to keep them safe. If I have to do things that appear soft on crime, then I must publicly state it and provide my reasoning." Another chief prosecutor said, "If an office gets a reputation for cutting corners, it ultimately affects the perception of juries." In Dallas County, Texas, which at one time had the highest number of exonerations in the country and a notoriously ethically challenged prosecutor's office, a newly elected district attorney sought to regain public credibility by adopting new disclosure policies along with new hiring, training, and supervision policies (Barkow 2010).

Accountability Mechanisms: Civil Liability, Criminal Liability, and Professional Discipline

Prosecutors are highly unlikely to be influenced by concerns about criminal or civil liability for noncompliance with disclosure obligations. Criminal liability is not a meaningful risk for prosecutors. Although lawyers are generally subject to regulation by criminal law (Green 1998), and the intentional failure to disclose evidence to the defense might be characterized as obstruction of justice, we know of only one criminal prosecutor who was indicted for such alleged misconduct, and he was acquitted (Shenon 2007). Prosecutors can be expected to be generally sympathetic to fellow prosecutors who fail to make legally required disclosures and to perceive the conduct as erroneous but not venal.

Civil liability for illegally withholding evidence is also unlikely because prosecutors have absolute immunity from civil liability for trial conduct as well as for administrative activities of prosecutors in the areas of "training, supervision, or information system management" (*Van de Kamp v. Goldstein*, 2009). There is limited qualified immunity solely for investigative functions, but prosecutors have a good-faith defense that all but eliminates the risk of civil liability (*Imbler v. Pachtman*, 1976). It is also difficult to hold district attorneys' offices civilly liable for inadequate disclosure obligation training in the absence of a clear pattern of *Brady* violations (*Connick v. Thompson*, 2011). Thus, regulatory considerations that are presumed to play a significant role in promoting legal and ethical compliance for privately retained lawyers are virtually irrelevant to prosecutors.

We also found little evidence that regulation through formal attorney disciplinary processes had a significant effect on prosecutorial disclosure decisions. Prosecutors are subject to professional discipline for illegally withholding evidence, but only when they do so "knowingly." If prosecutors had a realistic risk of discipline, they might err on the side of disclosure in close cases, but even when courts find that a prosecutor intentionally violated disclosure obligations, sanctions are rare. Disciplinary authorities have been reluctant to examine alleged prosecutorial ethical violations (Yaroshefsky 2004; Barkow 2010). Commentators have long lamented the lack of effective disciplinary sanctions for prosecutorial misconduct (Rosen 1987; Zacharias 2001). Our interviewees could not identify any instances in which prosecutors' colleagues had faced professional discipline, even after a court found that a *Brady* violation had been committed (Mosteller 2008). As one prosecutor acknowledged, "It's not a fear of being called into question later on that dictates behavior because prosecutors do not tend to get punished anyway."

In rare situations, judges impose professional sanctions, exclude evidence, or dismiss indictments for violations of disclosure obligations. However, the supposed "stigma of appellate reversal" for failure to disclose *Brady* information does not appear to be relevant in most prosecutors' discretionary decision making because of its unlikely occurrence. Most cases result in guilty pleas, as discussed by Nicole Martorano Van Cleve (chapter 14). In the small percentage of cases that go to trial, the chances of appellate reversal for disclosure violations are slim (Burke 2009), and even in those cases, courts do not typically name the prosecutors who were to blame.

Informal Peer Influences: Defense Lawyers and Judges
Wholly apart from formal processes of professional discipline, informal peer pressures in the form of "local legal culture" may influence prosecutors'

conduct (Church 1985; Feeley 1979). In particular, individual prosecutors or their offices as a whole may respond to how other local actors and agencies regard their behavior, preferring others to regard their behavior as legitimate and consistent with established practices and conventions.

Local judges appear to influence prosecutors' disclosure practices, most commonly through informal expressions of concern or disapproval that imply a potential withdrawal of goodwill, on which prosecutors depend for the smooth management of their work. It matters whether the judge displays an interest in pretrial disclosure. In jurisdictions in which the court exercises some authority over the discovery process—either informally or pursuant to court rules—prosecutors appear to be more diligent in complying with their obligations in gray areas. One prosecutor complained that a particular judge believes "discovery is whatever the defendant wants." As a result, prosecutors from this office rarely fight discovery motions and review their cases to ensure legal compliance: "We would rather give the defense everything than face the wrath of this particular judge." However, most judges tend to be "hands off." In another jurisdiction, a judge expressed dismay that the judiciary "enabled" prosecutors to fail to disclose exculpatory evidence by its inattention to discovery issues.

Prosecutors often are more forthcoming with defense lawyers whom they trust. They may maintain generous disclosure practices to build cooperative relationships with defense lawyers. In some jurisdictions, opposing counsel tend to see each other frequently, and they understand that conflicts have high costs in compromising their ability to negotiate guilty pleas and achieve other efficiencies; these lawyers "are likely to treat one another with respect and to avoid combative tactics" (Eisenstein, Flemming, and Nardulli 1999, 269–270). Despite potential strategic disadvantages to making earlier or fuller disclosures, prosecutors may be more accommodating if they perceive that defense counsel will not misuse evidence and that the disclosures are valuable to maintaining cooperation. In rural and small jurisdictions, information may be shared more quickly between the police, prosecutor, and defense lawyer because all of the actors know each other and interact frequently. Even in large urban counties, the same dynamic may exist because the prosecutors and defense lawyers may interact with each other regularly in courtroom workgroups (Eisenstein and Jacob 1977). It appears that open file policies, in particular, increase trust between prosecutors and defense counsel. Contrary to initial fears, early access to information by the defense has made prosecutors' work more efficient, increasing guilty pleas and improving counsels' relationships (Chisolm 2010).

Conversely, when witness intimidation or tampering is of concern, prosecutors can be circumspect about disclosing to a distrusted lawyer as much information or in as timely a fashion as to other lawyers. One district attorney said that his office would certainly comply with disclosure obligations in dealing with a distrusted lawyer but would stick to the letter of the law. Another said the extent of disclosure would be no different, but that everything would be put in writing. A third said he might seek protective orders from the court to prevent the misuse of information.

Organizational Influences on Prosecutors' Disclosure Practices

Office Policies

Organizations operating in the same field tend to converge on similar ways of working, a process known as isomorphism (DiMaggio and Powell 1983). Prosecutors' offices are something of an exception, partly because of their highly localized character. Since they are not directly in competition for business, the homogenizing pressures are much weaker. They do not adopt similar policies. The few offices with written disclosure policies do not make them public and would not provide them to us. We found that office policies adopted or endorsed by the chief prosecutor or supervisory prosecutors are a significant factor in shaping prosecutors' disclosure practices. If taken seriously, they become, in effect, the "law" of the particular office.

Many offices had some version of an open file policy, but their definitions varied considerably (Yaroshefsky 2004). One office might invite defense counsel to view all information gathered in a case, while another office may simply give the defense substantial, but not total, access to its files. However, all open file policies entail significantly broader disclosure than legally required. This definition is typical: "We turn over everything to the defense as soon as possible including all investigative reports, all reports from experts and labs, grand jury testimony, the defendant's criminal history and anything else we have that would not be our own work product." One office had a system in which the police automatically provided the prosecution with two copies of every document so that they could be handed to the defense as soon as practicable. In all open file systems, exceptions exist when prosecutors are concerned about witness safety or the protection of confidential informants. One jurisdiction's open file policy excludes all homicides and most sex crimes because witness safety is an issue in a large number of such cases.

Prosecutors perceived that open file policies remove most of their individual discretion in disclosure (Mosteller 2008). In the words of one prosecutor,

"Due to my office's open file policy, I have no individual discretion. I must hand everything over to the defense." However, an open file policy does not wholly dictate prosecutors' decisions, in part because (1) prosecutors must interpret office policy; (2) they must sometimes decide whether to disclose information that is not recorded and filed (e.g., unrecorded information provided by witnesses as the prosecutor prepares them to testify); (3) they must decide what documents to put in the particular case file; and (4) they must determine how strongly to make demands for information that the police have not conveyed. Prosecutors often note the difficulty of complying with their *Brady* obligations because of the police agency's failure to disclose information to them (Gershman 2007).

In open file and other robust disclosure jurisdictions, other players confirmed prosecutors' reports that the office's disclosure policy defines the practice. For example, a defense lawyer in one of these jurisdictions reported that, in general, the prosecutors are "highly ethical and very competitive in trial. . . . In big cases we get information months before trial. The police department brings the file to the prosecutor's office and we review it. Often we find information that the DA has not seen. . . . There are rare prosecutors in that office who do not turn over information until the last minute to obtain an advantage, but that is the exception not the rule."

By contrast, in narrow compliance jurisdictions, it is far more significant how the particular prosecutor interprets the law. Some prosecutors in these jurisdictions might err on the side of disclosure by reading the law liberally, but that is not generally the practice. The narrow compliance policy tends to influence both the culture of the office and the attitudes of individual prosecutors, who perceive themselves as participants in a highly adversarial, often noncooperative process. This may be true even in jurisdictions in which prosecutors are told that they have individual discretion to disclose more information than legally required. A former prosecutor in a narrow compliance jurisdiction said, "There was no intentional hiding of information or malicious acts. We did what the law said and nothing more. . . . I used to be a jerk and held onto material until trial was actually starting. I held onto material until the last moment. We did no favors for the defense. . . . Unless you have an open file policy, the adversarial dynamic will influence prosecutors."

Informal Office Understandings and Culture

Prosecutors' offices may develop understandings about whether to disclose or withhold information—particular ways of doing things—that are not expressed in, or acknowledged as, office policies but that are communicated informally by one prosecutor to another, especially by senior to junior prosecutors. For example, in one office with a narrow compliance policy, prosecutors have developed a shared understanding that they need not disclose certain information relating to the credibility of an eyewitness who has identified the defendant. They do not disclose evidence that the victim was intoxicated at the time of making the identification, on the theory that it "has nothing to do with whether the defendant committed the crime." Prosecutors in this jurisdiction appear to "resist disclosure of [evidence relating to an] investigation of law enforcement officers as a matter of course without looking to determine whether those police internal investigations contain exculpatory evidence." Similarly, arguably false statements by the police may not be disclosed because a prosecutor considers them immaterial to the police officer's proposed testimony. Prosecutors learn from peers or supervisors that the accepted practice is not to make disclosure in those particular situations and do not make decisions on their own about what the law requires.

Different understandings may develop in an office or among units that handle different types of cases based on differences among types of cases. Experienced prosecutors in large white-collar cases are more likely to disclose information earlier because there is extensive material to review and failure to disclose will delay proceedings and be criticized by the court. Further, there is little physical danger to witnesses. In all jurisdictions, disclosure is more carefully guarded in homicide or other cases involving potential danger to witnesses. Judicial orders of protection are sought to prohibit disclosure of the witness or identifying information. Similar to corporate culture in which informally developed "practice norms" govern litigation (Kirkland, chapter 8), prosecutors' offices may develop cultural attitudes that are conveyed to and assimilated by junior lawyers. A judge in a jurisdiction in which the prosecutor's office had a policy of narrow legal compliance said that its prosecutors "resist disclosure as a matter of course," which they justified by adopting questionably narrow legal interpretations. For example, the office looked at particular appellate decisions in which nondisclosure did not lead to appellate reversal of a conviction because the evidence of guilt was so strong; it interpreted the decisions to mean that the kind of exculpatory evidence at issue in the case did not have to be disclosed in general. Prosecutors also withheld exculpatory evidence on the dubious ground that the evidence did not in itself prove the defendant's innocence.

Office culture may reinforce office policies. For example, in one office with an open file policy, a laudatory story about a prosecutor's compliance with the policy to the office's strategic disadvantage had entered office lore: Several different prosecutors recounted it independently. That defendant was charged with stealing the victim's car and forging checks, but claimed that he had authority to write the checks and take the car. The prosecutor had information that the victim, a convicted felon, had severe problems recalling information accurately. The prosecutor disclosed this information to defense counsel, who used it to help secure an acquittal. Prosecutors told the story in the office to convey the importance of complying with the full disclosure policy, even at the cost of a conviction, because doing so furthers the office's broader mission to do justice.

Conversely, office culture and informal understandings may subvert office policies. Several former prosecutors and judges identified an office in which prosecutors are told to comply with the law and "if in doubt, disclose," but actual practice differs. One former prosecutor explained, "What we learned in training is not what happened in practice. We were told that if it was debatable, you should turn it over. In practice, supervisors would not tell you not to turn it over, but there was pressure and you were carefully scrutinized if you did not hold on until the bitter end with discovery."

Leadership

Strong, effective leadership shapes and drives an office's culture. The chief prosecutor sets the tone. One prosecutor drew the analogy that "a sports team adopts the personality of its coach, and something like that happens in the prosecutor's office." In setting the office's tone, many district attorneys specifically articulate a definition of "success" that is broader than simply winning at trial. One assistant describes the tone set by the district attorney in his office: "As prosecutors we're not just out to win but to see that justice is done. We follow the principle that full disclosure is better in order to protect the process and the people subject to the process. Our office provides full disclosure and by adhering to the idea that we want to see justice done we protect the process and avoid wrongful convictions." Chief prosecutors who adopt open file discovery policies create an environment encouraging broad disclosure, which influences prosecutors' general approach to discovery. Office-wide attitudes that favor disclosure are encouraged by chief prosecutors who consistently educate their staffs that the standard for disclosure is "whether [information] is favorable to the defense" and not whether it meets the legal definition of "materiality," or who espouse the view: "If it's not going to hurt you, then turn it over, and if you think it's going to hurt you, then you *must* turn it over." Junior prosecutors in offices in which the chief prosecutor conveyed these views reported, "We must disclose unless witness safety is at issue." Effective leadership also conveys a message of "shared responsibility." In the words of another prosecutor: "When we toss out our ethics, we not only ruin our own reputation, but we also ruin our office's reputation." If the chief prosecutor conveys that ensuring a fair trial and protecting the judicial process is paramount, then prosecutors who are led to have a sense of shared responsibility are more likely to err on the side of disclosure in gray areas.

Organizational Structures

The structure of a prosecutor's office may also affect ethical conduct, including disclosure practices. Organizational structures can differ significantly. In a small rural community, the elected county attorney may personally try cases and work with only one or two full-time or part-time lawyers. In a large city or county, where the office has several hundred prosecutors and a smaller number of senior lawyers who staff specialist trial units or act as supervisors, the chief prosecutor must delegate greater decision making to others. In both small rural and large urban offices, the line prosecutors may be recently hired lawyers with less than five years' experience.

Large urban offices are characteristically bureaucratic (Eisenstein, Flemming, and Nardulli 1999, 277). Prosecutors are divided into units, arranged by tasks and/or kinds of cases, and headed by supervisors and/or deputies. The more senior prosecutors typically handle the more important tasks (e.g., trials) or types of cases (e.g., homicides). These large offices generally have "regular procedures . . . set up for checking the behavior of assistant prosecutors and for formally evaluating their performance" (Eisenstein, Flemming, and Nardulli 1999, 277; Bibas 2009; Scheck 2010). Junior prosecutors can easily consult with more experienced colleagues or supervisors. In theory, such offices have the manpower to form executive committees or panels to review disclosure and other ethical issues as they arise (Burke 2009). In practice, supervisory review of disclosure decisions is rare, and there are often inadequate mechanisms to review disclosure and track problems (Barkow 2010). The effectiveness of large offices is strongly influenced by the available resources. High caseloads and underfunding significantly undermine supervision and management. This creates an environment with insufficient documentation of witness statements, failure to follow up on police evidence, and lack of attention to items of evidentiary value (Barkow 2010). Discretion may be driven less by carefully considered ethical judgments than by time constraints preventing careful file review. We rarely found formal or informal retrospective reviews of disclosure decisions, such as spot-checking case files to determine compliance with disclosure requirements or random audits of entire case files. When disclosure errors are made, offices do not examine them to determine how to improve internal practices (Scheck 2010; Green 2010). In one office, random audits were reserved for those prosecutors with a reputation for handling cases poorly. In another, a relatively inexperienced prosecutor said that supervisors randomly reviewed all first-year prosecutors' cases and that the audit may have influenced him to ensure that he was complying with the office's disclosure policy.

Small offices have little hierarchy: In the smallest we studied, all prosecutors worked on a variety of tasks and cases and, when questions arose, went either to another prosecutor or directly to the chief prosecutor. The chief prosecutors in smaller offices tended to have better knowledge of cases and, in some jurisdictions, routinely met with defense counsel in felony cases. When all prosecutors are trying cases, however, there may be little time for formal training, although less-experienced prosecutors may have more direct and regular access to the chief prosecutor and more experienced prosecutors in the office, assuming that their workload permits it. We found one small office in which the chief prosecutor reviewed junior prosecutors' decisions, including disclosure decisions, in every case except routine DUI cases. Such direct supervision had an immediate impact on discretionary disclosure in that office; disclosure mistakes were caught in time because there was early oversight.

In small offices, the office "culture" may more directly reflect the practices and policies of the chief prosecutor, who may have a stronger personal incentive to control junior prosecutors' decisions. As a recently retired small-town district attorney told us, "They were going to court in my name and were going to do it my way, which was to disclose harmful information to the defense." He stressed the importance of consistency, and said, "I created a culture where prosecutors erred on the side of giving up information and learned how to deal with the information strategically in the courtroom." One chief prosecutor in a small office believed that his active role in trying cases contributed to his conclusion that a broad disclosure policy was necessary. He observed that in large offices the "supervisors may have forgotten what it is like to actually try cases. This can affect the policies that they implement and the instruction that they provide to the prosecutors trying cases."

Hiring Policies

Hiring policies in theory may have an impact on pretrial disclosure decisions insofar as it is possible for those responsible for hiring to assess the values and character of applicants and select for those who have the preferred traits—for example, a commitment to fair process, on the one hand, or aggressiveness, on the other. If an office values certain ethical standards, it will seek to employ people who will act in accordance with those standards (Bibas 2009). Some prosecutors believe that the most important way to ensure ethical practice is to hire prosecutors with "good character." However, it is by no means clear that it is possible to do so, that prosecutors' offices make credible efforts to do so, or that they succeed.

Regardless of whether hiring practices can distinguish among those with desired values or philosophical approaches, they can foster a kind of office culture (Bibas 2009). For example, the district attorney in Dallas, inaugurated in 2007, sends all potential candidates *Brady* and other cases and tells them to be prepared to discuss the issues during the interview, hoping to impart the values of full and fair disclosure. Some offices also seek to hire former defense attorneys to alter the "us against them" mentality and provide the perspectives of seasoned defense counsel. One prosecutor said that his former work as a defense attorney contributed to his view that turning over all information as quickly as possible benefits both sides and that sharing his perspective as a former defense attorney with colleagues had had an impact on some of the other prosecutors.

Training

Once recruited, all prosecutors experience a process of both formal and informal organizational socialization as they learn what is expected of them as members of the office team. Larger offices more commonly run formal training programs, although resource constraints have curtailed some of these. Most programs are lecture-based and provide prosecutors with written materials on cases, ethics rules, and office procedures. Those manuals typically do not contain written disclosure policies (Barkow 2010). Some programs include case scenarios that prosecutors found helpful in understanding their obligations. Most programs include training about relationships and information exchange with police departments (Reiter 2010). Few offices have defense lawyers or judges participate in training programs. Some academics have suggested the trainings should include discussion of cognitive biases that may influence disclosure decisions, such as the risk that prosecutors who are persuaded of the defendant's guilt may minimize the importance of exculpatory evidence that is inconsistent with their theory of the case (Burke 2007). However, no office in our study trained prosecutors to understand the possible effects of cognitive biases.

Formal training programs are regarded as necessary by the chief prosecutor, but their impact is limited (Yaroshefsky 2004). Informal socialization through ongoing discussion with other prosecutors and supervisors ultimately appears to have a greater effect on prosecutors' resolution of disclosure questions. A midlevel prosecutor said, "Formal training provides a foundation of a prosecutor's disclosure obligations, and you build upon that foundation with experience and informal training." Informal socialization takes place on a daily basis. It occurs during conversations and e-mails with colleagues about cases and in case review sessions with supervisors and more experienced prosecutors. Prosecutors learn from their own mistakes. Several prosecutors said training was "trial by fire," and one said, "Once you get burned, you make sure not to make that mistake again." Another prosecutor recounted receiving a stern lecture from a judge and the chief prosecutor for failing to disclose information in a timely manner. He now "works very hard to avoid making a similar mistake," notably maintaining a better case file system to ensure that he has complied with all of his disclosure obligations as soon as possible.

Internal Regulation and Performance Management

In theory, performance review systems may enhance or impair adherence to ethical standards. However, many prosecutors do not regard themselves as "career prosecutors." Rather, they intend to gain trial experience and secure other jobs. Consequently, performance review and advancement within the office may not be a significant reward.

None of the offices we interviewed have mechanisms in place to reward good disclosure practices, and some have cultures that affirmatively discourage good disclosure practices. In offices that emphasize prosecutors' won-loss records and measure individual performance by conviction rates, the concept that a prosecutor's "success means more than winning" is less likely to be translated into practice (Findley and Scott 2006, 328; Barkow 2010). As one former prosecutor explained, "The trial atmosphere is that you're there to win and have to win. That was really pushed, not a spoken rule but there was that pressure. You got it from the supervisor, his boss and those around you. It's celebrated when you win." In other words, regardless of what the chief prosecutor says to the public or within the office about the importance of procedural fairness, prosecutors get the message that winning at trial is the key to career success and that fair-process values are comparatively unimportant (Medwed 2004; Barkow 2010; Burke 2007).

In most offices, internal discipline for failure to disclose is unlikely to occur. However, in one office a supervisor recalled that another prosecutor engaged in "discovery games" and was disciplined by reassignment, but this appears to be unusual. Particularly in offices with narrow legal compliance practices, failures to disclose, even when criticized by appellate courts, do not appear to result in meaningful internal sanctions (Rosen 1987; Yaroshefsky 2004).

In many instances, office culture values cohesion and tolerates disclosure violations for fear of undermining morale (Barkow 2010). This is not necessarily a conscious decision. Prosecutors may have implicit understandings of the limits of acceptable behavior and publicly support one another, even when there may be internal disagreements about proper conduct. There may also be institutional barriers to the use of disciplinary mechanisms. While a new chief prosecutor may bring in new senior lawyers, lower-level prosecutors can stay from one administration to the next. In some jurisdictions, prosecutors can be replaced "at will" by the chief, but in others, prosecutors have civil service protection and can be fired only for good cause. While this may give them a valuable measure of independence in professional judgment, it may also create difficulties in weeding out poor or inappropriate performance.

There is some suggestion that offices may be shifting toward better oversight and accountability of their attorneys. One large office had created an ethics oversight panel to review cases and the ethical conduct of individual prosecutors regarding decisions that it deemed to be "very important on a global level." The panel's work had resulted in the recent firing of two prosecutors for "ethical violations coupled with low level performances." This type of structure not only serves as an accountability mechanism for the particular prosecutor, but encourages compliance by others. In Dallas, the district attorney established a Conviction Integrity Unit (CIU) to review alleged wrongful conviction cases. The CIU uncovered unethical and marginal disclosure practices; the office imposed significant internal sanctions. This signaled a shift in office culture (Scheck 2010).

Prosecutors' Individual Philosophies, Motivations, Predispositions and Idiosyncrasies

Different prosecutors in an office often make different disclosure decisions in similar situations. Environmental and organizational influences do not account for all the variation. Individual personality, personal philosophy, and individual character traits and motivations may also be significant. Prosecutors who more highly value procedural fairness or who seek to cultivate a professional reputation for fairness or reasonableness may be more forthcoming in situations in which prosecutors who more highly value securing convictions or who seek a reputation for toughness may withhold discovery. Decisions may also be affected by the extent of the prosecutor's self-confidence: Those with confidence in their trial skills may make disclosure in situations in which less self-confident prosecutors will seek an edge by withholding or delaying the production of evidence and information.

The recent professional literature puts substantial weight on prosecutors' cognitive and experiential limitations as an influence on disclosure decisions, among others (Burke 2007). A recurring criticism in jurisdictions that do not have open file discovery is that prosecutors do not disclose information because they do not accurately perceive that it is exculpatory or impeaching information. Defense lawyers say, "They are thinking like prosecutors, not recognizing how the defense lawyer may use the evidence at trial." As District Judge Paul Friedman reflects, "most prosecutors are neither neutral (nor should they be) nor prescient" (*United States v. Safavian*, 2005, 14).

Some prosecutors attributed colleagues' unwillingness to make liberal pretrial disclosure to their being "too much of an advocate," setting the goal to "get this guy," being "overly paranoid and a little too competitive," and being "well intentioned" but too "strongly believ[ing] in the defendant's guilt." Aggressive prosecutors were referred to as "trial jocks." In one office, we were told that "there are committed ideologues particularly in sex offenses and child pornography cases" who will not disclose any information unless forced to do so by the court. Others who are less forthcoming may be driven by fear: of losing; of a dangerous person being released onto the streets; of the consequences of losing in terms of office respect, promotion, and future career goals (Scheck 2010). Conversely, many prosecutors have a "deeper commitment to the values that support disclosure" (Wright 2010, 1997).

Particularly in narrow compliance jurisdictions, the lawyer's level of experience may affect disclosure practices. As Elizabeth Chambliss discusses (chapter 3) and contrary to Bibas's (2009) report, it seems that experienced lawyers are more likely than junior ones to make fuller and earlier disclosures. One experienced prosecutor said, "These lawyers are more confident, they have been 'burned by experience' and if there are bad facts, they would rather turn them over early. Experienced prosecutors can deal with discrepancies in information." But this is not invariably true. Experience may also translate into "playing discovery games." One younger prosecutor observed that some veteran prosecutors are less concerned about office policy or supervisors' views. "They are not in it for the money and they don't have room to move up in the office. They are tired and burned out. Some are lazy. All they have to hang onto is their power and they take out their frustration on the system."

Conclusion

Prosecutors have a unique role among lawyers. Sworn to "seek justice," they operate with different constraints than other lawyers because they are buffered from market forces and client influences. The ethical decision making of the individual prosecutor is guided by a range of factors from environmental influences, including statutory and regulatory frameworks, to organizational influences such as office structure and policy as well as an individual's experience, personality, and idiosyncrasies. A study of the various factors and the interplay among them in the context of prosecutorial decision making regarding disclosure of information to the defense reveals that while an individual prosecutor's ethical compass may play a role, disclosure decisions are primarily influenced by other systemic factors. Potential civil and criminal liability and professional discipline play little or no role. Law substantially shapes prosecutors' decisions but is not dispositive, both because the law is unclear and underenforced and because the law leaves much to prosecutors' discretion. The most significant factors influencing prosecutors' decisions are office policy, informal understandings, culture, and internal regulatory and supervisory practices. Offices vary by size, locale, personnel, and policy, and each office develops its own formal and informal culture and practices that guide and drive disclosure policies. Whether prosecutors comply with rules and law, and even more so whether they exercise discretion wisely and fairly, is likely to be an outcome of the complex interplay of environmental and organizational factors and prosecutors' own professional values.

Although we have not interviewed federal prosecutors, our conclusions are likely to apply in the federal system. Disclosure practices can be expected to vary less among Offices of the US Attorney since the Department of Justice sets policy that narrows the range of offices' and individual prosecutors' discretion. In exercising the discretion afforded by law and centralized policy, however, federal prosecutors are likely to be influenced by the same general organizational, environmental, and individual factors that shape state prosecutors' disclosure decisions.

References

American Bar Association (ABA) Standing Committee on Ethics and Professional Responsibility. 2009. "Prosecutor's Duty to Disclose Evidence and Information Favorable to the Defense." Formal Opinion 09-454, July 8.

Barkow, Rachel E. 2010. "Organizational Guidelines for the Prosecutor's Office." *Cardozo Law Review* 31:2089–2118.

Bibas, Stephanos. 2009. "Prosecutorial Regulation Versus Prosecutorial Accountability." *University of Pennsylvania Law Review* 157:959–1016.

Blasser, Jennifer. 2010. "Prosecutorial Disclosure Obligations and Practices." In "New Perspectives on *Brady* and Other Disclosure Obligations: Report of the Working Groups on Best Practices." *Cardozo Law Review* 31:1962–1971.

Burke, Alafair S. 2007. "Neutralizing Cognitive Bias: An Invitation to Prosecutors." *New York University Journal of Law & Liberty* 2:2512–2530.

———. 2009. "Revisiting Prosecutorial Disclosure." *Indiana Law Journal* 84:481–519.

Chisolm, John. 2010. "How Individuals Are Processed Through the Criminal Justice System." In "Voices from the Field: An Inter-Professional Approach to Managing Critical Information." *Cardozo Law Review* 31:2074–2077.

Church, Thomas W., Jr. 1985. "Examining Local Legal Culture." *American Bar Foundation Research Journal* 10:449–510.

DiMaggio, Paul J., and Walter W. Powell. 1983. "The Iron Cage Revisited: Institutional Isomorphism and Collective Rationality in Organizational Fields." *American Sociological Review* 48:147–160.

Eisenstein, James, and Herbert Jacob. 1977. *Felony Justice: An Organizational Analysis of Criminal Courts*. Boston: Little, Brown.

Eisenstein, James, Roy Flemming, and Peter Nardulli. 1999. *The Contours of Justice: Communities and Their Courts*. Boston: Little, Brown.

Feeley, Malcolm M. 1979. *The Process Is the Punishment: Handling Cases in a Lower Criminal Court*. New York: Russell Sage.

Findley, Keith A., and Michael S. Scott. 2006. "The Multiple Dimensions of Tunnel Vision in Criminal Cases." *Wisconsin Law Review* 2006:291–397.

Galin, Ross. 2000. "Above the Law: The Prosecutor's Duty to Seek Justice and the Performance of Substantial Assistance Agreements." *Fordham Law Review* 68:1245–1284.

Gershman, Bennett L. 2007. "Litigating *Brady v. Maryland*: Games Prosecutors Play." *Case Western Reserve Law Review* 57:531–565.

Green, Bruce A. 1998. "The Criminal Regulation of Lawyers." *Fordham Law Review* 67:327–392.

———. 1999. "Why Should Prosecutors 'Seek Justice'?" *Fordham Urban Law Journal* 26:607–643.

———. 2010. "Beyond Training Prosecutors about Their Disclosure Obligations: Can Prosecutors' Offices Learn from Their Lawyers' Mistakes?" *Cardozo Law Review* 31:2161–2186.

Griffin, Leslie C. 2001. "The Prudent Prosecutor." *Georgetown Journal of Legal Ethics* 14: 259–307.

Hooper, Laura L., Jennifer E. Marsh, and Brian Yeh. 2004. *Treatment of* Brady v. Maryland *Material in United States District and State Courts' Rules, Orders, and Policies: Report of the Advisory Committee on Criminal Rules of the Judicial Conference of the United States.* Washington, DC: Federal Judicial Center.

Innocence Project. 2011. Home page. http://www.innocenceproject.org.

Justice Project, 2007. *Expanded Discovery in Criminal Cases: A Policy Review.* Washington DC: Justice Project.

Levine, Samuel J. 2004. "Taking Prosecutorial Ethics Seriously: A Consideration of the Prosecutor's Ethical Obligation to 'Seek Justice' in a Comparative Analytical Framework." *Houston Law Review* 41:1337–1370.

Lewis, Neil A. 2009. "Tables Turned on Prosecution in Stevens Case." *New York Times*, April 7.

Medwed, Daniel S. 2004. "The Zeal Deal: Prosecutorial Resistance to Post-Conviction Claims of Innocence." *Boston University Law Review* 84:125–183.

Mosteller, Robert P. 2008. "Exculpatory Evidence, Ethics, and the Road to the Disbarment of Mike Nifong: The Critical Importance of Full One-File Discovery." *George Mason Law Review* 15:257–318.

Reiter, Lou. 2010. "Police Departments." In "New Perspectives on *Brady* and Other Disclosure Obligations: Report of the Working Groups on Best Practices." *Cardozo Law Review* 31:2056–2061.

Rosen, Robert A. 1987. "Disciplinary Sanctions against Prosecutors for *Brady* Violations: A Paper Tiger." *North Carolina Law Review* 65:693–774.

Scheck, Barry. 2010. "Professional and Conviction Integrity Programs: Why We Need Them, Why They Work, and Models for Creating Them." *Cardozo Law Review* 31:2215–2256.

Schwartz, Irwin H. 2010. "Beyond *Brady*: Using Model Rule 3.8(d) in Federal Court for Discovery of Exculpatory Information." *Champion*, March, 34.

Shenon, Philip. 2007. "Ex-Prosecutor Acquitted of Misconduct in 9/11 Case." *New York Times*, November 1.

Terzano, John F., Joyce A. McGee, and Alanna D. Holt. 2009. *Improving Prosecutorial Accountability: A Policy Review.* Washington DC: Justice Project.

Wilson, Duff, and David Barstow. 2007. "All Charges Dropped in Duke Case." *New York Times*, April 12.

Wright, Ronald F. 2009. "How Prosecutor Elections Fail Us." *Ohio State Journal of Criminal Law* 6:581–610.

———. 2010. "Systems and Culture." In "New Perspectives on *Brady* and Other Disclosure Obligations: Report of the Working Groups on Best Practices." *Cardozo Law Review* 31:1995–2010.

Yaroshefsky, Ellen. 2004. "Wrongful Convictions: It Is Time to Take Prosecution Discipline Seriously." *University of the District of Columbia Law Review* 8:275–299.

———. 2010. "Foreword: New Perspectives on *Brady* and Other Disclosure Obligations: What Really Works?" *Cardozo Law Review* 31:1943–1959.

Zacharias, Fred C. 2001. "The Professional Discipline of Prosecutors." *North Carolina Law Review* 79:721–778.

Cases and Rules

Brady v. Maryland, 373 U.S. 83 (1963).

Connick v. Thompson, 131 S. Ct. 1350 (2011).

Giglio v. United States, 405 U.S. 150 (1972).

Imbler v. Pachtman, 424 U.S. 409 (1976).

Kyles v. Whitley, 514 U.S. 419 (1995).

United States v. Bagley, 473 U.S. 667 (1985).

United States v. Safavian, 233 F.R.D. 12 (D.D.C. 2005).

Van de Kamp v. Goldstein, 555 U.S. 335 (2009).

Federal Rules of Criminal Procedure 16 (2011).

Reinterpreting the Zealous Advocate

Multiple Intermediary Roles of the Criminal Defense Attorney

Nicole Martorano Van Cleve

How do criminal defense attorneys interpret their obligations to their clients as advocates in the context of today's criminal courts? With the expansion of the criminal justice system, defense attorneys are forced to confront extralegal issues traditionally in the domain of social workers and even psychologists. Their clients are not only confronting a criminal charge but often a confounding mental illness or addiction.[1] Consequently, defense attorneys must expand their advocacy strategies and tactics beyond *adjudicative processes* like negotiation or trial work and add *treatment processes* like mental health and drug interventions. Rather than defense attorneys assuming one categorical role, they are often navigating between different types of "advocacy" orientations—trial advocacy or treatment advocacy.

In today's criminal justice system, zealous advocacy requires attorneys to determine what advocacy strategies are in the best interests of their clients. As in other practice specialties, defense attorneys must integrate traditional adjudicative principles, elements of social work, insider bargaining, and other disciplines of law—such as family law or immigration law—to advocate for clients (Mather, McEwen, and Maiman 2001). Rather than seek lesser sentences or acquittal, many defendants seek treatment and rely on defense attorneys to navigate treatment resources on their behalf or even to mentor them on more personal levels. Ethical boundaries are stretched when attorneys represent defendants whose needs are complex and whose judgments are impaired;

---

1. This chapter focuses on representation for the typical criminal defendant in state court who is prosecuted for street crime (including nonviolent felony offenses and violent offenses such as sexual assault and murder) rather than the more affluent white-collar criminal defendants who are prosecuted for financial crimes.

attorneys must persuade defendants as to what constitutes their "best interest" in the system.

I examine the challenges of criminal defense attorneys practicing in a large metropolitan courthouse in Cook County–Chicago. In the first section, I outline traditional accounts of advocacy within the criminal justice system. In the second section, I present an empirical account of criminal defense in Chicago and discuss the particular frameworks and strategies adopted by defense attorneys as they interpret advocacy for their clients. Throughout, I discuss the implications of these practices for the criminal justice system and for lawyers' understanding of what constitutes "legal work."

Zealous Defenders, Double Agents, or Beleaguered Brokers

According to the American Bar Association (ABA) Model Rules of Professional Conduct, a lawyer is supposed to act "with zeal in advocacy upon the client's behalf" (Model Rule 1.3 cmt.). Yet, the professional rules governing lawyers neither elaborate on the specifics of zealous representation (Uphoff and Wood 1998) nor acknowledge the social context that impacts advocacy. Zealous advocacy is not a fixed standard but is subject to interpretation. It is informal and discretionary decisions that define the formal legal processes (Rosett and Cressey 1976) and professional standards. Advocacy is not an autonomous project in which individual attorneys develop their own approaches to clients, but rather it is created and constrained by social and organizational factors, cultural norms, and clients to varying extents (Mather 2003). Lawyers define and share norms of professional conduct through interactions and exchanges in their "communities of practice" (Mather, McEwen, and Maiman 2001). Factors such as anticipating the reaction of courtroom actors, gauging the quality of the legal case, or preserving their reputation within the legal community structure the experience of representation (Skolnick 1967). It is the practice of "doing" advocacy and managing these multiple variables that defines it.

The academic literature on zealous advocacy examines various constraints on the representation provided by criminal defense lawyers. Blumberg's (1967) classic article addressed how the organizational structure of the criminal justice system impacted criminal defense lawyers. Blumberg prioritizes trials as a central indicator of the zealousness of a lawyer. Since few cases went to trial, the defense attorney was seen as a second-class attorney. Pressured by excessive case volume, dependencies on prosecutors (Alschuler 1968; Casper 1972), and cohesive memberships within the courtroom workgroup[2] (Eisenstein and Jacob 1977), defense attorneys surrender their ideological commitments to due process and instead adopt a competing set of organizational priorities that co-opt them into being a "double agent." In this role, defense lawyers facilitate guilty pleas that move cases along in the best interest of the court organization rather than the client (Blumberg 1967). At best, defense attorneys are brokers or middlemen for quick deals; at worst, they become "double agents" for expeditious prosecution (Blumberg 1967).

Subsequent works critiqued this characterization and widened the notion of advocacy to include tactics such as negotiating a plea agreement. In addition, researchers examined the social, organizational, and cultural contexts that structured the clients' "best interest" in the system. The two central advocacy objectives were reduction of sentence or acquittal. For instance, Mather (1979) used anthropological methods to expose the taxonomy of decision making amongst these options for case disposition. Other works studied discretion by examining the language, rhetoric, and backstage process of negotiation (Maynard 1988; Neubauer 1974; Rosset and Cressey 1976). Rather than plea bargaining constituting a lesser form of representation or a reaction to outside social pressures, it was an "enaction" of the practitioner's own cultural knowledge and praxis toward advocacy (Maynard 1984, 2). Since there may be strong incentives for defense lawyers to assume cooperative postures in court—as well as harsh penalties for seeming adversarial—the "best interest" of the client may be for the defense attorney to "perform" a nonconfrontational stance.[3] As a result, adversariness in advocacy may be indiscernible to laypersons—hidden in pretrial stages or the rhetoric of backstage bargains (Maynard 1988; Neubauer 1974; Rosset and Cressey 1976). Given such contextual factors, Uphoff (1992)

2. "Courtroom workgroup" refers to all the central players who have an ability to affect case disposition, including the prosecutors, defense counsel (public defenders or private attorneys), the judge, and the bailiff. Courtroom work is a group activity, and attorneys constantly interact with other workgroup members to efficiently dispose of cases (Eisenstein and Jacob 1977).

3. McIntyre (1987) argues that public defenders are adversarial, even combative, opponents of state prosecutors, but they pursue this advocacy in covert and subtle ways. Public defenders are cautious not to advertise their successes or embarrass the state, even going to lengths to feign incompetence since they depend on the state for continued and expanded funding. I refer to these efforts as a "performance" since they mirror the principles of Erving Goffman's (1959) dramaturgical model of social behavior. In this model, Goffman uses a theater metaphor to explain how social actors present themselves to others within the cultural boundaries of their social group.

challenged Blumberg's notion of a "double agent" broker and argued that such organizational and social constraints changed the "zealous defender" into a "beleaguered dealer" who was short of resources and incentives to challenge the state but who maintained an ideological commitment to clients.

Rather than attempt to further categorize and compare the behavior of defense attorneys, this chapter considers zealous advocacy as a social process. Zealous representation is shaped by the social attributes and needs of the client, the complexity of the case, emotional and financial stress, and even the client's views of the lawyer and the law. Under most circumstances, the client's goals should shape the advocacy through a collaborative process that respects client autonomy (Binder, Bergman, and Price 1990), but lawyers retain a significant amount of influence by controlling the framing of the case, by considering alternatives, and by making other discretionary decisions that affect case outcome (Mather 2003).

The formal rules governing lawyers are of limited use to criminal defense lawyers as they state simply that clients are to determine the objectives of the representation (including whether to plead guilty), while lawyers are to determine the means (Model Rule 1.2). Given this vague guidance regarding such decision-making practices, lawyers have a large amount of discretion in determining the level of participation clients have in the strategic and tactical decisions of their cases (Uphoff and Wood 1998). In addition, many clients in today's criminal justice system are impaired by significant challenges that compromise their ability to define or express their "case objectives." Defendants are asking attorneys for help in battling mental illness, homelessness, trauma, and addictions. While Binder, Bergman, and Price's (1990) account of client-centered lawyering (which is taught in many law schools) focuses on responding to the client's legal problem, it says little about addressing co-occurring problems outside the scope of traditional legal services—problems that may have caused the client to enter the criminal justice system. In addition, works like Mather's (1979) provided an account of how defense attorneys determined whether cases were handled via a plea or a trial. The clients' objectives were assumed to be acquittal or reduction of sentence. However, with the advent of treatment courts and postconviction services, attorneys are widening their advocacy objectives and strategies to include various rehabilitation alternatives. The next section addresses these changes from the vantage point of defense attorneys and addresses how these treatment options have posed considerable ethical challenges for attorneys in today's criminal justice system.

Zealous Advocacy in Practice: The Case of Cook County

This section looks at the practices of criminal defense attorneys working on the state court level in Chicago. This research incorporates data from (1) participant observation of the work of public defenders and private attorneys;[4] (2) 104 interviews with prosecutors, defense attorneys, and judges;[5] (3) 200 hours of court-watching observations in the public gallery of 25 courtrooms (including of court-call, plea bargains, and hearings); and (4) supplementary interviews conducted with "lawyer regulars" (Blumberg 1967)—both private and public defense attorneys—in order to probe the rationale and motivations behind courtroom behavior and practices.

Criminal courts vary from jurisdiction to jurisdiction. Yet, there are basic similarities in all criminal court processes (Rosset and Cressey 1976, 45; Mather 1979, 2). All courtroom workgroups share expressive goals (e.g., "doing justice") and instrumental goals (e.g., disposing of cases), regardless of the city (Eisenstein and Jacob 1977). All workgroups also have a common composition—judge, prosecutors, and defense attorneys who are familiar with one another's specialized roles but who retain their own unique tasks and vantage points in the system. This case study focuses on how defense attorneys incorporate new objectives and tactics toward advocacy as they cope with limited resources, additional treatment options, and expanded recognition of the nonlegal needs of their clients.

Context of Cook County

The main Cook County Criminal Courthouse is the biggest and busiest felony courthouse in the United States (Bogira 2005). The 36 Criminal Division judges hear more than 28,000 felony cases, half of which are nonviolent, drug-related charges. At any one time, these judges have about 275 pending cases

4. In 2004, with the intention of collecting data, I clerked for the Office of the Public Defender, which provided access to front- and backstage environments including the Public Defender's Office, the courtroom, the courtroom lockup, and judges' chambers. In addition, my status as a courtroom regular allowed for observations of private attorneys working in these same courtrooms. Participant observations were conducted in both the main felony courthouse as well as one of its largest satellites.

5. In 2006, Chicago Appleseed Fund for Justice, a public policy and advocacy organization, conducted a comprehensive study of the Cook County Criminal Justice System. As project director for this organization, I had access to considerable field data, including 104 intensive interviews with prosecutors, defense attorneys, and judges, and observations of courtroom proceedings.

on their dockets. The defendants awaiting trial are decidedly male, minority, and poor. The Cook County Public Defender's Office represents between 22,000 and 23,000 indigent defendants each year. These individuals are determined by a judge to be too poor to secure private defense counsel (Chicago Appleseed 2007). The vast majority are pretrial detainees unable to make bond. Compounding these disadvantages, many inmates suffer from drug addiction, mental illness, or both.

Adjacent to the main criminal court is a jail complex that houses 10,000 criminally accused defendants (Chicago Appleseed 2007). More than two-thirds of the jail population meets the criteria for drug dependency or abuse. In 2003, 82% of all male arrestees and 61% of all female arrestees in Chicago tested positive for at least one illegal drug at the time of arrest (Chicago Metropolis 2006). In addition, the Cook County Jail holds so many inmates with serious mental illness that it is one of the largest providers of psychiatric care in the country (Chicago Metropolis 2020 2006). It is estimated at least 20% and perhaps as many as 50% of these defendants suffer from untreated mental illness (Chicago Appleseed 2007).

For both mental health and drug treatment, Treatment Alternatives for Safe Communities (TASC) is a sentencing and treatment alternative for some nonviolent offenders postconviction. TASC also acts as a service provider for specialty courts like Mental Health Court and Drug Court and is the only agency designated by the state to provide substance abuse assessments and recommendations to the Illinois courts. If defendants meet both clinical and legal criteria, defendants may receive TASC-supervised probation as an alternative to regular probation.[6] TASC case managers design individualized service plans that link defendants with community-based substance abuse treatment and social services like medical/mental health services and vocational/educational programs. TASC then monitors defendants' progress through case management and toxicology screens and provides reports to the court. For Drug Court and Mental Health Court, TASC provides assessment and advocacy services to help offenders successfully complete probation and achieve community reintegration (Treatment Alternatives for Safe Communities 2011).

---

6. TASC assesses defendants' eligibility by examining their previous criminal records, the nature of their addictions, their readiness for treatment, and the likelihood of treatment success. Legal exclusions from supervised TASC probation (e.g., defendants charged with a violent crime) are spelled out in the Alcoholism and Other Drug Abuse and Dependency Act (20 Ill. Comp. Stat. 301/40-5).

Judges contend that given the high number of eligible defendants and the limited resources for mental health and substance abuse programs, TASC is grossly insufficient. Defense attorneys are quick to emphasize that it is only through pleading guilty that such services are even a possibility for offenders. As for specialty courts, since the funding is so limited and the assessment criteria so stringent, the eligible defendant population for them is extremely low (Chicago Appleseed 2007). Yet jails and criminal courts provide the only mental health care system for many criminal defendants because there are no other social services being provided by the state.

How Defense Attorneys Understand the System

Defense attorneys conceptualize their work as being structured by two central challenges: (1) defendant-based challenges fueled by addiction, poverty, and/or mental illness; and (2) system-based challenges that compromise the quality and character of justice. System-based challenges include limitations in treatment resources and cultural norms that stigmatize zealous advocacy within the courtroom workgroup. Regardless of the lawyers' inclination to be client-centered in their approach to decision making, defense attorneys are acutely aware that they are representing defendants with co-occurring problems like poverty, addiction, and mental illness and there may be more than just their client's freedom at stake. Many defendants stand to be deported, lose custody of their children, or forfeit their jobs or benefits because of the possibility of felony conviction. Yet, system-based challenges confound defense lawyers' obligations and decisions. Defense attorneys describe a criminal justice system that is woefully underfunded. Treatment options are particularly limited.

In addition, defense attorneys are navigating advocacy in what Blumberg (1967, 21) described as an "organized system of complicity"—where informal and covert evasion of due process are institutionalized in the practices of participants. Defense attorneys describe pressure applied by judges and prosecutors that borders on intimidation for zealous representation that appears too "combative" (McIntyre 1987). In particular, public defenders describe being "punished" by some judges and/or prosecutors for adversarial strategies via harsher consequences for their clients. As a result, defense attorneys often balance how to meet their advocacy obligations in a system where fighting for their client could undermine the client's interests.

Such challenges, whether client-based or system-based, contextualize the ethical context of decision making by defense attorneys. Client-based concerns help guide the attorney as to the type of advocacy to provide the client—whether treatment advocacy or trial advocacy. There was no "one size fits all" model of representation where individual attorneys could be characterized as "brokers" (Uphoff 1992), "double agents" (Blumberg 1967), or zealous advocates. Rather, zealous advocacy was an interpretive process that was contingent on the needs of the defendant—whether extralegal or legal—and the social terrain of the criminal justice system. The following sections review the defendant-based and system-based challenges that confront defense attorneys, the strategies they pursue in practice, and the ethical boundaries they must manage in the process.

Defendant-Based Decisions: "Trial Advocacy" or "Treatment Advocacy"

Cook County criminal defense attorneys identify two distinct types of advocacy in criminal defense—"zealous trial advocacy" or "zealous treatment advocacy." Client objectives and other considerations help attorneys frame the general advocacy approach to the case—whether adjudicative or rehabilitative (Model Rule 1.2). Trial advocacy addresses the client's legal needs while treatment advocacy addresses the client's rehabilitative needs and social challenges.

For many defense attorneys, justice is not based on an acquittal or a reduction of charge but on understanding and responding to the clients' needs—both legal and extralegal. Adopting such an approach transforms criminal courts from simply a "legal system" to an actual "justice system." As a private defense attorney (PA) explained:

> The consent of the defendant changes the role of the attorney—the defense attorney—be it a private attorney or public defender. 'Cause if the defendant says: "I gotta bad habit. I need help. Can you get me some help?" . . . Then, the role of the lawyer is to do whatever necessary to get him help. Even if the lawyer thinks, "I can beat this case on a Fourth Amendment violation" . . . the linchpin that has to control all of that . . . [pause] is the desire of the defendant. So, the defendant is the one that controls whether we're a legal system or a justice system. Our system of laws is defendant-centered. The Bill of Rights goes to the defendant. I take that back. The Bill of Rights goes to all citizens. The only ones that use them are people that become a defendant. So, we are defendant-centric in that way. . . . Though the decision about being a zealous trial advocate or a zealous treatment advocate is made by the defendant.

According to this perspective, the traditional definition of "zealous advocacy" is incomplete and insufficient for the realities of representation. Defense attorneys must navigate between "treatment advocacy" and "trial advocacy," and this process changes the role of the attorney. Defendants often requested more of their attorneys than just seeking acquittal or reduced incarceration time. For example, through his public defender, one defendant made an appeal to the judge to seek a longer intensive probation with drug treatment rather than a shorter term in the state penitentiary. As the defendant appealed in open court, "I need to change and be there for my six children. I want this longer sentence for the drug program. I need the structure in my life." In another more dire case, a defendant with full-blown AIDS, a low T-cell count, and a recent contraction of TB while in jail asked his public defender to save him from dying in prison.

In both advocacy roles, lawyers must define "winning" by the value system of the clients. Although in some cases this may involve winning a motion or trial, other times it requires the attorney to take a less adversarial strategy and advocate by pursuing rehabilitative resources. As one private attorney explained:

PA: If your client wants you to get the best deal for him, then you have to zealously get the best deal for him. If your client wants you to get out there and fight that trial, then you get out there and fight that trial. If your client wants you to get him into a treatment program, then that's what you do. Let's get back down to the basics here. Lawyers are mouthpieces. And, lawyers have a job to do and their job is dictated by what the client wants. But, the main difficulty that I've seen is on the defense side with egotistical defense lawyers who say, "I can beat this case; you don't need treatment."

NVC: When you talk about these egotistical defense lawyers . . . it sounds like the banter of getting the "best" deal or fighting the good fight in a trial or motion can take priority over asking a defendant: "What type of advocate do you want me to be?"

PA: Right. But, this is what you should do. It's our ethical obligation.

Defense attorneys must assume different roles and draw on multiple disciplines and competencies as they develop advocacy strategies—especially for the treatment needs of clients.

PA: One of the beautiful things about being a lawyer is the opportunity to learn all these different disciplines to be effective. You've got mental health issues, you've got drug issues, you got trauma, you got all sorts . . . sometime economic issues, medical issues . . . if you're a zealous advocate, you've got to be able to draw upon all these resources in order to achieve a just result and when you're representing poor people, of course, you've got to multiply your effect. Because the system is not designed to help poor people so it makes it that much more difficult but much more rewarding when you accomplish a just result.

While this standard is the ideal that many attorneys strive to achieve, it is challenging on two fronts. First, younger lawyers describe more entrenched and experienced attorneys as believing that treatment aspects of advocacy are outside the scope of "real law." The tendency is to narrowly define representation as being adjudicative rather than rehabilitative, and to see clients as one-dimensional rather than multidimensional. One defense attorney described this difference as "generational," as though the behavior of defense attorneys was evolving with the demands of the criminal system and its defendant-consumers:

> I think the concept of lawyer in the past has been much more about being the person who goes to court and makes the arguments in front of the judge or the jury and writes the motions. They might work with the investigator to get the facts that they need but they were doing legal tasks. They became lawyers, not social workers.
>
> The problem with that perspective is that it ignores the fact that the people you represent are not one dimensional and if you were looking to be able to serve the people you're representing, you have to treat people as whole people and you can't do that without the assistance of folks that have more than just legal skills. And, I don't by any means see myself as having the same sorts of skills that a social worker develops, but I have no problem doing more than just being the guy who goes to court, looks up cases in the library or something. You're helping people. It just boils down to . . . if I were on the other side of the table, and I needed help, I may not be able to express what it is I need help with and I would hope that whoever was trying to help me . . . would be willing to look beyond just the fact that I came here for a legal problem.

Despite defense attorneys' client-centered approach to interpreting their advocacy orientation, they face considerable ethical challenges given the impaired judgment of many clients. As described above, many defendants suffer from mental illness (short of statutory impairment), and their judgment is compromised. As a public defender (PD) explained, many defendants were unable to understand the consequences of particular decisions, discussions with their attorneys, or their previous legal cases: "When you think of these defendants and their personality disorders . . . they have paranoid [sic] and mistrust. It's like the defendants and attorneys are talking in no-man's land." In addition, defense attorneys describe defendants as lacking basic education and cultural knowledge to understand the consequences of their decisions in the criminal justice system. As one PD explained, "Some defendants say 'I got rid of that case' or 'I beat that case' and they think that a charge doesn't count. Whenever they don't get 'time,' they think it doesn't count on their record, but then I have to tell them it does." Another defense attorney described his clients as follows:

> There is no denying the fact that you do represent people who sometimes are knuckleheads. . . . [Y]ou're dealing with a group of individuals who in large part, don't make the best decisions. That's not the only reason but a good chunk of the time that's how they get involved in the criminal justice system in the first place. And, when it comes time then to mapping out a way to best deal with the predicament they've got themselves in, it shouldn't come as any surprise that they aren't going to magically have good decision making skills all of a sudden. And, that is . . . as far as being able to be an effective advocate . . . a dynamic that [it] helps to be aware of because sometimes, what you're really trying to do is just help them understand the process you go through to making a decision in a way that's different than the way they've always made decisions.

Criminal defense lawyers find themselves widening the scope of the practice of law into areas traditionally viewed as "social work." This is particularly true when the client is battling addiction or mental illness and the "word of the client" is not reliable. In these instances, like a social worker, the attorney must reach out to other resources, family networks, and specialists to investigate and piece together the best interest of the client and help define his rehabilitative and/or adjudicative goals. In a sense, attorneys are looking for surrogates or proxies for the client's voice. A private attorney described the difficulty of not being able to take the word of the client at face value and detailed the strategies required to mine for the client's best interests:

> It is a complex matter . . . sometimes you have to work with others . . . if there are others available . . . in that person's larger familial, community or

social network to be able to figure out what's actually going on. I've had situations where I have dealt with people—especially with substance abuse—where it's hard to figure out what to believe and what not to believe. And, what I've found very helpful, is that I've at least gotten enough information from the individual to know that they've been involved with these sorts of support programs or services of a particular nonprofit group. If I can figure out who they've been working with and I can contact them, I can at least get a better handle on who they [the clients] are. Now, that doesn't tell me how to go about determining what the actual goals are for the case . . . it sort of helps counterbalance the deficiencies that might exist based on what you're not getting from the one-on-one with the client you're representing.

Binder, Bergman, and Price's (1990, 34) definition of client-centered decision making assumes that clients have the cultural and intellectual skills necessary to assess the most satisfactory decisions and corresponding outcomes. They argue that "clients are likely to be more adept at predicting the nonlegal consequences of a decision than an attorney" (1990, 34). Yet, in the absence of these important skills and a social or familial network to help the client, some attorneys find themselves compensating and advising on nonlegal consequences like a social worker—similar to the legal services lawyers discussed by Corey Shdaimah (chapter 15). Defense attorneys describe themselves acting as parental figures or mentors to defendants by personally counseling and giving advice on the nonlegal consequences of particular decisions. One private attorney explained:

The most difficult thing is when I am dealing with somebody who is not as intelligent as they could be, but they're not statutorily retarded. Or they're not insane or they're not in need of treatment. They're just slow. And, I have to almost fill a parental role because they don't have anyone else to bounce ideas off of and talk to. And, you find yourself talking someone into taking 35 years in the penitentiary because you know, from all of your experience and background, that the evidence the State has got at its disposal, will be enough to convict him and will be enough to execute him if they go forward on that. That becomes very difficult to maintain boundaries on.

Yet, as defense attorneys cross these personal boundaries, there are ethical issues that arise if the attorney disagrees with the defendant, especially in cases in which the mental fitness of the client is in question. The attorney quoted above described a case in which taking on the role of "mentor" on nonlegal matters pushed his tactics precariously close to the ethical limits of representation:

> I had a client . . . no felony background. Had within his grasp, a future. Was in a trade school; could've done something good. He gets arrested on an absolutely bogus case and we went out and proved it. Through investigation, and photography and everything else, it was simply impossible and we were going to go to trial. He [the defendant] goes, "I gotta get home. I gotta see my baby. My baby's gonna be born. Give me probation."
>
> "If I get you probation, it's going to be felony probation. You will never be able to have your CDL [Commercial Driver's License]; you'll never be able to do anything. And, if you're concerned about being a daddy to that baby, you got to put in some time [to go to trial]. 'Cause I got to tell you . . . I got two kids. I don't think that they remember the fact that I was there when they were born. They remember when I was there when they were about two. So, you got to put time into this case now and let us take this case to trial."

Here the defense attorney imparts his own advice and opinion from his life to guide the young man. When the defendant would not budge and go to trial, the attorney emphasized the inherent ethical issues that arose:

PA: He [the defendant] wouldn't do it. I had him BCXed [evaluated for mental fitness]. "Judge I think he's unfit." Because I was looking to buy time to convince him to let us go to trial. BCX comes back. I knew the BCX would come back fit. But, I just couldn't get his family on board, I couldn't get him . . . and I laid the case out for them and I said, "Look, I can never guarantee you an outcome but in every case I've ever tried in my life, this is a really good case. I could win this case." And, even the judge knew it because we did a pretrial ruling and the judge said, "Based on the fact that we have to look at this ruling in the light most favorable to the state, I'll have to deny your ruling. I don't know *what's* going to happen at trial" [inflection like judge was exaggerating and winking].

NVC: So, did the defendant take probation?

PA: He did. We ended up having to get off the case because he wanted some lawyer who would plead him. I was pushing the bubble. I was telling my students, we're right up to that ethical obligation here, but I'm trying to figure out how to save this guy's life or let him destroy it. It was a very difficult thing for me to figure out. How far can I push? And, the BCX was about as far as I could go.

This example illustrates how treatment advocacy and trial advocacy are not mutually exclusive. Attorneys must integrate these orientations to effectively represent their clients. This may require engaging (like a social worker) with the client's family, imparting advice and opinions on nonlegal matters, and assuming the role of a mentor while also assessing the potential legal outcomes of the case from the attorney's experience. Yet, given the impairments of the client, well-meaning attorneys can find themselves close to the ethical boundaries of professional standards when the client's goals and the attorney's view of the client's "best interest" sharply diverge.

System-Based Considerations: "Saving" and "Selling Out" Clients

Saving Defendants from the System

Defense attorneys' views of the criminal justice system also structure their approaches to advocacy and influence how they handle the ethical obligations they have to their clients. Rather than interpret their obligations within a normative framework of how the system *should* work, attorneys are contextualizing representations within the social realities and pitfalls that riddle the criminal justice system.

In the Chicago Appleseed (2007) report on the Cook County felony courts, the overwhelming consensus among criminal defense attorneys was that drug cases were not handled effectively by the court system.[7] Overall, attorneys felt that the laws themselves were overly harsh and even draconian in nature. For instance, possession of under a gram of drugs is classified as a felony—thereby disenfranchising many nonviolent, first-time offenders. As one public defender explained:

> You should write about this whole felony disenfranchisement. . . . Dave [a PD who has a desk next to hers] always does this example. In our country, this amount of drugs [holding up a packet of sugar], can get you four years in the pen . . . when I started as a PD, the laws were not as harsh, but now, with this "war on drugs," you have all these poor people being put behind bars . . . the people who make the laws are not affected by the laws.

Beyond the severity of the laws, defense attorneys were critical of the resources available to those addicted to drugs. As one public defender elabo-

---

7. Of the 26 public defenders and 25 private attorneys in their sample, 24 public defenders and 23 private attorneys, respectively, agreed that drug cases were handled ineffectively.

rated, "There should be more drug diversion, drug treatment programs; now, they [criminal justice officials] don't do anything to change their [defendants'] behavior—defendants are put back in the same conditions that have brought them here."

In addition, defense attorneys were nearly universal in their criticism of the mental health resources available to defendants. One public defender described what she called the "biggest scandal" in Cook County: "The jail is the largest mental health hospital." Another defense attorney also cited this statistic, commenting that the treatment of defendants was both biased toward the state and substandard since some defendants wait six months in jail to be accepted into a program. One public defender described the court psychiatric/clinical forensic services as "biased—they work for the State. They have a one-time, 10 minute interview for malingering that doesn't meet the DSM-IV standards."[8] Another attorney noted that even for those who did not have a diagnosed mental illness, most defendants were often trauma survivors living without treatment. This group was particularly neglected, as one attorney explained:

> When a person is obviously [mentally ill], they have them BCXed, but one level below that is a group of people who are being missed. The criminal justice system should provide better rehab services, social work services . . . these are people who are victims of urban trauma, they have been sexually abused, neglected . . . who better to provide that stability?

In addition to these inadequate resources, defense attorneys viewed judges and prosecutors as being intolerant or lacking compassion for defendants and their medical needs. As a public defender walked to court, she explained how prosecutors and judges disregarded and stigmatized defendants based on these issues: "I look at them as people . . . not as criminals. . . . This judge does not have a clue about addiction or alcoholism . . . not a clue. She is a little better with the mental illnesses. . . . It's not that they're [prosecutors and judges] bad people, they just don't show any compassion."

For example, I observed a public defender representing a 19-year-old sailor in the US Navy who was charged with possession of a controlled substance. He told his attorney that he had a drug problem but since he could not post bond, the defendant had remained in the Cook County Jail for a month. During this

---

8. The DSM-IV is the *Diagnostic and Statistical Manual of Mental Disorders,* 4th edition, published by the American Psychiatric Association. It provides standardized criteria for the evaluation and classification of mental disorders.

time, the Navy categorized him as absent without leave. The public defender attempted to get the charge dropped by leveraging his military service, his commitment to getting treatment, and his desire to return to military service. The state's attorney (SA) responded in anger, even misreading the defendant's charge:

SA: I don't care about the guy in the Navy. He was dealing.
PD: No, it was straight possession.
SA: Fine, the guy is in the Navy and he's a drug addict. I don't care.

Given the inadequacies of the system and the intolerance of prosecutors and some judges, defense attorneys are placed in a precarious ethical position when they advocate for treatment. While their client may desperately need social services and/or treatment, many attorneys try to "save" their clients from the system itself—hiding the client's mental health issues or addiction. The best they can do is minimize time for their client, as one public defender explained:

I'm a good person to ask about this because I have more crazy people in my courtroom than any other; I have two BCXed every week. . . . I've found that Mental Health probation rats your clients and turns them in more often than regular probation so I try not to get my clients involved with them even if they are not all there.

In another example, a public defender named "Mark" described what he called a "weird little case" that was going to trial, one case he admitted that he would most likely lose. The defendant was standing outside of a drug store ringing a Salvation Army bell. Witnesses observed the defendant grab change from the bucket. The defendant then went to a random car, opened the door, sat down in the passenger side, and rustled through the glove compartment. He took out papers, left more valuable items, and threw the papers in the garbage. As Mark explained, since stealing the money was only a misdemeanor, the police charged the defendant with burglary, a felony offense, by focusing on the items removed from the car.

During the trial, the defendant sat expressionless. His mouth slightly hung open. His eyes stared at the witness speaking as though he was watching TV rather than listening to his trial. Given the nature of his strange crime and his lack of affect in court, I asked Mark if the defendant was "all there."

MARK: No, he is definitely not all there.
NVC: Why didn't you order a BCX?

MARK: I try to keep people out of the mental health system . . . especially on these little cases.

Mark explained that getting the defendant "lost" in the mental health system could mean that he cannot get "out." In his experience, if defendants are deemed unfit for trial, they are kept and given therapy until they are "fit." Given the lack of quality therapy and the tendency to just "drug" the defendants, this process could be longer than the maximum sentence.

With such a view of the system, these defense attorneys, without professional training in psychology or social work, must make judgments on whether their clients are "sane enough" to pass through the system to "save them" from the system itself. Rather than ordering a BCX to protect a client, they must consider the consequences of these decisions within the limitations of the criminal justice system. From a professional standpoint, Mark described this move as risky, and, of course, there was the possibility of his actions being seen as a gross, professional misjudgment. According to Mark, "I don't care about covering myself. I take little or no notes and in 15 years, I haven't gotten sued. . . . [B]ut this is by no means official office policy."

Given the limits of the system, advocacy requires the public defender to assume professional risk on behalf of his client. Mark ultimately lost the trial, but the defendant was released after a short minimum sentence.

"Selling Out" Clients in the System

In advocating for their clients, defense attorneys must navigate and adjust to the court culture itself—anticipating how their strategies and tactics will be received by their prosecutor and the judge. Cook County is characterized by a horizontal representation system in which public defenders and prosecutors are assigned to a single courtroom as consistent members of a courtroom workgroup. Defendants who pass through these courts are randomly assigned to these public defenders.[9] This consistent arrangement creates a set of competing organizational priorities that allow the workgroup to dispose of cases in an efficient manner (Eisenstein and Jacob 1977). Defense attorney Edward Bennett Williams equates the chronic interdependence of prosecutors and defenders with two wrestlers who must face off in a different city each night.

---

9. In a vertical representation system, in contrast, public defenders, like private attorneys, follow clients, rather than act as permanent courtroom actors. Horizontal representation allows for more efficient case disposition, but vertical representation may allow for more adversarial representation.

Over time, they become friends, and their biggest concern is to be "sure not to hurt each other too much" (Skolnick 1967, 60). In Cook County, public defenders described this organizational arrangement as exerting strong incentives to assume a cooperative posture—as well as harsh penalties for seeming adversarial. Some public defenders discussed a relative "power imbalance" between them and the prosecutor and judge. Public defenders were careful "not to annoy them, or otherwise their clients would receive poor deals in the plea bargaining process" (Chicago Appleseed 2007, 36). As a result, the best results for the client may be achieved when the defense attorney "performs" a nonconfrontational stance (McIntyre 1987). In the most extreme instances, defense attorneys described this power imbalance as taking a decidedly unethical turn. They encounter unprofessional behavior and intimidation by judges and prosecutors, ex parte communication, and police perjury. One public defender described it as follows:

> Very often, it's the culture in this building . . . the prosecutor is in chambers with the judge every morning . . . they justify by saying that they are just talking about their families, but inevitably when you come in, they are talking about a case. Certain judges will threaten and intimidate, if you want a jury trial . . . they will make reductions on other people . . . the judges and prosecutors will work in tandem.

As for the police's tendency to perjure themselves on the stand, defense attorneys describe this phenomenon as "testilying"—a practice that prosecutors were well aware of but did little to rectify. One public defender recalled:

> In a case recently, I caught a police officer lying on tape, and I thought the prosecutor would drop the case; instead, he just made a better offer, which my client took, because he just wants to get out of jail. But what can they do? They [prosecutors] don't have any discretion; and they're worried about upsetting their supervisors.

These "insider" norms pressure and intimidate defense attorneys as they defend their clients. Defense attorneys—in particular, public defenders—describe overt negative consequences for "fervent representation." Fervent representation, defined by courtroom participants as exercising basic due process rights like calling witnesses, filing motions, or demanding trials, was met with hostility for fighting "too hard." During fieldwork, prosecutors often classified which defense attorneys were "good" or "bad" based on whether the attorney was able to "control" her client into pleading guilty. Defense attorneys who pursue "too many" motions and trials often find that their reputations suffer as a result. This was especially true for public defenders who were accountable to the same workgroup on a daily basis. Prosecutors labeled these defense attorneys as "clueless," "difficult," or "incompetent." Nonverbal cues like rolling their eyes, shaking their heads, or exchanging glaring stares with other courtroom players punctuated these labels during court proceedings and hid the policing of these norms from the court record. The reputational consequences caused defense attorneys to hold back on their defense as they weighed the cost of certain efforts on their clients or on subsequent cases. One public defender described this pressure as bordering on abuse. She also described how she compromised her representation:

> Have I had a judge storm off the bench? Yes, there have been times when the judge was bullying me; it doesn't create warm feelings. . . . [O]ne of the things that, as PDs, we need to stop doing is pretending that we read the judge better than we do. I didn't call a witness because the judge yelled at me, and I thought, "If the judge yells at me, then the jury will see it and it will work to my advantage." And he didn't actually yell; he leaned over the bench and glared at me, so not to go on the record. It was a jury [trial], and I don't think the case would have changed if I had called the witness, but I made a mistake not to call the witness. . . . I also have a law license, and I shouldn't have backed down, but neither should I have been in that situation.

Beyond the reputational consequences, defense attorneys were "punished" by some judges or prosecutors vis-à-vis harsher consequences for their clients. Some defense attorneys described a court culture of prosecutors and judges that often punished defendants for the zealous actions of their attorneys. Defense attorneys were often balancing how to navigate their own advocacy obligations in a system where the "right" ethical action could actually undermine the "best interest" of their client. A public defender illustrated this point:

> The prosecution filed a motion to revoke my client's bond because they got mad when they found out that I had submitted a motion to suppress evidence. . . . When you take cases to trial, they might withdraw offers or give worse offers to other clients. There was one judge I worked with who liked to plead out cases . . . if you went to trial he would slam the guy if you lost. He did give fair warning about it; he was honest that this is what would happen.

Defense attorneys also expressed concern about discrimination and the level of decency afforded to clients. They described prosecutors and judges who acted "desensitized" to the individual circumstances of defendants primarily due to the fact that clients are from minority communities. In the vernacular of court culture, defendants are known by many slurs including "scum," "piece of shit," "bad guys" and "banana suits" (referring to the jail jumper detainees must wear in court). One commonly used epithet is "mope"—a catchall term for someone who is uneducated, incompetent, degenerate, and lazy. While this term is primarily used for defendants, it can also be wielded at attorneys who violate central courtroom norms. As a result, defense attorneys may conceal adversarial moves by leveraging the mope framework in their plea-bargaining appeals to gain concessions and avoid any implied personal sympathy for clients.

With both the pressure to appear cooperative and the pressure to personally distance themselves from their clients, it is no surprise that the rhetoric of plea bargaining, where defense attorneys are asking for individual concessions for their clients, takes a decidedly negative tone. Defense attorneys seemingly distance themselves from any personal sympathies, disassociate themselves from their clients, and adopt the language of the workgroup. In some cases, private attorneys would give brief back stories as to why they were "stuck" defending their clients, as illustrated by the following excerpt from a private attorney making such an appeal to the judge during a plea:

> Actually, his mother took care of my mother-in-law when she was in the nursing home. I'm doing this as a favor to her—help her with her renegade son. She took care of my mother-in-law so well. What can you do? . . . [Defendant is] one of those street people. . . . I can't just ask for probation; he deserves more time. Basically, he's crap but I'm just asking for the best possible scenario. I'm doing the lady a favor.

Although the defendant is the recipient of any "deal," he is vilified in this quick appeal for leniency. In this case, the private attorney spoke the "language" of the prosecution by stating the expectation that the defendant "deserved" more time. Furthermore, he positioned the defendant's mother as a more sympathetic character who is coping with a "renegade" son. Any deal was not for the defendant but was actually for the mother.

In another example, a private attorney used a similar strategy. The defense attorney asked the prosecutor to consider a long-shot request to reduce the defendant's charge. To disassociate from any personal sympathies, the attorney mocked his client shortly after the request. This strategy was similar to the strategy used by many of the public defenders who expressed personal sympathies toward their clients—only to mock them in front of the workgroup. The following is the hallway exchange between the state's attorney ("Roger"), and a private defense attorney ("Steve"):

SA: Steve, I'm not reducing it . . . he's a bad kid. . . .

PA: It's not *his* fault, it's poverty. (laughing)

SA: Well, poverty isn't my fault so I guess I can't do much for you.

The negotiation continued as a formal conference in the judge's chambers.

PA: I'll start by saying that he deserves to be put away. I want to string him. There's certainly no more money in this for me. . . . Let's just get this over with. Last time, I waited in court all day. . . . I worked on that deal . . . then, he [the defendant] skipped out.

SA: The guy's a bum. . . .

PA: Listen Roger, I don't care if you hang the guy . . . do whatever you want.

JUDGE: I'm going to give him one extra year IDOC [Illinois Department of Corrections]. . . .

SA: Steve, take it, and consider it a gift.

PA: Well, he's not going to take it, and I'm going to have to go to trial. . . . Don't punish me and make me stay. . . .

JUDGE: Eighteen months more and that's the best I can do.[10]

In this example, the attorney appropriated the rhetoric of the prosecutor to appeal to the language and point of view of the prosecutor and judge. In addition, the private attorney positioned himself as a "prisoner" of the defendant forced to represent a client who "deserves" punishment. Any deal would actually be helping the attorney rather than the defendant. At one point, the "threat" to go to trial was masked as an abuse of the defense attorney—"punishing" him for defending a client who "deserved" to be "strung."

Such a performance raises its own ethical dilemmas, even though it may be in the defendant's best interest for his attorney to speak in these rhetorical

---

10. The judge initially added a year to the defendant's sentence, which pushed the sentence to nearly 24 months in prison in total. Ultimately, the total sentence was reduced to 18 months—a small win for the defense.

frames common to the workgroup. When asked about these strategies, defense attorneys admitted to the practice but emphasized that it was beyond the normative, ethical bounds of what *should* happen.

NVC: Despite all the personal sympathies that defense attorneys have for their clients, they appear to "sell them out" in backstage realms. Can you explain that?

PA: I've observed that too and I've probably fallen victim to it on occasion. I don't agree with it, you know. I think that there's a lot of ways to get to a just result. . . . I think maintaining and respecting the dignity of your client is important . . . not only for that individual client but for yourself as a person. And, for the system as a whole. So, I frown on that. I've seen that. As I said, I probably have done it more than I'd care to admit but I don't think it's right. I don't think it's right to demean or disrespect your client in order to achieve a short-term result.

Despite the intentions of defense attorneys to take a defendant-centric approach to advocacy, the character of plea bargaining is decidedly hostile toward defendants. To advocate within the culture of the Cook County Criminal Courthouse, defense attorneys are forced to speak the language of the system in front-stage domains while they privately confess to being "bullied" by the courtroom workgroup. While zealous advocacy implies fighting on their clients' behalf, defense attorneys must make difficult decisions about how far they are willing to "sell out" their clients to get them the best deals. Often, "ethical decisions" to protect their clients' integrity and dignity in front of the workgroup may correspond to worse case outcomes.

Conclusion

Traditional accounts of criminal defense miss the multiple ways attorneys interpret advocacy within the constraints of today's expanding criminal justice system. To fulfill their ethical obligations, defense attorneys must decide what *type* of advocacy orientation is in their client's best interest and assume multiple intermediary roles to achieve a zealous defense. Often, these roles are not mutually exclusive, and attorneys find themselves integrating adjudicative and rehabilitative strategies. With the increased social and legal needs of their clients and new treatment alternatives, defense attorneys are forced to expand their notion of what constitutes a criminal defense and "legal work" in general. Beyond a trial or a plea bargain, legal work means harnessing rehabilitative resources, problem solving like a social worker, or even acting as a mentor to a young defendant on legal and nonlegal matters. Yet, confounding this ideal are the defendant-based and system-based constraints imposed on defense attorneys that force them to navigate precariously close to the ethical limits of their responsibilities. Gauging the best interest of the client is highly interpretive in the context of a woefully underfunded system, which responds negatively to adversarial actions by defense attorneys. This is made worse by the impairments of the clients. Ironically, defense attorneys must cross ethical lines to live up to their advocacy obligation in today's criminal justice system.

References

Alschuler, Albert W. 1968. "The Prosecutor's Role in Plea Bargaining." *University of Chicago Law Review* 36:50–112.

Binder, David, Paul Bergman, and Susan Price. 1990. "Lawyers as Counselors: A Client-Centered Approach." *New York Law School Law Review* 35:29–86.

Blumberg, Abraham S. 1967. "The Practice of Law as a Confidence Game: Organizational Cooptation of a Profession." *Law & Society Review* 1:15–40.

Bogira, Steve. 2005. *Courtroom 302: A Year Behind the Scenes in an American Criminal Courthouse.* New York: Random House.

Casper, Jonathan D. 1972. *American Criminal Justice: A Defendant's Perspective.* Englewood Cliffs, NJ: Prentice Hall.

Chicago Appleseed Fund for Justice. 2007. *A Report on Chicago's Felony Courts.* Chicago: Chicago Council of Lawyers, Chicago Appleseed Fund for Justice.

Chicago Metropolis 2020. 2006. *2006 Crime and Justice Index.* Chicago: Chicago Metropolis 2020.

Eisenstein, James, and Herbert Jacob. 1977. *Felony Justice.* Boston: Little, Brown.

Goffman, Erving. 1959. *The Presentation of Self in Everyday Life.* New York: Anchor.

Mather, Lynn. 1979. *Plea Bargaining or Trial?* Lexington, MA: Lexington.

———. 2003. "What Do Clients Want? What Do Lawyers Do?" *Emory Law Journal* 52:1065–1086.

Mather, Lynn, Craig A. McEwen, and Richard J. Maiman. 2001. *Divorce Lawyers at Work: Varieties of Professionalism in Practice.* New York: Oxford University Press.

Maynard, Douglas W. 1984. *Inside Plea Bargaining: The Language of Negotiation.* New York: Plenum Press.

———. 1988. "Narratives and Narrative Structures in Plea Bargaining." *Law & Society Review* 22:449–482.

McIntyre, Lisa J. 1987. *The Public Defender: The Practice of Law in the Shadows of Repute.* Chicago: University of Chicago Press.

Neubauer, David W. 1974. *Criminal Justice in Middle America.* Morristown, NJ: General Learning.

Rosett, Arthur, and Donald R. Cressey. 1976. *Justice by Consent: Plea Bargains in the American Courthouse.* Philadelphia: J. B. Lippincott.

Skolnick, Jerome H. 1967. "Social Control in the Adversary System." *Journal of Conflict Resolution* 11:52–70.

Treatment Alternatives for Safe Communities. 2011. Home page. http://www.tasc-il.org/preview/index.html.

Uphoff, Rodney J. 1992. "Criminal Defense Lawyer: Zealous Advocate, Double Agent, or Beleaguered Dealer?" *Criminal Law Bulletin* 28:419–456.

Uphoff, Rodney J., and Peter B. Wood. 1998. "The Allocation of Decisionmaking Between Defense Counsel and Criminal Defendant: An Empirical Study of Attorney-Client Decisionmaking." *Kansas Law Review* 47:1–60.

Statutes

Alcoholism and Other Drug Abuse and Dependency Act, 20 Ill. Comp. Stat. 301/40-5 (2009).

Legal Services Lawyers

When Conceptions of Lawyering and Values Clash

Corey S. Shdaimah

Legal services lawyers provide free civil legal services to low-income clients in areas such as housing, family law, government benefits, and employment. The main federal funding source for these programs is the Legal Services Corporation (LSC). However, the LSC has long been unable to provide sufficient funding to meet the legal needs of millions of low-income people.[1] According to recent estimates, one eligible client is turned away from LSC-funded programs for each client served, and 80% or more of the civil legal needs of low-income individuals go unmet (Legal Services Corporation 2007). This means that legal services lawyers handle large caseloads and must make difficult decisions about allocating their scarce resources. This may limit who is served, which practice areas are addressed, and what range of legal services is provided. Despite stressful working conditions and lower salaries that go with underresourced programs, there is tough competition for legal services jobs, which are often filled by graduates of elite schools (Jones 2005). Current legal services practice is therefore not usually a default career choice.

Legal services lawyers' norms and values are influenced by their shared commitments to communities or individuals who have been marginalized by poverty and other forms of societal oppression, such as racism, anti-immigrant sentiment, or incarceration (Houseman and Perle 2007). These norms and values include a desire to foster client empowerment, to work against the oppression of vulnerable people and communities, and to achieve equity within the

---

1. Client eligibility for LSC-funded legal services is set at or below 125% of the federal poverty guidelines.

legal system and elsewhere. Entering this field out of a desire to achieve social change, legal services lawyers are frequently troubled by what they perceive as the limited scope of their work for individual clients (Cummings and Rhode 2009), the scarcity of available resources that limits services and raises caseloads (Tremblay 1999), and the possibility that their efforts may be incompatible with the values that led them to choose to become legal services lawyers (Shdaimah 2009b).

This chapter summarizes prominent conceptions of legal services lawyering found in the social science and clinical law literature. It then turns to engaged practice, focusing on two dilemmas that legal services lawyers confront. The first stems from lawyers' concerns that their actions will foster client dependency instead of client autonomy. The second dilemma revolves around the gap between the ideals and realities of legal services lawyering. Most lawyers feel that their practices fall short of what they would like to accomplish given their broader visions of social justice, and they worry whether this makes them complicit in maintaining the status quo. Using case studies, this chapter explores how two legal services lawyers grapple with these dilemmas in their day-to-day practice. Although we use the word "dilemma" easily in conversation, true dilemmas are relatively rare, "arising when two or more principles or values conflict. More than one principle applies and there are good reasons to support mutually inconsistent courses of action. Although it seems terrible to give up either value, a loss is inescapable" (Kälvemark et al. 2004, 1077). Dilemmas have no perfect outcomes; they cannot be resolved without compromising fundamental values. In the final section of the chapter, I offer concluding thoughts about legal services lawyering *with* dilemmas, which by definition are not amenable to resolution.

Background

The case studies in this chapter are drawn from a sample of more than 50 interviews with legal services lawyers and clients conducted during 2002–2003 at Northeast Legal Services (NELS), a large urban legal services practice.[2] NELS has one office in Northeast City's central business district and another in a

2. One important limitation is that data from this study are based on self-reports. The bias inherent in self-reports was to some extent mitigated by conducting interviews with clients as well as lawyers. Lawyers were also eager to share concerns regarding their own work and identified need for improvement, indicating some level of candor. A detailed description of study

neighborhood from which NELS draws clients.[3] NELS is comprised of units that serve specific populations, such as children or the elderly, or address substantive practice areas. Units operate with wide discretion, including with regard to case acceptance criteria. Lawyers and clients were drawn from both offices and worked with six different units.

At the time of my interviews, NELS employed approximately 100 lawyers, paralegals, and administrative staff. All but one of the lawyers in this sample were white; 6 were women and 8 were men; and their practice experience ranged from less than a year to nearly 30 years. While most of the more experienced lawyers were from middle-tier local law schools, those hired since the mid-1980s had graduated from elite law schools. Clients included 27 women and 3 men; 4 were white, 24 were African American, 1 was Indonesian, and 1 was Nigerian. I was told that this sample was representative of NELS's clients, who are predominantly racial and ethnic minority women. Public interest lawyers are well aware of their privileged status relative to clients due to their professional and socioeconomic standing and, often, their race and gender. Lawyers sought to minimize the impact of status in their interactions with clients; they also saw leveraging power on behalf of clients in representing them against their more privileged adversaries as one of the goals of legal services practice.

NELS is well resourced. It is supported by the public interest and private bars in Northeast City, which has a robust and cooperative public interest law community. NELS relies on both government and private funds. It is better off than many beleaguered legal services programs that weather substantial funding cuts and the vagaries of changing attitudes toward low-income individuals and communities. The struggles that NELS lawyers face, therefore, may be mild compared to those faced by legal services programs without NELS's resources.

For dilemmas of client dependency, I draw on two interviews with Liz, who worked with elderly clients. For dilemmas arising from the ideals and realities of legal services lawyering, I draw on two interviews with Marjorie, who specialized in consumer advocacy. Both practiced at NELS for approximately five years, and both had prior experience in other advocacy arenas. I highlight

---

methods, including sample selection and discussion of possible bias, and of the research site can be found in Shdaimah (2009b, 1–11, 31–34, appendix A).

3. NELS, Northeast City, and study respondents' names are pseudonyms.

day-to-day ethical concerns rather than dramatic examples, as these are more representative of the sample and of what legal services lawyers face in practice. The two case studies provide depth and nuance when exploring the dilemmas; the dilemmas reported here were common among the other 12 legal services lawyers.

Legal Services Lawyering and Ethical Concerns

Contemporary legal services programs trace their roots to the 1960s, when lawyers influenced by the civil rights movements criticized the legal aid model that was designed to alleviate private troubles without confronting the status quo. These critics advocated for legal practices that would challenge the decisions and policies of government agencies and be more responsive to the self-identified needs of underserved communities (Cahn and Cahn 1964). They were also influenced by the social change efforts of the NAACP's Legal Defense Fund. After the American Bar Association (ABA) joined the push for legal services under a less radical agenda, federal funding was provided to support legal services for low-income clients through the Office of Economic Opportunity (OEO) and, later, through the creation of the Legal Services Corporation in 1974 (Hilbink 2006; Houseman and Perle 2007). The new LSC-funded programs often pursued political change-focused strategies that challenged government decisions in both individual cases and as matters of policy (such as in the context of welfare benefits). A political backlash dismantled many of the OEO programs but did not eliminate the LSC. However, the LSC was weakened over decades by reduced funding. Restrictions placed on LSC-funded agencies also undermined legal services programs across the country (Udell 1998). Although these restrictions were challenged in court, they continue to have a severely limiting impact on the breadth and type of legal services that LSC-funded programs can provide (Diller and Savner 2009).

There are few empirical studies of legal services practice. The existing studies provide a complex picture of legal services practice in which lawyers strive to maintain their ideals and commitments in challenging practice settings. Carl Hosticka (1979) found that legal services lawyers shaped their clients' stories and directed representation in ways not always consonant with client understanding. However, even when clients complained, their lawyers worked on their behalf and expended greater efforts. Jack Katz (1982) found that Chicago legal services lawyers who were committed to using the law to challenge government practices sought ways to increase the significance of their work, such as impact litigation and representation of high-profile cases and clients. They continued to challenge the legal system and private sector practices throughout the 1970s, after the more radical social movement efforts of the 1960s subsided. Handler, Hollingsworth, and Erlanger (1978) reported that legal services programs faced many obstacles and that legal services lawyers often viewed their employment as temporary. Lawyers still entered legal service practice, however, with high ideals and were largely satisfied with their work and accomplishments. Common themes in these studies are the need to ration services, the engagement of clients with the legal process, and a desire to expand the repertoire of legal tools and arenas of practice lawyers exploited on behalf of low-income clients.

There seems to be little connection between the empirical studies described above and the critiques of legal service practices during the 1980s and 1990s. The majority of legal services critiques are self-reflective, often written by practitioners and academics—many of whom are clinical law professors—about their own experiences. Most are heavily normative; together with critiques of prevailing practice, they offer prescriptions for ideal practice. Perhaps the most famous of these is Gerald López's (1992) critique of regnant lawyering. Regnant lawyering is hierarchical, lawyer directed, and inattentive to the narratives and goals of clients. López's alternative model, called "rebellious lawyering," focuses on the amelioration of unfair treatment not only within the legal system but within the lawyer-client relationship itself, which can serve as both a model and a vehicle for client empowerment and social justice. One common focus of these critiques is client autonomy. Client autonomy, as conceived in these critiques, includes the importance of client decision making shared by mainstream legal ethics (e.g., ABA Model Rule of Professional Conduct 1.2(a)), which affords the client the right to determine the goals of the representation. In legal services practice, however, autonomy is primarily valued because it reaffirms human dignity and is a challenge to the subordination that clients regularly experience outside of the lawyer-client relationship (Shdaimah 2009a).

Sameer Ashar (2007, 1904–1905) notes that decades of important and valuable critical scholarship have shaped the practice of public interest law, including legal services practice. The values of rebellious lawyering and client empowerment resonate with practicing lawyers and are a fair reflection of their aspirations and motivations. Tensions can arise between legal services values and mainstream professional practice norms or when different legal services values conflict. For example, autonomy may become problematic when lawyers' respect for client dignity and self-determination appears to conflict with the need for expert knowledge and legal skills as well as clients' desires to delegate decision-making responsibility to the lawyer (Simon 1994). Legal services lawyers are often frustrated by these tensions, which highlight the limits of the law as a tool for radical social change (Shdaimah 2009b, 58–59). Lawyers in my sample entered legal services practice with high ideals and hopes, despite awareness of practice constraints that they would face. Most chose this path before law school and told me that they would not be lawyers if they could not practice in legal services or some other form of public interest law. Their concerns about client autonomy, dependency, and systems advocacy, although informed by legal practice norms, primarily stemmed from prior commitments to serve low-income clients and a desire to work toward sometimes amorphous notions of social justice (Shdaimah 2009b, 36–40; Shdaimah 2006). For some, this was reinforced in law school where they read the work of critics such as Lucie White and Gerald López, who were explicitly cited by two lawyers in my sample. Whatever their law school experience, all lawyers described NELS as a workplace where colleagues shared and reinforced their overarching commitments and concerns.

I focus here on two dilemmas stemming from legal services lawyers' self-described values, which are often at the root of their motivation to become lawyers. The first is the problem of perceived client dependency on lawyers, which conflicts with the values of self-determination and autonomy. The second is the tension between the larger goals of legal services and actual practice, which occurs within institutional, legal, and societal constraints. I draw from the interviews to illustrate the dilemmas as the lawyers perceive them and to show how they reason through them.

It is important to note that the problems described here also arise in other areas of legal practice. Small firm attorneys and solo practitioners face resource constraints that shape and limit their practice (Levin, chapter 5; Seron 1996); divorce lawyers deal with clients who often seek help with concerns that go beyond their legal problems (Sarat and Felstiner 1995; Mather and McEwen, chapter 4). Lawyers share a professional ethics code that may lead them to perceive these problems similarly. The strong influence of law school socialization is well documented and likely influences lawyers' perceptions, framing, and problem-solving approaches in ways that lawyers might not fully apprehend (Mertz 2007). This should lead us to question the belief of legal services lawyers that they are different from other lawyers (Shdaimah 2008). Most notably, they share similarities with public defenders, who provide services to similarly marginalized and multiply-challenged clients under severe practice constraints (Van Cleve, chapter 14) and high-impact public interest lawyers who may draw from a similar value base (Cummings, chapter 16). There are some undeniable differences, however, including that legal services lawyers experience such concerns within a framework of values that include equality, empowerment, anti-oppressive work, and human dignity, often with a focus on individual representation.

Dilemmas of Dependency

Liz first envisioned a career in public policy. She told me about her frustration trying to work at the state policy level before she attended law school, which was dominated by lawyers who used a process that was opaque in a way that left her feeling powerless. She saw law as a way of tapping into power to change policy on behalf of low-income individuals and communities. Liz also desired to work with individual clients. A summer job with an impact litigation practice had her "just researching and writing a 12 to 15 page memo each week and that wasn't at all what I envisioned for the kind of practice I wanted to do." Liz was frustrated to be so far removed from actual clients because she wanted to hear directly what her clients wanted and what the cases meant for them, and to have a sense of the direct impact of her work. Subsequent experiences in a different legal services setting "providing direct services but hopefully being in a position to be able to do some policy work as well" turned out to be a better fit. This is how she described her work at NELS, which was her second job out of law school and where she served elderly clients, many of whom spoke little English.

Despite her satisfaction in working with clients directly, Liz worried that the relationships she developed might cause clients to become too reliant on her for legal and technical assistance with state agencies, as well as for more personal or nonlegal affairs:

> Well, I have had some clients I feel become a little bit too dependent on me. And that's you know, from time to time I identify things that I need to work on in my own relationships with my clients or my practice in general and one of the things is trying to be less of a social worker.

Legal service lawyers are discomfited by the possibility that they may replicate the more troubling aspects of their clients' interactions with private entities (such as employers and mortgage companies) and government agencies, particularly paternalism and oppression. Legal services lawyers see themselves as fighting oppression, helping to empower their clients, and fostering self-determination, self-confidence, and social change to equalize resources (including power and influence) in society. The thought that they might foster dependence and reinforce hierarchical systems that take away from their clients' dignity and self-worth are anathema. Most lawyers in my sample, like Liz, believed that their own good intentions and motives are not enough to justify harm that they might cause. A few also feared that their moral reasoning might be little more than a post hoc rationalization to justify their improper actions.

In talking about her concerns, Liz identified aspects of her practice that create greater risks of client dependency. One is the ongoing nature of her relationships with clients, which she characterizes as personal and long-term:

> They can be very grateful; they can develop a closer relationship with us and sometimes, that's nice on the one hand. I mean it's nice to feel connected to your clients and not just feel like you're just doing all this legal stuff in a box. But on the other hand, I really want people to become [reflective pause] independent is not really the right word, but to be able to feel comfortable handling some issues on their own. . . . [S]ometimes I think that I should be more of a resource person [and] not volunteer to do everything that I could. I mean we really, we are constantly making decisions about, can this client take this information and handle the issue herself or should we volunteer to help her with this? Or should we volunteer to just take care of it?

Asked why she was concerned about client dependency, Liz responded: "For me it comes from a sense of respect for individuals and their ability to—trying to inspire confidence in them." She further notes that there are some clients with whom she is more willing to engage in what she calls "hand holding," which includes offering more services and expecting less from them. When deciding which approach to take with a particular client, Liz considers each client's particular circumstances. She is also influenced by her level of empathy. She describes what she calls a "classic scenario" to exemplify the kind of clients she is most likely to assist and for whom she worries that she is fostering dependency:

> Elderly women who have not had, never had a lot of money, worked, you know may have worked or worked sporadically while raising children. Husband, primary income earner—illness to the husband—they try to care for the husband as long as they can. Husband goes into a nursing home and then wife is just alone with having to manage her grief over the loss of her

spouse and the loss of his companionship—physical separation—which is very lonely. Having to deal with a bunch of confusing financial issues. Not understanding the laws regarding nursing home care, eligibility for grant, that sort of thing. And so all that kind of stuff, I feel like they've done—they've been the very good person that they thought they should be and still, when this sort of thing happens we don't have a . . . public system that supports them adequately.

Liz's clients are often emotional. Many of them cry a lot, and she showed me her supersized box of tissues. Liz believed that the combination of confusion and vulnerability renders her clients more likely to be dependent; these are also the very same factors that make her want to take on more responsibility in their cases.

While Liz wondered whether the risk of dependence is more acute with elderly clients, these same concerns were raised, using similar language, across my interviews with legal services lawyers practicing with a variety of clients in different substantive areas. Legal services clients live at or below the poverty level and often juggle concerns that can include health problems, employment challenges, and unstable housing. Most are confused by bureaucracies that are opaque and frequently hostile. The confusion and vulnerability that Liz and other NELS lawyers described were corroborated by clients, who spoke of tremendous stress and often sought to delegate responsibility to their lawyers as a way to manage overwhelming circumstances.

One response to the dilemma that Liz experiences is to "empower" clients by enhancing their ability to understand and successfully tackle the problems they face: "The role that I identify with was sort of information and resource giver." She explained, "I don't mean just in an emotional way, I mean to be able to give them concrete information that they can then apply to their own lives." Part of what makes her work at NELS so appealing is that "there's community education which I think is incredibly important and I think the public interest community doesn't do enough of, to try to help people identify problems early and prevent them. And also to empower them to help."

Her experience with state government taught her that lack of knowledge and understanding are barriers to action and create power imbalances:

I was really frustrated by my own *ignorance* of how language could be interpreted by the courts. I'd go in to the legislative committee meetings and these corporate attorneys for [a corporate state lobby group] would be there talking about changing this one word and I couldn't always grasp why is it that that one word will make such a difference and I really hated it that they had a lot of *power* because of that.

Much of Liz's policy work, therefore, focuses on enhancing autonomy for legal services constituents by forcing agencies to make their policies consistent and comprehensible to clients. One example that she provided was that nursing home administrators told many of her clients or their families that the family would lose the rights to the patient's home once the nursing home patient died if they had received medical assistance funding for care. However, there were federal regulations that provided little-known hardship exceptions to this surrender. Neither social workers assisting patients and their families nor many nursing home administrators were aware of the exceptions; the policies were also vague and open to discretion. Liz's long-term advocacy work with local agencies helped create a written policy that clarified the hardship exceptions and made clients and social workers aware of their availability. She then worked with state agencies to ensure that the policy was implemented and followed, and to develop educational materials to help family members and case workers understand the policy and how to apply for the exemptions. Liz works to create situations in which clients are better informed and able to act without the assistance of lawyers—trying to eliminate an ongoing practice dilemma by attacking its root causes.

Even when Liz's policy reform efforts to enhance autonomy are successful, she conceded that people are likely to still find themselves in situations where they need lawyers. Clients to whom she referred me all required assistance with bureaucracies, where legal knowledge helped. Liz's clients are often so "bewildered by the process that they become more dependent on me as an attorney who seems to know what's happening and can explain it. And so they contact me a lot. A lot." Government agencies and other bureaucracies respond (when they do respond) to her, not only because she is knowledgeable but *because* of her status as a lawyer. This means that no matter how much information and knowledge is passed on, even to Liz's savviest clients, the agencies with which they interact often remain impervious to independent resolution of problems in the absence of a lawyer. When clients' abilities to self-advocate are further compromised by grief, stress, or other problems, the "independence" that Liz seeks to foster is elusive. She is keenly aware of herself as broker and resource guide. She is troubled that her own role as a lawyer might be a necessary feature of representation, but understands that clients may be dependent on the expertise and authority of lawyers to prod otherwise unresponsive agencies into action.

Liz turns to other lawyers to help manage her discomfort, especially her direct supervisor: "I'm so glad I work with her because when I feel, you know, my humanity slipping [laughs] I can think of her." The assistance, inspiration, and encouragement of her colleagues is typical of NELS's work environment:

> We have incredible resources to serve our clients, incredible support collegially and administratively. And very strong leadership. . . . And people like [Nadine] who have been doing this work for—well she's been at NELS for 22 years. '79 I think. And who's still as fresh and aggressive and creative and committed. . . . She's a really good model and I feel very fortunate to be working with all these senior attorneys who've made it work for them all these years.

Liz recognizes that hand holding and relationship building have their roots in other deeply held values that are central to her work as a legal services lawyer. It is clear, as is the case with all the other lawyers in my sample regardless of gender, experience level, or practice area, that empathy (which Liz defined as not feeling too distant from her clients) and compassion almost always trump concerns about dependence. They tell stories of clients for whom they performed distinctly nonlegal activities due to a perception that the client was close to a breaking point or so overwhelmed that the lawyer felt compelled to help. Lawyers who engage in direct service are touched by their clients. This leads to a desire to help, which troubles lawyers who worry about the dependence that such help engenders. It is a problem when lawyers believe, as Liz does, that systems change rarely reaches far enough for most clients to handle complex legal and bureaucratic matters on their own.

As I have argued elsewhere (Shdaimah 2009b), the perception of dependence as a "problem" in legal services lawyering stems, at least in part, from an overly narrow understanding of dependence that focuses on the clients' legal problems. A wide-angle lens into clients' lives would show that most clients delegate problems to lawyers to increase agency in other spheres. Liz described her clients' dependency as connected to their lives as wives and mothers who were dependent on husbands. Yet these women were also people who were depended on by others, although their home-based work made them less able to be independent in spheres outside of the home due to lack of income and status.

Lawyers like Liz struggle with the feeling that, although they have done their best, their desire to empower clients and fears of fostering dependence leave them with lingering worry about the harm that they cause. This is the root of the dilemma. Even though lawyers like Liz believe that the actions they characterize as fostering dependence are justified under the circumstances, they still represent a compromise of core values of legal services lawyering.

Law as a Limited (and Limiting) Tool

Marjorie had been practicing at NELS's consumer housing unit for about five years at the time of our interview, focusing on "mortgage foreclosure defense and predatory lending, home equity scams, home improvement scams." Marjorie's work was both personally compelling and professionally stimulating:

> I love it. I absolutely love it . . . my clients are complete victims of these really bad scams so it's really easy to have sympathy and empathy for what has happened to them. And it's intellectually stimulating, the laws that we use are really interesting and my bosses are very creative and historically this has been a creative unit in a creative organization so they're always coming up with new legal theories, and trying to push the envelope.

Marjorie told me, "I wanted to go to law school because I wanted to save the world [laughs]." She did not believe that law was the only tool to achieve her goal but was drawn to the law due to an assessment of her skills and capabilities. After six years in practice, Marjorie was tempered in her assessment of the law, and many of her frustrations stemmed from her experiences with the law as a tool with limited efficacy in achieving social change. She struggled with the gap between the rewarding day-to-day work and its limited contribution to her larger vision of social justice, which she described as "getting treated fairly and rightly," a definition influenced by her work in the consumer housing unit with victims of predatory lending and foreclosures:

> You know you never feel like [pause]—it's hard to step back and see how much of a difference if *any* you're making, and you don't necessarily feel like you're making much of a difference on a day-to-day basis, so then you start to look around and say, "Well who is making a difference or how could I better make a difference if that's what drives you?"

Marjorie experienced three major frustrations with her work as a legal services lawyer. The first was the limited assistance that she can provide to clients, which is circumscribed by their immediate legal needs around consumer housing. These are often just a small part of the legal and other troubles in her clients' lives. Second, Marjorie did not believe that even successful resolution of legal problems necessarily gets to the root causes of client troubles, which are more societal than legal. She worried that her work may amount to tinkering that leaves oppressive systems intact, their legitimacy unchallenged. The third frustration was her sense that the law (at least in her field) pushes toward individual rather than systemic or collective solutions, and that the work she is able to accomplish usually has little impact beyond the individual cases. Despite these limitations, Marjorie believes in the importance of her work and is able to manage her disappointment. However, like Liz, the frustrations leave her troubled and uneasy.

Marjorie describes herself as empathic and compassionate. She frequently toggles back and forth between the benefits and risks of her compassion. On the one hand, compassion keeps her motivated: "It would be hard to practice this kind of law if you lost that." The compassion that motivates her to be a zealous advocate for her clients also makes her uncomfortable: "I mean that's one of the difficult things like how much you delve into the other issues in your clients' lives." She spoke of taking her cases "too personally," even to the point that she may "get angry with opposing counsel and the other side." Twice in the course of our interviews she described crying with clients.

Marjorie's legal training has provided her with skills in certain areas (and not in others); like several other lawyers, she lamented her lack of social work case management and counseling skills. She is also limited by her large caseload. When Marjorie learns of her clients' troubles, she would like to be able to help them: "I regret that I don't have more time to be more of a full service person for clients 'cause you do get into their lives and you do know about things." Her need to comply with legal requirements in her cases, such as procuring documents and meeting deadlines, leaves her less attuned and less able to take time to learn what is going on in clients' lives, even with issues that might affect their cases. Marjorie described a client who called and told her that she had been in the hospital after she had been out of contact for months:

> So she finally gets home and I get her on the phone and I'm [talking quickly] like "Okay so you need to call this person, you need to call that person, and you need to do this." Like in the next 10 days sort of thing. And so, I found myself just kind of rattling this off to her. And she's like [in slow, soft voice] "I hope—well you know I just got out of the hospital and I'm really"—or no, she needed to get me information. And I was like, "Okay, can you get that

for me now?" And she was like, "Well I have to find it, and I'm not moving too—" She said something that made me realize, "Okay Marjorie, give it a break, she just got out of the hospital [laughs ruefully] and she's really hurting and she just can't, just can't jump off the couch because you need this information right now." But it's almost like I can't stop and say, or I feel like I can't stop and say, "Okay well when you're better," or like be a little nicer about the fact that she's really hurting. I'm just like on this: "Well we need to [snaps fingers]!"

Marjorie regretted her inability to be more empathic. She did not feel she had the time to commiserate and ask about her client's hospitalization. This made her feel callous, but she reflected that she had no choice but to avoid learning more about her clients' troubles:

A client came in the other day and she's 32—she looks 52—she looks so old. And she's legally blind and really behind on her mortgage. And she has 2 kids and she's living in this house but she said half of it doesn't have electricity; the gas is turned off so she's cooking off of a stove.

Marjorie went on to describe the rest of her day. She wanted to see if she could help the client. This detailed description provides a window on the day-to-day work of legal services lawyers:

I was on intake and I was interviewing all these other people, so I had like maybe a half an hour, 45 minutes, to kind of devote to her and figure out what her situation is. You know I want to start asking her—'cause then she had a job issue. And she just had to pass a test and they wouldn't give her a test to—with her eyesight! So then I start thinking like, ADA [Americans with Disabilities Act] violation and is she getting any assistance for that and you know is she getting the right amounts of money for her kids and you know like there are a bazillion other things I could ask about? . . . I went and talked to our social worker afterwards and said, "Can you guys help her find other housing because she really needs to get out of that place and just get an apartment?" But then [our social worker] started asking me all these questions; I'm like, "I don't know. I didn't want to know. I didn't ask."

Not wanting to ask, Marjorie noted, is typical. She explained:

One of the hardest things about my job is that we aren't delving into every aspect of their life and it's almost like I don't want to ask questions because I don't want to know because I either don't have the expertise to do anything about it, or I don't have the time to do anything about it; or I don't want to know and say that I can't do anything about it or I don't know how to do anything about it. So you just don't ask.

Like all legal services offices, NELS limits the scope and type of assistance it provides due to resource constraints. It sets times and days when clients can apply for services and also determines what kinds of cases it will take (Shdaimah 2009b, 3–5), a phenomenon that is common in the legal services sphere (Tremblay 1999). NELS maintains resource lists of legal and nonlegal services, and nearly all the lawyers provided examples of advising clients or referring them to pro bono or fee-for-service lawyers or to other legal services programs that specialize in cases that NELS cannot address, even though clients are often so concerned about the problem that brought them to NELS that they may not take the information or follow up when they do. This was corroborated by clients, including one of Marjorie's clients who told me that she had provided him with advice on a negligence case he had with another lawyer. All of Marjorie's clients described her as honest, empathic, and responsive. Her description of walling herself off to clients reflects her need to create some kind of boundaries so as not to be overwhelmed and paralyzed by empathy in the face of pressing need.

Marjorie is also troubled by the insufficiency of legal remedies to get at the root causes of her clients' troubles. Describing her clientele as predominantly low-income African American women, many of whom are elderly, she believes that the dual plagues of poverty and racism are at the root of predatory lending and home foreclosures. Legal remedies, however, rely on improper actions of individuals (like lenders) but do not challenge societal or structural conditions (like poverty or lack of affordable housing) that disadvantage some people and make them more vulnerable than others. Although Marjorie would like to challenge the underlying structural conditions, the law does not provide a means to do so. This means that when it comes to home foreclosures resulting from poverty or unemployment rather than wrongdoing on the part of a lender or broker, she can do little more than explain the situation to a prospective client:

If it's just a regular purchase money mortgage and they fell behind because they lost a job I won't necessarily do that long of an interview. I'll just ask why they fell behind and what their income is and what their family situation is. . . . And we'll usually just complete the interview right there—tell them that, at the end, some people if they don't have any income there's no chance they're going to save their house and I tell them that "Some people are just too poor to live in [America]" [says this sarcastically, sounding pained].

One of the hardest parts of her job "is telling people that they're too poor to own a house that's only costing them $150 a month." The law cannot address poverty, and she does not have the tools to ameliorate it, except in her limited way of treating people respectfully and offering information.

Even in cases in which individual wrongdoing gives rise to legal remedies, Marjorie often feels helpless in getting at root causes of her clients' problems. She is angry at people and institutions that prey on her clients and will chastise "the other side" (and their lawyers):

And I actually had an opportunity to ask [a broker and contractor] one day on the phone: "You met my client Mrs. Smith and you saw that she was living on the edge of the badlands and that she was blind and paralyzed and 90 years old and how can you [live] with yourself when you steal $10,000 from her?"

She cannot fathom what causes people to scam others, and she believes that a disregard for others is the basis for such behavior. Like other lawyers in my sample, Marjorie often felt that other tools, such as journalism or education, may be better suited for bringing about change because legal remedies leave underlying prejudices unchallenged.

Marjorie is frustrated not only by the limitations of legal remedies but also by her own ability to effectuate more broad-scale change. NELS's successful campaign to pass legislation to curb predatory lending practices at the city level backfired when it faced a backlash at the state level, resulting in legislation favorable to banks and lenders. Since Marjorie sees consumer law as designed to be driven by individual lawsuits rather than systemic challenges, she and her colleagues are often caught in the middle between litigating the best solutions for their clients and more general solutions (Shdaimah 2009b, 53–55).

Often NELS does not have the resources to get clients as much relief as it would if its staff had lower caseloads. Its resources, therefore, must be apportioned to serve more clients:

If I only had 10 cases I could probably—these cases are probably worth more money. Yeah, surely. If I wanted to go down to state court and really litigate these cases to death. . . . I think of the client case I probably mentioned to you because I mention it a lot, you know a 90-year-old blind and partially paralyzed woman, I probably could have taken that into state court if I was like a flashy state court lawyer and gotten a big award for her. I mean I can't imagine not being able to do that with a Northeast City jury.

While they do not get large individual victories for clients, Marjorie and her colleagues are able to restructure loans and renegotiate payments for individual clients that are meaningful. Their work often allows people to stay in their homes and relieves them of predatory loans. Marjorie is aware of the importance of her work with individual clients, despite what she sees as its limited focus. It provides her with a sense of satisfaction to see clients doing well, and she hopes that relief from mortgage or predatory lending troubles lifts a burden that allows them to turn to other areas of their lives:

Like this one client that I have, he was just really in crisis mode for a year. And now I see him periodically because his mortgage company keeps screwing up. But he's fine and he's in this stable job now; it's been three years. He's always pleasant. He's not stressed when I see him. He's just stable now; he's just going on in life, just stable.

Marjorie speculated that "maybe the fact that I stabilized his situation got him to a place where he could just be making payments that were affordable. . . . [T]he goal is always to get a client an affordable mortgage payment, so if you can do that then it's going to stabilize the rest of their lives." The satisfaction that she gets from providing meaningful assistance to individual clients helps make her frustrations manageable.

However, Marjorie and her colleagues see the same problems again and again, causing them to question the value of their work outside the context of individual cases. Due to limited resources and immediate client needs, most of NELS's consumer housing cases settle. The ones that are litigated rarely have an impact beyond her individual clients. Marjorie also says that she is often conflicted about counseling clients to participate in a class action lawsuit because they can get a lot more relief in individual settlements, if they succeed. This means that the best interest of the individual client might conflict with the interest of the larger group that NELS represents as well as NELS's own needs to manage overwhelming caseloads. She is careful to fully inform clients of their options, and in one recent class action case, her unit set up a panel of private attorneys to whom they could refer clients who opt out of the settlement to pursue individual remedies.

Marjorie's opportunities to engage in impact work are another way that she is able to live with her frustration. Class action lawsuits, when she does pursue them, provide her with the deep satisfaction of creating change for a broader group of people that she hopes will affect lenders' practices. Talking about one class action lawsuit that she worked on, which mostly involved people who would not qualify for LSC-funded legal services, she said:

> Many people said, in just having conversations with them about this, "Well I'm so glad somebody went after this company" and different people have thanked us, "Thank you for bringing this lawsuit against them." Not because they're personally getting so much money out of it, but because they're just happy because somebody stood up to this company.

While each individual might not receive much, the hope is that the aggregated blow to the lender will have a larger impact than individual cases. Marjorie sees clients as empowered when their foes are taken to task in such a public manner. She also leverages her resources through education. "I tend to train professionals who are then working with clients. They're housing counselors or I've done trainings with senior care professionals."

Marjorie faces competing interests in her practice that she sees as dilemmas because, for her, they have no satisfactory resolution. But she has been able to find a way to live with them as part of the price of her work, which she believes is meaningful to individuals and, sometimes, to a larger group. Like Liz, Marjorie turns to supervisors and colleagues for assistance in managing her dilemmas and will ask: "What would you do in this situation?" Consultation with colleagues and supervisors is typical at NELS:

> We've got a really good working relationship in our unit, we're really lucky—although that's probably most of the units at NELS, if not all. But my two bosses here are just great. Their doors are always open and if I think something's wrong their attitude is "okay go fix it." They have always given me a lot of independence from the beginning and yet would give me all the supervision and assistance that I need.

Most NELS units have regular meetings in which they discuss cases. There is a culture of mutual assistance and mentoring at NELS, and nearly all the lawyers in my sample mentioned instances of informal mentoring and consultation, as well as support in difficult times.

Dilemmas as a Hallmark of Practice

Contrary to earlier critiques, recent empirical scholarship on public interest law and legal services lawyers provides evidence that these lawyers are well aware of the damage that paternalism, oppressive practices, and "doing for" can have (Rhode 2008; Shdaimah 2009b). They often manage these dangers explicitly and self-critically. Liz and Marjorie both developed strategies to live with the dilemmas they confront in practice and not feel overly compromised. Although they were less experienced than other lawyers in my sample, all the lawyers interviewed in this study faced similar frustrations that often rose to the level of dilemmas.

Both Liz and Marjorie experience what has been called "moral distress" over their chosen courses of action, despite firm beliefs that in the majority of individual cases they make the "right" choices. A concept that has been developed extensively in the nursing literature, moral distress is defined as knowledge of one's inability to make decisions that are entirely consonant with deeply held values either due to value conflict or structural and practice constraints. Moral distress can give rise to unease, guilt, and burnout (Raines 2000), even as it may also have positive effects such as providing an impetus for reflection and growth (Hardingham 2004). For professionals who experience moral distress, debriefing, open communication, and the creation of a trusting and supportive environment are helpful coping mechanisms (Rushton 2006).

The extensive narratives reveal some of the moral reasoning Liz and Marjorie use to balance contradictions in their day-to-day legal services practice. Liz wants to foster clients' dignity and decision making; she challenges agencies that make things difficult for clients with opaque rules and hostile bureaucrats. However, she often finds herself dealing with these same bureaucracies that she tries to reform on behalf of her clients, and she uses her legal expertise and authority in ways that her clients cannot, replicating some of the same hierarchies that she is so eager to dismantle. Even though Liz obtains material relief for her clients, they remain supplicants who have less power than she does, rather than equal citizens who are empowered to make demands on the government that is supposed to serve them. Marjorie's empathy compels her to want to alleviate the heavy and immediate burdens faced by clients and stirs a desire to help as many clients as possible, but also causes her to avoid learning more about clients' lives when she knows she cannot help them. The legal tools that are so important to individual clients are adequate neither to bring full relief for individual clients nor to effect the deeply rooted social change that Marjorie desires.

Liz's and Marjorie's dilemma management strategies were similar to those of other legal services lawyers, regardless of gender or years of experience (Shdaimah 2009a; Shdaimah 2009b). Liz and Marjorie rely on mentors at NELS to help them clarify the values at stake and better understand the range of alternatives and risks of any given action. These mentors help Liz and Marjorie figure out whether they face a true dilemma and whether they made a reasonable decision given competing commitments and values. In the examples provided by all of the lawyers, most advice came after decisions had been made and so had more the character of a post mortem that was both a learning experience and a strategy for managing the guilt, frustration, and disappointment that often comes with difficult decisions.

Liz and Marjorie both try to place boundaries on their emotions and moral distress. While they both are extremely empathic, they know they must place limits on their empathy to avoid being overwhelmed or incapacitated by it. Thomas and Otis (2010), in their study of 171 randomly sampled licensed clinical social workers, reported that social workers who were effectively able to manage a balance between empathy and distancing were less likely to experience compassion fatigue and burnout while remaining open to their clients. Striking such a balance is difficult; too much distancing can inure service providers to client suffering while too much empathy can exact a high emotional toll. Each lawyer in my study struggled with how to set boundaries on the extent to which they were affected by their clients; they worried about the negative impact their work had on clients, while also being open enough to clients to remain motivated to work on their behalf. Marjorie, for example, purposely walls herself off from knowledge of her clients' lives that will make her feel only more helpless as a lawyer in the face of their troubles. Liz, too, tries to keep her identification with clients at bay. For instance, she tries to fight off her discomfort with wearing a six-year-old raincoat as she walks past clients without hats, umbrellas, or jackets as they stand in the rain.

Probably most important to Liz, Marjorie, and others was the overriding imperative that they must continue to serve clients and to *act*. Inaction, or abandoning clients due to the frustrations and dilemmas they face, was not an option that they entertained. In fact, the face-to-face contact that comes with conducting intake and with any direct services practice is part of what made their jobs so compelling to both lawyers. Liz and Marjorie, nearly eight years after these interviews, still practice legal services law. The overwhelming majority of my sample has remained in legal services or other form of public interest law, and just over half still work at NELS.

It is the hallmark of a reflective practitioner to be troubled (Addams [1889] 2002; Schon 1983). Legal services lawyers must identify, work on, and do their best in an imperfect world. Louise Trubek (1998) urges critical-thinking public interest lawyers to "live in the contradiction." This does not mean abandoning critical thinking or throwing deeply held values to the wind with the excuse that at least one is doing something. The sense of dilemma that is expressed by Liz and Marjorie is precisely the evidence that they do not abandon values in an imperfect situation, but rather strive to do their best. They try to resolve tensions by seeking creative and satisfactory solutions to the problems that they face whenever possible. When value conflicts cannot be resolved or avoided, and thus rise to the level of true dilemmas, they manage their responses to value conflicts as best they can. They do so by reflecting on dilemmas to make decisions that they can live with, discussing them with colleagues, and maintaining a balance between engaged commitment to their clients and their work and a necessary detachment from what they are (un)able to accomplish to avoid being overwhelmed to the point of paralysis.

Like many others who provide direct services under severe resource constraints, legal services lawyers will always have to make difficult decisions, some of which will involve compromises of fundamental values. The main challenges they face are to continue the work without becoming desensitized to the risks that it inescapably involves. The lawyers highlighted in these case studies offer strategies to recognize and manage these tensions and remain in practice, learning to live with imperfection.

References

Addams, Jane. (1889) 2002. "The Subtle Problems of Charity." In *The Jane Addams Reader*, edited by Jean B. Elshtain, 62–75. New York: Basic.

Ashar, Sameer M. 2007. "Public Interest Lawyers and Resistance Movements." *California Law Review* 95:1879–1926.

Cahn, Edgar S., and Jean C. Cahn. 1964. "The War on Poverty: A Civilian Perspective." *Yale Law Journal* 73:1317–1352.

Cummings, Scott L., and Deborah L. Rhode. 2009. "Public Interest Litigation: Insights from Theory and Practice." *Fordham Urban Law Journal* 36:603–652.

Diller, Rebekah, and Emily Savner. 2009. "Restoring Legal Aid for the Poor: A Call to End Draconian and Wasteful Restrictions." *Fordham Urban Law Journal* 36:687–712.

Handler, Joel, Ellen J. Hollingsworth, and Howard S. Erlanger. 1978. *Lawyers and the Pursuit of Legal Rights*. New York: Academic Press.

Hardingham, Lorraine B. 2004. "Integrity and Moral Residue: Nurses as Participants in a Moral Community." *Nursing Philosophy* 5:127–134.

Hilbink, Thomas, M. 2006. "Constructing Cause Lawyering: Professionalism, Politics, and Social Change in 1960s America." PhD diss., New York University.

Hosticka, Carl J. 1979. "We Don't Care about What Happened, We Only Care about What Is Going to Happen: Lawyer-Client Negotiations of Reality." *Social Problems* 26: 599–610.

Houseman, Alan W., and Linda E. Perle. 2007. *Securing Equal Justice for All: A Brief History of Civil Legal Assistance in the United States*. Washington, DC: Center for Law and Social Policy.

Jones, Lynn C. 2005. "Exploring the Sources of Cause and Career Correspondence among Cause Lawyers." In *The Worlds Cause Lawyers Make: Structure and Agency in Legal Practice*, edited by Austin Sarat and Stuart Scheingold, 203–238. Palo Alto, CA: Stanford University Press.

Kälvemark, Sofia, Anna T. Höglund, Mats G. Hansson, Peter Westerholm, and Bengt Arnetz. 2004. "Living with Conflicts—Ethical Dilemmas and Moral Distress in the Health Care System." *Social Science & Medicine* 58:1075–1084.

Katz, Jack. 1982. *Poor People's Lawyers in Transition*. New Brunswick, NJ: Rutgers University Press.

Legal Services Corporation. 2007. *Documenting the Justice Gap: The Current Unmet Civil Legal Needs of Low-Income Americans*. 2nd ed. http://www.lsc.gov/JusticeGap.pdf.

López, Gerald P. 1992. *Rebellious Lawyering: One Chicano's Vision of Progressive Law Practice*. Boulder, CO: Westview Press.

Mertz, Elizabeth. 2007. *The Language of Law School: Learning to "Think Like a Lawyer."* New York: Oxford University Press.

Raines, Marcia L. 2000. "Ethical Decision Making in Nurses: Relationships among Moral Reasoning, Coping Style, and Ethics Stress." *Journal of Nursing Administration's Healthcare Law, Ethics and Regulation* 2:29–41.

Rhode, Deborah L. 2008. "Public Interest Law: The Movement at Midlife." *Stanford Law Review* 60:2027–2086.

Rushton, Cynda H. 2006. "Defining and Addressing Moral Distress: Tools for Critical Nursing Leaders." *AACN Advanced Critical Care* 17:161–168.

Sarat, Austin, and William L. F. Felstiner. 1995. *Divorce Lawyers and Their Clients: Power and Meaning in the Legal Process*. New York: Oxford University Press.

Schon, Donald A. 1983. *The Reflective Practitioner: How Professionals Think in Action*. New York: Basic.

Seron, Carroll. 1996. *The Business of Practicing Law: The Work Lives of Solo and Small-Firm Attorneys*. Philadelphia: Temple University Press.

Shdaimah, Corey S. 2006. "Intersecting Identities: Cause Lawyers as Legal Professionals and Social Movement Actors." In *Cause Lawyering and Social Movements*, edited by Austin Sarat and Stuart Scheingold, 220–245. Stanford, CA: Stanford University Press.

———. 2008. "Not What They Expected: Legal Services Lawyers in the Eyes of Legal Services Clients." In *Cause Lawyers and Cultural Studies: Structure and Agency in Legal Practice*, edited by Austin Sarat and Stuart Scheingold, 359–387. New York: Cambridge University Press.

———. 2009a. "Losses of Professional Identity and Career Aspirations." In *Grief and Loss across the Lifespan: A Biopsychosocial Perspective*, edited by Carolyn Ambler Walter and Judith L. M. McCoyd, 241–245. New York: Springer.

———. 2009b. *Negotiating Justice: Legal Services Lawyering, Low-Income Clients, and the Quest for Social Change.* New York: New York University Press.

Simon, William H. 1994. "The Dark Secret of Progressive Lawyering: A Comment on Poverty Law Scholarship in the Post-Modern, Post-Reagan Era." *University of Miami Law Review* 48:1099–1114.

Thomas, Jackie T., and Melanie D. Otis. 2010. "Intrapsychic Correlates of Professional Quality of Life: Mindfulness, Empathy, and Emotional Separation." *Journal for the Society of Social Work Research* 1:83–98.

Tremblay, Paul R. 1999. "Acting 'A Very Moral Type of God': Triage Among Poor Clients." *Fordham Law Review* 67:2475–2532.

Trubek, Louise M. 1998. "Poverty Lawyering in the New Millennium." *Yale Law & Policy Review* 17:461–468.

Udell, David S. 1998. "Legal Services Restrictions: Lawyers in Florida, New York, Virginia, and Oregon Describe the Costs." *Yale Law & Policy Review* 17:337–368.

The Accountability Problem in Public Interest Practice
Old Paradigms and New Directions

Scott L. Cummings

An ethical paradox is built into the very concept of public interest lawyering. Public interest lawyers, by definition, seek to use law to achieve external benefits beyond their immediate clients; yet they remain ethically bound to advance those clients' interests. The centrality of the client is codified in the American Bar Association (ABA) Model Rules of Professional Conduct. Rule 1.2(a) requires a lawyer to "abide by a client's decisions concerning the *objectives* of representation" (emphasis added). The lawyer, in turn, is given broad discretion to select the *means* by which client objectives are pursued (Model Rule 1.2(a) cmt. 2).

This conventional means-ends dichotomy is meant to protect client autonomy by ensuring that the lawyer remains accountable to the client's definition of goals—while leaving flexibility to shape legal strategy to achieve them. There is a long-standing debate about the degree to which public interest lawyers, by advancing some vision of the collective good, undercut client autonomy—and whether this is sometimes necessary. Concerns about client autonomy are heightened in the context of *lawyering to achieve policy reform*, in which the goal of the representation is not simply to win client redress, but to change existing law for the benefit of a broader community. The most commonly identified vehicle of policy reform is the "impact lawsuit," in which public interest lawyers bring cases in court designed to achieve a particular legal outcome that has broad policy application. The classic example is the school desegregation campaign conducted by the NAACP Legal Defense and Educational Fund (LDF), which culminated in *Brown v. Board of Education* (1954). Typically, such cases are carefully selected by the lawyers to test the validity of a specific legal theory (hence the label "test case"), building scrupulously on precedent and presenting the legal issue in the context of facts and clients that the lawyers believe are most sympathetic. The premise is that a victory in court can create real change on the ground. This pursuit of policy reform crystallizes the "double agent" dilemma faced by public interest lawyers (Luban 1988, 319), who simultaneously seek to advance the interests of client and cause. As Sarat and Scheingold note (1998, 3), it is the lawyer's commitment to cause, and the rejection of professional role neutrality that it entails, which distinguishes her from the conventional "hired gun"—and envelopes her in controversy about to whom (or to what) she is ultimately accountable.

This chapter examines the "accountability problem" in public interest practice, focusing specifically on the case of lawyering for policy reform. In it, I make two basic claims. First, I suggest that contemporary analyses of public interest lawyer accountability, while raising legitimate concerns, have generally focused on the classic civil rights impact litigation model, in which strong lawyers (who work full-time in nonprofit groups to control case selection and execution) represent weak clients (who are diffuse and disorganized) in the pursuit of policy change through courts. Although this model of lawyering continues to be important, it represents only one slice of contemporary reform efforts, many of which diverge significantly from the classic impact model and raise a distinct set of ethical issues for public interest lawyers who engage in them.

This leads to my second claim, which is that an accurate appraisal of the accountability problem in public interest practice requires attention to the complex ways in which lawyers pursue policy reform in the contemporary legal and political arena. My focus in this chapter is on the emerging model of "multidimensional advocacy" that seeks policy reform, but does so across different domains (courts, legislatures, media), at different levels (federal, state, local), using different tactics (litigation, legislative advocacy, public education) (Cummings and NeJaime 2010, 1242). I draw on my own research to provide two contemporary illustrations. The first involves the pursuit of better conditions for low-wage workers, in which lawyers represent community-labor coalitions (relatively strong, but organizationally complex clients) to advance policy reform from the *bottom up*—in the sense that the community-based client groups (not the lawyers) are driving the policy reform strategy, which takes place in the local legislative arena. The second example comes out of the campaign for marriage equality in California, where public interest lawyers have pursued a more *top-down* reform strategy (led by the lawyers) across multiple policy domains (at the state rather than the local level) on behalf of a diverse constituency of same-sex couples. I conclude by exploring the accountability problems raised in each case.

The examples I use—the campaign to stop Walmart from developing a big-box store in the Los Angeles area and the campaign to advance marriage equality in California—draw on detailed case studies I produced (with Douglas NeJaime in the case of marriage equality) examining the relationship between legal mobilization and political change (Cummings 2007; Cummings and NeJaime 2010). For both case studies, I conducted in-depth, semistructured interviews with key actors (both lawyers and nonlawyers), which I supplemented with additional data from sources including media reports, legal cases and briefs, organizational documents, and secondary academic sources. The accounts in this chapter, including the firsthand reflections of the lawyers involved, come from those studies.

The Accountability Problem in Public Interest Practice

What constitutes the "public interest" is a deeply contested notion claimed by lawyers across the ideological spectrum (Southworth 2005). No definition of "public interest law" or its rivals (such as "cause lawyering") avoids debates on the margins of what qualifies (Scheingold and Sarat 2004, 5). Nonetheless, I use the term "public interest law" to refer to advocacy that promotes the interests and causes of constituencies that are relatively disadvantaged in the private market or political process—for instance, by serving those unable to afford a lawyer or advancing the policy aims of less powerful groups challenging governmental or corporate practice. The iconic public interest law groups—such as LDF—have been structured as nongovernmental organizations (NGOs), yet the NGO sector is only one part of the broader public interest law industry, which includes for-profit and governmental lawyers (Handler, Ginsberg, and Snow 1978). On the for-profit side are small firms that pursue public interest missions by taking on cases in areas like civil rights, environmental justice, and consumer law; collecting court-awarded or contingency fees; and sometimes supplementing mission-driven cases with commercial ones to pay the bills (Cummings, forthcoming). Government lawyers in places such as the US Department of Justice, state attorneys general, and local prosecutors' and public defenders' offices may also be considered public interest lawyers. Across these locations, the nature and degree of client accountability issues are shaped by the type of clients, fee arrangements, and organizational practice norms in these distinct venues.

While opponents of public interest lawyers have often couched their opposition in terms of concerns about lawyer accountability, critiques have also been leveled by those generally sympathetic to the aims of the public interest law movement (Simon 2004). The central target of critical scholarship is the liberal public interest lawyer working in an NGO—and financially independent from clients—who undertakes impact litigation asserting rights that affect a larger community. Accountability concerns relate to the appropriate allocation of control among the actors with a stake in such cases: lawyers, clients, and the community. Such concerns center on two different phases of litigation.

The first is client selection. For impact-oriented legal groups like the American Civil Liberties Union (ACLU) or LDF, client selection is closely linked to the group's substantive aims: Clients are chosen if their cases present issues that promote the group's policy agenda. As a doctrinal matter, it is at the selection stage that lawyer autonomy is at its apex. Lawyers have a constitutionally protected right to solicit clients for cause-advancing cases, subject to limits on abusive practices that involve "coercion, duress or harassment" (Model Rule 7.3).[1] Yet critics of cause-driven case selection have focused on its potential to confer unaccountable power on individual lawyers to advance a political agenda through courts (Hegland 1971).

The strong version of this critique holds that the public interest lawyer, by effectively manufacturing test cases to advance substantive legal rights identified as important *by the lawyer,* uses the legal system to engage in policy-making without having to answer to the very group he purports to help. Under this view, the lawyer lacks accountability either to clients or the broader community, from which he usurps the right to pursue redress through democratic channels.

The weaker version of this accountability critique focuses on differences of opinion within the affected community and the lawyer's role in facilitating the assertion of some political views over others. Here, the claim is not that the public interest lawyer is a rogue rights claimer, but rather that she effectively chooses sides in a contested policy debate—perhaps helping minority factions to pursue a policy agenda that is at odds with the will of the majority of the affected community.

Similar accountability problems may also arise during litigation, when the public interest lawyer must negotiate a set of conflicts either (1) between the

---

1. The First Amendment right of public interest law groups to solicit clients for cases that advance their political missions was upheld in *In re Primus* (1978).

lawyer's policy goals and the client's interests or (2) among different factions within the client constituency (Rhode 1982). The first problem relates to the potential for the divergent interests of lawyer and client to distort representation in ways that undermine client or community autonomy. This problem arises either because the individual clients are relatively weak or the class of clients is relatively diffuse, which permits the lawyer to make crucial case decisions, persuading the clients (or their representatives) to go along. The classic formulation of this problem is posed by Luban (1988, 320), who posits a situation in which a client wants to settle a case that the lawyer thinks should be litigated to judgment to establish a broader precedent. Model Rule 1.2(a) requires deference to the client's wishes should she desire to settle. But the issue is whether her lawyer, who has many tools of persuasion that can be deployed (Simon 1991), may convince the client otherwise for the good of the cause. This act of persuasion may doubly disempower clients: Not only do they fail to get what they want out of the lawsuit, but their experience with their lawyers reproduces their sense of marginalization in society (Alfieri 1991; White 1990).

The problem is heightened in the context of multiparty representation in which the community's interests are diverse and even conflictual. Lawyers may exercise their power to favor some factions over others in ways that are unaccountable to the broader community—and may end up serving a different set of "masters." Bell (1976) articulated this concern most forcefully when he questioned whether LDF's commitment to desegregation—supported by its middle-class white and black constituents—ignored the needs of black communities by privileging litigation to achieve integration over political strategies to promote educational quality.

The Strategic Context: Beyond Impact Litigation

Are these accountability concerns salient for contemporary public interest practice? To answer requires close attention to what public interest lawyers actually do in practice, which pushes us to look beyond the civil rights impact litigation paradigm to new models of lawyering for policy reform. This section explores two case studies of lawyering that point in very different directions. One is toward the grassroots level, where "community lawyering" strategies have evolved to promote change from the "bottom up." The other looks to courts, but through the lens of a multidimensional advocacy model that operates across policymaking domains; it remains relatively lawyer driven, however, and hence still "top down."

Law Reform from the Bottom Up: Accountable Development

Bottom-up styles of lawyering have been associated with the community economic development (CED) movement, which has focused on mobilizing community participation in economic revitalization efforts, especially the creation of partnerships to promote affordable housing and job creation (Cummings 2001). In contrast to the impact litigator, the CED lawyer's role requires the type of nonadversarial transactional skills that are the stock-in-trade of the corporate bar. One criticism of the CED movement has focused on its lack of a policy reform agenda. This criticism has contributed to an alternative vision of grassroots practice that builds on community organizing, labor organizing, and social movement models to enact legal reforms that promote "economic justice" (Cummings 2001, 478–483). A prominent example has been the emergence of the "accountable development" movement in Los Angeles, in which community-labor coalitions have sought to change city redevelopment practices through grassroots campaigns aimed at increasing community participation in the planning process and forcing local developers and governmental officials to commit to redevelopment projects that are responsive to the needs of low-income residents. In these campaigns, "the lawyer is not the protagonist" (Gordon 2007, 2133). Instead, the lawyer is asked to represent a coalition of organizations in situations in which grassroots organizing and community building have already occurred and objectives defined.

To illustrate this type of bottom-up reform lawyering, I draw on a case study (Cummings 2007) of legal advocacy involving the community-labor campaign to exclude Walmart from Inglewood, California—a separately incorporated city in Los Angeles county. That campaign was developed and led by the Los Angeles Alliance for a New Economy (LAANE), a community organization formed in 1993 by the Hotel Employees and Restaurant Union Local 11 to move beyond conventional union organizing to more effectively address the growth of low-wage work. The group, financially supported by labor unions and philanthropic sources, scored its first major success spearheading the enactment of the Los Angeles living wage law in 1997. It was directed by Madeline Janis (a public interest lawyer by training with substantial advocacy and policy experience) and staffed by researchers and organizers who developed "comprehensive campaigns" (Janis-Aparacio and Tynan 2005)—which combined organizing, policy advocacy, research, communications, fundraising, and legal advocacy—to advance local policy reforms to improve conditions in geographically stable low-wage sectors, such as the hospitality, transportation, and grocery industries.

Beginning in 2003, LAANE collaborated with the United Food and Commercial Workers Union (UFCW) Local 770 to stop the development of what would have been the first Walmart Supercenter in metropolitan Los Angeles. This "site fight" campaign was advanced by the Coalition for a Better Inglewood (CBI), an alliance of groups organized by LAANE (which played the key leadership role in the coalition) that included the UFCW and ACORN (Association of Community Organizations for Reform Now), in addition to several other community-based organizations and progressive faith-based groups. The campaign was framed by the threat that Walmart's Supercenter format—which housed a nonunionized grocery department—posed to the unionized grocery sector in Southern California, which Walmart was targeting for expansion. Inglewood was the line in the sand drawn by the UCFW and its allies, which believed that Walmart's entry into the Los Angeles area would weaken union bargaining power in negotiating with local grocery chains (that could invoke Supercenter competition as a reason to cut wages and benefits). To defend Inglewood against Walmart's entry, CBI deployed a strategy that combined grassroots organizing and litigation to mobilize Inglewood voters to defeat a 2003 Walmart-sponsored ballot initiative, Measure 04-A, which would have circumvented the normal environmental and land use review process to automatically authorize the proposed Supercenter—taking the decision away from a city council hostile to the development.

On the organizing side, CBI pursued a two-pronged strategy—developed primarily by organizers at LAANE—that combined a sophisticated public relations campaign with a get-out-the-vote drive to defeat Measure 04-A at the ballot box. This organizing was coordinated with a legal campaign that was designed to give CBI an opportunity to defeat the Walmart initiative in court, while also reinforcing the grassroots effort. CBI's leaders therefore viewed the legal campaign as part of a comprehensive strategy to use all available tools to gain a "win"—in this case, thwarting the Supercenter development.

To advance the legal campaign, the UFCW and LAANE jointly retained Margo Feinberg, a longtime labor lawyer at a small union-side firm, to coordinate strategy. Feinberg, an expert in neither land use nor election law, contacted Jan Chatten-Brown, an environmental and land use lawyer whom she knew through their work on progressive causes. Chatten-Brown was also not an election law expert, but her practice background was deemed critical to challenging an initiative that sought to circumvent conventional environmental and land use processes. Her firm, Chatten-Brown & Associates, was a small private public interest law office that represented citizen groups and environmental organizations. Chatten-Brown formally represented both LAANE and CBI, although client communications were generally with LAANE representatives, and LAANE paid for the legal work on a reduced-fee basis.

Chatten-Brown's firm focused on analyzing the legality of the initiative from constitutional and statutory perspectives. Meanwhile, CBI assembled a larger team of lawyers to consult on the case. Feinberg was heavily involved in coordinating the team, which included practicing and academic lawyers who were identified for their capacity to contribute relevant expertise and bring legitimacy to the cause. One member of this team was David Pettit, a partner at Caldwell Leslie, a small commercial litigation firm. Pettit started out as a legal aid lawyer and had worked for more than a decade at Caldwell Leslie as a land use specialist. He joined the Inglewood team as pro bono counsel to LAANE. LAANE's Janis was also on the team, where she was joined by then-USC law professor Erwin Chemerinsky and Sean Hecht, executive director of UCLA's Environmental Law Center.

A key question faced by the legal team at the outset was whether to file a pre-election challenge to block the initiative or to wait until after the election to sue in the event that Measure 04-A passed. Though Chatten-Brown was confident about winning a post-election challenge, she and other members on the legal team were less sanguine about the prospects of prevailing on pre-election review, given the strong judicial bias against preempting the electoral process absent a clear showing of an initiative's invalidity. Nonetheless, the legal team agreed to pursue a pre-election challenge to block the initiative based on two considerations. First, the legal team, in consultation with LAANE organizers Tracy Gray-Barkan and Lizette Hernandez, agreed that they should take advantage of the outside chance to succeed on the merits to halt the initiative. In fact, LAANE was concerned about its ability to win the ballot initiative outright and thus viewed litigation as perhaps its best chance of gaining victory in Inglewood. Second, LAANE believed that even if the pre-election lawsuit proved unsuccessful, it would still put Walmart on notice that, if it won the ballot initiative, it would face a strong legal challenge that would at the very least tie up the plan in court. In addition, even if the lawsuit did not stop the ballot initiative, CBI believed that the publicity it created would amplify its central argument: that Walmart was attempting to place itself "above the law."

The court, in what came as no surprise, rejected the pre-election challenge, holding that the petitioners had not made a "clear/compelling showing of invalidity" that would warrant interfering with "the people's constitutional right of initiative." The legal team then turned to prepare for a post-election lawsuit to invalidate Measure 04-A if it passed. Chatten-Brown's firm again took the role of lead counsel in drafting the post-election filing, with Pettit, Feinberg, and Hecht involved in strategy discussions and substantive reviews of the pleadings. In addition, Feinberg coordinated an effort to put together lawyers who would file a range of amicus briefs with the court on behalf of organizations opposing the initiative from different legal perspectives. The CBI organizers focused their energy on mobilizing voters to defeat Measure 04-A at the ballot box.

In the end, the success of the grassroots campaign rendered a post-election lawsuit moot as Inglewood voters sent Measure 04-A to defeat by a decisive margin. It was Walmart's first ballot-box defeat and an embarrassing setback in the company's Southern California expansion plans, particularly in light of the fact that Walmart had spent over $1 million to secure the initiative's passage.

The momentum from the campaign carried over to the enactment of innovative citywide Superstore Ordinances—first in Los Angeles, then in Inglewood—that made any future effort by Walmart to open a Supercenter more difficult. UFCW and LAANE lawyer Margo Feinberg took the lead in coordinating with the Los Angeles City Attorney's Office on drafting the new ordinance. She started by discussing the central policy objectives with John Grant, general counsel at the UFCW, along with Roxana Tynan, a nonlawyer who directed LAANE's Accountable Development project, and Madeline Janis. Feinberg produced and circulated drafts based on this policy input and then made revisions based on feedback from the group. Feinberg also testified and prepared other community members to testify at a Los Angeles city council hearing to build a strong public record for the ordinance. She was further involved in briefing the council on the goals of the ordinance and coordinating with council member staff on executing changes. LAANE staff and the UFCW's Grant managed the process of educating council members and coordinating community input. Grant also mobilized new constituencies in support of the ordinance such as affordable housing groups and legal aid lawyers. Despite early hostility, Walmart eventually accepted the ordinance once it became clear that it had the overwhelming support of the city council. In August 2004, after roughly three months of negotiations, Los Angeles passed the nation's first

Superstores Ordinance requiring an economic impact analysis demonstrating the absence of adverse economic impacts prior to big-box approval. A similar ordinance, also drafted by Feinberg, was enacted in Inglewood two years later.

Law Reform from the Top Down: Marriage Equality

The bottom-up reform strategy exemplified by the Inglewood Walmart case may be contrasted with the movement for marriage equality, which shares much in common with the classic top-down litigation model of the civil rights movement. Yet there are also crucial distinctions, as a recent analysis of the California campaign for marriage equality suggests (Cummings and NeJaime 2010).

In contrast to the classic test case approach, marriage equality lawyers in California did not define the legal right to marry as their immediate objective and initiate a litigation campaign to achieve it. Rather, comprehensive domestic partnership (DP)—achieved legislatively—was the initial goal. The tactical decision to deemphasize marriage and avoid courts was devised by a group of leading LGBT rights movement lawyers in California. Lawyers affiliated with the key LGBT legal organizations—Lambda Legal, the National Center for Lesbian Rights (NCLR), and the ACLU's national Lesbian and Gay Rights Project—combined elite academic credentials with deep experience in the LGBT movement. At Lambda Legal, the main lawyers were Legal Director Jon Davidson and Jennifer Pizer (who became National Marriage Project director in 2008); at NCLR, it was Executive Director Kate Kendell and Shannon Minter; and at the ACLU, it was Matt Coles, director of the national Lesbian and Gay Rights Project. These lawyers worked in a national coalition with their East Coast counterparts, particularly Lambda Legal's Evan Wolfson in New York.

After the US Supreme Court's decision in *Bowers v. Hardwick* (1986) upholding state sodomy laws, movement lawyers reached a consensus in the late 1990s that the marriage campaign had to proceed state by state. They concluded, according to Pizer, that "California would not be the place" where marriage litigation was launched. By far the most important factor militating against litigation was the ease with which California's constitution could be amended to erase any gain won through the courts. The key question, according to Pizer, was: "If we were to win in the [California] Supreme Court, what would we need to do to hold on to it?" The answer was clear: Marriage equality supporters would have to be able to mobilize enough voters to thwart the initiative to bar same-sex couples from marriage that would surely come. This, they decided, they could not yet do.

Instead, the lawyers pursued a strategy to enact a statewide comprehensive DP regime. The quest for DP initially reflected the broader—and longstanding—ambivalence about the centrality of marriage within the LGBT community. In the late 1980s, Lambda Legal's executive director, Tom Stoddard, and legal director, Paula Ettelbrick, debated the merits of the marriage question in a series of articles in an LGBT publication (Stoddard 1989; Ettelbrick 1989). Stoddard argued that the right to marry was essential to lesbian and gay citizenship and that marriage itself could remedy many of the inequities lesbian and gay families faced. Ettelbrick, in contrast, urged the movement to continue to serve diverse family forms rather than prioritize marriage, which was steeped in gender stereotypes.

The debate around the first DP legislation in California in the late 1990s—a DP registry bill known as AB 26—reflected the two poles of this disagreement. One side viewed DP as a way to move the legal status of same-sex couples incrementally closer to marriage, eventually setting the stage for marriage equality. The second, expressed by Davidson and Coles, viewed DP as a true alternative to marriage: In their view, the goal was "to have a world in which marriage would be open to everyone, and something that provided a less highly defined but still significant safety net—like domestic partnership—would also be available to everyone."

This view, however, gradually lost sway as the focus on marriage as the ultimate goal became ascendant within the LGBT rights community. One reason for this was the vigor with which *opponents* of marriage equality pursued their agenda—which had the effect of heightening the political importance of marriage within movement circles and drawing more resources to its defense. In 2000, marriage equality opponents succeeded in the passage of Proposition 22, amending the Family Code to prohibit California from recognizing any marriage by same-sex couples. The success of Proposition 22 provoked LGBT community dissatisfaction with the absence of a strong pro-marriage political group and thus sparked the development of Equality California—headed by the lawyer and political activist Geof Kors—as the public education and legislative advocacy arm of the marriage equality movement.[2] The emergence of a powerful pro-marriage political organization began to focus the movement's agenda more directly on marriage equality as the principal objective. Toward

2. Equality California's precursor was a group called the California Alliance for Pride and Equality (CAPE), which was formed in 1998. After Proposition 22 passed, CAPE's leader stepped down in the face of criticism; Kors took over and became executive director in 2001.

this end, Equality California spearheaded the drive for comprehensive DP benefits—not simply as a goal in its own right but as a "stepping stone" for moving incrementally closer to marriage.

Comprehensive DP was achieved in 2003, in a bill drafted by Lambda Legal's Davidson and Pizer, and advanced through the legislature with Kors coordinating pressure on key members. The bill provided in sweeping language that domestic partners "shall have the same rights, protections, and benefits, and shall be subject to the same responsibilities, obligations and duties under law . . . as are granted to and imposed upon spouses." Although this victory was significant on its own terms, the language of the bill also showed how the lawyers had come to view DP with an eye toward eventual marriage litigation. According to Kors, the advocates "were able to create through the legislative process a body of findings and policy on same-sex couples [showing] how they are equal in every way . . . [to] set up suspect class arguments" for eventual marriage litigation.

Yet litigation was not yet what movement lawyers wanted. To the contrary, at a 2003 meeting at the UCLA School of Law held to debate the merits of an affirmative marriage challenge, the idea of launching a marriage case was roundly rejected. The meeting was attended by all of the major LGBT rights lawyers and leading legal academics whose work touched on LGBT themes. Davidson circulated a persuasive memo on the ballot initiative process, which warned that "failure to consider [whether an anti-marriage initiative could be defeated at the polls] could make affirmative marriage litigation not only futile, but . . . set back future attempts to obtain both judicial and legislative reform to the marriage laws." Marriage litigation was again deferred. As Lambda Legal's Pizer put it: "Smart people had thought about it. We had a plan."

The plan unraveled in early 2004 when newly elected San Francisco Mayor Gavin Newsom, dismayed by President George Bush's State of the Union speech vowing to "protect" marriage from "activist judges" and emboldened by the Massachusetts Supreme Judicial Court's decision affirming the right of same-sex couples to marry, decided to start issuing marriage licenses to same-sex couples. Despite warnings from NCLR's Kendell and Minter, who "initially tried to talk him out of it," Newsom proceeded with his plan, which was immediately challenged in court by Christian Right legal groups. For the lawyers who had labored so carefully to control the timing and nature of any marriage challenge, the Newsom decision immediately transformed the political landscape. Overnight, as Pizer recalled, the question for the lawyers became: "What part of our strategy can we salvage?"

The consequence of Newsom's decision was that the lawyers' efforts to keep the marriage issue out of court broke down. In the immediate aftermath, legal challenges were filed by two groups: one by the Proposition 22 Legal Defense and Education Fund, represented by the Christian conservative Alliance Defense Fund (ADF), and the other by the Campaign for California Families, represented by Liberty Counsel. The San Francisco City Attorney's Office defended the legality of the marriages.

The movement lawyers sought to maintain involvement by moving to intervene. In the ADF suit, NCLR, Lambda Legal, and the ACLU intervened on behalf of a selected group of married same-sex couples, which included long-time partners and activists Del Martin, 83, and Phyllis Lyon, 79. Their goal was to shape the arguments on the question of the constitutional validity of California's ban on marriage by same-sex couples, which would inevitably be raised in the cases. The adjudication of the constitutional issue was made even more likely with the filing of a private lawsuit directly challenging the constitutionality of California's marriage scheme. Movement lawyers also intervened (on behalf of client Equality California) in this private suit, which was brought by high-profile Los Angeles attorney Gloria Allred on behalf of two same-sex couples denied marriage licenses. This was followed by a suit to enforce existing California marriage laws brought by the California attorney general and ultimately led to a pivotal California Supreme Court order that invited an affirmative constitutional challenge to the marriage laws.

With the constitutionality of the marriage statutes clearly in play, the immediate question—for both the San Francisco city attorney and LGBT rights lawyers—was: "Do we file a direct constitutional challenge?" Movement lawyers acted decisively to do so. They recognized the risks of litigating the constitutional question, but believed that if they did not strike at that moment, someone else would, with potentially damaging effects. Thus, on March 12, 2004, the day after the San Francisco city attorney filed a similar suit, NCLR, Lambda Legal, and the ACLU, along with pro bono lawyers from the law firm Heller Ehrman, brought a constitutional challenge, titled *Woo v. Lockyer* (2004), on behalf of Equality California and 12 same-sex couples selected by the attorneys.

The California Supreme Court ultimately decided this case in a sweeping victory for the marriage equality movement. The court held that California law limiting marriage to a man and a woman violated state constitutional due process and equal protection guarantees (*In re Marriage Cases*, 2008). What was seen as a pipe dream only five years earlier had become a legal reality in

California. Despite themselves, lawyers for marriage equality had succeeded in establishing it as a state constitutional right.

Yet the taste of victory was short lived. As predicted, foes of marriage equality swiftly organized a ballot initiative to amend the California constitution to prohibit marriage by same-sex couples. After a bitter and divisive campaign, California voters narrowly passed the ban, known as Proposition 8, in November 2008. Movement lawyers filed a state challenge to Proposition 8 on technical voting law grounds, which the California Supreme Court rejected. Yet just after the state supreme court issued its decision upholding Proposition 8, a federal lawsuit was announced—not by movement lawyers, but by legal elites and ideological opposites: Ted Olson, who represented George W. Bush in the 2000 recount and then served as his solicitor general, and David Boies, a prominent trial lawyer who represented Al Gore in the 2000 election recount. The case was orchestrated by Los Angeles political strategist Chad Griffin, who had worked on Bill Clinton's 1992 presidential campaign and then ran a foundation for Rob Reiner. A mutual friend put Olson in touch with Griffin, who selected the plaintiffs and set up the American Foundation for Equal Rights (AFER) to fund the litigation. Olson's firm, Gibson Dunn & Crutcher, agreed to take the case on a hybrid-fee arrangement in which it would donate the first $100,000 worth of services and then collect "flat fees for the various stages," ultimately amounting to millions of dollars. Olson then brought in Boies.

In May 2009, Olson and his colleagues discussed the merits of a possible suit with Lambda Legal's Davidson and Pizer and ACLU of Southern California Director Ramona Ripston and Legal Director Mark Rosenbaum. After the conclusion of these discussions, Olson decided to proceed with the lawsuit, *Perry v. Schwarzenegger* (2010). Leaders of LGBT legal groups claimed they did not learn of the filing until it was officially announced. On that same day—and without knowledge of the pending announcement of *Perry*—LGBT rights lawyers issued an updated version of a joint statement called "Why the Ballot Box and Not the Courts Should Be the Next Step on Marriage in California," arguing that "we need to go back to the voters."

Movement lawyers then faced a decision about how to respond to the federal suit they had fought for so long to prevent. Their initial strategy was to cooperate with Olson and Boies, but not to intervene or file a parallel suit. They asked themselves: "Would our participation make a difference?" Based on their assessment of the risks of the lawsuit, coupled with their respect for the litigation skills of Olson and Boies, they determined that the answer was no. Instead, they decided to play an amicus role. District Court Judge Vaughn Walker's call for an evidentiary hearing changed the lawyers' position. Olson initially resisted having a hearing, preferring to tee up the constitutional issues for eventual review by the US Supreme Court. The movement lawyers were concerned that Olson's resistance to a hearing meant that he would not mount a strong effort if one were ordered. Accordingly, the ACLU, Lambda Legal, and NCLR moved to intervene to assist in the development of the factual record. Their intervention motion was also a way to put pressure on Olson and Boies to take the call for evidence seriously. The *Perry* lawyers resisted the intervention, not wanting to have "five captains of the ship." In the end, the district court denied the LGBT rights groups' motion on the ground that the interests of same-sex couples were already represented by the plaintiffs, but permitted the San Francisco City Attorney's Office to intervene as the entity responsible for enforcing the law.

Back in their amicus capacity, the movement lawyers in *Perry* sought to emphasize "the singular nature of the case presented by Proposition 8, and the California-focused analysis that accordingly is warranted." By asking the court to rule in favor of the plaintiffs on narrow state-specific grounds, the lawyers sought to frame the issues in a way that had the greatest chance of being upheld by the US Supreme Court on review. Thus far, their strategy has seemed to work: After trial, Judge Walker struck down Proposition 8 on due process and equal protection grounds in an opinion that emphasized the unique nature of the California case (*Perry v. Schwarzenegger*, 2010). His order was stayed pending appeal, which analysts agree will ultimately wind up in the US Supreme Court—precisely the place that movement lawyers spent the last decade trying to avoid.

Accountability in Multidimensional Advocacy

These cases point to alternative models of lawyering for policy reform that raise distinct ethical challenges for the public interest lawyers who engage in them. In particular, they highlight the power of "multidimensional advocacy," which departs from the impact litigation paradigm by (1) decentering courts as the desired venue of policy change; (2) deemphasizing the federal level as the primary advocacy arena; (3) broadening the tactical repertoire of reform to include legislative and grassroots strategies; and (4) engaging different types of client groups, some highly organized, with distinct claims to represent broader constituencies. As I suggest in this section, multidimensional advocacy does not avoid accountability concerns; rather, it presents new challenges for lawyers to navigate.

Strong Clients at the Grassroots Level

In the accountable development context, the salient lawyering features are (1) the presence of organizationally complex clients, allied in a coalition, with relatively stronger and weaker members; (2) the assembly of legal teams based on expertise, but not (necessarily) long-term commitment to an overarching (in this case, anti-Walmart) cause; and (3) the clients' formulation and execution of a discrete policy objective targeted at the local policy arena. As the case study suggests, this structure mitigates the problem of lawyer domination of clients, but potentially aggravates the problem of the more powerful and vocal client constituency (here, organized labor) disproportionately influencing the agenda setting and tactical aspects of the campaign.

In the anti-Walmart campaign, the nature of the client group and the approach of the lawyers diminished concerns about the disempowering impact of legal expertise on client mobilization. On the client end, LAANE was a relatively powerful community organization, drawing political clout and resources from its labor affiliation, and governed by politically savvy and influential leaders—particularly its executive director, Madeline Janis, who understood when and how to use law as a strategic tool and who would not be intimidated by other lawyers. The strength and coherence of LAANE's leadership structure tended to insulate it from undue influence from outside lawyers; moreover, LAANE operated as a sophisticated consumer of legal services, selecting outside counsel based on how well the lawyers advanced LAANE's objectives. In making this selection, LAANE's representatives sought out the best technical lawyers for the specific legal tasks, which meant that they evaluated outside counsel based on conventional metrics of legal expertise and capacity—they did not look for lawyers to undertake organizing functions, which they viewed as appropriately kept within LAANE's purview. Because LAANE and CBI approached the lawyers as empowered political actors, the lawyering itself focused on achieving a result defined by the coalition rather than on promoting goals envisioned by the lawyers who represented them.

For their part, the lawyers who worked on the campaign approached their engagement with LAANE and CBI from a perspective that mitigated concerns about client autonomy. For one, they were generally private sector lawyers retained by the clients to achieve a well-specified result. Their role conception, informed by their position in the market, was quite conventional. The Chatten-Brown lawyers were specifically brought into the case because of their legal expertise in land use, not because of their ideological allegiance to the labor movement. From this perspective, the lawyer-client relationship looked to some degree like a conventional outside counsel arrangement, in which a law firm is retained to assist an organizational client with a discrete objective.

David Pettit, the small firm lawyer retained by LAANE to be part of the legal team, adopted what he termed the "David Binder method" of client representation, referring to his UCLA Law School professor and one of the founders of clinical legal education—famous for his seminal text in client counseling that advocates a "client-centered" approach designed to protect client autonomy in all aspects of representation (Binder et al. 2004). Thus, Pettit approached his ongoing relationship with LAANE from a very deferential counseling perspective, talking to its representatives about their short- and long-term objectives and basing his approach in any particular campaign on their articulated goals. Feinberg approached her role as coalition lawyer from a similar perspective. Particularly when it came to drafting the Superstore Ordinances, she listened to what coalition members emphasized as their policy interests and then produced multiple drafts based on their input, leaving it to the coalition members to provide feedback for additional changes and to accept the version they believed best served their objectives.

Though Inglewood was, at bottom, a labor rights campaign, its focus on leveraging labor reform through local land use planning meant that land use and environmental lawyers were enlisted in the service of labor movement objectives. Though all of the lawyers involved contributed to the ultimate union-defined goal of blocking Walmart to advance labor standards, each approached the engagement with a unique notion of the "cause." Chatten-Brown accepted the Inglewood case (at a reduced-fee rate) as a way of challenging what she viewed as an instance of bad land use planning on behalf of a company that she held in low regard from an environmental perspective. For Pettit, the land use attorney, the cause was framed in terms of promoting community participation though the framework of land use planning. Because these lawyers were not driven by the same goal as the UFCW (or even LAANE), they may have been less invested in the overarching labor strategy and thus less likely to exert strong control over the campaign. Unlike the impact litigation context in which lawyers work over long time periods to put together interlocking cases to build precedent, here the architect of broader strategy was the community group, LAANE, and the lawyers contributed technical skill to advance LAANE's articulated plan.

The conventional nature of the lawyer-client relationship nonetheless raised its own accountability questions. Even within the confines of the lawyer-client relationship as constructed by the parties, the potential for conflicts was ripe. First, there were complexities involved in representing both a multi-organizational coalition (CBI) and the lead organizing group (LAANE) within the same case. Group representation raises difficult questions about who speaks for the group, but here those questions were exacerbated because CBI itself was an amalgam of several groups, which operated with a range of organizational formality and were endowed with very different resources. On the one hand, CBI included representatives from LAANE and the UFCW, who brought critical financial and organizational resources; on the other, CBI contained more loosely constituted resident and faith-based groups that lent credibility and authenticity, but did not have the same decision-making clout. This created inherent questions of governance and authority to make decisions on behalf of the entire coalition—made more difficult by the fact that LAANE was also named as a separate party to the litigation and was paying for the legal representation. Thus, during the course of the lawsuit, the Chatten-Brown lawyers coordinated primarily with LAANE representatives as the spokespersons for the broader group. This arrangement, in part, proceeded by necessity, with LAANE serving as the nodal point in a broader network and thus well positioned to assimilate the views of coalition members and present a unified point of view to the lawyers. However, the lack of formal specification of any type of governance structure within the coalition format complicated the lines of client communication.

This fluidity was apparent in the ways that the other members of the legal team perceived the "clients" to whom they owed allegiance. Pettit viewed himself as LAANE's lawyer and dealt with Janis as the ultimate decision maker. The UFCW's Grant viewed his role less as legal counsel than as an officer of the union accountable to its membership (and leaders) and made decisions based on how campaign actions would affect the broader labor movement. Feinberg was on retainer with the UFCW, where she communicated with its president and Grant; she was also on retainer with LAANE, where she dealt primarily with Janis. When conflicts arose, she let the two organizations work them out and then pursued the commonly agreed-on strategy.

The existence of multiple attorneys representing relatively powerful client groups may have mitigated the potential for client domination, but it also underscored the possible divisions between those clients and the broader "community" represented by CBI, suggesting how difficult it is for public interest lawyers to be accountable to the community at large, rather than a particular interest group within it. An important division revealed in the anti-Walmart campaign was between class- and race-based conceptions of community. In Inglewood, Walmart was able to drive a wedge between the labor-backed CBI and traditional African American groups like the Urban League and NAACP, which supported the Supercenter development. As a result, CBI lawyers could not claim to represent an entire working-class community of color in its fight against Walmart—but rather simply one faction within it. In this way, the lawyers could be viewed as choosing sides in an intracommunity dispute in a similar fashion to the LDF desegregation lawyers criticized by Bell (1976). One crucial difference is that in a bottom-up campaign, it is the power of nonlegal client groups—such as LAANE—that drives the policy choice, rather than the lawyers themselves. But this also highlights the central trade-off of the bottom-up model: As client groups take the lead in shaping and executing the policy objective, the more powerful among them wield disproportionate influence in the process of defining what constitutes the authentic "community" interest. The lawyers then facilitate the groups' exercise of power. In this sense, bottom-up strategies do not avoid accountability problems, but rather transfer the central locus of conflict from the relationship between lawyers and clients to that between clients and the broader communities they purport to represent.

Strong Lawyers across Policy Domains

The marriage equality case was characterized by (1) a stable and coherent team of movement lawyers involved in the long-term planning and execution of strategy; (2) contests over the ultimate policy objective and how best to achieve it; (3) simultaneous advocacy within multiple policymaking venues, in which the lawyers' formal connection to clients varied; and (4) the existence of a diffuse and diverse constituency. On one level, these factors interacted to enhance lawyer decision-making power over means and ends—particularly when the marriage issue was squarely presented in court. However, the fact that the lawyers were embedded in larger policymaking networks also brought them into connection with, and made them more responsive to, other stakeholders in ways that limited their ability to dominate the policy agenda and thereby enhanced accountability to the community.

A key similarity between the marriage equality and classic civil rights litigation model is the nature of the legal team, composed of activist lawyers with strong normative commitments who work to promote well-defined agendas over long periods of time. Thus, in contrast to the accountable development case, in which disparate lawyers came together in an ad hoc alliance to advance an anti-Walmart campaign that attracted them for different policy reasons, the marriage campaign is marked by the constant presence of a core team of committed lawyers whose dedication to the ultimate goal of marriage equality has powered their more than decade-long support of the movement. The lawyers from Lambda Legal, NCLR, and the ACLU, in particular, have been the chief architects of the policy reform strategy, have participated in every stage of movement building, and have struggled to control the agenda so as to avoid a federal constitutional showdown. Because from an early stage the marriage equality movement has been highly legalized, the lawyers have been the central "policy entrepreneurs" (Mather 1998) and have often acted based on their own sense of strategic necessity. Although they have collaborated with other lawyers—notably the San Francisco City Attorney's Office in the California Supreme Court marriage case—the continuity of their leadership over time is striking. This continuity allowed them to assert control over the definition and execution of the policy agenda. Their control of the agenda, however, has never been absolute—but rather always shaped by interactions with activists and community members in other domains and constrained by the presence of powerful opponent groups.

From the beginning, the question of who got to decide whether marriage should be the central movement goal was deeply contested. This contest was evident in the initial push to pass a statewide DP registry in 1999. Although some marriage advocates had already begun to view DP as a "stepping stone" toward marriage, others saw DP as an end in itself—a distinct system of legal protections that would make sense for those to whom marriage was undesirable or inapplicable. Over time, calls for marriage became more univocal, but this occurred against the backdrop of complex political dynamics. Within movement circles, a key development was the success of marriage proponents in pushing their agenda in the face of broader ambivalence about alternative family structures. In California, the key moment came with the passage of comprehensive DP, which incorporated legislative findings designed to "set up suspect class arguments" in an eventual marriage case. Yet for those who were uneasy with giving priority to marriage, the merger of DP and marriage was less a strategic innovation than a cause for concern. From this point of view, DP "was hijacked by marriage folks."

Control of the tactical agenda was similarly contested throughout the marriage equality movement. Early on, the movement lawyers were relatively successful in dissuading others from litigating what the movement lawyers viewed as ill-advised marriage cases. As James Esseks, director of the ACLU LGBT Project, put it, "We spent lot of time talking people down from that particular ledge." The 2003 UCLA meeting was convened, in part, to dissuade some younger lawyers from moving forward with a contemplated lawsuit. But this control unraveled in the face of events. Mayor Newsom's decision to issue marriage licenses provoked legal challenges that ultimately led to the favorable California Supreme Court decision—swiftly reversed by Proposition 8. After Proposition 8 was passed, movement lawyers issued a statement opposing a federal challenge and attempted to dissuade Olson and Boies from filing one—but to no avail.

The fact that the marriage equality lawyers operated across policy domains—courts, the legislature, and the ballot initiative process—also produced accountability trade-offs. On the one hand, it was clear that they were only loosely constrained by formal client obligations. Indeed, there appears to be greater lawyer flexibility in multivenue campaigns because the lawyers move into policymaking domains where they may represent a constituency's interests—but not clients per se (and thus the rules and norms governing client accountability do not apply). For example, in the lawyers' legislative advocacy around DP rights (and later a failed state marriage bill), there were no formal clients, and thus the lawyers operated based on their best sense of the community's interests. Here, the legal groups' collaboration with Equality California offered an important counterbalance to the movement lawyers' discretion to define the terms of the ultimate policy objectives: It was Equality California that played a prominent role in building political support for DP and helping the lawyers shape its ultimate contours. So, too, was Equality California the key representative organization in the voter drive to defeat Proposition 8. Although Kors, the director of Equality California, was a lawyer, his organization's explicit focus on political mobilization meant that it was centrally involved in the democratic policymaking process and therefore answerable to the broader LGBT community for its political choices.

In certain cases, Equality California also served as the client, again allowing the lawyers to plausibly claim that their legal advocacy was on behalf of a group that stood for the broader community interest in promoting marriage equality. In this formal sense, the lawyers were acting in the interest of an organizational client, to which they were ultimately accountable. However, it is fair to view this relationship more as a collaboration than a conventional client-centered arrangement. Kors was cut from the same legal cloth—a former ACLU and LGBT rights litigator—and interacted with the movement lawyers as a strategic ally. The lawyer-client relationship, therefore, was more akin to a strategic partnership that allowed the lawyers to make legal arguments advancing predefined policy goals. Thus, the presence of Equality California as one of the intervenor clients in the Gloria Allred suit and the client of record in the *Woo* litigation reflects lawyer-driven strategic choices: Equality California was effectively selected by the lawyers as client rather than the other way around.

This was true in other lawsuits in which clients were handpicked. In the *Woo* case, the lawyers attempted to select individual plaintiffs who would be more broadly reflective of the state's gay population than the stereotyped version of the white, urban gay man. According to Lambda's Davidson, "We were trying to find plaintiffs who would be good spokespeople and representative of different parts of the state."

The degree of lawyer freedom to shape the ultimate policy outcomes was also evident in the way that movement lawyers used litigation to influence policymaking processes in the legislative arena—and vice versa. According to Davidson, "What was transformative across gay rights was relationship litigation that . . . made an incredible difference in making people think of lesbians and gay men as people with families." The litigation strategy, in Pizer's terms, was to present a "wrenching story, with powerful evidence, in which the legal step was relatively small." One example of this was the case of Keith Bradkowski, whose partner was a victim on the first American Airlines flight to crash into the World Trade Center on September 11, 2001. Lambda Legal's Pizer represented Bradkowski in his difficult effort to obtain money from victim compensation funds. Bradkowski's powerful testimony in front of the California legislature was credited with helping ensure the passage of a 2002 DP bill, which provided domestic partners with inheritance rights. Conversely, movement lawyers pursued a legislative strategy mindful of the prospect of future marriage litigation, carefully creating a record that would aid such litigation when it occurred. Thus, in the context of domestic partnership, lawyers made sure that the legislative record supported the potential legal arguments that the state did not have any legitimate interests in withholding marriage from same-sex couples and that such a denial was based on animus.

Yet, while marriage equality lawyers have enjoyed broad discretion in devising means and ends, they have not acted in a political vacuum, charting legal strategy in isolation from other political actors. And this is crucial to ultimately understanding the contextual factors that constrain their decision making and promote accountability. In the marriage equality context, there are countervailing forces that operate to cabin lawyer discretion: The lawyers are networked into a field of movement organizations, face challenges from countermovement groups, and experience divisions within their own movement on legal strategy (as evidenced in the *Perry* case). All of these forces require that the lawyers negotiate and compromise with other political actors, make legal decisions based on predictions about how they will play out in other policy arenas, and strike alliances with nonlegal groups to pursue legislative change and promote public education strategies. This complex decision-making environment means that movement lawyers have multiple community inputs into their deliberations about strategy and must ultimately respond to outside stakeholders to retain legitimacy as community leaders.

In the California campaign, this was evident in the lawyers' collaboration with nonlegal groups, like Equality California, to move policy through the legislature, where they had to present arguments persuasive to lawmakers keenly attuned to the reactions of constituents. Battles with movement opponents, like ADF, also limited the LGBT rights lawyers' ability to set the agenda by forcing them to defend the rights of same-sex couples against legal attack. In this way, movement lawyers were enlisted in legal fights not of their choosing. Key examples were the movement lawyers' responses to ADF lawsuits challenging the validity of the California comprehensive DP statute and Newsom's decision to issue marriage licenses to same-sex couples. Finally, the movement lawyers' negotiations with outside lawyers to stop (or reshape) rival litigation efforts also forced them to continuously reassess their no-litigation position and ask themselves: "Was the time finally ripe for a marriage challenge?" These forces contributed to a decision-making context in which the lawyers acted with relatively weaker accountability to clients but stronger accountability to the broader LGBT community.

Conclusion

What both the marriage equality and accountable development cases suggest is that multidimensional advocacy may position lawyers in roles that ultimately enhance democratic legitimacy by linking their legal work more closely to broader political efforts to advance causes. Whether *client* interests are served (and whether we should care if they are) depends on factors such as the degree and power of client organizations, whether clients pay fees (and how much), the extent to which multiple clients and client groups are involved (and how they interact), and the nature and scope of the policy reforms at stake. Yet, if we ultimately care about lawyers advancing policy claims that actually reflect the interests of the communities they purport to serve, the approach described in the cases—so far as they suggest that advocacy embedded in politics deepens community ties—may be a step in the right direction. At the very least, the cases present a much more complex picture of contemporary public interest lawyering that requires new analytical and ethical tools that reflect the post–civil rights practice reality and offer guidance for the next generation of public interest lawyers.

References

Alfieri, Anthony V. 1991. "Reconstructive Poverty Law Practice: Learning the Lessons of Client Narrative." *Yale Law Journal* 100:2107–2147.

Bell, Derrick A. 1976. "Serving Two Masters: Integration Ideals and Client Interests in School Desegregation Litigation." *Yale Law Journal* 85:470–516.

Binder, David A., Paul Bergman, Susan C. Price, and Paul R. Tremblay. 2004. *Lawyers as Counselors: A Client-Centered Approach.* 2nd ed. St. Paul: Thomson-West.

Cummings, Scott L. 2001. "Community Economic Development as Progressive Politics: Toward a Grassroots Movement for Economic Justice." *Stanford Law Review* 54: 399–493.

———. 2007. "Law in the Labor Movement's Challenge to Wal-Mart: A Study of the Inglewood Site Fight." *California Law Review* 95:1927–1998.

———. Forthcoming. "Privatizing Public Interest Law." *Georgetown Journal of Legal Ethics* 25.

Cummings, Scott L., and Douglas NeJaime. 2010. "Lawyering for Marriage Equality." *UCLA Law Review* 57:1235–1331.

Ettelbrick, Paula L. 1989. "Since When Is Marriage a Path to Liberation?" *Out/Look*, Fall, 14.

Gordon, Jennifer. 2007. "The Lawyer Is Not the Protagonist: Community Campaigns, Law, and Social Change." *California Law Review* 95:2133–2145.

Handler, Joel F., Betsy Ginsberg, and Arthur Snow. 1978. "The Public Interest Law Industry." In *Public Interest Law: An Economic and Institutional Analysis*, edited by Burton A. Weisbrod, Joel F. Handler, and Neil K. Komesar, 42–79. Berkeley: University of California Press.

Hegland, Kenney. 1971. "Beyond Enthusiasm and Commitment." *Arizona Law Review* 13:805–817.

Janis-Aparicio, Madeline, and Roxana Tynan. 2005. "Power in Numbers: Community Benefits Agreements and the Power of Coalition Building." *Shelterforce Online*, November/December. http://www.nhi.org/online/issues/144/powerinnumbers.html.

Luban, David. 1988. *Lawyers and Justice: An Ethical Study.* Princeton, NJ: Princeton University Press.

Mather, Lynn. 1998. "Theorizing about Trial Courts: Lawyers, Policymaking, and Tobacco Litigation." *Law & Social Inquiry* 23:897–940.

Rhode, Deborah L. 1982. "Class Conflicts in Class Actions." *Stanford Law Review* 34: 1183–1262.

Sarat, Austin, and Stuart Scheingold. 1998. *Cause Lawyering: Political Commitments and Professional Responsibilities*. New York: Oxford University Press.

Scheingold, Stuart, and Austin Sarat. 2004. *Something to Believe In: Politics, Professionalism, and Cause Lawyering*. Palo Alto, CA: Stanford University Press.

Simon, William H. 1991. "The Dark Secret of Progressive Lawyering: A Comment on Poverty Law Scholarship in the Post-Modernist, Post-Reagan Era." *University of Miami Law Review* 48:1099–1114.

———. 2004. "Solving Problems vs. Claiming Rights: The Pragmatist Challenge to Legal Liberalism." *William and Mary Law Review* 46:127–212.

Southworth, Ann. 2005. "Conservative Lawyers and the Contest over the Meaning of 'Public Interest Law.'" *UCLA Law Review* 52:1223–1278.

Stoddard, Thomas B. 1989. "Why Gay People Should Seek the Right to Marry." *Out/Look*, Fall, 9.

White, Lucie E. 1990. "Subordination, Rhetorical Survival Skills, and Sunday Shoes: Notes on the Hearing of Mrs. G." *Buffalo Law Review* 38:1–58.

Cases

Bowers v. Hardwick, 478 U.S. 186 (1986).

Brown v. Board of Education, 347 U.S. 483 (1954).

In re Marriage Cases, 183 P.3d 384 (Cal. 2008).

In re Primus, 436 U.S. 412 (1978).

Perry v. Schwarzenegger, 704 F. Supp. 2d 921 (N.D. Cal. 2010).

Woo v. Lockyer, No. CPF-04-504038 (Cal. Super. Ct. filed Mar. 12, 2004).

Epilogue

The chapters in this book powerfully demonstrate that lawyers' ethical decisions are affected by a variety of factors including—perhaps most important—their particular practice context. Now, with the research gathered in this volume, we can look across those contexts and ask which features transcend practice contexts and which are context specific. To do that systematically would require far more research—and, indeed, another book. Nevertheless, in these last few pages, we would like to offer some tentative concluding thoughts.

Lawyers do not practice entirely as independent agents. Their conduct is shaped by the social setting of practice—that is, the workplace—and, more specifically, by the formal and informal controls at work. In order to understand lawyers' ethical decision making, we must focus on the social organization of law practice and the incentives and possible sanctions that shape lawyers' norms and values and constrain their behavior.

Lawyers are also crucial intermediaries between *clients* and *the law.* Those two poles generate two important contextual features: first, clients—who they are (e.g., individuals or organizations, wealthy or poor, repeat players or one-shot users of legal services), and second, the law—both substantive and procedural—and enforcement mechanisms. Although considerable research has focused on the impact of workplace and client differences on lawyer decision making, much less attention has been given to the impact of law itself, the normative values and quality of justice embedded in it, and how lawyers think about the law and the system in which they are working. Lawyers' perceptions of the law's morality, as we suggest below, may affect how lawyers approach ethical dilemmas.

Formal and Informal Controls in the Workplace

Each practice context contains its own combination of formal and informal constraints, which shape the norms, values, and conduct of the lawyers working within it. Lawyers in some areas of practice have considerable autonomy while lawyers elsewhere face more formal and informal controls.

Formal bar rules and positive law (e.g., malpractice, criminal law) unquestionably play a role in shaping lawyers' norms and values. But the likelihood of enforcement and the severity of the formal sanctions seem to affect lawyer behavior depending on the practice context. For example, patent lawyers demonstrate a healthy respect for disclosure requirements, in part because of the US Patent and Trademark Office's controls and because the consequences of patent invalidation for clients can be severe (Conley and Mather, chapter 12). Similarly, securities law has a significant regulatory framework and enforcement system that causes securities lawyers to favor disclosure (Schmidt, chapter 11). In contrast, corporate litigators, who rarely face sanctions for speaking objections, regularly flout the rules prohibiting such conduct (Kirkland, chapter 8). Prosecutors—who are virtually immune from formal sanctions—may only grudgingly comply with their constitutional obligations to disclose exculpatory information to criminal defendants (Yaroshefsky and Green, chapter 13). Likewise, transnational lawyers engaged in complex business deals face few formal controls and will manipulate the "truth," for example, about the actual location of a corporate transaction (Flood, chapter 9). These examples strongly suggest that it is not just the content of the professional conduct or other legal rules, but their actual enforcement in particular practice contexts, that shape lawyers' views of acceptable conduct.

Informal regulation within the workplace also influences lawyers' behavior. When insurers require that firms implement certain safeguards, such as calendaring and conflict checking procedures, in order to obtain malpractice insurance at the lowest available premiums, they informally regulate lawyers. Office policies also reduce lawyers' autonomy: in prosecutors' offices with respect to disclosure, in small law firms with respect to the provision of reduced-fee services to a divorce client (Mather and McEwen, chapter 4), and in large law firms that require lawyers to consult with ethics partners on certain kinds of issues (Chambliss, chapter 3). Office hierarchies create informal pressures for lawyers to view ethical issues from the perspective of those in charge, such as junior lawyers seeking to please senior partners to gain support in their quest for partnership or in-house counsel seeking more responsibility and advancement (Kim, chapter 10).

Informal controls also operate through lawyers' repeated interactions with colleagues within and outside of their offices who constitute their communities of practice. We have seen how public defenders in Chicago sometimes advocate for their clients by denigrating them in plea discussions, thus appealing to the expectations and views of the judges and prosecutors who these defense attorneys work with on a daily basis (Van Cleve, chapter 14). Colleagues' expectations also shape the views of divorce lawyers with their norm of the reasonable lawyer. Likewise, personal injury lawyers influence one another through referrals and reputational interests; and public interest lawyers' longstanding relationships with one another promote cooperation and accountability (Cummings, chapter 16). These examples highlight the importance of informal collegial controls within different practice contexts.

Clients and the Economics of Practice

To the extent that lawyers compete for business and struggle to earn a living, they may behave in ways that push the limits of the positive law or even overstep those boundaries. This feature is most relevant to private practitioners, but can also be seen in the in-house counsel context. This is not a new insight, as Jerome Carlin noted in *Lawyers' Ethics* that lawyers with low-status clients were more likely to have an unstable clientele, face more competition, earn less, and be more likely to "adjust their attitudes" with respect to the bar's ethical duties than lawyers with high-status (i.e., corporate) clients. But research on corporate lawyers shows their ethical vulnerabilities as well, particularly as increased economic competition, the rise of in-house counsel, and outsourcing and globalization have weakened client relationships, making it more difficult for large firms to retain their lucrative corporate clients (Wilkins, chapter 2).

Lawyers who represent individual clients often do so on a one-shot basis; for example, divorce and personal injury clients may need their lawyers only once in a lifetime. Consequently, lawyers who predominantly represent individuals are constantly looking for new clients. As Daniels and Martin (chapter 6) found in their interviews with personal injury lawyers, because of the need for new business, some lawyers push the norms of acceptable conduct, using certain types of advertising to attract clients. Some divorce lawyers will take on more cases than they can competently handle—and risk neglecting their

clients—to maintain their high-volume practices. Certain immigration lawyers who compete for business with lawyers and nonlawyer providers are
sometimes willing to include a false statement on a visa application or take a
potentially fraudulent case to earn the fee (Levin, chapter 5).

The economics of practice also affect the norms of lawyers who represent
organizations that are sophisticated repeat players in the legal system. Corporate litigators are mindful of the need to adjust their behavior to accommodate their clients, especially as those clients have shown more willingness to
spread their legal work around to a number of firms or to bring it in-house.
Senior lawyers, who may have only one major client, recognize that their client may leave the firm if the lawyer fails to achieve the client's goals or comply with its requests. Securities lawyers often have disagreements with their
clients about the need for disclosure, but these lawyers are reluctant to "fire"
a client in the event of such conflict. Insurance defense lawyers struggle to determine how to properly represent their nominal clients (the insureds) while
also satisfying the insurance companies that pay their fees (Kritzer, chapter
7). In-house counsel, whose bonuses and promotions may be directly affected
by their client's satisfaction with their efforts, may adopt the entrepreneurial
perspective shared by others in the organization rather than the role of gatekeeper. In all of these cases, clients and the economics of practice subtly and
not-so-subtly shape lawyers' norms and values.

Views of the Law and the Legal System

While the economics of practice and workplace controls explain a good deal of
the ethical behavior of any professional, lawyers are unique in that the content
of their job is to apply and do *law*. This is an inherently normative task and
one that varies according to the law in different practice contexts. Sometimes,
as we have seen in these chapters, lawyers' willingness to push the envelope
stems from their commitment to a broader or different set of normative values, while lawyers' readiness to comply reflects their positive views of the law.
Moreover, if lawyers feel that the legal system is fair and just and that the law
serves normatively valuable goals, then they may be more likely to create and
abide by norms of practice that will reinforce positive law.

For example, patent lawyers, who believe in patent law to protect new scientific inventions, generally find little difficulty in being open and honest about
the prior art to maintain the integrity of the system. Similarly, securities law-

yers, who view securities regulation as necessary to protect the public and the integrity of financial markets, take disclosure obligations seriously.

The opposite may also be true: Lawyers' perceptions that the particular law or systems within which they operate are unfair, unjust, or unreal may lead lawyers to behave in more problematic ways or to develop norms that are at odds with the positive law. Some immigration lawyers—many of whom believe the system is unfair—will not turn down clients who may be lying, reasoning that it is the government's job to discover whether this is the case. Corporate litigators' views that the adversarial system is a game, not a justice system, permit them to construct the "truth" by culling through evidence to create the most favorable version of events. Litigators justify their signaling norms in discovery by relying on the rules of the game, which assume that all lawyers are equally competent and that all clients can afford good lawyers. Similarly, transnational lawyers, who work with the laws of many different countries to which they have little allegiance, see legal rules as setting up an elaborate game that requires legal creativity to play.

Lawyers' attitudes toward the legal system within which they work also seem to lead them to develop norms that they think will be more just, fair, and appropriate. For example, legal services lawyers are acutely concerned about respecting client autonomy as a response to a legal system that they view as disempowering and unfair (Shdaimah, chapter 15). Divorce lawyers' experiences with litigation that produces so much acrimony and distress have caused many of them to seek alternatives to protect children from the effects of a prolonged and bitter divorce. Criminal defense lawyers also redefine traditional legal advocacy to do what they believe will create more just and beneficial outcomes for their clients. As all of these examples suggest, we need to look more closely at the fairness and efficacy of law itself to more fully understand the conduct of lawyers in different areas of practice.

Concluding Thoughts

The chapters in this book raise more questions than they answer, but in so doing, we also hope that they lead to ideas for improving lawyers' ethical decision making. The economic, social, and organizational features of practice contexts deserve at least as much attention as the formal bar rules in light of the powerful impact of context on lawyers' decisions in practice. New lawyers should be taught about the influence of these features when they are first socialized into the profession—in law school. The one-size-fits-all approach of the ABA Model Rules of Professional Conduct also needs to be revised. At a minimum, the Rules should recognize and encourage compliance with codes for specialty practices that articulate public-regarding standards of conduct. Specialty bar codes should be written to reflect the true challenges of the practice specialties and to account for the power of clients and the workplace to shape norms. Unless rules are enforced, or are otherwise consistent with lawyers' values or self-interest, they will have limited impact on the conduct of lawyers. Finally, attention must be paid to the justice and fairness of the positive law itself and the system for realizing legal entitlements or rights. If the law that lawyers are asked to uphold does not garner their respect, they are more likely to engage in conduct that lawyers themselves define as appropriate.

Leslie C. Levin
Lynn Mather

Index

Made in the USA
Middletown, DE
28 January 2020

83848996R00223